International Political Economy Series

General Editor: **Timothy M. Shaw**, Professor of Commonwealth Governance and Development, and Director of the Institute of Commonwealth Studies, School of Advanced Study, University of London

Titles include:

Glenn Adler and Jonny Steinberg (*editors*)
FROM COMRADES TO CITIZENS
The South African Civics Movement and the Transition to Democracy

Glenn Adler and Eddie Webster (*editors*)
TRADE UNIONS AND DEMOCRATIZATION IN SOUTH AFRICA, 1985–1997

Einar Braathen, Morten Bøås and Gutermund Sæther (*editors*)
ETHNICITY KILLS?
The Politics of War, Peace and Ethnicity in Sub-Saharan Africa

Deborah Bräutigam
CHINESE AID AND AFRICAN DEVELOPMENT
Exporting Green Revolution

Gavin Cawthra
SECURING SOUTH AFRICA'S DEMOCRACY
Defence, Development and Security in Transition

Jennifer Clapp
ADJUSTMENT AND AGRICULTURE IN AFRICA
Farmers, the State and the World Bank in Guinea

Neta C. Crawford and Audie Klotz (*editors*)
HOW SANCTIONS WORK
Lessons from South Africa

Susan Dicklitch
THE ELUSIVE PROMISE OF NGOs IN AFRICA
Lessons from Uganda

Kevin C. Dunn and Timothy M. Shaw (*editors*)
AFRICA'S CHALLENGE TO INTERNATIONAL RELATIONS THEORY

Kenneth Good
THE LIBERAL MODEL AND AFRICA
Elites Against Democracy

Kees Kingma
DEMOBILIZATION IN SUBSAHARAN AFRICA
The Development and Security Impacts

Vijay S. Makhan
ECONOMIC RECOVERY IN AFRICA
The Paradox of Financial Flows

Clever Mumbengegwi (*editor*)
MACROECONOMIC AND STRUCTURAL ADJUSTMENT POLICIES IN ZIMBABWE

Nana Poku
REGIONALIZATION AND SECURITY IN SOUTHERN AFRICA

Howard Stein, Olu Ajakaiye and Peter Lewis (*editors*)
DEREGULATION AND THE BANKING CRISIS IN NIGERIA
A Comparative Study

Peter Vale, Larry A. Swatuk and Bertil Oden (*editors*)
THEORY, CHANGE AND SOUTHERN AFRICA'S FUTURE

International Political Economy Series
Series Standing Order ISBN 0–333–71708–2 hardcover
Series Standing Order ISBN 0–333–71110–6 paperback
(*outside North America only*)

You can receive future titles in this series as they are published by placing a standing order. Please contact your bookseller or, in case of difficulty, write to us at the address below with your name and address, the title of the series and one of the ISBNs quoted above.

Customer Services Department, Macmillan Distribution Ltd, Houndmills, Basingstoke, Hampshire RG21 6XS, England

Macroeconomic and Structural Adjustment Policies in Zimbabwe

Edited by

Clever Mumbengegwi
Dean of the Faculty of Social Studies
and
Senior Lecturer
Department of Economics
University of Zimbabwe

palgrave

First published 2002 by
PALGRAVE
Houndmills, Basingstoke, Hampshire RG21 6XS and
175 Fifth Avenue, New York, N. Y. 10010
Companies and representatives throughout the world

PALGRAVE is the new global academic imprint of
St. Martin's Press LLC Scholarly and Reference Division and
Palgrave Publishers Ltd (formerly Macmillan Press Ltd).

ISBN 0–333–80177–6

This book is printed on paper suitable for recycling and made from fully managed and sustained forest sources.

A catalogue record for this book is available from the British Library.

Library of Congress Cataloging-in-Publication Data
Macroeconomic and structural adjustment policies in Zimbabwe / edited by Clever Mumbengegwi.
p. cm. — (International political economy series)
Rev. papers selected from an international conference entitled: "Zimbabwe: macroeconomic policy, management and performance since independence: lessons for the 21st century."
Includes bibliographical references and index.
ISBN 0–333–80177–6
1. Structural adjustment (Economic policy)—Zimbabwe—Congresses. 2. Zimbabwe—Economic policy—Congresses. I. Mumbengegwi, Clever. II. Series.

HC910 .M333 2001
338.96891—dc21

2001021732

10 9 8 7 6 5 4 3 2 1
11 10 09 08 07 06 05 04 03 02

Printed and bound in Great Britain by
Antony Rowe Ltd, Chippenham, Wiltshire

To my late father Chivandire, my late mother Dzivaidzo, my mother Haruperi and my beloved daughter Ndinatsei Rumbidzai Nathalie, in memory of her late mother

Contents

Part IV Trade Liberalization: CGE Analyses

Part V Sectoral Perspectives

List of Tables

List of Figures

List of Abbreviations

ACF	Autocorrelation Function
ADF	Augmented Dickey–Fuller
AFC	Agricultural Finance Corporation
AGRITEX	Agricultural Extension and Technical Services
AIDS	Acquired Immune Deficiency Syndrome
AIM	AIDS Impact Model
AMA	Agricultural Marketing Authority
ARCH	Auto-Regressive Conditional Heteroscedasticity
ARV	Antiretroviral
BA	Banker's Acceptances
BLR	Base-Lending Rate
BOP	Balance Of Payments
BWI	Bretton Woods Institutions
CAD	Current Account Deficit
CD	Certificate Of Deposit
CES	Constant Elasticity of Substitution
CGE	Computable General Equilibrium
CIMAS	Commercial and Industrial Medical Aid Society
CMB	Cotton Marketing Board
CPI	Consumer Price Index
CSAE	Center for the Study of African Economies
CSC	Cold Storage Commission
CSO	Central Statistical Office
CSS	Central Statistical Services
DEER	Desired Equilibrium Exchange Rate
DLMA	Direct Local Market Allocation
DMB	Dairy Marketing Board
ECM	Error Correction Model
EIS	Export Incentive Scheme
EIU	Economic Intelligence Unit
EMCOZ	Employers' Confederation Of Zimbabwe
ERER	Equilibrium Real Exchange Rate
ERF	Export Revolving Fund
ERS	Export Retention Scheme
ESAF	Enhanced Structural Adjustment Facility
ESAP	Economic Structural Adjustment Program
EU	European Union
FAO	Food and Agriculture Organization
FCA	Foreign Currency Account

FDI	Foreign Direct Investment
FEER	Fundamental Equilibrium Exchange Rate
FIC	Foreign Investment Committee
GARCH	Generalized Autoregressive Conditional Heteroscedasticity
GDP	Gross Domestic Product
GFCF	Gross Fixed Capital Formation
GMB	Grain Marketing Board
GNP	Gross National Product
GoZ	Government of Zimbabwe
HIV	Human Immuno-deficiency Virus
IBDC	Indigenous Business Development Centre
ICOR	Incremental Capital Output Ratio
IFC	International Finance Corporation
IFS	*International Finance Statistics*
ILO	International Labor Organization
IMF	International Monetary Fund
IPC	Industrial/Investment Projects Committee
ISI	Import Substituting Industrialisation
JSE	Johannesburg Stock Exchange
LES	Linear Expenditure System
LR	Lending Rate
LSCF	Large-Scale Commercial Farmers
MLR	Minimum Lending Rate
MOHCW	Ministry of Health and Child Welfare
MPLSW	Ministry of Public Service, Labor and Social Welfare
MSE	Micro and Small Enterprises
NACP	National Aids Co-ordination Program
NBER	National Bureau of Economic Research
NCD	Negotiable Certificates of Deposit
NER	Nominal Exchange Rate
NSSA	National Social Security Authority
OECD	Organization of Economic Co-operation and Development
OGIL	Open General Import License
OLS	Ordinary Least Squares
OMO	Open Market Operations
PASS	Poverty Assessment Survey Study
PEs	Public Enterprises
POSB	Post Office Savings Bank
PPP	Purchasing Power Parity
QDS	*Quarterly Digest of Statistics*
QESR	*Quarterly Economic and Statistical Review*
QJE	*Quarterly Journal of Economics*
RBZ	Reserve Bank of Zimbabwe
REPO	Repurchase Arrangements

RER	Real Exchange Rate
SAM	Social Accounting Matrix
SAP	Structural Adjustment Program
SDF	Social Dimension Fund
SEDCO	Small Enterprise Development Corporation
SSCF	Small-Scale Commercial Farmers
STI	Sexually Transmitted Infections
SUR	Seemingly Unrelated Regression
TFP	Total Factor Productivity
TNDP	Transitional National Development Plan
TOT	Terms of Trade
UDI	Unilateral Declaration of Independence
UMB	United Merchant Bank
UNAIDS	United Nations AIDS
UNDP	United Nations Development Program
USA	United States of America
VoC	Vote of Credit
YTC	Youth Training Centers
ZANU PF	Zimbabwe African National Union Patriotic Front
ZCTU	Zimbabwe Congress of Trade Unions
ZIMPREST	Zimbabwe Program for Economic and Social Transformation
ZISCO	Zimbabwe Iron and Steel Company
ZSE	Zimbabwe Stock Exchange

Notes on Contributors

Hans Bjurek is an Associate Professor at the Department of Economics, School of Economics and Commercial Law, University of Göteborg in Sweden. His research areas are micro-productivity and efficiency studies, mainly with applications to the public service sector, and productivity and growth in development.

Margaret Chitiga-Mabugu is a Lecturer in the Department of Economics at the University of Zimbabwe. She currently teaches Public Finance and Policy Modeling. Her current research interests lie in the areas of poverty and income distribution, environmental economics and macroeconomics.

Dick Durevall is a Senior Lecturer at the Department of Economics, School of Economics and Commercial Law, University of Göteborg, and at the Department of Economic and Political Sciences, University of Skövde in Sweden. His main research area is applied development macroeconomics. Since the end of the 1980s, Durevall has followed the developments in Zimbabwe for SIDA (Sweden) and written several reports on the Zimbabwean economy.

James Gordon, a Zimbabwean national, is the IMF's Senior Resident Representative in India. He has worked for the IMF for 12 years, initially in the Africa Department. Before joining the IMF, he was a Lecturer in Economics at the London School of Economics, where he completed a PhD in Economics. He also has degrees from the University of Natal, Durban, and the University of New England, Australia.

Phineas Kadenge is a Lecturer in the Department of Economics at the University of Zimbabwe. He holds a PhD from the University of Göteborg, Sweden. He has been teaching microeconomics, macroeconomics, economic planning and development and monetary economics for the past 11 years. He has, among other issues, researched and published on the impact of structural adjustment, inflation, money demand and the real exchange rate.

John Knight is a Professor of Economics, Head of the Department of Economics, and member of the Centre for the Study of African Economies at the University of Oxford. He has written extensively on human resource issues in Africa and China, with publications including *Education, Productivity and Inequality: the East African Natural Experiment* (with

Richard Sabot) and *The Rural–Urban Divide: Economic Disparities and Interactions* (with Lina Song). The chapter in this volume is part of his wider research project comparing Zimbabwe and South Africa after the arrival of democracy.

Ramos Mabugu is a lecturer at the University of Zimbabwe in the Economics Department. He is currently teaching Macroeconomics, International Economics and Policy Modeling. His current research interests lie in the areas of environmental economics, macroeconomics and policy issues.

Halvor Mehlum is a researcher at the Frisch Centre of Economic Research, University of Oslo. His doctoral thesis 'The Political Economy of Failing Reform' discussed the problems of self-fulfilling expectations in the implementation of economic reform. He is presently working on a project titled 'Inequality, Social Conflict and Development'.

Chandima Mendis is an economist in the Asia and Pacific Department of the International Monetary Fund. Prior to this, he worked for Emerging Market Economics (EME) Ltd, an international economic consultancy in London. He specializes in international macroeconomics, monetary policy and financial sector issues. His recent research has focused on the macroeconomics of external shocks, capital flows and financial crises in developing countries. He has also worked in Zimbabwe and Ghana. He obtained his DPhil from the University of Oxford.

Minsoo Lee is a Lecturer of Economics at the Commerce Division in Lincoln University, New Zealand. Prior to joining Lincoln University he was an Assistant Professor in the Economics Department at Washington State University. His research interests are economic development (transitional economies in Eastern Europe and Africa), international foreign exchange market, and time-series econometrics. In 1997, he was involved in a project 'Turnover and Duration Rates for Small Enterprises' funded by the Ministry of Industry and Commerce, Government of Zimbabwe and he has published papers on that project. He holds MA degrees in Economics and Applied Mathematics from UCLA and a PhD in Economics from Washington State University, USA.

Clever Mumbengegwi is the Dean of the Faculty of Social Studies at the University of Zimbabwe. He is a graduate of Monash University, Melbourne, Australia and obtained his PhD from Washington State University, USA. His research interests are in agricultural policy issues in Zimbabwe and he has published several papers on the subject. More recently, he has developed research interests in macroeconomic policy and management issues in Zimbabwe.

Gladys Mutangadura was a lecturer at the University of Zimbabwe until July 1999. She holds a PhD in Agricultural Economics from Virginia Polytechnic and State University, USA. Her research interests are on agricultural development, gender, poverty, health and the socioeconomic impacts of the HIV/AIDS epidemic in Sub-Saharan Africa. She has written several articles focusing on rural household and community attempts to alleviate the impacts of the HIV/AIDS epidemic.

Daniel B. Ndlela was a Senior Lecturer in Economics at the University of Zimbabwe before proceeding to work as a senior regional policy adviser on economic cooperation at the United Nations Economic Commission for Africa based in Addis Ababa, Ethiopia. Currently he is an economic consultant with Zimconsult, an economic and planning consulting firm based in Harare. Dr Ndlela is a graduate of the Higher Institute of Economics, Sofia State University, Bulgaria and holds a PhD from the University of Lund, Sweden. His current research interests are in the areas of macroeconomic management, international trade and industrialization and he has published several papers on these issues.

Obert Nyawata is a Zimbabwean economist who has worked at the International Monetary Fund since 1989. He worked for the Ministry of Finance in Zimbabwe and later at the African Development Bank in Côte d'lvoire before joining the IMF. He is a graduate of the Universities of Zimbabwe and Sussex and is currently on study leave at the University of Surrey.

Mudzivirit T. Nziramasanga is an Associate Professor of Economics at Washington State University. He holds a PhD from Stanford University. In 1980 he joined the Government of Zimbabwe's Ministry of Economic Planning and Development. He also served on the Commission of Inquiry into Taxation (1985–86) and the Committee of Inquiry into the Administration of Parastatals. From 1990 to the end of 1993 he was the Secretary of Industry and Commerce, one of the key ministries in the economic reform program initiated in 1991. Dr Nziramasanga has participated in several projects for, among others, the US Agency for International Development, UNDP and the United Nations Industrial Development Organization and has also published research on the Zambian and Zimbabwean economies.

Jørn Rattsø is Professor of Economics at the Norwegian University of Science and Technology. He holds a doctoral degree from the University of Oslo and his prime interests are in the areas of development macroeconomics and fiscal federalism. In the area of development macroeconomics he has contributed to many books and published in international journals such as the *Cambridge Journal of Economics,* the *Journal of Development Economics, Open Economics Review* and *World Development.*

Peter Robinson is an economic consultant in Zimbabwe and the Southern African region. In nearly 20 years as a consultant, Dr Peter Robinson has carried out studies in a wide range of aspects of the economy. His current interests are in macroeconomic modeling and forecasting, trade negotiations, competitiveness and private sector participation in infrastructural development. Dr Robinson was responsible for the macroeconomic framework of ZIMPREST. He is a member of the macroeconomic and industrial task forces of the National Economic Consultative Forum – a government–private sector policy dialogue forum and think tank.

Ragnar Torvik is an Associate Professor at the Department of Economics, Norwegian University of Science and Technology. His doctoral thesis 'The Macroeconomics of Foreign Exchange Shortage: a Study with Reference to Zimbabwe' developed applied and theoretical models relevant to the discussion of Zimbabwean macroeconomic experiences and policies. He also holds a position at the Central Bank of Norway. His main areas of work are macroeconomics and development economics, and he has published in journals such as the *European Economic Review*, the *Journal of Development Economics*, the *Scandinavian Journal of Economics* and the *Cambridge Journal of Economics*.

Preface

During the first decade of independence (1980–90) Zimbabwe had a high degree of government intervention and a controlled macroeconomic policy environment. This was partly due to the government's continuation of the policy regime it had inherited from the UDI period that immediately preceded African majority rule and partly the result of the government's socialist orientation. In a major shift in the policy regime in 1991, the government embarked upon a structural adjustment program aimed at removing these regulations and controls and adopting a more market-based system of economic management. The results of the two decades of macroeconomic policy have been mixed, partly because of negative exogenous shocks and partly due to policy failures. What lessons has Zimbabwe learned from the 20 years of experience with macroeconomic policy and management? How has Zimbabwe's experience differed from that of other Sub-Saharan African and other developing countries? How can the observed outcomes be explained? At the turn of the twenty-first century, serious problems confront the economy with no clear consensus as to the way forward. What changes in macroeconomic management are needed in order to enhance the growth capacity of the economy? While valid criticisms of the government's past management of the economy have been made, much research remains to be done to generate viable policy options for the future. This book makes an important contribution in this direction.

The chapters contained in this volume were originally presented at an international conference entitled 'Zimbabwe: Macroeconomic Policy, Management and Performance since Independence: Lessons for the 21st Century', which was held in Harare, from 18 to 21 August 1998. The objective of the conference was to bring together policy makers, academic researchers and economists who have been analyzing these problems in order to provide guidelines for the future direction of policy. The participants included senior Zimbabwean policy makers and academics and several international scholars whose research interests focused on the Zimbabwean economy. The chapters included in this volume were selected from a total of 38 papers presented at the above conference. The selection was based largely on their thematic and policy relevance to the overall argument of this book. The papers were subsequently revised and updated by the authors in the light of comments received at the conference and also in line with editorial requirements. In several cases, related conference papers were merged to become co-authored chapters in this book. The editor is extremely grateful to the authors for agreeing to this.

The Department of Economics, University of Zimbabwe and the Professional Development and Training Program in Economics (PDTPE) Project organized the conference. The latter was a Government of Zimbabwe training and capacity building project in macroeconomic policy analysis and management, funded by a grant from the African Capacity Building Foundation (ACBF). As Director of the PDTPE project and editor of this book, I wish to express my most sincere gratitude and indebtedness to the ACBF for financing the conference and the editorial expenses for this book. Sincere gratitude and appreciation are also due to President Robert Gabriel Mugabe who set aside time from his busy schedule to open the conference and address the delegates on many of the issues that have become the subject of this book. I am extremely grateful to my colleagues at the Department of Economics for their support in organizing the conference. In particular, but without implicating him in the shortcomings of this book, I am especially grateful to my colleague Ramos Mabugu who collaborated with me in the paper-selection process and gave me support and encouragement to persevere with the editing of this book. Last but not least, I owe tons of appreciation and gratitude to my secretary, Jessica Tsarara, who, with cheerfulness and diligence, handled all the pre-and post-conference practical details and logistics and provided secretarial services needed to get this manuscript ready for publication.

CLEVER MUMBENGEGWI
Harare

Part I

Introduction and Overview

1

Macroeconomic and Adjustment Policies in Zimbabwe (1980–2000): an Introduction and Overview

Clever Mumbengegwi and Ramos Mabugu

1 Introduction

Macroeconomic policy and performance in Zimbabwe since independence in 1980 present an interesting case study on the problematic and pitfalls involved in the process of economic policy reform. During the first decade (1980–90), the macroeconomic policy framework was highly controlled. Current economic wisdom advises that this was 'a very bad thing' for the economy. As a result, a standard IMF/World Bank-supported structural adjustment package was adopted in 1991, because it was felt that this would be 'good' for the economy. Performance indicators show that the economy grew by a respectable average of 4.3 per cent per annum under the 'bad' control policies of the 1980s but by only a miserly 0.8 per cent under the so-called 'good' policies pursued during the period of economic structural adjustment (ESAP 1991–95). Thus, despite the 1980s having been described as a 'lost decade' for Africa in terms of growth performance, Zimbabwe stands out as one of the few African countries that registered growth rates comparable to those of other developing regions of the world, notwithstanding the government-controlled macroeconomic framework at this time.[1] Further, other performance indicators of macroeconomic stability, employment, income distribution and poverty also worsened after the launch of the market-based economic reforms of the 1990s. That growth and other indicators of performance were significantly higher during the control regime of the 1980s than during the period of the structural adjustment reforms is an apparent paradox that begs serious analysis and explanation. The chapters in this book provide valuable insights into this apparent paradox and the pitfalls involved in the transition from a controlled to a market-oriented macroeconomic policy regime.

2 Macroeconomic policy and performance: an overview

Zimbabwe's post-independence macroeconomic history can be easily divided into two major policy episodes: (i) the control regime of 1980–1990; and (ii) the structural adjustment period (1991 to date). This distinction is not meant to simply reflect the chronological sequence of events – it is also intended to capture fundamental changes in the macroeconomic policy framework and a major shift in the development paradigm.

2.1 The control regime of the 1980s (1980–1990)

In order to understand Zimbabwe's post-independence macroeconomic policy successes and failures, it is important to bear in mind that many of the policies and instruments adopted soon after independence have their origins in the period immediately preceding African majority rule. During the period of the Unilateral Declaration of Independence (UDI) (1965–79), Ian Smith's Rhodesian government had adopted inward-looking, import-substituting policies in response to international economic sanctions and the country's isolation from the rest of the world. The objectives of this government were to promote domestic manufacturing and to achieve self-sufficiency in major consumer goods. Government intervened extensively in the economy. Economy-wide controls on prices, wages, interest rates and in foreign exchange markets became a pervasive feature of the UDI period. An elaborate system of foreign exchange allocation and import rationing was introduced to avert an ever-looming balance of payments crisis. Although the first decade of UDI (1965–1974) was a successful experiment in rapid import substitution, this could not be sustained once the early and easier stages of import substitution became exhausted. The initial growth rate of about 7 per cent per annum turned to negative figures from 1974 onwards due partly to economic dislocations associated with the intensification of the national liberation war, the oil price increases and the world recession. This was the immediate background against which Zimbabwe attained political independence on 18 April 1980.

The new black majority government proceeded to maintain many of the macroeconomic controls inherited from UDI as instruments of macroeconomic management and to try and achieve a more equitable pattern of economic growth. Indeed its first economic policy statement was entitled 'Growth with Equity'. Extensive price controls were maintained in output, labor and capital markets. New regulations regarding higher minimum wages, and hiring and firing restrictions were added with respect to labor markets in a bid to protect workers and to redress racial discrimination in employment. Foreign exchange rationing, import licensing and restrictions on capital mobility were also maintained, again to protect jobs and domestic industry from foreign competition. In essence, the ailing import substitution strategy from UDI was given a new impetus in the name of the 'socialist transformation' of the economy.

High government spending and deficit financing combined with foreign exchange allocation to priority sectors were used with some effort at redistribution to achieve growth-compatible outcomes. These policies could be rationalized using both structuralist and neo-Keynesian arguments. The government's redistributive objectives necessitated a large public sector. As a result, the number of people employed in the civil service grew considerably while existing public enterprises (parastatals) were strengthened and many new ones were created. Invariably, most operated on 'soft' budget constraints with losses being met by direct subsidies from the fiscus. Increased government spending on education, health, basic social services and physical infrastructure achieved significant improvements in health, education and other social indicators during the 1980s. However, these were achieved at a high cost in terms of unsustainably high budget deficits whose harmful economy-wide effects remained hidden behind the plethora of economy-wide controls.

Performance

The 1980s started on an optimistic note, with growth rates of 10.7 per cent and 9.7 per cent being recorded in 1980 and 1981 respectively. These unprecedented growth rates were made possible by initially favorable exogenous growth conditions such as the end of the liberation war, the lifting of economic sanctions, favorable world market conditions and two consecutive and exceptionally good rainfall seasons. High growth, in turn, made it easier for government to pursue fiscally driven redistributive policies. Because Zimbabwe's is an agriculture-driven economy, good rainfall combined with high producer prices raised incentives to farmers, resulting in rapid agricultural growth. Higher agricultural incomes and industrial minimum wages fueled consumer demand, which gave a growth impetus to other sectors of the economy, such as manufacturing. The opening up of external markets gave an initial boost to exports, which facilitated higher foreign exchange allocations to industry. Thus, a short-lived real economic boom was experienced in the immediate aftermath of independence.

However, as exogenous growth factors began to evaporate towards the middle of the 1980s, the economy was plunged into a deep recession, sparked by two consecutive droughts (1983/4–1984/5) and falling demand in world markets. Agricultural output declined by almost 20 per cent, reducing incomes and effective demand for manufacturing sector output. Gross fixed capital formation (GFCF) as a percentage of GDP declined after 1982 and stabilized at around 12–13 per cent throughout the decade, which was hardly adequate to cover replacement capital. Exports also declined and then stagnated with balance of payments problems necessitating a nominal devaluation in 1982 and tighter foreign exchange controls on imports. The resulting import compression and reduced capacity utilization in industry reduced the average growth to 4.1 per cent for the period 1980–85, which was well below the 8 per cent growth target envisaged by the Transitional National Development Plan (1982–1985) (see Table 1.1).

The second half of the decade saw an increasing realization by policy makers that import substitution had reached its limits as a strategy for

Table 1.1 Zimbabwe: GDP growth, inflation, employment, investment and factor shares

Period	*GDP growth (%)*	*Inflation rate (%)*	*Employment growth (%)*	*Investment ratio (%)*	*Wage/GDP ratio*	*Profit/GDP ratio*
1980–85	4.1	8.7	2.3	9.8	56.7	41.6
1986–90	4.6	10.8	1.9	7.7	57.3	40.5
1991–95	0.8	25.1	1.4	21.0	45.0	54.8
1996–98	4.2	24.0	2.8	16.1	42.3	57.7

Source: CSO, *National Accounts and Quarterly Digest of Statistics*, Harare.
Notes: 1997 and 1998 are provisional figures.

promoting long-term growth and that different policies were required if growth was to be accelerated and sustained at higher levels. Thus, although most of the macroeconomic controls were kept in place, tentative steps towards economic reform were slowly introduced. Through various incentive schemes, export promotion was adopted as a complement to rather than a substitute to the import-substitution strategy. The essence of these schemes was to give exporting firms greater access to foreign exchange with which to import intermediate inputs and capital equipment. The relaxation of import and foreign exchange constraints eased the import compression and resulted in increased capacity utilization. Signs of recovery began to appear in the second half of the decade. Although annual growth rates were erratic and subject to wild fluctuations, Zimbabwe managed to achieve a respectable average growth of 4.6 per cent in the period 1986–90. Whereas the 'boom–bust' pattern can be explained by exogenous factors (especially drought), the tendency for growth to decline[2] is related to the controlled macroeconomic environment that failed to provide adequate incentives for long-term investment. This notwithstanding, Zimbabwe achieved a 4.3 per cent average annual growth rate over the first decade of independence which compares favorably with other developing regions of the world.

2.2 The decade of economic reform (1990–2000)

Zimbabwe is a relatively late adopter of structural adjustment reforms. Global trends and the declining growth performance in the last three years of the 1980s persuaded its government to abandon the existing system of macroeconomic controls. Furthermore, these controls had become difficult to administer and there was growing belief that growth performance could be improved upon. Thus, a World Bank/IMF-supported structural adjustment program was officially adopted in January 1991, although tentative moves towards reform had begun a few years earlier. The first phase of the reforms was the *Economic Structural Adjustment Programme (ESAP)* 1991–1995.[3] ESAP had many of the standard prescriptions from the Bretton

Woods institutions – the deregulation of domestic markets and decontrol of prices, trade liberalization, macroeconomic stabilization measures, public sector reforms, financial liberalization and monetary sector reforms and social safety nets to protect vulnerable groups. The rationale was to effect a shift from a controlled to a more market-based system of macroeconomic management. Market forces were to play a more significant role than state controls in determining prices and resource allocation.

Although ESAP had a lot in common with the standard World Bank/IMF reform prescriptions, there were some significant differences. Firstly, it sought to improve upon an already respectable growth performance rather than to rescue a collapsed economy,as had been the case in several African countries. Secondly, it was not really an agreement between the IMF/WB and the government, but rather a government program supported by these institutions. Donor support did not come up-front but only started to be negotiated eight months into the program,and largely involved diverting funds from old projects to the new reforms. Thirdly, the duration of the Zimbabwean program was much longer (five years) than standard IMF stabilization programs.

It is now widely accepted that many of the anticipated results from structural adjustment did not materialize. Despite the considerable progress that was made in implementing the reforms, especially in the areas of trade liberalization and domestic deregulation, the economy failed to generate the desired supply response. The program design had underestimated the inherent lag in output and export supply response such that economic growth and other indicators of performance were disappointingly low. Not only do growth figures compare very unfavorably with those achieved during the control regime of the 1980s; they also fell far short of their planned targets, as shown in Table 1.2. Real GDP growth was a meager 0.8 per cent per annum between 1991 and 1995, while GDP per capita actually declined by over 2 per cent per annum. Furthermore, the functional distribution of income shifted away from labor to capital, as shown in Table 1.1, so that the share of salaries and wages decreased from 57 per cent of GDP in the 1980s to 45 per cent by 1995. In contrast, profit share rose from 41 to 55 per cent over the same period.

Table 1.2 Zimbabwe: planned targets vs actual growth rates

TNDP 1980–85		*FFYNP 1986–90*		*ESAP 1991–95*		*ZIMPREST 1996–98*	
Target	*Actual*	*Target*	*Actual*	*Target*	*Actual*	*Target*	*Actual*
8.0	4.1	5.1	4.6	4.6	0.8	6.0	4.2

Source: Actual growth rates calculated from CSO *National Accounts* and *Quarterly Digest of Statistics*. Targets obtained from the Transitional National Development Plan (TNDP), the First Five-Year National Development Plan (FFYNDP), the ESAP and ZIMPREST policy documents.

The economic structural adjustment reforms had been designed on the assumption that they would lead to resources shifting from notradable and protected import-competing to tradable and unprotected import-competing sectors. The contraction of the former would be more than compensated by an expansion of the latter. This improvement in resource allocation would stimulate growth. That this did not occur to any significant degree is an apparent paradox that can be easily explained by the failure of government to adhere to the internal logic of the reforms. For example, fiscal stabilization, which was required up-front, was never seriously attempted because the Zimbabwean government found it politically difficult to reduce its expenditure levels. Exogenous factors, in particular the worst drought in living memory, which devastated the country very early in the reform process, served merely to aggravate the situation. However, these drought-related government expenditures were compounded by delays in public sector and public enterprise reforms resulting in high budget deficits – above 8 per cent, compared to the target of 5 per cent of GDP by 1995. Further, incompatibilities in implementing the various elements of the program undermined the credibility of the reforms and rendered them prone to policy reversals, as occurred on several occasions. The vigorous pursuit of trade liberalization while failing to reform the public sector and to reduce the budget deficit was, therefore, an important source of the many difficulties that confronted the economy during ESAP. Thus, if promoting growth was the main purpose of ESAP, then it was a dismal failure.

The second phase of reforms was implemented as the *Zimbabwe Program for Economic and Social Transformation (ZIMPREST, 1996–2000)*. ZIMPREST sought to continue the unfinished reforms from ESAP, and, in particular, the reduction of the budget deficit, public sector and public enterprise reforms, financial liberalization and the enacting of a more effective supervisory and regulatory framework for the financial sector. However, it also had a broader social and political focus than ESAP – to include issues of poverty reduction, land reform, black economic empowerment and the indigenization of the economy.

ZIMPREST started with strong overall GDP growth of 7 per cent and a lower than anticipated budget deficit in 1996, with every indication that the worst was now behind. However, it too, soon faltered for reasons identical in nature, if not worse in magnitude, than those responsible for ESAP's failure to achieve its objectives. On this occasion the villain of the piece was government fiscal imprudence, which threw all the macroeconomic fundamentals into disarray. Persistent revenue and expenditure mismatches made the budget deficit problem *the* cause of Zimbabwe's macroeconomic instability since the start of economic reforms. During ZIMPREST, the method of its financing shifted from borrowing from the non-banking to borrowing from the banking and financial sector, a change which fueled money supply growth, rampant inflation and high interest rates. Although annual inflation had been controlled at around the 22 per cent level, the factors discussed above soon led to runaway levels, reaching an all-time peak of 70 per cent by the end of 1999 while interest rates also skyrocketed to similar levels in line with inflation. As a result, Zimbabwe's central bank responded by adopting tight monetary policy as domestic demand management measures but without the necessary support from the fiscal side. Firms, especially new firms, were subjected to a severe credit squeeze, which dampened down investment. Deficit financing from the domestic money market at interest rates of over 60 to 70 per cent brought the country to the brink of a domestic debt trap, with interest on debt the largest single item of the government budget. The high domestic inflation relative to the country's major trading partners caused the real exchange rate to appreciate, thus undermining export competitiveness. The weak export supply response had adverse consequences on the balance of payments and foreign exchange reserves.

Thus, the ZIMPREST period witnessed unprecedented macroeconomic instability which manifested itself in low overall economic growth, high budget deficits, high inflation, low foreign exchange reserves, a weak balance of payments position and generally negative macroeconomic fundamentals. This eroded market sentiment and uncertainty which led to a currency crisis and a squeeze on the Zimbabwe dollar in 1997 and again in 1998. The immediate response by policy makers to the currency crisis was a set of measures which amounted to another policy reversal. Eventually the nominal exchange rate became fixed in January 1999 in a bid to reduce exchange rate instability. Furthermore, political events that unfolded towards the end of the decade exacerbated macroeconomic instability. The government's handling of the land issue, the granting of Z$3 billion in unbudgeted-for gratuities to veterans of the 1970s liberation war, the country's involvement in the Democratic Republic of the Congo conflict and the government's failure to meet agreed targets with the IMF led to the suspension of IMF support to the reform program. This had 'snowball' effects on funding from other donors and the drying up of private foreign investment. The result was severe shortage of foreign exchange and balance of payments crisis,which has affected the country's capacity to meet external debt obligations. The country's external debt of 82 per cent of GDP by the end of 1999 and its external debt service ratio above the 20 per cent level recommended for sustainability has affected its credit worthiness, resulting in the suspension of some credit lines.

Thus, Zimbabwe entered the twenty-first century in a deep economic crisis. Whereas it is generally agreed that structural adjustment reforms have not been successful in reversing the downward growth trend in Africa, in the case of Zimbabwe, the reforms have actually been associated with much worse performance compared to the decade prior to reform. Such comparisons have generated a growing domestic perception that the reforms are at the center of the economy's decline and the root cause of current economic crisis to an extent that it has become a fertile breeding ground for Zimbabwe's political resistance to further reforms. The corollary is that Zimbabwe is increasingly perceived, internationally, as a reluctant traveller along the rocky road to economic reform.

3 About this book

This book makes an important contribution to the analysis and understanding of Zimbabwe's macroeconomic and structural adjustment experience since the attainment of independence in 1980. Collectively and individually, the chapters shed light on the causes of why and how Zimbabwe has ended in the worst economic crisis it has witnessed in its 20 years of independence. The major insight from this book is that partial and non-implementation of structural adjustment reforms may lead to worse outcomes than strict adherence to macroeconomic controls. Thus, all aspects of reforms need to be implemented simultaneously if growth is to be realized because partial implementation has led to the apparent paradoxical outcomes witnessed in Zimbabwe, which we have outlined above. Thus, the book provides valuable insights into the problematic involved in the transition from a controlled to a market based economy.

4 Organization of the book

The rest of the book is divided into four parts.

II Macroeconomic policies and performance

The four chapters in Part II give insightful analyses and explanations of the effects of macroeconomic controls and structural adjustment policy reforms on economic growth, inflation, labor markets and employment and other macroeconomic aggregates. They confirm the paradoxical finding that the paradigm shift from controls to market reforms neither enhanced growth, nor contributed to macroeconomic stability and improvements in other indicators of performance. They attribute this failure to the non-implementation rather than implementation of structural adjustment reforms. In Chapter 2, Peter Robinson explains the reasons for the failure in terms of a medical metaphor. The analogy of the relationship between a patient and a physician is put to good effect in evaluating the efficacy of policy prescriptions emanating from the Bretton Woods Institutions vis-à-vis home-grown ones. The typical sequence of medical treatment, from diagnosis of the problem, the recommended treatment regime to the extent to which the patient adheres to the course of treatment drugs is instructive in understanding what went wrong with Zimbabwe's structural adjustment program. Robinson argues that while the physician's diagnosis of pre-ESAP economic problems and the recommended treatment regime were not fundamentally wrong, the patient's (Zimbabwe's) unwillingness to adhere to the recommended treatment regime is what derailed the reforms. Instead Zimbabwe opted for a disastrous strategy of selecting and arbitrarily combining different elements from different treatment regimes. This lack of appreciation that structural adjustment reforms are a 'package deal' with their own internal logic and their own set of mutually reinforcing measures that have to be properly synchronized, if desired results are to be realized, is what explains the paradoxical outcomes realized from structural adjustment reforms.

However, the physician is not spared from criticism either. Robinson is also critical of the IMF's actions as having caused 'iatrogenic effects', that is, illnesses caused by the physician's actions or the unforeseen ailments that the patient would not have had to endure if he had not consulted the physician in the first place. In particular the suspension of IMF support to Zimbabwe in 1995 and on several subsequent occasions comes under severe criticism as having contributed to the failure of economic reforms. Robinson's chapter concludes with a set of recommendations if the reforms are to be brought back on track. Among these is the need for Zimbabwe to take greater charge of its policy formulation in order to avoid the possibility of iatrogenic effects. Arresting the decline in public sector investment, budget deficit reduction, lowering inflation, interest rates and the domestic debt trap are the key issues that need to be immediately addressed if Zimbabwe is to realize the intended benefits from structural adjustment. Institution-building, especially those measures which strengthen the financial sector regulatory framework is also recommended as a matter for immediate policy concern.

In chapter 3, Mudziviri Nziramasanga and Minsoo Lee use intervention analysis in order to assess the short- and long-run impacts of the two most important events in Zimbabwe's macroeconomic policy after independence. These are the attainment of independence in 1980 (*essentially the removal of economic sanctions*) and the adoption of the economic reform program (*essentially trade liberalization*). Their analysis shows that independence gave a boost to economic growth while ESAP did not. Several mutually reinforcing explanations are given that account for these outcomes. Firstly, although there was an increase in both private savings and investment during the period of ESAP, this did not translate into higher growth due to the prevailing unstable macroeconomic conditions. Other macroeconomic aggregates of relevance to growth, such as imports and exports both increased immediately following independence and the implementation of economic reforms. However, imports increased faster than exports during ESAP, exarcebating pressures for further macroeconomic instability. Secondly, the decline in capital expenditures and government investment in infrastructure relative to recurrent expenditures that occurred during ESAP resulted in the budget being less growth-oriented. The budget became dominated by recurrent expenditures because the government found it easier to sacrifice capital expenditure in the face of mounting pressure to achieve the 5 per cent budget deficit target. Thus, the reform program's focus on reducing the global size of the budget deficit as a percentage of GDP without regard for its composition is raised as an issue of concern. Thus, they suggest, a reversal of the fiscal trend of increasing recurrent at the expense of government capital expenditures; would augur well for the economy's future growth prospects. Thirdly, Nziramasanga and Minsoo Lee agree with Robinson that the post-1990 reforms were hamstrung by being only partly implemented. The government's emphasis on trade liberalization, with no corresponding reform of the public sector contributed to trade liberalization failing to have any significant positive impact on GDP. Their econometric estimation of an economy-wide production function finds no meaningful growth in total factor productivity. The only changes found were in output elasticities that suggest that production has become more capital-intensive. This finding, combined with the lack of growth, trade liberalization with no fiscal adjustment and rising inflation considerably reduced real wages such that labor bore the brunt of the adjustment process. The chapter concludes by emphasizing the need to implement all aspects of the reforms simultaneously if growth is to be realized. Partial implementation may well lead to a decline in growth; but, as the authors point out, it would not necessarily be correct to attribute the decline to those aspects of the program that are implemented.

In Chapter 4, Dick Durevall and Phineas Kadenge tackle the formidable task of estimating the determinants of inflation, which has been a major source and indicator of macroeconomic instability in Zimbabwe during the structural adjustment period. They apply single equation error-correction models to estimate the underlying factors driving inflation during the first phase of economic reforms (ESAP 1991–1995). Their exploration of the link between inflation, money supply growth, real interest rates and the nominal exchange rate suggests that before 1991, long-run inflation was determined by excess money supply. Later, the exchange rate and foreign prices replaced money supply as the major determinants of the domestic price level during ESAP. The view that high real interest rates cause cost-push inflation by raising the cost of financing working capital is also weakly supported. Overall, they find weak support for the link between inflation and changes in money supply. From their analysis, Durevall and Kadenge conclude that targeting money alone to fight inflation may be ineffective. Other sources of inflation, like exchange rate depreciation, wage growth and food prices have to be tackled if inflation is to be effectively contained.

Low employment growth has been a major feature of Zimbabwe's economy since independence. In chapter 5 John Knight provides a lucid account and analysis of Zimbabwe's labor market policies and outcomes with the objective of enhancing understanding, informing policy and distilling labor market policy lessons for the future. Knight argues that, although well intentioned, the labor market interventions pursued by the government soon after independence resulted in unintended harmful effects on employment. Many of the interventions, such as minimum and maximum wages, and hiring and firing restrictions were largely ineffective due to general equilibrium effects not unanticipated by policy makers. For example, the state's strict and well-intentioned dismissal regulations designed to defend jobs had the opposite effect on employment, making employers reluctant to hire if they could not fire, while they also weakened workers' incentives for effort, which reduced employment. He suggests that interventions which harness market forces might well have been more effective, as exemplified by the government's policy of investment in education, training and human capital formation. He argues that the most successful of the policy interventions during the 1980s was the expansion of the supply of educated labor relative to demand because this was a powerful means of compressing the earnings structure and one, which could rely on market forces.

Although the labor market reforms of the 1990s reduced the extent of government intervention on wages and employment, Knight argues that it cannot be concluded that they were beneficial overall. His assessment of the labor market effects of the ESAP strategy shows adverse effects on the welfare of wage earners as evidenced by the sharp fall in real wages and the reduced security of employment. Furthermore, the employment growth that was anticipated to flow from ESAP did not materialize. However, a 'no-change' counterfactual may, with time, have produced even worse outcomes.

In view of the poor employment growth effects realized during the period of ESAP, Knight advocates the fostering of a productive urban informal sector as a complementary strategy to employment creation and development. However, this requires a less regulatory and more promotional framework, with government intervention needed to help overcome the informational, credit and training constraints, which hinder the educated unemployed from opting for entrepreneurial careers. There needs be a relaxation of restrictions and assistance to would-be small entrepreneurs and to remove the web of laws and regulations, which obstructs the establishment of and operation of small businesses. These would be the most fruitful government interventions in labor markets in that they redress failures in capital market by promoting human capital accumulation. Whether through direct action, subsidization or loans, Knight argues the case for government to concentrate on helping people – particularly the young, educated and unemployed workers – to accumulate human capital in all its forms.

III Financial liberalization, monetary policy and currency crisis

Financial liberalization and monetary policy reforms were integral components of the economic structural adjustment program. The objectives were to improve financial intermediation, financial depth, breadth, and competitiveness and market orientation. Monetary policy sought to achieve the intermediate objective of price stability. Part III of this book contains three chapters focusing on Zimbabwe's monetary and financial sector reforms and the currency and financial crisis that hit the country so soon after the Asian financial crisis of 1997.

In Chapter 6 Obert Nyawata and Clever Mumbengegwi review the theoretical basis for financial liberalization and provide an account of the main facts and major episodes of Zimbabwe's financial sector reforms. They argue that prior to reform, Zimbabwe's financial sector exhibited many of the features common to financially repressed economies – interest rate ceilings, directed lending and various other types of controls. The reforms essentially involved a shift from administrative controls on credit, interest rates and a move from direct to indirect instruments of monetary policy. They find that although considerable progress was made towards liberalizing the financial sector, some controls, market segmentation, asset prescription and distortionary taxes on some financial assets still remain in place.

Using simple criteria, Nyawata and Mumbengegwi find some evidence of financial deepening and improvement in the efficiency of the financial sector. However, monetary policy is found to have failed to achieve its intermediate objective of a stable and low rate of inflation. As full transition to indirect instruments of monetary policy had been premised on reduction of the budget deficit to 5 per cent by 1995, failure to achieve this target was what undermined monetary policy effectiveness which, in turn, influenced the incomplete liberalization of some interest rates. Thus, they point to fiscal inertia, the high budget deficits and levels of domestic debt as the Achilles' heel of Zimbabwe's financial liberalization process. However, delays in reforming the prudential and regulatory framework, especially in amending the Banking and Reserve Bank Acts, also created problems for the financial sector, contributing to the financial crisis that resulted in the collapse of one bank and the rescue of two others.

Chandima Mendis (chapter 7) and James Gordon (chapter 8) respectively address the currency and banking crisis experienced in Zimbabwe after November 1997 and whether there is anything Zimbabwe can learn from the Asian crisis. In chapter 7, Chandima Mendis applies the 'new' theories of financial and exchange rate crises in order to explain the November 1997 currency crush and the subsequent banking crisis. He observes that the crush of the Zimbabwe dollar occurred against the backdrop of severe balance of payments pressure and weak macroeconomic fundamentals – low economic growth, high budget deficits, high inflation and low foreign exchange reserves. The exchange rate was, thus, incompatible with macroeconomic fundamentals and other policies. The resulting market uncertainty regarding the sustainability of the exchange rate is what led to speculative attacks on the local currency.

Using an econometric approach, he estimates a logit model to identify the factors that could have influenced the probability of occurrence of the November 1997 event. The candidates considered as possible determinants of currency crises include monetary and fiscal shocks, current account imbalances, foreign indebtedness, maturity and composition of foreign debt, levels of international reserves, world interest rates, the exchange rate and a weak banking system. Although preliminary in nature, Mendis' econometric results suggest that low level of foreign reserves, the budget deficits and the current account balance increase the probability of a currency and financial crisis. He also investigates the possibility of contagion but finds no evidence to support the argument that contagion from the Asian crisis or sudden capital outflows caused the crash of the Zimbabwean dollar in November 1997.

Mendis concludes that macroeconomic instability influences economic agents' perception of Zimbabwe's policy environment and risk rating. If these agents are skeptical about the macroeconomic fundamentals and sustainability of a policy regime, they are likely to devise strategies that may lead to speculative attacks, currency instability and financial crisis. Therefore, macroeconomic stability and paying attention to those political and social indicators which affect agents' perceptions is crucial to reducing the likelihood of future currency and financial crisis.

In chapter 8, James Gordon compares Zimbabwe with certain stylized facts about the Asian crisis and poses the question of whether there is anything Zimbabwe can learn from the Asian currency and financial crisis. The dissimilarity in the macroeconomic structures and fundamentals between Zimbabwe and the Asian economies leads him to conclude that the turbulence in Zimbabwe's financial markets was due to factors specific to Zimbabwe rather than contagion from Asia. To a country characterized by weak macroeconomic fundamentals were added the war veterans' gratuities,[4] and the easing of monetary policy. Both of these threatened to fuel the fiscal deficit and inflation; in addition, there was wave of labor discontent, the handling of the land question and uncertainty about the future direction of economic policies. These country-specific factors acted to erode market sentiment such that Zimbabwe became a real candidate for crisis given the tendency of market analysts to focus on a limited number of variables in assessing an economy's fundamentals. Among these are low reserve cover, high external debt ratios, exchange rate appreciation and weak macroeconomic balances. Zimbabwe exhibited several of these weaknesses and hence was a candidate for the financial and currency crisis. This militates against the existence of contagion, although a mild influence could have operated through the indirect effect of weak Asian demand and low world prices of Zimbabwe's mineral exports.

For the future, Gordon advises on the need for full disclosure and transparency in the conduct of economic policy as currency and financial crisis are often triggered not by what policy makers are actually doing, but rather by what financial markets perceive them to be doing. Disclosure of data on variables such as official reserves, forward exposure, short-term external debt, and other macroeconomic fundamentals which financial markets focus on is vitally important. Opaque and incomplete information on these matters tends to inflate fears, thus triggering speculative attacks on the currency. He further cautions policy makers to avoid the Asian example of resisting interest rate increases or easing of monetary policy and avert the threat of a much larger fiscal deficit. Further, the avoidance of exchange rate overvaluation, maintenance of international reserves to cover short-term debt and commitment to economic reforms, deficit cutting, better regulation of the banking system would go a long way towards restoring confidence after financial markets have become turbulent.

IV Computable General Equilibrium models and trade liberalization

The three chapters in Part IV use Computable General Equilibrium model simulations to examine growth and income distributional effects of trade liberalization. In chapter 9 Ramos Mabugu simulates the quantitative impacts of alternative policy scenarios in order to generate insights into why Zimbabwe's economic performance has been so poor since the introduction of economic reforms. The model is also useful for understanding the problematic involved in the economic reform process. He poses two major questions: (i) was the modest growth achieved during the1980s sustainable? and (ii) would the full implementation of reforms have yielded outcomes superior to those achieved from partial implementation? With respect to the first question, he finds the fiscally driven growth policies of the 1980s to be unsustainable on fiscal, equity and balance of payments grounds. With respect to the second question, partial implementation involving trade liberalization with no fiscal adjustment, has adverse consequences for GDP growth, income distribution and the trade balance. However, trade liberalization with a devaluation,even in the absence of fiscal adjustment, is found to have positive growth effects of 5 per cent and other favorable impacts on overall macroeconomic balance. Thus, he concludes that the non-aggressive use of devaluation as an active instrument of policy reform partly accounts for the poor growth outcomes during ESAP. However, the cost of devaluation is found to be inflationary pressures that worsen income distribution in favor of profit earners.

The simulation of full implementation of reforms involving simultaneous trade liberalization, devaluation and fiscal adjustment (*cuts in government spending*) illustrates the problematic involved in the economic reform process. The simulation produces mixed results. GDP falls by 11 per cent, suggesting that the ESAP package was contractionary. Imports also fall but exports increase, thus yielding a large improvement in the trade balance. However, a simulation involving the full implementation of the structural adjustment package accompanied by an exogenous increase in investment generates the most unambiguous growth outcome. According to Mabugu's analysis, this yields a 10 per cent higher GDP level and an output shift towards manufacturing as compared to the base-line scenario. However,the high import content of investment leads to a worsening of the current account balance.

Mabugu's conclusions are that Zimbabwe's vigorous trade liberalization without fiscal adjustment generated persistent balance of payments crises, reduced demand and loss of market share. The decline in the production of importables with no commensurate increase in manufactured exports meant that the current account deteriorated to unsustainable levels. Ultimately this led to deindustrialization and the decline in manufacturing share in GDP.

Thus the low rates of growth recorded in the 1990s is traced back to the lack of fiscal adjustment, deteriorating balance of payments, inadequate investment and negative distributional shifts, which is largely consistent with Nziramasanga and Minsoo Lee's conclusions.

The short- and long-run effects and dynamics of investment response after trade liberalization are analyzed by Halvor Mehlum, Jorn Rattsø and Ragnar Torvik in Chapter 10. They conduct counterfactual experiments involving the elimination of import rationing. This is done in two steps – the first is the elimination of intermediate imports rationing and the second adds final goods market to intermediate imports liberalization. The model predictions show the short-run effects of liberalization of intermediate imports to be expansionary, while the results of liberalizing finished goods is output contraction. To take into account the fact that the liberalization of finished goods coincided with the severe drought of 1992, they simulate the combined effects of these two events. This experiment predicts a 9.3 per cent decline in total GDP; which is very close to what was actually observed in that year. In contrast, the experiment of liberalization without the drought gives a fall in GDP of only 4 per cent. They also perform an experiment in which investments are increased by 5 per cent to take into consideration the fact that a strong investment response can counteract the contractive elements usually included in liberalization packages. The result is found to be a worsening of the trade balance rather than the avoidance of output contraction, mainly due to the high import content of investments. The removal of final goods protection is found to have a much larger short-run contractionary effect than the expansionary effect of intermediate imports liberalization. They conclude that deindustrialization was the net result.

Thus the first two years of ESAP are characterized as a case of successful liberalization, while from 1992 onwards, when final goods protection was removed as a case of unsuccessful liberalization in terms of its less favorable economic outcomes. The effects of the latter were output contraction, deindustrialization,external imbalance and erratic investments. Furthermore, the expected favorable effects of liberalization on living standards did not materialize, largely due to the fact that the short-run contractive effects of liberalization were larger and more long lasting than had been expected.

The long-run effects and dynamics of trade policy reform is argued to depend on the extent to which investments respond to changes in profit rates. If the process of trade liberalization is credible, it stimulates profitability and investments in the export sector. The result is increased exports and growth. However, if investors have doubts about the credibility of reform, investment response will be weak and the negative short-term effects will prevail. They find Zimbabwe's experience to accord with this expectation. Therefore, they conclude that Zimbabwe's trade liberalization needs to be credible in order to be successful.

In chapter 11, Margaret Chitiga also uses a Computable General Equilibrium model to analyze the income-distributional effects of trade liberalization. She uses functional income-distributional shifts to make assessments on the equity effects of policy. She concludes that trade liberalization has hurt the poor, and in particular the urban poor. She suggests complementary policies to be used and finds that, in all instances, the outcome with complementary policies dominates trade liberalization alone.

V Sectoral perspectives

Part V of the book contains three chapters that assess the sectoral impacts of macroeconomic and adjustment policies on the agriculture, manufacturing and health sectors respectively. In Chapter 12, Clever Mumbengegwi reviews the policy environment facing agriculture since independence. He argues that despite positive sectoral policies, agriculture's aggregate performance was below levels consistent with the country's resource and technological potential. He traces the cause of this to the negative macroeconomic environment, which, he argues, counteracted the positive effects of these positive sector-specific policies. Although structural adjustment reforms were meant to eliminate the anti-agriculture bias of macroeconomic controls, this objective was undermined by implementation failures. Mapping from a poor mix of fiscal, monetary and trade policies to real exchange rate appreciation, Mumbengegwi argues that this hurt agriculture, especially exportables.

The mechanism through which macroeconomic policies are transmitted to agricultural incentives is the real exchange rate. Therefore, the chapter highlights the sharp appreciation in the real exchange rate that accompanied the low growth and stagnation in agricultural output and real exports. The tendency for the real exchange rate to appreciate is located in the negative macroeconomic environment, both before and after the reforms. Descriptive and econometric evidence is provided to show that poor performance was the result of real exchange rate appreciation, which negatively affected the price incentives structure facing producers. The major conclusion and policy lesson from Mumbengegwi's chapter is that policies that cause a long-run appreciation of the real exchange rate are particularly harmful to agriculture. Therefore, he cautions that policy makers need to take a more serious view of the significance of macroeconomic factors in their design of policies aimed at stimulating agricultural performance.

In chapter 13, Hans Bjurek, Dick Durevall and Daniel Ndlela provide an overview of Zimbabwe's manufacturing sector and assess the impact of macroeconomic policies on its performance. They argue that the inward-looking strategies pursued in the 1980s acted as a disincentive to investment for firms and made the sector and the economy especially vulnerable to exogenous economic shocks. The piecemeal trade and investment incentives introduced during the period had a positive but small impact on manufacturing performance. The introduction of an outward-oriented policy regime in the 1990s did not improve matters, mainly because domestic firms were not appropriately geared to external competition. As a result, increased competition and high input costs hurt the sector. They call for a new industrial policy with an explicit outward orientation,complemented by efforts addressed towards macroeconomic stability.

The second part of the chapter analyzes whether ESAP has contributed to total factor productivity growth in the manufacturing sector. A Malmquist index of productivity is estimated for 31 manufacturing sub-sectors for the years 1980–95. They find that productivity increased in most sub-sectors during the periods 1981–85 and 1986–90, while for the period 1991–95 more than half of the sub-sectors show decreasing productivity. Their conclusion is that, contrary to expectation, there has been no growth in manufacturing total factor productivity during ESAP. Further, using panel data econometric methods, they investigate whether trade reform and market liberalization have contributed to an increase in total factor productivity growth. None of the trade reform measures are found to have had any significant impact on TFP while two variables related to ESAP (growth of imports and foreign aid) are found to have had an impact on TFP growth.

In Chapter 14, Gladys Mutangadura presents an analysis of the impacts of macroeconomic policies on the public health sector since 1980. She argues and presents evidence to show that the period 1980–90 was characterized by macroeconomic policies supportive of the health sector. Her findings indicate that tremendous gains in health were achieved, with all the major health indicators showing spectacular improvements. In contrast, the period 1991–98, when economic reforms were implemented, was characterized by cutbacks in the health budget, cost recovery measures, and declines in real incomes and increasing poverty of the potential health users. This resulted in the poor performance of the health sector, with some health indicators declining to below-1980 levels. Included in Mutangadura's discussion is how the HIV/AIDS epidemic has placed additional pressure on the health sector.

Drawing on her review of macroeconomic policies and the health sector, experiences from other countries, and basic projections of the HIV/AIDS epidemic, she outlines recommendations that can enable health to be more securely embedded in future macroeconomic policies. Among these is the need to set priorities in the allocation of the limited resources available in the face of a tightening budget and the AIDS epidemic. This can be done by measuring the social and economic benefits of investing in each of the sectors against the costs. Further, concerns with the impact of HIV/AIDS need to be grounded in the broader context of the initiatives already underway in health education, as well as improvements in demographic planning.

The analyses contained in this volume offer important lessons and advice to Zimbabwean policy makers (and indeed other developing countries in similar circumstances) as to which pitfalls to avoid and the policy options to consider in the transition from a controlled to a market-based economy. Since the authors concluded writing, Zimbabwe's economy has collapsed into an even deeper crisis. The conclusions and policy recommendations contained in this volume are even more relevant and valid than they were when the conference on which this book is based was held. Had policy-makers who attended the conference heeded the conclusions and recommendations, the current economic crisis could have been avoided. This notwithstanding, the book remains an important reference for policy-makers, researchers, students and others concerned with the issues and problematic involved in the transition from a government-controlled to a market-based economy.

Notes

1. Africa's average per capita growth declined by 1.3 per cent per annum while other developing regions of the world averaged positive growth of about 3.7 per cent per annum.
2. This is evidenced by the Figures of 7.3 per cent, 4.6 per cent and 2.2 per cent recorded in the last three years of the decade respectively (1988–90).
3. *Zimbabwe: A Framework for Economic Reform, 1991–1995* (GoZ, 1991).

References

Collier, P. and Gunning J.W. 'Explaining Africa's Economic Performance', *Journal of Economic Literature*, vol. XXXVII (March 1999) pp. 64–111.

UNDP (1997) *Human Development Report*. New York: Oxford University Press.

World Bank (1994) *Adjustment in Africa – reforms, results and the road ahead*. New York: Oxford University Press.

World Bank (1997) *World Bank 1998. World Development Indicators*. New York: Oxford University Press.

Part II

Macroeconomic Policy and Performance

2

Macroeconomic Performance under the Economic Structural Adjustment Program: an Essay on Iatrogenic Effects

Peter Robinson

1 Introduction and background

This chapter seeks to analyze and, in the process, provide an explanation for Zimbabwe's macroeconomic policies and performance during the period of the economic structural adjustment program (ESAP) which has been being implemented since 1991. In order to appreciate the problems that faced Zimbabwe's black majority government soon after it achieved independence in 1980 and the economic policies pursued during the ESAP period, it is important to understand the sequence of events, especially the economic policies and strategies pursued prior to the attainment of independence. Firstly, successive settler colonial regimes had culminated in the Unilateral Declaration of Independence (UDI) in 1965 by the then Prime Minister, Ian Smith. This was followed by the imposition of economic sanctions by the British government, with the support of the United Nations, which forced the rebel white colony of Rhodesia to pursue inward-looking policies that were supported by a panoply of controls over the economy. This ushered in a phase of economic development characterized by intensive import-substituting industrialization, accompanied by expansion in agriculture, mining and service sectors. The first decade of UDI experienced rapid growth of both GDP and employment – in excess of 7 and 3.8 per cent respectively. The manufacturing sector expanded its share in GDP from 19.3 per cent in 1965 to 23.7 per cent in 1974 (see Table 2.1). This was in response to the sanctions-induced incentives for import substitution, complemented by carefully targeted interventions to facilitate the broadening and deepening of the industrial base. The expansion was achieved without extracting a surplus or imposing other forms of burden on agriculture and mining, which also diversified and expanded over the period. The share of trade (exports plus imports) in GDP dropped rapidly, from 93 per cent in 1965 to 57 per cent in

1974. The second part of the UDI period (1975–79) was characterized by a decline in both GDP and employment such that by the time of independence in 1980, the economy had been significantly weakened. An ideology of racial superiority of whites over the black majority also characterized the UDI period, resulting in a system of economic management designed to provide for the white minority at the expense of the black majority. Thus, the first black majority government inherited one of the world's most unequal societies, with high levels of poverty, especially in the marginalized communal lands where the majority of the population live.

During the first decade of independence (1980–90), the policy stance of the new government was to maintain the panoply of controls and then characterize them as instruments for socialist transformation. The removal of economic sanctions and resumption of normal world trade, which coincided with two successive good rainy seasons in 1980 and 1981, provided an initial spurt of growth of 10.7 per cent and 9.7 per cent per annum respectively. Despite the next few years being characterized by drought and slower rates of growth, average GDP growth for the period 1980–85 was a respectable 4.7 per cent per annum. Slow growth of formal employment was a matter of considerable concern, with an average of 1.4 per cent – equivalent to an average of only 13 500 net new jobs per annum. The inward-looking character of the economic strategy is summarized by the decline in the trade ratio – from 57 per cent of GDP in 1979 to 44.2 per cent in 1985. Foreign exchange shortages became the binding constraint not only on investment, but also on capacity utilization, particularly in the manufacturing sector. Export incentives were introduced, and in the second half of the 1980s there was a reasonable GDP growth performance of 4 per cent per annum with more rapid growth in employment of 2.5 per cent, or an average of 28 000 net new jobs per annum. However, with new job seekers numbered in the hundreds of thousands each year, the unemployment gap remained enormous, thus turning an economic concern into a major political issue. However, considerable strides were made in extending the access of the population to health and education services and resources were also put into promoting communal agriculture and accelerating rural development. As a result of expenditure policies in the social sectors, there was considerable improvement in health, literacy and standards of living of the poor – during, especially, the first half of the 1980s.

2 Macroeconomic performance during the Economic Structural Adjustment Period (1991–95)

The economic structural adjustment program (ESAP) has been commonly perceived as a 'failure'. However, a major problem in assessing the performance of the Zimbabwean economy is the lack of consistent and reliable data. When the ESAP program was being designed in the early 1990s, it was widely recognized that the quality of the national accounts data had declined. As a result, the Central Statistical Office (CSO) carried out a major revision of the national accounts in 1996 and 1997. A new set of data covering the period 1985–96, with 1990 replacing 1980 as the base year for real values, was published in September 1997. These data were substantially different from the previous official figures. For example, GDP was approximately 40 per cent higher, domestic expenditure 66 per cent higher, gross fixed capital formation (GFCF) 20 per cent higher, GDP growth higher prior to 1991 and lower than previously estimated during ESAP. The 1990 base series has recently been extended to include 1997 and in so doing, some of the values in the 1997 document have been changed; in particular, the adoption of a lower 1995 GDP, giving rise to different 1994–95 and 1995–96 growth rates.[1] There is a general consensus that the revised national accounts are a great improvement on the data published prior to 1996; and, by and large, give a credible recent history of the Zimbabwean economy. Nonetheless, there remain some anomalies. For example, as shown in Table 2.2, inflation in 1995 as measured by the GDP deflator is 9.3 per cent as against a rise in the consumer price index for that year of 22.5 per cent. Some series are still subject to revision; notably the series for formal employment, which is thought to have captured a declining proportion of those actually employed and thus to give an unduly pessimistic view of the employment outcomes of ESAP.[2]

The data used in this chapter are from these latest revisions. The aim of this chapter is to compare the path of development intended under ESAP with the actual outcome, as reflected in these latest available data. In the main table of the ESAP policy document,[3] the targets are given in terms of proportions of GDP. So, clearly, the proportions are going to be different when a new GDP base is used. Rather than try to assess performance in relation to a GDP series now thought to be irrelevant, or try to modify the ESAP numbers to correspond to the new series, the data in Tables 2.2 and 2.3 show the year-to-year changes as planned at the start of ESAP and the outcome, as reflected in the July 1998 national accounts data. The ESAP targets themselves were set in relation to the performance of the economy in the preceding five-year period. So there are two five-year sub-periods to be examined (1986–90 and 1991–95). Because they have a different GDP base, the year-to-year figures are not directly comparable. A relevant comparison of relative performance is, however, the difference between the 1991–95 and 1986–90 averages, which are given in the last column of each table.

The judgment that the economic structural adjustment program (ESAP) has been commonly perceived of as a 'failure' arises from comparing the data in Table 2.1 and the first panel of Table 2.2. This shows that the economic strategy not only failed to provide improved performance, but was also associated with a considerable deterioration in what were generally thought to be the main objectives of ESAP – increasing growth and creating

Table 2.1 Macroeconomic performance indicators under various national development strategies and political regimes

Period	*Annual av. GDP Growth (%)*	*Employment growth (%)*	*End year Pop. (m)*	*Formal employment (% pop)*	*End-year GDP shares (%)*				*National Development Strategy*
					Agriculture	*Mining*	*Manu-facturing*	*Exp + Imports*	
1965–74	7.1	3.8	5.979	17.4	17.6	7.6	23.7	57.1	Import-substituting industrialization + development of other sectors
1975–79	−1.4	−1.1	6.951	14.2	12.1	8.5	23.6	56.8	Intensification of liberation struggle
1980–85	4.7	1.4	8.837	11.9	17.6	4.7	20.7	44.2	Growth spurt at Independence slowed by drought & inward orientation
1986–90	4.0	2.5	9.789	12.2	14.8	3.9	20.5	45.7	Export incentives superimposed on tightly controlled economy
1991–95	0.8	0.8	11.212	11.1	14.1	4.2	16.8	79.0	Economic Structural Adjustment Program ESAP + 2 droughts
1996–00	6.0	3.2	12.701	11.4	15.6	4.2	18.6	81.1	ZIMPREST

Source: Central Statistics Office, various publications (later GDP data from *National Accounts 1985–1997*, published July 1998; some discontinuities in pre- and post-1985 series. Population estimates: Updated from *1997 Inter-Censal Demographic Survey Report*, 1996–2000 are planned figures from ZIMPREST document).

Table 2.2 Key macro indicators for 1986–1990 and the ESAP period (1991–1995)

Calendar Year	*Item and Source*	*1986*	*1987*	*1988*	*1989*	*1990*	*1991*	*1992*	*1993*	*1994*	*1995*	*Av. 1986–90*	*Av. 1991–95*	*Difference*
GDP growth rate (%)	PLAN KMI	2.6%	−1.5%	5.8%	5.6%	4.2%	4.3%	4.4%	4.6%	4.8%	5.0%	3.3%	4.6%	1.3%
(factor cost – real)	ACTUAL T2.2(c)	1.8%	1.6%	5.9%	3.6%	7.2%	3.2%	−5.5%	2.0%	5.3%	−1.1%	4.0%	0.8%	−3.2%
Employment increase (%)	ACTUAL C-T7.7	28 600	4 000	46 100	35 500	25 500	51 900	−7 700	3 400	23 800	−24 000	27 940	9 480	−18 460
Growth rate (%)	ACTUAL C-T7.7	2.7%	0.4%	4.2%	3.1%	2.2%	4.4%	−0.6%	0.3%	1.9%	−1.9%	2.5%	0.8%	−1.7%
Consumption per capital(%)	PLAN KMI			−3.4%	5.9%	2.8%	2.1%	0.8%	1.1%	2.1%	1.8%	1.8%	1.6%	−0.2%
Growth rates (%)	ACTUAL C-T3.1(a)	−8.4%	−6.3%	−2.4%	39.5%	0.6%	17.1%	−24.6%	−7.8%	0.9%	−8.3%	4.6%	−4.5%	−9.1%
	ACTUAL Revised	−8.4%	−6.3%	−2.4%	39.5%	0.6%	17.1%		−7.2%	1.7%	−7.5%	4.6%	−4.1%	−8.7%
(GFCF+Stocks)/GDP(%)	PLAN KMI	19.4%	19.1%	19.7%	20.7%	21.0%	23.0%	24.3%	25.2%	25.1%	25.3%	20.0%	24.6%	4.6%
(market prices – nom.) (%)	ACTUAL T3.1(b)	18.0%	14.9%	18.7%	15.0%	17.4%	19.1%	20.2%	22.8%	23.5%	19.4%	16.8%	21.0%	4.2%
GFCF/GDP (%)	ACTUAL T3.1(b)	15.1%	16.1%	15.6%	14.0%	18.2%	20.6%	22.4%	23.6%	21.2%	24.3%	15.8%	22.4%	6.6%
Stock changes (%)	ACTUAL T3.1(b)	3.0%	−1.2%	3.1%	1.0%	−0.8%	−1.5%	−2.1%	−0.8%	2.4%	−4.9%	1.0%	−1.4%	−2.4%
National Savings/GDP (%)	PLAN KMI	18.5%	19.1%	21.0%	19.2%	18.0%	17.1%	17.9%	19.2%	19.9%	21.3%	19.2%	19.1%	−0.1%
(market prices – nom.) (%)	ACTUAL C-T6.2	18.2%	15.7%	20.2%	15.0%	15.7%	13.8%	11.3%	20.6%	21.5%	16.5%	17.0%	16.8%	−0.2%
Foreign Savings/GDP (%)	PLAN KMI	1.0%	0.0%	−1.3%	1.5%	2.9%	5.9%	6.4%	6.0%	5.2%	4.0%	0.8%	5.5%	4.7%
(market prices – nom.) (%)	ACTUAL C-T6.1	−0.1%	−0.7%	−1.5%	0.0%	1.7%	5.3%	8.9%	2.1%	2.0%	2.9%	−0.1%	4.2%	4.4%
Inflation (% change)	PLAN KMI	15.2%	9.2%	12.6%	10.8%	16.0%	16.0%	14.0%	12.0%	10.0%	10.0%	12.8%	12.4%	−0.4%
GDP (fc deflator) (%)	ACTUAL C-T2.2(d)	11.2%	6.7%	18.2%	18.7%	14.9%	31.6%	26.1%	21.4%	23.7%	9.3%	13.9%	22.4%	8.5%
CPI (%) Interest –	ACTUAL CSO	14.2%	11.9%	7.1%	11.6%	15.5%	23.3%	42.1%	27.6%	22.3%	22.5%	12.0%	27.6%	15.5%
treasury bonds (%)	ACTUAL RBZ	8.1%	9.3%	9.0%	8.8%	9.3%	14.0%	26.6%	33.1%	29.2%	28.0%	8.9%	26.2%	17.3%

Note: PLAN figures from ESAP document table Zimbabwe – Key Macroeconomic Indicators; ACTUAL figures from CSO *National Accounts* 1985–1997, July 1998, unless otherwise indicated. C = calculated from indicated table. Population figures for 1993–1995 extrapolated from 1997 *Inter-Censal Demographic Survey Report*.

employment. Both GDP and employment growth rates averaged a mere 0.8 per cent over the period 1991–95. Annual job creation in the formal sector fell from nearly 28 000 per annum in the late 1980s to 9500 per annum during the period of ESAP. There was a basic failure of the economy to provide an adequate number of new jobs – particularly, for the increasingly well-educated school-leavers, numbering some 300 000 per annum. Furthermore, those who were lucky enough to be employed experienced a sharp decline in real wages, the average being –7.4 per cent per annum over the period of ESAP. As a result, the share of wages in GDP fell from 44.5 per cent in the 1986–90 period to 36.9 per cent in 1991–95. This slow employment growth and reduced real wages were major contributing factors in producing falling consumption levels. Far from growing at +1.6 per cent per annum, as envisaged in the ESAP program, consumption per capita *fell* at a rate of –4.0 per cent per annum (based on the latest population figures from the 1997 Inter-Censal Survey). Thus, if employment creation was the main reason that propelled policy makers into embracing structural adjustment, then the severe curtailment of net new jobs created over the ESAP period can be regarded as a serious indictment of the program.

The opening up of the economy to international competition is encapsulated in the increase in the trade ratio to 79 per cent by 1995. However, the manufacturing sector was hard hit – its share in GDP fell to 16.8 per cent of GDP by 1995, 7 per cent lower than it had been a decade earlier. The planned targets for the successor program to ESAP, known as the Zimbabwe Program for Economic and Social Transformation (ZIMPREST), are ambitious. However, even if they are achieved, they would only return the economy in the year 2000 to where it had been in 1990. The explanation for this poor performance lies partly in the severe droughts experienced during the period – in 1992 and 1995. However, whatever the combination of causes, performance under ESAP was much lower than under the control regime of the 1980s. A point which was not adequately spelt out in the ESAP document, however, is that transformation of a highly regulated economy into a liberalized environment, in which high rates of growth are sustained, was not going to be completed in a period as short as five years. The first paragraph of the ESAP document states that 'the Government of Zimbabwe has embarked on a program of economic policy reform aimed at stimulating investment and removing impediments to growth'. In relation to those more modest objectives, the ESAP program can be said to have achieved a considerable measure of success. The second panel of Table 2.2, for example, shows that total investment increased by 4.2 per cent of GDP during ESAP, as compared to the 1986–90 period, which was close to the program target of an increase of 4.6 per cent of GDP. Of the components of investment, stocks actually declined on average during ESAP, perhaps reflecting the lower stock policies of firms once they were assured of access to imported inputs, this being a net efficiency gain for the economy. The remaining component, gross fixed capital formation, thus increased by more than total investment (6.6 per cent of GDP), attaining a respectable average of over 22 per cent of GDP over the ESAP period. This was not, however, financed through higher domestic savings, which declined on average by 0.2 per cent of GDP, but rather by increased foreign savings (a higher current account deficit) and by reduced stock holdings. Even if the relatively high investment figures during ESAP are taken as reflecting the success of the program, there are nonetheless some pertinent questions to be asked. Why is it that investment, which, on average, was 59 per cent higher in real terms than during the previous five-year period, was associated with much lower GDP growth? Can the economy be expected, during the next program of adjustment (ZIMPREST, 1996–2000), to take advantage of the investments already made and have a spurt of growth without putting a much higher level of resources into investment? These issues are analyzed in Annex 3 of the ZIMPREST document. An Incremental Capital Output Ratio (ICOR) of 22.2 was calculated for the ESAP period, as compared to 4.2 for 1986–90. This suggests a very low efficiency of investment during ESAP. Among the reasons suggested for this are that investments made were to modernize and replace equipment, rather than to expand capacity; and these were in areas with long gestation lags, such as infrastructure, rather than in productive activities which would more directly raise output. Furthermore, despite rapid increases in exports (especially from pure manufacturing), the droughts and decline in domestic demand sharply reduced production levels, so that new capacity was not fully utilized.

During ZIMPREST, provided macroeconomic balance is restored, a lower ICOR of 3.5 is envisaged, in part because of the level of underutilized investment available from the ESAP years. With roughly the same level of investment in relation to GDP, the ZIMPREST document argues that the target rate of growth of 6 per cent per annum (averaged over drought and non-drought years) can be achieved during the period 1996–2000. The performance during the first part of the UDI period (see Table 2.1) suggests that such an average growth is by no means impossible in this economy. Indeed, in 1996, the first year of the new program, GDP grew by 7 per cent (even though real GFCF declined by 8.8 per cent). However, in 1997 real GFCF declined by a further 13.5 per cent and GDP grew by only 2 per cent, leading to negative growth rates in 1998 and 1999 such that for the entire ZIMPREST period (1996–2000) average GDP growth was negative.

One of the key objectives of ESAP was to restore macroeconomic balance. The major problem during the ESAP period was the government's lack of budgetary control. In fact, fiscal indiscipline has been the Achilles' heel of Zimbabwe's post-independence government since it took power in 1980. In contrast to the UDI period, when external pressures from international isolation required the government to maintain strict fiscal discipline, the budget deficit was allowed to rise to an average of over 11 per cent during most of the

1980s, although on the recently revised GDP figures discussed above, the average is calculated to be 8 per cent. The interest payments resulting from the rapid accumulation of national debt rose from 10.5 cents per dollar of revenue collected in 1980/81 to 15 cents in 1985/86. Whatever the exact magnitudes, the persistent budget deficits of the 1980s were large enough to set the stage for the debt problems which were to increasingly overshadow attempts to restore balance to the national budget during the 1990s.

The government's unwillingness or inability to significantly reduce the budget deficit during ESAP worsened macroeconomic imbalances – especially high inflation and interest rates. As can be seen from Table 2.3, the average budget deficit, excluding international aid grants, of 8.3 per cent of GDP, was not significantly more than the average of 8 per cent for the period 1986–90. The significant difference is that, in the environment of financial repression that existed in the 1980s, high budget deficits could be financed largely through appropriating private sector savings which could not be channeled into investment because of the lack of foreign currency to purchase the imported component of investment projects. Thus, inflation and interest rates remained relatively stable (see the last panel of Table 2.2). With price decontrol, interest rate and financial market liberalization under ESAP, private investment increased to make use of savings previously channeled into budget financing, resulting in prices and interest rates rising rapidly. Reducing inflation became the chief target of monetary policy, with the Reserve Bank's rediscount rate being the main, but extremely blunt, instrument at its disposal. Thus, the size of the budget deficit and its method of financing through short-term instruments (Treasury Bills) led to a rapid accumulation of domestic debt and an even more rapid increase in interest payments on debt due to the much higher interest rates. These became the underlying reasons for the loss of macroeconomic balance. Thus a connection was established between the high budget deficit, excess demand in the economy, rapid monetary growth, high inflation and high interest rates as new issues of Treasury Bills attracted progressively higher interest rates during the period 1991–93 (see the last row of Table 2.2). In 1994 and 1995, Treasury Bill interest rates declined from the peak of nearly 40 per cent per annum reached during 1993, but rates remained at levels close to 30 per cent for the rest of the ESAP period. Combined with a continually increasing debt stock, the interest burden in the budget grew in real terms by an average of 12.2 per cent per annum over the period 1990/91–1994/95. This compares with growth rates of 1.2 per cent per annum for revenue and 1.6 per cent per annum for non-interest recurrent expenditure[4]. By 1995/96, interest payments consumed 36 cents out of every dollar collected in revenue (compared with 17 cents in 1990/91) and interest payments exceeded the combined expenditure of the health and education ministries. With the role of interest becoming more dominant in the budget, the aim of reducing expenditure sufficiently to allow a reduction in inflation and hence interest

Table 2.3 Salient features of national budget 1985/86–1989/90 and the ESAP period (1990/91–1994/95)

Financial year	*Item and source*		*1985/ 86*	*1986/ 87*	*1987/ 88*	*1988/ 89*	*1989/ 90*	*1990/ 91*	*1991/ 92*	*1992/ 93*	*1993/ 94*	*1994/ 95*	*Av. 1986–90*	*Av. 1991–95*	*Diff.*
Central Govt Revenue/GDP	PLAN	C-KMI	33.1%	37.0%	37.2%	37.9%	37.4%	37.6%	37.9%	37.4%	37.1%	36.5%	36.5%	37.3%	0.8%
(without grants) (%)	ACTUAL	C-FS	25.9%	27.4%	28.9%	27.0%	26.6%	25.6%	28.3%	26.0%	25.9%	26.1%	27.2%	26.4%	–0.8%
C Govt Expenditure/,	PLAN	C-KMI	37.8%	41.3%	40.2%	40.1%	39.6%	38.2%	36.9%	35.3%	34.1%	33.6%	39.8%	35.6%	–4.2%
GDP (excluding interest) (%)	ACTUAL	C-FS	29.5%	32.7%	32.0%	29.7%	28.2%	28.2%	30.0%	28.9%	26.0%	31.0%	30.4%	28.8%	–1.6%
Interest payments/	PLAN	C-KMI	6.8%	8.0%	7.8%	8.2%	8.0%	8.7%	8.8%	8.7%	8.5%	7.9%	7.8%	8.5%	0.8%
GDP at market prices (%)	ACTUAL	C-FS	4.4%	4.9%	5.0%	4.9%	4.8%	4.4%	4.9%	6.0%	6.1%	7.8%	4.8%	5.8%	1.1%
Central Govt Primary	PLAN	KMI	–4.7%	–4.3%	–3.0%	–2.2%	–2.2%	–0.6%	1.0%	2.1%	3.0%	2.9%	–3.3%	1.7%	5.0%
deficit– *surplus + GDP* %	ACTUAL	C-FS	–3.6%	–5.3%	–3.0%	–2.7%	–1.6%	–2.6%	–1.7%	–2.9%	0.0%	–5.0%	–3.2%	–2.4%	0.8%
Central Govt Deficit–	PLAN	KMI	–11.5%	–12.3%	–10.8%	–10.4%	–10.2%	–9.3%	–7.8%	–6.6%	–5.5%	–5.0%	–11.0%	–6.8%	4.2%
GDP (excluding grants) (%)	ACTUAL	C-FS	–8.0%	–10.2%	–8.0%	–7.6%	–6.4%	–7.0%	–6.7%	–8.9%	–6.1%	–12.7%	–8.0%	–8.3%	–0.3%
Salaries and wages	ACTUAL	C-FS	8.5%	9.9%	12.0%	11.0%	11.0%	11.4%	10.6%	10.6%	9.5%	10.5%	10.5%	10.5%	0.0%
Budgetary Investment/	PLAN	KMI	3.3%	5.5%	6.2%	5.3%	5.2%	5.0%	4.8%	4.6%	4.5%	4.5%	5.1%	4.7%	–0.4%
GDP at market prices (%)	Investment	C-FS	2.3%	2.7%	3.8%	3.4%	3.1%	3.4%	3.7%	3.7%	3.6%	5.0%	3.1%	3.9%	0.8%
	Investment and Net Lending	4.0%	4.8%	6.8%	6.6%	6.1%	5.9%	7.6%	5.3%	6.1%	9.0%	5.7%	6.8%	1.1%	

Note: PLAN figures from ESAP document table 'Zimbabwe – Key Macroeconomic Indicators', ACTUAL figures from Financial Statements, various years and CSO July 1998 GDP data (C = calculated from indicated source).

rates became ever more difficult to achieve. In other words, by the end of the ESAP period, continued high budget deficits, financed predominantly from the local capital market, had brought the country to the brink of a debt trap.

Changes in the national budget as a proportion of GDP for the ESAP period and the five preceding years are reported in Table 2.3. Looking at five-year averages, the targets set in the ESAP program were a marginal increase in revenue of 0.8 per cent of GDP, a larger reduction in non-interest expenditure of 4.2 per cent of GDP and a concomitant increase in interest of 0.8 per cent of GDP. The revenue and interest targets thus balance, leaving expenditure reduction to achieve the required reduction of 4.2 per cent of GDP in the budget deficit (exclusive of grants). In the event, revenue during ESAP declined by 0.8 per cent of GDP, and non-interest expenditure was reduced by 1.6 per cent of GDP while interest expenditure grew by 1.1 per cent when compared with the 1985/86–1989/90 average. As a result, the primary deficit did not improve nearly as much as the program had envisaged, and the overall budget deficit increased by an average of 0.3 per cent of GDP. In terms of expenditure components, on average, salaries and wages remained a constant proportion of GDP, while public investment as a proportion of GDP actually increased. Investment from the national budget was thus a contributor to the pattern of increased investment during ESAP, as discussed earlier.

Changes in the levels of revenue and expenditure did not take place smoothly. In 1991/92, revenue increased mainly because of a surcharge imposed on Open General Import Licence (OGIL) imports. When the OGIL surtax was reduced and subsequently the OGIL distinction fell away in 1995, revenue from border taxes declined, contributing to the downward trend of revenues arising from lower tax rates, low growth and declining collection efficiency. Non-interest expenditure rose as a proportion of GDP during the drought (though not in absolute real terms), but declined thereafter until the 1994/95 financial year.

Two particular aspects of that year's budget,[5] resulted in the deficit being recorded as 12.7 per cent of GDP, instead of the 6.1 per cent it would have been. If, in addition, the measures relating to the public enterprises had been postponed to the next financial year, the budget deficit for 1994/95 would have been well inside the target level of 5 per cent. Despite this, the IMF judged the program to have gone 'off track' and suspended its support. Given the 'knock-on' effect of other donors also withdrawing their support, the adjustment process was put under enormous pressure. Fortunately, there was strong growth in the first year of ZIMPREST, which allowed revenue growth to exceed expenditure increases in financial years 1995/96 and 1996/97 and the budget deficit to decline to 9.1 per cent and 6.1 per cent of GDP respectively. However, when growth slowed in 1997, the underlying imbalance between revenue and expenditure, continually augmented by a rising interest burden, clearly emerged. With high inflation relative to Zimbabwe's trading partners, the currency was allowed to become overvalued; a situation which resulted in a slowing in the growth of exports (which had been at satisfactory levels during ESAP) and a major currency crisis in November 1997, repeated in August 1998.

3 What went wrong?

As already outlined above, far from giving rise to higher economic growth and other desirable goals, the period of ESAP is associated with reduced growth and lower standards of living for the majority of the population. The main interest of this section is to tackle the question *'what went wrong?'* and, in so doing, to present an analysis of the change in economic policy paradigm in terms of a *medical metaphor*. An analogy is drawn between different stages of the policy metamorphosis and a typical sequence of medical treatment. The process of diagnosis, issuing of advice and different forms of treatment (drugs, surgery and so on) is not perfect because of the difficulty of making accurate diagnoses and limitations in knowledge about or ability to provide treatment. Thereafter, the process is greatly complicated by factors which affect the degree to which advice is taken and drug regimes adhered to, and the impact of side-effects.

Finally, there is the possibility of *iatrogenic* effects. These are illnesses caused by the physician's actions – unforeseen ailments which the patient would not have had to endure if he had not consulted the medical profession in the first place. It is the iatrogenic effects which are of particular interest in the debate about the structural adjustment policy prescriptions in Africa, particularly those emanating directly or indirectly from the Bretton Woods institutions rather than from indigenous sources. Thus, an important sub-theme of this chapter is that a country such as Zimbabwe needs to be much more proactive in formulating and sticking to an economic strategy appropriate to tackling the economic situation that the country now faces. In so doing, a more specific and holistic approach, encompassing the political context as well as economic circumstances, can be adopted. This should prove to be less prone to adverse side-effects and unforeseen iatrogenic influences. This conclusion follows directly from the medical analogy, where a growing response to modern high-tech medicine is for patients to take greater charge of their own medical care and ensure that specific interventions fit into an overall process of improving their state of health and well-being.

3.1 Medicine and economics

Modern medicine is widely, although not universally, regarded as having a firm 'scientific' basis. The style of modern medicine, with its reliance on expensive testing procedures for diagnosis, its tendency to prescribe a large number of drugs, each targeted to addressing specific symptoms, and its sophisticated surgical procedures, is certainly geared to reinforce that image in the mind of the patient. Without seeking to detract from major medical achievements, the situation of the medical profession in many highly developed countries is that patients have become alienated from the process of looking after their own health. Many tests and procedures are carried out in order to protect doctors from possible litigation arising from allegations of negligence or malpractice. The dispensing of drugs is strongly influenced by the commercial interests of an increasingly oligopolistic global pharmaceutical industry. Thus, iatrogenic diseases arise largely from the oversophistication of modern medicine.

The dominant strand of the economics profession works hard to give a 'scientific' appearance to the subject. There is an obsession with numbers, but many of the econometric procedures which are carried out on data of extremely dubious quality are entirely spurious. They are not treated as spurious, because attention is focussed on the sophistication of the methodologies which are used to produce the 'precise' numerical answers.[6] The ready availability of high technology tools is partly to blame, but so, in the view of this observer, is the way economics is now taught, as though it were a hard science and not a branch of politics and sociology, which is closer to the truth of the matter. The creation of an image of sophistication in the minds of new initiates to the 'profession' as well as in the mind of the 'patients' is a significant feature of economics as much as it is of medicine.

The mainstream of both disciplines also exhibit a high degree of consensus and defensiveness about the fundamental approach that is being adopted, explaining away problems and difficulties rather than being open to the possibility of a shift in paradigm. The convergence of opinion about economic strategy has become increasingly evident in economics as the process of globalization has continued to gather momentum, and as ideological positions have changed, particularly since the fall of the Berlin Wall and the end of the Cold War. With nearly all countries striving to make their way in the global capitalist economy, the main lines of economic policy, such as the need for macro stability and openness to trade and investment flows, are almost universally endorsed. The policy debate has become more narrowly circumscribed to issues concerning how great a role government should play relative to markets in promoting growth, industrialization and reducing poverty. The Bretton Woods Institutions (BWI) have been very influential in forging the current consensus and equally skilful in shifting the ground when the consensus is challenged.[7] The doctor and patient metaphor is especially apt in the case of Africa, where the World Bank and the IMF are so influential in the formulation and even the execution of economic policies.

In the analogy with modern medicine, a particular point of concern about the Bank and the Fund is their tendency to consider all patients in the same way, treating particular problems, in isolation from historically determined circumstances, with uniform prescriptions. The preferred alternative would be to assess the patient's overall condition and provide a holistic solution (taking into account psychological – political – factors, and socioeconomic circumstances as well as the clinical details of the patient's specific economic problems). Such an approach may produce less dramatic short-term results in respect of specific problems, but there will be lower risks of side-effects and iatrogenic problems and the patient will be more committed to the strategy. There will thus be a much higher level of assurance of the patient's continued well-being in the medium term.

In Zimbabwe's case, work on the program for the first five years of structural adjustment had reached an advanced stage in 1990. However, at that time it was as difficult to have health insurance companies cover treatments by *n'angas* (traditional healers) as it apparently was for the donor community, led by the BWI, to support a 'home-grown' program of reform. Instead, the ESAP document *A Framework for Economic Reform (1991–95)* bore the hallmark of the World Bank in its orientation and presentation. The prescription it contained was a mixture of specific interventions and recommendations on changes in lifestyle. The reasons for the outcome by 1995 being so different from the projections in the document are analyzed in the following sub-sections – from diagnosis through to anticipated side-effects and unforeseen iatrogenic effects.

3.2 Diagnosis

As has already been indicated above, the macroeconomic information available at the time that ESAP was formulated is now considered to have been quite inaccurate. The extensively revised national accounts give a quite different picture of the economy over the five years prior to ESAP. They show higher GDP and per capita consumption growth, despite considerably lower national and foreign savings and hence investment, and somewhat higher inflation. An interesting question to speculate about is whether the Zimbabwean government would have pursued structural adjustment had it known that the growth rate over the previous five years (1986–90) had averaged 4 per cent per annum? By the standards of Southern Africa, as opposed to South-East Asia, 4 per cent per annum could be considered quite acceptable. However, on the ground, at the end of the 1980s both government and the private sector had reached the conclusion that the complex system of controls was unworkable and hence counterproductive. There was a general view that a change of strategy was needed even for growth to be continued at 1980s levels and certainly if higher rates of growth were to be attained. The lack of sustainability of the 1980s, policy regime is evident from the figures in Table 2.2. With a national savings rate of 17 per cent of GDP, negative foreign savings and an investment rate (GFCF) of less than 16 per cent, the economy was fortunate in achieving 4 per cent growth. More rapid growth would have required higher savings levels (including being able to run a higher current account deficit) and a higher investment rate.

The structural adjustment route – reducing the burden of bureaucratic controls, opening the economy to investment flows, removing capital goods and imported input constraints, and encouraging national savings but having external bridging finance to get the process started – seemed an obvious course of action to pursue. Given the growing consensus within the economics profession, augmented by offers of financial support by those influential in forging that consensus, there was, perhaps, a certain inevitability about Zimbabwe embracing ESAP. What is at stake are issues of detail rather than of principle. In other words, the diagnosis and proposed line of treatment were not fundamentally wrong.

3.3 Advice on changes in lifestyle

The ESAP document envisaged the budget deficit being halved, from over 10 per cent in the late 1980s to 5 per cent by the financial year 1994/95. The document argued that 'Given Zimbabwe's relatively high tax ratio, this target will be achieved mainly through a containment of recurrent expenditure.' The lifestyle changes envisaged were 'the virtual elimination of subsidies to public enterprises', a 'reduction in the civil service wage bill' and 'increased cost recovery', these being partially offset by 'compensatory expenditures required to alleviate the burden of adjustment on the poor'.[8]

To what extent were these desired changes in lifestyle in the above three areas achieved? Direct subsidies were reduced sharply over the period, from a peak of Z$961 million in 1991/92 to Z$49 million in 1994/95. However, the practice of subsidization continued to a significant extent under the guise of other budget headings. For example, as shown in Table 2.4, the Zimbabwe Iron and Steel Company (ZISCO) received a number of 'loans' over the period.

Furthermore, as discussed earlier, past subsidies and debts of public enterprises had to be taken over in order to strengthen their balance sheets prior to commercialization or privatization. In respect of salaries and wages, the envisaged reduction in the civil service wage bill, from 16.5 per cent of GDP in 1990/91 to 12.9 per cent by 1994/5, did not materialize. After real reductions in the salaries and wages bill in the first three years, there was an increase of nearly 14 per cent in 1994/95, followed by a smaller increase in 1995/96. This was partly because those leaving the service had to be paid retrenchment packages, and the subsequent reduction in wage requirements

Table 2.4 Loans to the Zimbabwe Iron and Steel Company (ZISCO) 1990/91–1996/97

Financial year	*1990/91*	*1991/92*	*1992/93*	*1993/94*	*1994/95*	*1995/96*	*1996/97*
ZISCO allocation Z$$_m$	100	100	100	100	—	297	203

was not sufficient to offset the increases granted to those remaining in post. However, had there been higher economic growth, the reduction would have been achieved.

The third point mentioned above was increased cost recovery. A significant increase in non-tax revenues (from 2.9 per cent of GDP in 1990/91 to 4.3 per cent in 1994/95) was recorded over the period. This was largely due to increases in investment income (interest and dividends from state-owned companies), increased civil servant pension contributions and privatization proceeds as from 1994/95 ($525 million, or 0.9 per cent of GDP in that year). In respect of cost recovery itself, sector-level studies suggest that a great deal more should have been achieved in this area. The introduction of cost recovery in health and education rightly attracted attention because of its impact on those unable to pay, while other, potentially more lucrative, areas were neglected. For example, a comprehensive study of water pricing revealed that not only were prices too low, but that the collection of water fees had fallen to around 20 per cent of what was due to the government. In 1995, the total implicit subsidy on publicly supplied water was estimated at Z$400 million,[9] 2.4 times the amount collected in the education and health sectors and corresponding to a significant 0.7 per cent of GDP.

3.4 Prescription items – package deal

Once a patient has consulted a doctor and been given a treatment regime, the instructions he or she receives – for example, about which combinations of medicines to take at specified times – should be followed. Not doing so can significantly diminish the efficacy of the prescription. Another doctor may prescribe a different set of measures, which would also need to be adhered to in their entirety. While both packages might be to some degree efficacious, a strategy where different elements from the two different regimes are selected and arbitrarily combined could well be disastrous. In the economic sphere, the strategy that Zimbabwe had been following prior to 1990 had its own internal logic, but once structural adjustment was embraced there was a need to recognize that ESAP was a package deal with a different set of mutually reinforcing measures which had to be properly synchronized. There appears to have been a logical inconsistency in Zimbabwe pursuing, with vigor, trade liberalization, the relaxation of investment controls, the deregulation of agricultural marketing and, crucially, the removal of direct controls on interest rates while not taking measures to reduce the budget deficit to levels where its financing did not pose a threat to macroeconomic stability. As already highlighted, the consequence was an inflation–debt trap spiral which became a threat to the whole reform program.

3.5 Exogenous factors

Exogenous factors – influences outside the immediate purview and control of the doctor – can certainly disrupt the treatment envisaged for a patient. In the case of ESAP, slow growth in the region and low commodity prices for some key export products were a problem, but the significant exogenous event was the most severe drought since records began which occurred in 1991/92 at the start of the period of ESAP. The main impact of droughts is to reduce domestic agricultural production and increase pressure on foreign currency to import food and agricultural raw materials. In Zimbabwe's case, with a diversified manufacturing sector dependent on the local market, a secondary income effect (which often lasts into the following year) is a reduction in the demand for manufactured products. The 1991/92 drought was so severe that supplies of water and electricity were disrupted. Water and power rationing had marked supply-side impacts, while the income contraction corresponding to the 5.5 per cent reduction in GDP were also severe.

Was being in the midst of a structural adjustment program a help or a hindrance when the country had to cope with the 1991/92 drought? There can be little doubt that the response of the economy was made easier by the liberalization measures already in place by that stage, particularly in respect of trade. For example, without having to wait for a protracted bureaucratic process to respond to the changed circumstances, manufacturers were able to respond to the severe contraction of the domestic market by finding export markets, in many cases requiring companies to immediately improve their products and management systems to service much more demanding external markets. Growth of 'pure' manufactured exports (excluding ferrochrome, iron and steel, cotton, lint and sugar) was negative in 1991, but rose by 32 per cent in 1992, 30 per cent in 1993, 20 per cent in 1994 and 10 per cent in 1995, giving an annual average of over 15 per cent for the ESAP period as a whole. It is very doubtful that such growth would have been possible under the previous constrained regime.[10]

3.6 Anticipated side-effects

Medical treatments often involve trade-offs between desirable and undesirable outcomes, otherwise known as side-effects. Economies, like human beings, are complex organisms and all treatments involve some degree of risk that the unwanted side-effects may turn out to be much more severe than anticipated. In the ESAP document, the only side-effects which were acknowledged were the adverse impact on the poor of food subsidy removal and cost recovery in education and health, and the issue of fairness in respect of those retrenched as a consequence of the adjustment process.

With donor support, the Social Dimensions Fund (SDF) was set up in order to provide social safety nets for the poor. Retraining and subsidized loans to those retrenched from the civil service were to assist them in establishing their own businesses. The main problem with the SDF program was the fact that it only became properly operational in the 1993/94 financial year. Difficulties in establishing operationally manageable targeting mechanisms also meant that the coverage of the underprivileged was not satisfactory. The eligibility criteria have remained fixed in nominal dollars from the start of the program, with the result that the responsibilities of government to those requiring support have dramatically diminished due to the high level of inflation in the Zimbabwean economy. The actual criteria applied by SDF did not match the official thresholds. So in practice a broader coverage has been maintained, but the trend has been one of declining payments per beneficiary in real terms. At the same time, government acknowledged that the combined effect of the droughts and structural adjustment was an increase in the overall level of poverty in the country. The 'social dimensions' program was therefore broadened to a Poverty Alleviation Action Plan, with the SDF being recast as the Social Development Fund.

4 Iatrogenic effects

Iatrogenic diseases were characterized above as illnesses caused by the physician's actions – unforeseen ailments which the patient would not have had to endure if he had not consulted the medical profession in the first place. The essence of this definition is 'unforeseen', at least by the patient. The doctor may know about the risks involved in a particular course of treatment, but choose not to inform the patient. However, as experience is gathered, doctors will become more aware and, as public awareness is raised, it is likely that patients will begin to insist on being better informed. This is a process which is being worked through by institutions such as the IMF in the light of a growing body of experience of structural adjustment in a wide range of developing economies. In the case of ESAP, a number of iatrogenic effects can be identified.

4.1 Loss of capacity in government

Reduction in the civil service wage bill was one of the key elements in reducing the budget deficit during ESAP. A restrictive wage policy and a 25 per cent reduction in the number of civil servants, excluding the education sector, was to be effected over the first four years of ESAP to help achieve this. The reduction in numbers was to be in 'areas of redundancy and duplication, thus increasing efficiency in the government sector'. While average real wages would fall, differential wage adjustments would ensure that the 'policy does not result in shortages of specific skills in the civil service' (*A Framework for Economic Reform*, p. 6).

In practice, the reduction in numbers was achieved in part through a voluntary retrenchment program. Although ministries and the public service persuaded some would-be retrenchees to stay on, the inevitable result of a voluntary retrenchment program was for some of the most capable and experienced civil servants to leave government. At a time when government was supposed to become more commercially minded and innovative, those that left also tended to be those with business sense and, in some cases, entrepreneurial drive. The opening up of private sector opportunities, reduction in investment barriers under ESAP and the availability of retrenchment packages ironically played some part in weakening the civil service.

4.2 Revenue-raising ability compromised

A particular area of weakness which emerged within the civil service was in respect of accountancy skills. Demand for people with accountancy qualifications, but more particularly for those with work experience, increased rapidly outside government. It became very attractive for accounting officers to leave the civil service, with or without redundancy packages. The effect on the revenue-raising capability of government was disastrous. This applied first and foremost to the Department of Taxes. The reduction in the efficiency of collection of taxes had the immediate effect of reducing revenue and hence increasing the budget deficit, with the dire feedback consequences for the ESAP program already discussed. The likely longer-term effects of undermining that most precious of public goods – the willingness of taxpayers voluntarily to declare all their sources of income and to pay their taxes – is potentially far more serious.

It is difficult to estimate with any precision the impact on revenues of the reduction in the efficiency of the Department of Taxes. Davies (1996) has provided an interesting decomposition of revenues over the ESAP period, distinguishing separately a 'collection effect' from the 'real growth' and 'inflation' effects'. His collection effect was a combination of changed tax rates and collection efficiency and has a large negative magnitude. Tax rates were lowered as part of the ESAP program on the supply-side assumption that the tax burden was 'too high' and lower tax rates would encourage investment and growth, thereby maintaining the volume of tax revenues despite lower rates. It is difficult to separate the effect of lower rates (in the absence of economic growth) from lower collection efficiency, without having proper data on the tax base for each category of tax. However, direct observation of the collapse of the Department of Taxes suggests that the efficiency aspect must account for a significant portion of the reduced collection effect.

The increase in revenues expected of the proposed semi-autonomous National Revenue Authority has been variously estimated at between one and two percentage points of GDP. Such optimism about the expected impact of creation of the National Revenue Authority arises, in part, from the record of the 'door-to-door' exercise carried out in the first quarter of 1996. During this exercise, the provision of a few vehicles and the time of tax officials to visit firms at their place of business resulted in the collection of hundreds of millions of dollars of unpaid taxes in the space of a few weeks. Analysis of the tax payments of listed companies also reveals some interesting patterns, with some of the biggest companies consistently paying the lowest taxes. At present the Department of Taxes does not have the capacity to match the smart accountants employed by these large firms.

While there is doubt over the degree to which collection efficiency deteriorated during ESAP, there is clear evidence of the critical importance of declining revenue in the emergence of the deficit–debt trap. This author was part of a team that developed a macroeconomic model for the successor program to ESAP, ZIMPREST. The budget component of that model can be used to explore the implications of higher revenue collection during ESAP. The model is a suitable tool for such a counterfactual because it explicitly takes account of the dynamics of Zimbabwe's budget-related debt. Higher revenue implies lower deficits, lower financing requirements and a smaller debt stock for the next year. Maintaining revenue while having a lower interest burden in the next year quickly produces a marked impact on the overall macroeconomic environment. For example, if the level of revenue in 1991/92 (28.3 per cent of GDP) had been maintained over the following three financial years, the budget deficit would have fallen to below the target of 5 per cent of GDP by 1995/96 and below 3 per cent of GDP in 1996/97. The average revenue over the ESAP period would then have been 27.8 per cent of GDP, as compared with the actual figure of 26.4 per cent (see Table 2.3). This implies that an increase in average revenue of just 1.4 per cent of GDP would have been sufficient for the debt trap to be avoided and macro-stability to be achieved. This sensitivity of the macroeconomic system to revenue collection augurs well for the proposed National Revenue Authority.

4.3 Structural change reducing the tax base

With the reduction in constraints on investment and the encouragement given to the informal sector and the self-employed, the extent of wage and profit earning outside the formal tax system has clearly increased significantly. As part of the deregulation component of ESAP, the relaxation of restrictions on the use of domestic premises for business purposes (Statutory Instrument 216 of 1994) is particularly important in this regard.[11] As pointed out by Davies (1996), these changes have had the unanticipated effect of making taxes more difficult to collect, thereby effectively reducing the size of the tax base. Davies adds an interesting speculation about the loss of a likely side-benefit of the regulatory system which previously would have contributed to ease of tax collection: 'firms vying for import allocations had an incentive to provide information on their activities. Although this was not done for tax purposes, it created a climate in which better information was available to government'.

4.4 Increased nominal and real interest rates fueling the debt trap

The debt trap syndrome of a high budget deficit increasing inflation and interest rates, feeding back into worsening the budget deficit, became a major cause for concern by the end of the ESAP program. The basis of this problem was the liberalization of interest rates before the budget deficit had been reduced to a sustainable level. Like reading the small print on a medicine bottle, a careful scrutiny of the *'Framework for Economic Reform'* document might have alerted policy makers to the dangers. Annex II, p. 3 of the document, notes that

> far reaching and enduring financial sector and policy reform is predicated on firm control of the fiscal deficit. If the fiscal deficit is not reduced, the pace of financial liberalization of which interest rate deregulation is an important component, will have to be slower as the resulting higher market-determined interest rates will have an adverse impact on the budgetary position of the government.

However, once consumer price inflation had risen to over 40 per cent during the 1991/92 drought, there was intense pressure to raise nominal interest rates. Attempts thereafter to use monetary policy in order to control inflation resulted in significantly positive real interest rates. This did not immediately discourage investment, but probably only because of the lead time on investment projects. After 1995, when the projects initiated at the start of ESAP had been completed, gross fixed capital formation as a proportion of GDP has been falling. The main macroeconomic impact of high interest rates has been the feedback into the budget, making it increasingly difficult for the authorities to pull the economy back from the brink of the debt trap. At a micro level, high interest rates have been a particular burden for emergent businesses, making it more difficult to indigenize the economy.

While continued deficits in the pre-ESAP era had resulted in ongoing debt accumulation, the interest burden only became a matter of overriding concern once interest rates had been liberalized. If interest rates on Treasury Bills in the remaining years of the program had been kept at 1991/92 levels, a second counterfactual exercise using the ZIMPREST macroeconomic model[12] indicates that the target 5 per cent budget deficit would have been achieved by 1995/96, instead of the actual figure of 9.1 per cent of GDP. Thereafter, with a lower stock of debt (66 per cent rather than 80 per cent of GDP), lower inflation and interest rates, the task of maintaining macroeconomic stability would have been relatively straightforward, as compared with the actual starting conditions for the ZIMPREST program.

4.5 Rentier profits attracting the brightest and the best into secondary activities

Another unforeseen effect of high market interest rates and macroeconomic instability were the exceptional opportunities to make quick fortunes which emerged in areas like trading, property and financial markets. The brightest and the best of a younger generation of indigenous entrepreneurs proved the point by setting up successful merchant banks and financial services companies. These new entrants helped to propel the 'Finance and Insurance' component of GDP at 5.4 per cent per annum during the period 1991–95, while the economy as a whole grew at an average of only 0.8 per cent per annum.

The important point here is that these entrepreneurs did not go into the main productive sectors of the economy, where they are needed if the long-term growth of the economy is to be assured. The present generation of entrepreneurs, particularly in agriculture and manufacturing, is literally dying out and there is a need for them to be replaced by younger people with the energy and vision to meet the new challenges posed by globalization. Instead, trade liberalization showed many Zimbabwean enterprises to be characterized by pre-1990 mindsets and not properly able to cope with the opening up of the economy.

4.6 Market orientation creating powerful groups inimical to growth

Industrialists, accustomed to nearly three decades of almost total protection, were an obvious source of pressure to slow or reverse the liberalization process. Industry was subject to much more rapid trade liberalization than had originally been intended. Once export retention proceeds were made tradable in January 1992, a wide range of imports became freely available within the economy, and this was followed not long after (July 1994) by total liberalization of the current account of the balance of payments. Against this background, government was surprisingly unsympathetic to the pleas from industrialists, taking comfort perhaps from the fact that, while the domestic market collapsed, dynamic firms managed to penetrate export markets and overall manufactured exports performed well.

When concessions were made (for example, tariff increases on clothing, motor vehicles and batteries in the 1994/95 budget) these seemed to be ad hoc. The Tariff Commission promised in the ESAP document was only established in 1998, as was the Competition Commission. Inheriting a highly oligopolistic industrial structure resulting from the period of foreign currency control, greater protection of consumer interests might have been assured by an active and professional Competition Commission being established at the start of the ESAP period.

The significant change which took place in respect of business interest groups was the emergence of organizations to promote the indigenization of the economy. While using the rhetoric of creating a stake for the majority of the population in the economy, most of the leadership of these organizations was bent on furthering their own personal interests, and was thus keen to have those interests protected in various ways antithetical to the liberalization process and inimical to economic growth. In this, ready allies were found amongst the political elite. The slow pace of commercialization and privatization of public enterprises was a particular casualty of this process, delays on the basis of the need to find modalities of achieving indigenization actually guaranteeing favored parties the opportunity to establish themselves in the sectors concerned.

Unfortunately, it cannot be claimed that the political elite and its partners in business had not taken advantage of opportunities for personal gain at the expense of the economy as a whole prior to liberalization. Such opportunities are glaringly obvious in a controlled regime, where items such as investment approvals and access to foreign currency are under the direct control of politicians and senior civil servants. Indeed, one of the gains anticipated by economists from liberalization is the reduction in the scope for discretionary apportionment of economic access and resources. However, in Zimbabwe's case, the change in the ideological climate may have given rise to the opposite result in that, in the epoch of rhetoric about 'socialism', the pursuit of private business was done discreetly and there seemed to be some degree of restraint, too, amongst the leadership in the amassing of private wealth. The adoption of structural adjustment, with its explicit market orientation, changed all that, making it possible for indigenization pressure groups to become publicly active and loosening whatever restraints there may have been amongst the political elite.

4.7 Program failure paralyzing government

A set of instructions from a doctor which result in an immediate improvement in the condition of the patient tend to have a cumulatively beneficial effect. The sense of well-being encourages the patient to take the medicines in the prescribed doses and combinations and to adhere to the lifestyle advice. With a more positive attitude to life, the patient may be able to dispense with the prescriptions earlier than expected and go from strength to strength. Unfortunately, the converse scenario, of treatment having little immediate benefit or, iatrogenically, of exacerbating the condition or causing new problems, tends also to be cumulative in effect. In these circumstances, attention shifts to treating the new problems, the patient becomes depressed and fractious, and the treatment regime is then likely to be neglected or only partially followed, which, as already discussed, may actually be worse than not pursuing it at all.

In the case of ESAP, its failure – in the sense of insignificant GDP growth, few new jobs and increasing hardship for the mass of the population – exacerbated tensions and differences and resulted in fractiousness within the political elite. The fact that the Ministry of Finance, at the hub of the adjustment process, was without a substantive minister for protracted periods, was a major cause for concern during ESAP. The lack of leadership from the Ministry of Finance was compounded by conflicting signals from President Mugabe and other quarters of government. This tended to mean that sensible programs remained on the agenda, but were simply never implemented. The failure to set up the National Revenue Authority perhaps provides the starkest example of this phenomenon. An institution which, as discussed above, is likely to give the quickest and politically cheapest boost to restoring macroeconomic stability, remains on the drawing board several years after its imminent creation was officially announced in the budget statement at the start of the 1996/97 financial year.

4.8 The suspension of IMF support in 1994/95

It was suggested in the last section that the malaise which presently afflicts the Zimbabwe government can be ascribed to the political spin-off of the failure of ESAP to provide tangible results. While it is explicable that politicians should react to the lack of short-term pay-offs, the significance of this chapter is that it has argued that account needs also to be taken of the positive changes which did take place and which can be built upon. The liberalization path that was chosen around 1990 has an internal logic which needs to be consistently followed if the sacrifices already made are to be rewarded with some positive outcomes. Many of the problems which have arisen are due to exogenous factors (the drought) and unanticipated problems which can now be systematically tackled. The most obvious and urgent of these iatrogenic effects is to restore the efficiency of revenue collection within government. By combining this with stringent expenditure control and reducing the budget deficit sufficiently to allow a reduction in inflation and interest rates, a virtuous cycle can be initiated which will pull the country back from the debt trap almost as quickly as it moved towards it.

While it is understandable that politicians should feel ambiguous about the reforms and resort to populist measures (such as price controls on basic items) the decision of the International Monetary Fund in 1994/95 to declare Zimbabwe's structural adjustment program to be 'off track' is puzzling. While it is true that, in that year, the civil service salary and wage bill increased by nearly 14 per cent in real terms, and non-interest current transfers (such as pensions) also increased substantially, significant reasons for the resulting very large budget deficit were the change in the handling of the Vote of Credit (recommended by the Fund) and the take-overs of parastatal debt. The underlying budget situation was thus not nearly as serious as the budget deficit, taken in isolation, seemed to imply. The Fund could have taken a more neutral view of the problems:

> In cases where a country fails to meet performance targets within an IMF financed program, the Fund may (a) regard the failure as minor within a program that is basically 'on track', or (b) it may judge it to be a 'temporary slippage' which leads to modified performance targets to enable the country to return to the program, or (c) it may judge the program to be 'off track' and suspend the agreement. In Zimbabwe's case, the most harsh of those judgements was made.[13]

In so doing, all major donors withdrew support, and the difficulty of keeping the program anywhere near 'on track' became considerably greater.

In order to try to estimate the impact of the IMF decision, the ZIMPREST macroeconomic model has again been used to construct a counterfactual. The impact of the Fund's decision was felt in 1995/96 and subsequent years. Increasing the level of grants and concessionary financing which would have been available had the Fund program remained in place, it is estimated that the budget deficit in 1995/96 would have fallen by nearly two percentage points, but would still have been above 7 per cent of GDP. However, there would have been a fall in the budget deficit to around 3.5 per cent of GDP in 1996/97, as compared with the actual figure of 6.1 per cent of GDP. With greatly reduced domestic financing requirements, these falls in the budget deficit would have been associated with inflation falling to below 20 per cent in 1996 and perhaps below 15 per cent in 1997, with corresponding declines in interest rates. This would have put the economy on a much sounder footing at the start of the second phase of structural adjustment.

In 1997, the IMF initiated a process of systematic evaluation of its Enhanced Structural Adjustment Facility (ESAF), the concessional finance mechanism through which the Fund had supported structural adjustment programs since the mid-1980s. An internal evaluation by Fund staff, completed in July 1997, was followed by an external evaluation, which was published in March 1998. A summary document, 'Distilling the Lessons from the ESAF Reviews', has been made publicly available for comment (by 4 September 1998) before being finalized. Zimbabwe was one of the case studies examined in the ESAF external evaluation. The team carrying out that evaluation was forthright in criticizing ESAP, characterizing it as being so poorly designed as to be unworkable from the start. Based on the program as laid out in the ESAP document, the evaluation claims that a 'combined reduction in non-interest expenditures of 15 per centage points of GDP over the four years 1992–95' was required and that 'such a severe reduction in social and redistributive expenditures would inevitably have put the reform program under great political strain'. The report identified two miscalculations in the ESAP program: an economic one, in respect of the magnitude of the fiscal adjustment required; and a political one, in that there was insufficient consensus to allow expenditure cuts and public enterprise reform to proceed with sufficient vigor.

While the justification given for the estimate of a reduction of 15 percentage points of GDP being needed is borne out neither by the original ESAP program nor by the actual outcome, the general thrust of the argument in the external ESAF evaluation supports the case being made here that the Fund was not justified in making the judgment that the Zimbabwe program had gone 'off track'. The evaluation does not specifically criticize the Fund for this measure, merely referring euphemistically to the '1995 interruption' in the program, but it does hint that the judgment may have been influenced by political factors internal to the Fund rather than by an economic analysis of the economic situation in the country.

The report notes that

> in 1994, in a speech given to the South African Parliament in Cape Town, the President (of Zimbabwe) called for a democratization of the Fund and accused the Bretton Woods institutions of 'financial imperialism' and 'dictatorship'. In 1995, he was also reported as speaking of 'disastrous reforms imposed by the World Bank and the Fund, adding ominously 'we are wiser than we were three years ago and we will not listen willy-nilly to what the international institutions will tell us to do'.

To what extent was the public expression of such views taken as a slap in the face by the Fund? From the Fund's viewpoint, is the 'patient' the government of the day or the country as a whole? Why is it that in mid-1998, when the macroeconomic situation is clearly far worse than it was in 1994/95 and a number of political commitments with dire implications for the budget have recently been made, that the Fund seems determined to sweep any inconvenient facts and trends under the carpet and continue with financial support?

The obvious conclusion from President Mugabe's remarks, quoted above, is that Zimbabwe should take much closer control of its economic strategy. The same sort of conclusion is also made by those concerned with the direction in which modern medicine is proceeding. They suggest that by taking charge of our own health, being better informed and smarter in our interactions with the medical profession, and having the willpower to persevere with treatments, we have a better chance of improving our state of health and well-being. The problem in Zimbabwe's case is that President Mugabe has failed to provide the leadership required to allow the government to shake off its malaise and take autonomy in economic policymaking to its logical conclusion. For example, the successor program, ZIMPREST, inexplicably languished for two years before finally being published halfway through the program period it was supposed to cover. During the intervening period, no significant differences of opinion were voiced and no great changes were made to the draft, other than to update the macroeconomic framework when the revised GDP data became available. The document that was eventually published was originally the executive summary.

The complete version of ZIMPREST, which spells out the fiscal and sectoral programs in more detail, may never be made available to government officials and the general public. This is symptomatic of a continuation of the old habits of secrecy, despite the current rhetoric about consultation and transparency, which surrounds the recently created National Economic Consultative Forum.

Autonomy in policy making is very much in vogue in Washington at present. For example, the first point made in the Executive Summary of the Fund paper 'Distilling the Lessons from the ESAF Reviews' is that '*ownership of a program by the authorities* should be fostered by widening the policy debate within government and considering alternative policy mixes that would be consistent with appropriate program objectives. The Fund can also assist governments in their task of building a "*national consensus for reform*"' (emphasis in the original). Taking the initiative in formulating economic strategy does not mean turning one's back on the Fund. On the contrary, it means understanding the direction in which the Fund is moving and exploiting whatever opportunities are presented to the full.

Amongst the points agreed by the Executive Directors of the Fund following the ESAF evaluations is that 'signs of official commitment' to whatever program is established by the country are to be treated as important in deciding on levels of access to Fund resources. Having decided on a program and prevailed upon the Fund to accept it in the spirit of local ownership, the leadership cannot then subsequently indulge in scoring populist points if external financial support is to be sustained. Securing the Fund 'stamp of approval' is particularly important because the support of other major donors is unlikely to be forthcoming without it.

5 What can go wrong again?

While it is interesting to examine the iatrogenic effects which made the execution of the ESAP program much more difficult than anticipated, the main cause for poor performance was the lack of diligence on the part of the patient. The Zimbabwean government's failure to adopt the structural adjustment prescription as a package, and particularly its deficient performance in respect of the budget, were fundamental. With the exogenous factors, side-effects and iatrogenic aspects superimposed, the political outcome was one of disassociation from the program and greatly increased high-level corruption, these factors exacerbating the downward tendencies in the economy.

As a result, the economy ended up in a worse state than it had been in at the start of ESAP. Growth was so low over the first five-year program that it will take at least another five years of strong growth to return per capita income and consumption levels to where they were in 1990. Strong growth requires the logic of the chosen strategy to be resolutely followed, which, in turn, is only going to be possible under forceful leadership. One of the unfortunate legacies of the ESAP years is a weakening in the resolve of the leadership, growing political dissent and perhaps a shortening of the perceived political time horizon. Once political lifespans are shortened, opportunism and populism are increasingly likely to override the more difficult long-term measures that the country really needs.

There are also other more specific iatrogenic-type problems which may continue to thwart development unless pre-emptive actions are taken:

- **Sequencing**
  How is the initial 'kicker' which will reduce the budget deficit sufficiently for domestic financing to be reduced, inflation and interest rates to come down and the self-reinforcing process of moving away from the debt trap to be set in motion? The easy place to start is on the revenue side, establishing a properly autonomous National Revenue Authority to collect taxes more efficiently and equitably (as well as making it possible to introduce taxation measures to promote goals such as employee ownership or export growth) and ensuring complete cost recovery for all public goods and services supplied to those who can afford to pay. At the same time, expenditure savings have to be made through restructuring the civil service for the twenty-first century and through efficient commercialization and privatization of public enterprises.
- **Institution-building**
  Far from liberalization eliminating regulation, it places increasingly sophisticated requirements on those responsible for protecting the national interest. For example, the need for very careful regulation of the financial sector is one of the major lessons to emerge from the 1997 crisis in East Asia. Zimbabwe has an antiquated financial regulatory framework, but the reform of the Reserve Bank and Banking Acts, mooted before the ESAP document was released, was only completed in 1999, eight years later. This has become extremely urgent following the failure in 1997 of one of the merchant banks, with its fraudulent activities putting several other banks in danger. Similar increases in the sophistication of regulatory systems are required in the infrastructural sectors as part of the process of commercialization and privatization. Fiscal constraints are such that government can no longer fund major infrastructural developments, and a clear, non-discriminatory framework to facilitate private investment (domestic or foreign) is needed to ensure that the required level of investment in infrastructure will be achieved. The objective of regulation in sectors where there is a mix of private and public investment is to ensure that competitive conditions prevail, whether directly through ensuring sufficient players, or through creating pseudo-competitive conditions amongst oligopolists. Without sophisticated regulation, opening the infrastructure sectors to private investment could leave both consumers and the economy as a whole worse off than before.
- **Public investment**
  The temptation to reduce public investment in response to the required initial reduction in the budget deficit should be resisted. Reduced levels of

public investment will make the economy less responsive to other adjustment measures and are likely to impact adversely on employment creation and poverty reduction. Given the limits on their overall size, public investment programs need to be increasingly carefully designed to 'crowd-in' private investment. In similar vein, health and education spending should be maintained not only for immediate reasons of equity, but from the perspective of investing in human capital to sustain economic growth over the medium and long term.

Notes

1. CSO *National Accounts 1985–1997*, July 1998.
2. This view is based in part on comparing CSO employment data with statistics for those in formal employment published by the National Social Security Authority. Given incentives to under-report numbers of employees for whom social security payments have to be made, it would be expected that NSSA figures might be lower, but after adjusting for differing sectoral definitions and so on, the NSSA data suggest formal employment levels by 1995 that are at least 0.3 million higher than the CSO figures of 1.2 million for 1995.
3. Government of Zimbabwe (1991) *A Government of Zimbabwe Framework for Economic Reform*. Harare: Government Printers.
4. If the financial years applying to ESAP are taken to be 1991/92 to 1995/96, the five year average growth rates are 18.1 per cent p.a. for interest, 1.8 per cent p.a. for revenue and 0.3 per cent for non-interest recurrent expenditure.
5. The two particular aspects of that year which resulted in exceptionally high apparent expenditure and a consequent increase in the budget deficit from 6.1 per cent of GDP in 1993/94 to 12.7 per cent of GDP in 1994/95 were:
   - *a re-assessment of the way the Vote of Credit was to be handled in the budget accounts*: the Vote of Credit [VOC] allows ministries to draw on the consolidated revenue funds to spend money on projects funded by foreign assistance. Typically, the expenditure is made prior to the funds being received by government. On the suggestion of the IMF, the change made in the 1994/95 budget was that funds spent before reimbursement should be counted as government lending. The Minister in his 1994/95 budget speech (paragraph 32) stated that "the additional expenditure is attributed to a cleaning up exercise involving the Vote of Credit.... This was, in reality, a bookkeeping exercise which did not require additional financing". However, the amount involved ($3892 million or 6.6 per cent of GDP) had a significant impact on 'investment and net lending' and on the overall deficit.
   - *Payments made to strengthen the balance sheets of various parastatals prior to commercialization and privatization*: an amount of $486 million had to be paid out to accommodate guaranteed loans, this being a consequence of past failure to meet subsidy obligations to public enterprises. Government also took over the debts of the Grain Marketing Board and the Cotton Marketing Board and in so doing had to meet additional interest obligations amounting to $395 million. Together, these items required $881 million or 1.5 per cent of 1994/95 GDP.

6. Fine (1998) describes 'the use of econometrics as an unproblematic test of theories, in lieu of conceptual rigor and depth'.
7. In a lecture in January 1998 to the World Institute for Development Economics Research entitled 'More Instruments and Broader Goals: Moving Toward the Post-Washington Consensus', the then recently appointed Vice President for Development Economics and the World Bank, Joe Stiglitz, codified the consensus and moved the debate to the next stage.
8. *A Framework for Economic Reform* (1991), pp. 5 and 6.
9. Zimconsult (1996, p. 4).
10. A more formal exploration of the adaptability of the economy to drought, using a CGE model, is available in Penrose et al. (1997), Annex A.
11. See Zimconsult (1997, p. 69). The likely undercounting of formal employment – see note 2 – is not unrelated to the development of businesses in what were previously purely residential areas. Sectors such as computers and information technology provide highly remunerative employment, often from a home base, without being counted by CSO and also, perhaps, escaping the notice of the tax authorities.
12. As in the revenue counterfactual, the model explicitly takes account of feedback within the dynamics of budgetary debt: reduced interest rates imply lower interest charges and hence lower deficits, lower financing requirements and a smaller debt stock for the next year. The combination of lower interest rates and lower debt stock rapidly allows the overall macroeconomic environment to stabilize. This forms the basis of the ZIMPREST strategy for achieving macro stability.
13. Penrose et al. (1997, p. 27).

References

Davies, Rob (1996) 'The budget deficit in Zimbabwe', paper prepared for a National Seminar on Adjustment, Employment and Labour Market Institutions in Zimbabwe, International Labour Organization, 30 July.

Fine, Ben (1998) 'Endogenous growth theory: a critical assessment', *SOAS Working Paper Series No. 80*, School of Oriental and African Studies, University of London.

Fischer, Stanley and Easterly, William (1990) 'The economics of the government budget constraint', *The World Bank Research Observer*, vol. 5, no. 2, July, pp. 127–42.

Government of Zimbabwe (1998) *ZIMPREST (Zimbabwe Program for Economic and Social Transformation 1996–2000)*. Harare: Government Printer, February.

International Monetary Fund (1998a) 'The external evaluation of the enhanced structural adjustment facility, report by a group of independent experts', IMF, March.

International Monetary Fund (1998b) 'Distilling the lessons from the ESAF reviews', IMF, July.

Ito, Takatoshi (1998) 'What can developing countries learn from East Asian economic growth?', in B. Pleskovic and J. E. Stiglitz (eds), *Annual World Bank Conference on Development Economics 1997*. Washington DC: World Bank, April, pp. 181–247.

Penrose, Perran, Laurence Harris, Gerald Bloom, Rob Davies, Peter Robinson and Sam McPherson (1997) *Evaluation of the EU's Structural Adjustment Support Program in Zimbabwe*, for the Commission of the European Communities, Cambridge, July.

Robinson, Peter (1997) 'Application of the systems approach to Zimbabwe', in Toru Yanagihara and Susumu Sambommatsu (eds), *East Asian Development Experience: Economic System Approach and its Applicability*. Tokyo: Institute of Developing Economies.

Stiglitz, Joseph E. (1996) 'Some lessons from the East Asian Miracle', *World Bank Research Observer*, vol. 11, no. 2, August, pp. 151–77.
Stiglitz, Joseph E. (1998) 'More instruments and broader goals: moving toward the post Washington Consensus', *WIDER Annual Lectures*, United Nations University World Institute for Development Economics Research, Helsinki, January.
World Bank (1996) *Zimbabwe: Fiscal Management Review*, vol. 1, Macro, Industry and Finance Division, Southern Africa Department, June.
Government of Zimbabwe (1991) *Zimbabwe: a Framework for Economic Reform (1991–95)*. Harare: Government Printer, January.
ZIMCONSULT (1996) 'Water pricing options and implications', report for Steering Group of Water Resources Management Strategy, Harare, May.
ZIMCONSULT (1997) 'The relationship between economic and physical planning in Zimbabwe: the spatial implications of medium and long-term economic policies, and positive planning responses', Department of Physical Planning, Harare, April.

3
Redistributive Policies and Economic Growth

Mudziviri T. Nziramasanga and Minsoo Lee

Introduction

Economic reform programs have the potential to yield significant benefits, yet in most cases the necessary policy changes are only implemented as a last resort, long after policy makers realize that the status quo is no longer sustainable. Programs have rarely been implemented in full, nor have they been successful the first time around. Reform programs have usually been motivated by dissatisfaction with the lack of economic growth, or with rates that are low relative to those of neighboring countries with market-oriented systems (Perkins, 1994). Delays in responding to the internal and external pressures are attributed to uncertainty over the distribution of gains and losses from the reform program (see, for example, Fernandez and Rodrik, 1991). Voters do not know with certainty ex ante those individuals who would derive positive net benefits, and therefore would be willing to pay the cost. Given this uncertainty the bias is toward maintaining the status quo. The evidence cited in such studies pertains to macroeconomic stabilization in the developed world. When it comes to developing countries, the lack of reform has been partly attributed to non-economic motives such as sheer ineptitude or predatory behavior (Krueger, 1993) and the initiation of programs due to exogenous shocks, political change, or even the emulation of economic performance in neighboring countries (Perkins, 1994). Assessing the validity of the above reasons as well as the impact of implementing gradual reform on such objectives as income growth and employment has proved problematic. In this chapter, we try to capture both the flavor and impact of the reform process by using time series data for Zimbabwe. First, we use intervention analysis to assess the impact of the actual implementation on the individual macro variables considered key to the reform process. The relative magnitudes indicate that the gradual reform process in Zimbabwe was hamstrung in that only trade liberalization, exchange rate policy and price reforms were implemented – and these measures were only introduced very gradually. Labor markets were also decontrolled. However, there was difficulty in controlling public consumption expenditures which would have allowed for a restructuring of the budget. We then use a production function to assess the impact on GDP of the liberalization process. Since the initial impact of reform is generally assumed to be changes in capacity utilization and allocative efficiency, we should be able to observe them as well as any long-term impact.

This chapter is divided into three sections. The first section discusses the historical background and the economic policies pursued in Zimbabwe in the period leading up to the economic reform program. The second applies intervention analysis to the key variables to assess the impact of the policy interventions of 1980 and 1990. The effects are likely to be dynamic in nature and we can expect overlapping effects of the 1980 and 1990 measures during the period 1990–96. Our model is designed to separate these effects. In the last section we estimate a production function, test for returns to scale and compute the annual levels of total factor productivity for the whole period (1954–96) and the period before reforms (1954–89).

1 Background

The economic policy measures which led to the adoption of the economic reform program in 1990 have their roots in the institutional and political environment established in 1954 with the formation of the Federation of Rhodesia and Nyasaland. The period can be divided into three parts: the federation era (1954–63); the period of sanctions and forced import substitution (1964–79); and the post-independence phase (1980–96). While the sociopolitical conditions changed and policy measures were intended to benefit first one group and then another, the result throughout the period was a decline in investment rates, capacity utilization and output growth.

The Federation (1954–63)

The Federation of Rhodesia and Nyasaland, formed in September 1953, was a customs union consisting of Southern Rhodesia (now Zimbabwe), Northern Rhodesia (now Zambia) and Nyasaland (Malawi). The idea behind the formation of the Federation was that economies of scale and tariff protection would foster more rapid industrialization.[1] By 1956 a common external tariff with four schedules had been adopted, with the revenues reverting to the Federal government. The constitution also gave the Federal government the power to levy an income tax. A portion of the revenues raised was then returned to the territories on the basis of an agreed formula. With regards to expenditure, the constitution vested control in the territorial authorities of those services which were particular to the indigenous population (that is, agriculture, primary education and social welfare) while the Federal government was responsible for non-African education and agriculture, as well as most of the health services and the public infrastructure. Major public sector investments in power and communications were completed during this period, financed mostly through overseas borrowing by the Federal government which passed on the loans to statutory bodies created for the purpose of operating the facilities. The customs union never gained popular support, however, and from the very beginning two of the member countries pressed for its dissolution. This inhibited private sector fixed investment and long-term growth in Southern Rhodesia. The Federation was finally dissolved in July 1963.

Sanctions (1965–1979)

The differences between the British and Southern Rhodesia government over the eventual political participation of the indigenous population escalated soon after the break-up of the Federation. In November 1965 the colony unilaterally declared itself independent. The United Nations responded by imposing economic sanctions on trade. The impact was more significant on oil and other raw material imports as well as agricultural exports previously destined for the European Community and, later, the European Union (EU). Two of the relevant policy measures which continued to be applied concerned land ownership and government expenditures on education by race. The Land Apportionment Act of 1930 divided the country into European Areas, which covered 49 per cent of the country, Native Reserves (including land available for purchase) occupying another 29.2 per cent, and State Land. The inequity in this division is clear from the fact that the indigenous people comprised over 80 per cent of the population. There were also disparities in the agricultural potential of the land, and market transactions across races were illegal. In 1964 the government of Southern Rhodesia assumed control over the expenditures on European education as well. Schools were segregated by race. During the Federation period, Southern Rhodesia had spent 2 per cent of the government budget on African education. After 1969 education comprised about 15 per cent of the annual budgets. The policy was to spend equal absolute amounts on each race. Since African children attending school outnumbered Europeans by 20 to 1, there was a wide racial disparity in expenditure per child. In addition, only 2 per cent of all apprentices trained using public funds during this period were Africans. This generated disparities in the distribution of skills and thus wage income.

In 1965 the currency was removed from the Sterling Area and became non-convertible. Exports were subject to sanctions but reached some markets anyway through indirect channels. The transactions costs, though not documented, were sizable. Fixed investment was stimulated by import substitution. In an attempt to maintain domestic employment, foreign exchange reserves were managed through a system of quotas on imports. Exporters were obliged to surrender all their foreign currency earnings to the central bank at the official rate of exchange. This added to the already strong upward pressure on prices which in turn triggered extensive controls. The prices of most major commodities were established after negotiations with producer organizations, and they allowed for guaranteed rates of return.

The first post-independence period (1980–90)

The government elected by universal suffrage in 1980 faced significant political pressures to redress the imbalances in favor of the new voter majority. Primary education was to be free for all, as were medical benefits for those below Z$150 a month. By 1989 educational salaries constituted 41.4 per cent of the budget and defense accounted for another 26.1 per cent. The economic management system in existence since 1965 continued, including price controls. Public corporation deficits grew, fueled by consumer subsidies and a burdening bureaucracy. Central government expenditures more than tripled, increasing its share from 32.5 per cent of GDP in 1979 to 37.6 per cent in 1983 and 44.6 per cent by 1989. Table 3.1 shows the major sources of growth in government expenditure.

When adjusted for outstanding subsidy obligations, the budget deficit's share rises from 7.8 per cent to 9.23 per cent of GDP in 1985, and 9.28 per cent to 14 per cent in 1990. Growth in government services increased public sector employment by 60 per cent between 1980 and 1989. Most of the additional employment was in education, administration, defense and health. On the other hand, industrial employment remained constant while the real wage declined by 3 per cent. The average real wage declined by 50 per cent between 1980 and 1989 on the strength of the decline in industrial capacity and capacity utilization.

Economic reforms (1989–95)[2]

By 1988 the budget deficit had risen to over 13 per cent of GDP. The private sector and government agreed that a program to stimulate growth would have to increase capacity utilization through import liberalization. It would also require a reversal of the government expenditure policies which had

Table 3.1 Real government expenditures on selected items, 1978/79, 1990/91 (Z$million 1980 prices)

Sector	*1978/79*	*1990/91*	*Growth rate*
Education	227.6	628.0	10.0
Subsidies	155.9	205.7	2.9
Interest payments	78.8	438.3	17.0
Health	66.4	188.6	10.0
Civil Service	347.9	1194.3	12.0

Sources: Government of Zimbabwe, *Financial Statements*, various issues; *Estimates of Expenditure*, 1981.

enjoyed some support until then. The program unveiled in 1991 was to be implemented over five years. The major components were foreign trade liberalization, price decontrols, reductions in the size and functions of government and the deregulation of business activity. Import restrictions would be relaxed on 45 per cent of intermediate inputs by the end of 1991. All intermediate inputs as well as capital goods would be freely importable by the end of 1994, and this would be extended to consumer goods during the final year of the program. Exchange rate management would be designed to protect export market shares. The currency had declined 78.4 per cent relative to the US currency between 1981 and 1990. Henceforth it would be pegged to a basket of currencies of the major trading partners. Fiscal balance would entail the reduction of government current expenditures and marginal tax rates in such a way that the deficit would be 5 per cent of GDP by 1993, compared to 12 per cent in 1990. A major component of the expenditure reduction was a projected 26 per cent reduction in the size of the civil service and the elimination of consumer subsidies. The latter were administered by public corporations through a reimbursement process that generated losses. The public enterprises would be privatized or closed down. Monetary policy was to be based on gradually decontroling interest rates and commodity prices.

Trade liberalization and price deregulation were implemented relatively fully, though not on time. The labor market was decontrolled in 1994, as were most consumer subsidies. The exchange rate for current transactions became market-determined through the establishment of foreign-currency-denominated accounts (FCA) for exporters in 1993, although the entitlements were not tradable until the end of the year.[3] Revamping government expenditures has proved to be more intractable at the time of writing and the process of privatization did not start until 1997. There has been a reluctance to reduce radically the size of the civil service or elimination of subsidies to cover the cumulative losses of public enterprises by liquidating them.[4]

Figure 3.1 summarizes the key macroeconomic variables, which we use to assess the reform program. The GDP (Y), government capital expenditures (G) and the value of private capital (K) and imports (M) are all expressed in millions of Zimbabwe dollars at 1987 prices.

2 Intervention analysis

We use intervention analysis to assess the initial and long-run impacts of the program on the magnitude of the changes in these measures over the period beginning with independence in 1980 and the economic reform program initiated in 1990. First, we used the Box–Jenkins (1976) method for estimating time series, and found that GDP (Y), public capital expenditures (G), total government recurrent expenditures, the real wage and imported

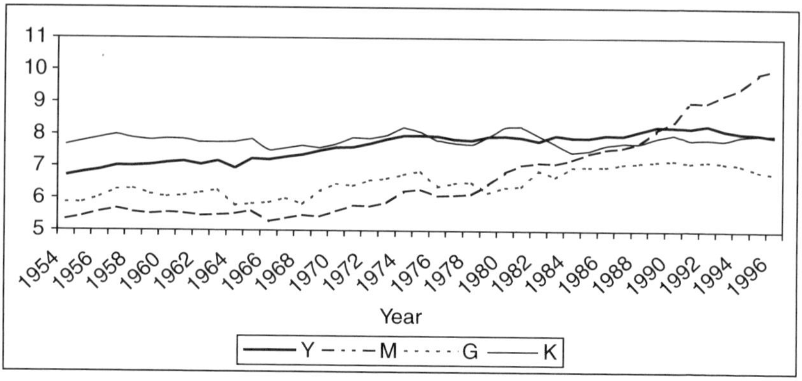

Figure 3.1 Log of Y, K, M and G

intermediate inputs (M) are AR(1) processes with a gradual decaying autocorrelation function (ACF) and a high spike at the first lag for the PACF. This indicates the need for the unit-root test. We performed the Augmented Dickey–Fuller (ADF) test on those time series data and each of those series is a random walk process with a drift. The exceptions were the private capital stock (K) and the degree of openness (the ratio of exports to GDP) which were MA(1) and AR(2) processes, respectively.

In general, basic intervention analysis only allows for a formal test of a change in the mean of pre- and post-intervention time series data using the following model

$$y_t = \alpha_0 + A(L)y_{t-1} + c_0\xi_t + B(L)\epsilon_t, \tag{3.1}$$

where $A(L)$ and $B(L)$ are polynomials in the lag operator L and $\xi_t = 0$ for the period before the intervention (1980 or 1990) and $\xi_t = 1$ afterward. Since we are interested in capturing the non-linear properties of the dynamic progress of the long run effects along with the initial impact, we extend this basic approach to the general rational transfer function

$$y_t = \alpha_0 + A(L)y_{t-1} + R(L)\xi_t + B(L)\epsilon_t, \tag{3.2}$$

where $R(L) = W(L)D(L)$ is the rational transfer function with $W(L)$ and $D(L)$ as polynomials in the lag operator L. $R(L)$ shows how the impact of the exogenous variable ξ_t is transferred to the dependent variable (y_t), with the coefficients of $W(L)$ and $D(L)$, denoted by ω_t and δ_t respectively, as the numerator and denominator transfer weights. The impulse response function $R(L)\{1 - A(L)\}$ represents the dynamic effects of a ξ_t shock on the (y_t) sequence.

We perform the analysis in three stages. First, we find a plausible set of ARIMA model for the longest data span (the pre-intervention observations) using the Box–Jenkins technique. Then we estimate the various models over the entire sample period, including measures of the impact of the intervention. Lastly, we perform diagnostic checks of the estimated equations. All coefficients were statistically significant at 5 per cent levels and we used a parsimonious model. The residuals were white noise, as they should be if the estimated model is to mimic the actual data-generating process.

Output

As previously stated, the log of the GDP for the pre-independence period (1954–79) display a random walk process, $(1 - L)\ln Y_t = \alpha_0 + \epsilon_t$. We found the best-fitting intervention model to be

$$(1 - L)\ln Y_t = R(L)\xi_t + \epsilon_t = \frac{W(L)}{D(L)}\xi_t + \epsilon_t = \frac{\omega_0 \xi_t}{(1 - \delta_1 L - \delta_2 L^2)} + \epsilon_t, \qquad (3.3)$$

where $\omega_0 = 0.09375, \quad \delta_1 = -1.1202, \delta_2 = -1.05454.$
$\qquad\qquad (1.66) \qquad\qquad (-9.57) \qquad\qquad (-6.74)$

The figures in parentheses are the t-ratios. The constant term was statistically insignificant so it was suppressed. The corresponding impulse response function can be written as a third-order difference equation in IR_t

$$IR_t^Y = -0.12025 IR_{t-1}^Y + 0.06571 IR_{t-2}^Y + 1.05454 IR_{t-3}^Y - 0.09375\xi_t \qquad (3.4)$$

where $\xi_t = 1$ if $t \geq 1980$ and $\xi_t = 0$ if $t < 1980$. Figure 3.2 shows the initial and dynamic effects of the impulse response function.

The estimated impact on real GDP of the independence intervention is given by a 10 per cent increase. The long-run effect implies a 1996 GDP that is 77 per cent higher than in 1979. These estimates are significantly higher

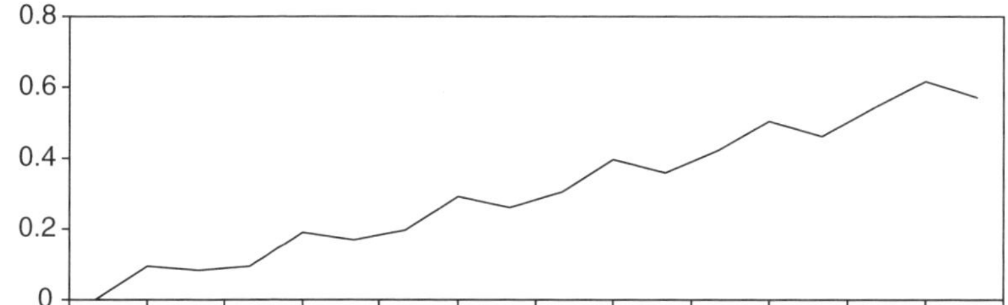

	79	81	82	84	85	87	88	90	91	93	94	96
IR(Y)	0	0.083	0.095	0.169	0.197	0.261	0.305	0.358	0.42	0.461	0.542	0.571

Year

Figure 3.2 Impulse response of Y

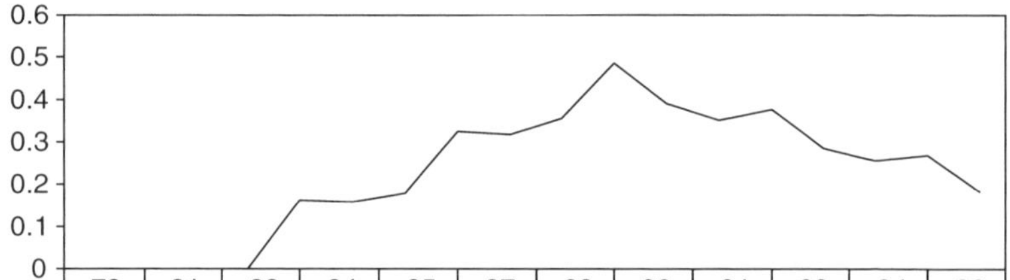

	79	81	82	84	85	87	88	90	91	93	94	96
IR(Y)	0	0	0	0.158	0.179	0.318	0.356	0.391	0.352	0.286	0.257	0.183

Year

Figure 3.3 Combined impulse response of Y

than the actual values. If we take the 1979 GDP as the initial observation then the estimated 1996 real GDP would be Z$49.9 billion, compared to the actual level of Z$28.60 billion. A more accurate estimate can be obtained by taking into account the impact of the known economic reform of 1990. The best-fit model that captures both interventions at the same time is

$$IR^Y = \frac{0.16298\xi_t}{(1-L)(1+1.03L+0.904L^2)} - \frac{0.08975\eta_t}{(1-L)},$$

where $\xi_t = 1$ if $t \geq 80$, $\xi_t = 0$ if $t < 80$, and $\eta_t = 1$ if $t \geq 90$ and $\eta_t = 0$ otherwise. The first term again captures the effect of the 1980 events while the second transfers the impact of the reform program of 1990. Figure 3.3 shows the combined effects on GDP.

The response for the first three years is negligible. The cumulative impact of the removal of economic sanctions in 1980 increases until 1989. The added impact of the events after 1990 obviously more than compensated for upward trend, and there is a monotonic decrease in GDP. This function provides estimated values that mirror the actual trend more closely. A plausible explanation of the decline in GDP after 1989 can be discerned in the behavior of government capital expenditures.

Public capital (G) and recurrent expenditures (TG)

The best fitting model generated a second order difference equation in IR^G and first order in ξ_t

$$IR^G = 0.2774IR^G_{t-1} + 0.7226IR^G_{t-2} + 0.3367\xi_t - 0.3362\xi_{t-1} \qquad (3.4)$$

with $\xi_t = 1$ for $t \geq 1980$ and zero otherwise. Figure 3.4 displays the immediate and dynamic impact of the advent of a new political regime on government investment levels.

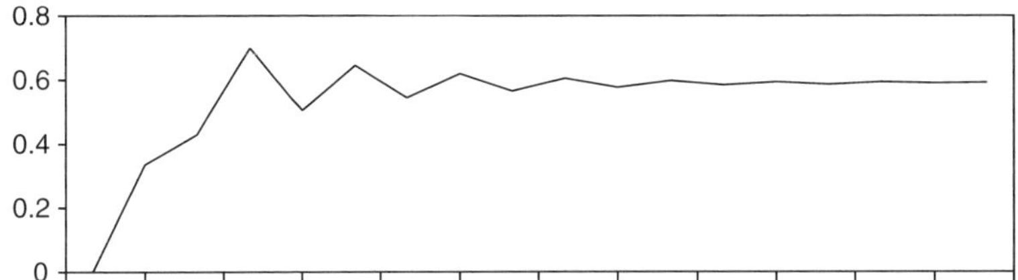

	79	81	82	84	85	87	88	90	91	93	94	96
IR(G)	0	0.43	0.699	0.646	0.545	0.565	0.604	0.597	0.583	0.586	0.592	0.591

Year

Figure 3.4 Impulse response of G

The response function estimates an immediate 40 per cent increase and the total impact by 1996 as an 81 per cent increase over 1979 levels. The reform program was supposed to have a further positive impact on public expenditures on economic services, but this has not been the case. The combined model gives the following results

$$(1 - L)\ln G_t = \frac{0.2265\xi_t}{(1 + 0.939L)} - 0.1795\eta_t + \epsilon_t, \tag{3.5}$$

where values for ξ_t are the same as in (3.4), $\eta_t = 1$ for $t \geq 1990$ and zero otherwise. Figure 3.5 shows this downturn in capital expenditures after 1989 and relates it to the GDP trend. Total government recurrent expenditures (TG), on the other hand, reflect the failure to reform the public sector. The combined impact of the two interventions gives us the following

$$(1 - L)\ln\ TG_t = \frac{0.185\xi_t}{(1 + 0.747L^2)} - 0.1114\eta_t + \epsilon_t$$

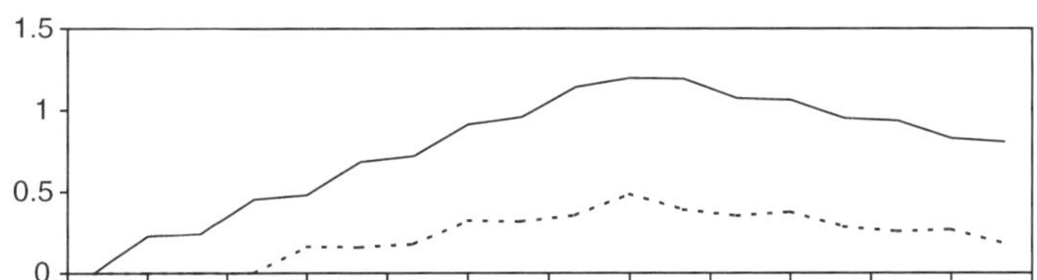

	79	81	82	84	85	87	88	90	91	93	94	96
—— IR(G)	0	0.24	0.454	0.682	0.718	0.956	1.14	1.19	1.071	0.949	0.932	0.804
- - - - - IR(Y)	0	0	0	0.158	0.179	0.318	0.356	0.391	0.352	0.286	0.257	0.183

Year

Figure 3.5 Impulse responses of G and Y

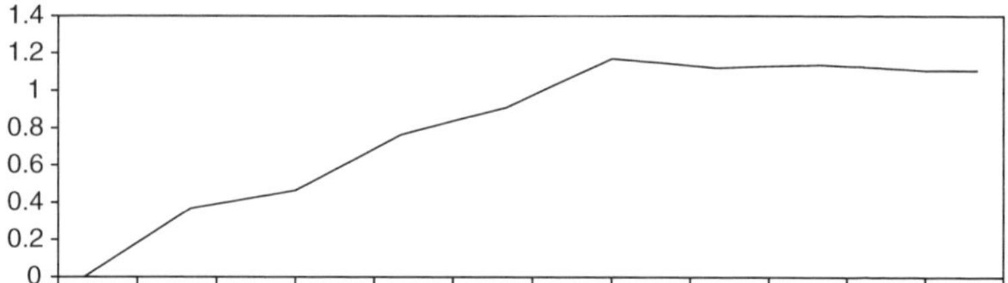

	79	81	82	84	85	87	88	90	91	93	94	96
IR(TG)	0	0.37	0.417	0.614	0.764	0.91	1.04	1.147	1.123	1.139	1.124	1.11

Year

Figure 3.6 Impulse response of TG

The restrictions on ξ and η are the same as in (3.4). The initial estimated effect of the new government was to increase recurrent expenditures by 20 per cent. The reform program acted to reverse the trend and the estimated total impact by 1996 is a 200 per cent increase. The results overshoot the actual levels partly because the previous government increased significantly the 1979 expenditures on social services for the majority population in a last-ditch attempt to convince the international community to remove sanctions without a change of government. If we take 1978 actual expenditure levels as the base year then the estimated values are more accurate. Figure 3.6 shows the result, and with Figure 3.5 the contrasting trends in capital and recurrent expenditures.

The budget apparently did not become more growth-oriented with the implementation of the reform program. An explanation for this lies in the primary focus of the reform program on the budget deficit as a percentage of GDP but not necessarily on the composition of the budget. As pressure mounted to reduce this ratio to 5 per cent by 1995 it apparently became easier to reduce the capital budget in the face of mandatory debt repayments and other expenditures considered to be politically desirable (Government of Zimbabwe, 1997).

Imported Inputs

The models that best capture the 1980 and the combined 1980 and 1990 interventions, respectively are

$$(1-L)\ln M_t = \frac{(\underset{(2.40)}{0.1911} - \underset{(2.18)}{0.4605}\,L + \underset{(-2.10)}{0.3327}\,L^2)\xi_t}{(1 - \underset{(3.03)}{0.7773}\,L)} + \epsilon_t \tag{3.6}$$

$$(1-L)\ln M_t = \frac{\underset{(4.24)}{0.2249}\,\xi_t}{(1 - \underset{(4.13)}{0.356}\,L + \underset{(-9.51)}{0.9167}\,L^2)} + \frac{\underset{(2.81)}{0.2944}\,\eta_t}{(1 + \underset{(-5.64)}{0.9158}\,L)} + \epsilon_t \tag{3.7}$$

with the same constraints on the values of ξ and η. The t-statistics are in parentheses. The respective third-order difference equation in $IR^M(t)$ for the 1954–79 period is

$$IR^M(t) = 1.7773IR^M_{t-1} - 0.7773IR^M_{t-2} + 0/1911\xi_t - 0.4604\xi_{t-1} + 0.3327\xi_{t-2} \tag{3.8}$$

for $\xi_t = 1$ if $t \geq 1980$ and $\xi_t = 0$ if $t < 1980$.

The estimated initial impact of the removal of international sanctions is a 21 per cent increase in the real value of imports while the long-run impact by 1996 would be a 34.65 per cent increase over 1979. The estimated value of imports, at US$1.262 billion, is only 53.37 per cent of the actual 1996 figures. We attribute a major portion of this discrepancy to the period beginning with the 1989 liberalization of the licensing regime. To capture this effect we now regard 1954–89 as the pre-intervention period but estimate the function by including terms that capture both the 1980 and 1990 effect. The third-order difference functions for the 1954–89 and 1990–96 periods, respectively are

$$IR^M(t) = 1.3535IR^M_{t-1} - 1.2703IR^M_{t-2} + 0.9167IR^M_{t-3} + 0.2249\xi_t, \tag{3.9}$$

where $\xi_t = 1$ if $t \geq 1980$ and $\xi_t = 0$ if $t < 1980$ and

$$\begin{aligned} IR^M_t =& \{1.354IR^M_{t-1} - 1.27IR^M_{t-2} + 0.917IR^M_{t-3}\} \\ &+ \{0.2249\xi_t + 0.084IR^M_{t-1} + 0.916IR^M_{t-2}\} + 0.2944\eta_t \end{aligned} \tag{3.10}$$

The brackets indicate the coefficients for the first and second interventions respectively. The impact of the 1980 measures alone would generate imports of US$1.32 billion by 1989, or 87.14 per cent of the actual value of US$1.5145 billion. When both 1980 and 1989 measures are included, however, the estimated imports in 1996 would be US$2.887 billion, compared to the actual value of US$2.365 billion. The model overestimates the joint impact. Other factors, such as the 1992–93 drought, account for the overestimation. We derive the estimated impact of trade liberalization alone on imports (the difference between the 1980 effect and the total impact by 1996) as 79.0 per cent of the total increase in imports between 1980 and 1996. Figure 3.7 shows the overall trend.

Private Capital

The pre-1980 time series for the capital stock is MA(1) process

$$\ln K_t = a_0 + (1 - \theta_1 L)\epsilon_t = \underset{(188.64)}{7.8055} + (1 + \underset{(-4.08)}{0.6611}L)\,\epsilon_t \tag{3.11}$$

The variance estimate is 0.01637 and the AIC, −29.364989. The best functional forms we could obtain gave us values of ω_0 and δ_1 that were not

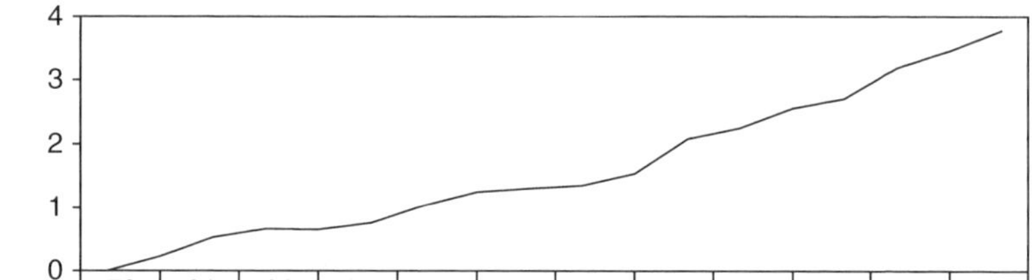

	79	81	82	84	85	87	88	90	91	93	94	96
IR(M)	0	0.529	0.655	0.752	1.023	1.302	1.342	2.079	2.246	2.714	3.192	3.788

Year

Figure 3.7 Impulse response of M

significantly different from zero. We concluded the events of 1980 and 1990 had no significant impact on private investment and the log of this variable fluctuated around its mean value.

Real wage (R_t)

The best-fitting impulse response function turned out to be

$$IR_t^R = 0.352IR_{t-1}^R + 0.648IR_{t-2}^R - 0.1999\xi_t + 0.0258 \qquad (3.12)$$

where $\xi_t = 1$ for $t \geq 1989$ and $\xi_t = 0$ for $t < 1989$. Figure 3.8 shows the total effect. The immediate effect of trade liberalization was an 18 per cent decrease in the real wage and by 1996 the estimated decline was 54 per cent.

Index of openness (EX_t)

One possible outcome from trade liberalization is the changed role of exports. We use the ratio of exports to GDP as a measure of the degree of

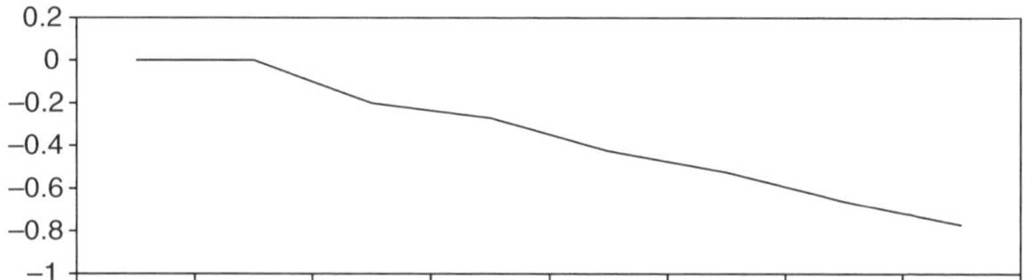

	89	90	91	92	93	94	95	96
IR(R)	0	0	−0.1999	−0.27	−0.424	−0.524	−0.659	−0.771

Year

Figure 3.8 Impulse response of R

openness and assess whether it changed after 1990. The data series for 1954–89 of this ratio exhibited the AR(2) process

$$\underset{(7.09)}{(1 - 1.1271L} + \underset{(-2.48)}{0.3991L^2})EX_t = \underset{(10.27)}{65.6658} + \epsilon_t \tag{3.13}$$

The response function is

$$EX_t = 70.53 + 26.13\xi_t + \frac{\epsilon_t}{(1 - 1.28L + 0.53L^2)} \tag{3.14}$$

The post-1989 period has a mean value of openness that is 40 per cent higher than prior to trade liberalization. Since GDP was on a downward trend it would seem that exports declined at a lower pace relative to the domestic share. Trade liberalization increased the role of exports.

Conclusions

The intervention analysis above indicates that the removal of sanctions in 1980 increased the level of imports and that trade liberalization then enhanced the trend. Government investment expenditures initially increased until 1989. The pressure to control the budget deficit as a ratio of GDP, together with a reluctance to reduce the civil service or subsidies, probably caused the reduction after 1990. Private domestic and foreign investment remained relatively stagnant. It is beyond this chapter to formally model the underlying causes. The World Bank (1989) estimated the elasticity of private investment with regard to lagged GDP at 1.8 and real interest rates at −1.3. Foreign investment had an elasticity of −1.4 with respect to the opportunity cost of investing in Zimbabwe, measured as the differential between an overseas bond rate adjusted for changes in relative exchange rates. As already stated, sanctions during the period 1965–79 caused excess capacity to emerge and this, along with the international sanctions, retarded significant additional foreign and domestic investment. Thereafter, nominal interest rates were decontrolled in 1992 and the higher real cost of borrowing must have had an impact. Deregulation of the economy, the second part of the reform package, had not been implemented by 1995. A restrictive environment for foreign investment was buttressed by a protracted project approval process and a complicated tax code which resulted in bureaucratic delays on new projects. The share of dividends that could be remitted depended on the age of the investment and were subject to the trend in export earnings. The lack of growth, higher rates of price increases and increased penetration by imports all contributed to a decline in the real wage, giving credence to the belief that labor paid much of the price for the adjustment program. Finally, both interventions had a much larger impact on imports which increased much faster than exports. However, the lack of growth cannot be exclusively attributed to the worsening of the balance of payments given the lack of investment, decline in infrastructure improvements and the increasing costs of capital.

3 Aggregate output relationships

It is useful to now establish the causal relationship between GDP, public and private investment expenditures and imports. We posit a generalized, log-linear production function to estimate any changes in output/input relationships with implementation of the structural adjustment program. The dependent variable is non-agricultural GDP (Y) with private capital stock (K), public capital expenditures (G), and imported intermediate goods (M) as the inputs:

$$\ln Y = \alpha_0 + \alpha_1 \ln K + \alpha_2 \ln G + \alpha_3 \ln \mathrm{M} + \epsilon \tag{3.15}$$

This functional relationship is patterned after Alesina and Rodrik (1994) and Barro (1990). We first obtained OLS estimates of the coefficients and carried out diagnostic tests. Phillips (1995) shows that stationary and non-stationary time series can be used in the same equation and produce optimal estimators provided the error terms are white noise. The ACF and PACF again showed that the residuals were autocorrelated. If the error term is autocorrelated, the efficiency of ordinary least-squares (OLS) parameter estimates is adversely affected and standard error estimates are biased. To correct for the autocorrelation we used the Yule–Walker autoregressive method to obtain the efficient parameter estimates. We also performed the generalized autoregressive conditional heteroscedasticity (GARCH) test and we found the error term is homoscedastic.

Since the gradual reforms were initiated with import liberalization measures at the end of 1989 the equation was fitted to the two time periods (1954–89 and 1954–96). We also obtained estimates for the pre-indepen-

Table 3.2 Production function estimates: dependent variable: non-agricultural GDP

Independent variable	*1954–79*	*1954–89*	*1954–96*
Imports	0.8230	0.2608	0.1075
	(6.98)	(2.57)	(2.20)
Public Capital	0.4243	0.3037	0.4189
	(3.89)	(2.80)	(4.19)
Private Capital	—	0.5039	0.5298
		(5.76)	(6.98)
MSE	0.0168	0.0192	0.0197
DW	1.77	1.66	1.53

Note: The t-ratios are in parentheses.

dence period (1954–79) in order to assess the impact of the removal of sanctions. The results are summarized in Table 3.2. In all the periods the constant term was not significantly different from zero, so it was suppressed and the equations re-estimated.

The Wald test statistic was less than the critical value of Chi-square at the 5 per cent significance level in each instance, so we cannot reject the null hypothesis of constant returns to scale. The coefficient for private capital for the sanctions period (1954–79) was not significantly different from zero. This supports the existence of excess capacity during sanctions when such intermediate inputs as oil were rationed. The removal of sanctions initially increased the inflow of imports of intermediate inputs from aid programs and allowed capacity utilization to rise. However, the rationing of foreign exchange continued until 1990. The allocation rules gave priority to intermediate inputs to existing firms and penalized most new projects aimed at supplying the domestic market. Imports of raw materials became more readily available, albeit at overvalued exchange rates (the elasticity declined from .82 to .26) but private investment became the major constraint. The impact of gradual trade liberalization after 1989 was to further increase capacity utilization and the import coefficient declined to 0.11. Domestic fiscal policy seems to have become more pertinent if output gains were to be realized given the elasticities with respect to public and private fixed capital formation.

Sources of growth

The log of the constant term was not significantly different from zero over the whole period. The strongest interpretation of the results would be that all changes in output during the period 1954–94 could be completely accounted for by changes in the level of input use. There is no residual that could be interpreted as due to the sources of total factor productivity (TFP), namely, technological change, efficiencies caused by the institutional, legal or regulatory changes.[5] We computed the estimated total annual contributions to GDP growth rates of each of the three factor inputs (fixed private capital, government investment expenditures and imported inputs). These estimates are the sum of the growth rates of each factor weighted by the respective output elasticity parameter. The difference between these estimates and the actual growth rates gives the residual which could be attributed to the above factors. The results are plotted on Figure 3.9. Again, the shift factor over the total sample period was not significantly different from unity, with a mean value of 1.0299 and a standard deviation of 0.0351.

There are, however, three slight, but discernable trends. We can only surmise at the underlying causes. The first upward trend (1954–69) reflects the initial industrialization period when public investments in hydroelectric power and transportation infrastructure attracted significant foreign capital equipment and skilled personnel inflows. These must have generated some

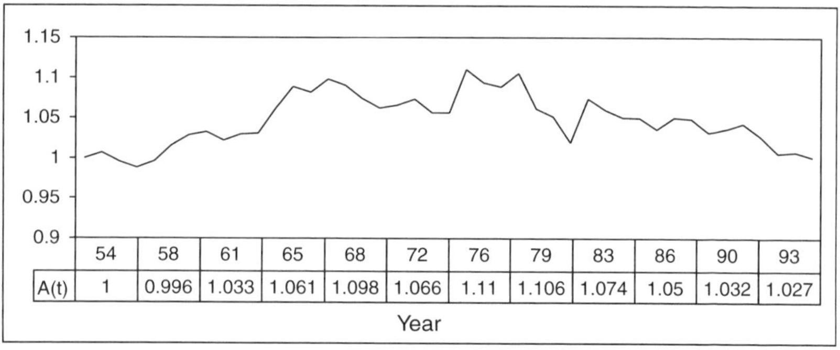

	54	58	61	65	68	72	76	79	83	86	90	93
A(t)	1	0.996	1.033	1.061	1.098	1.066	1.11	1.106	1.074	1.05	1.032	1.027

Figure 3.9 Impulse response of t

spillover effects, particularly in the domestic capital goods and services sectors. There were also gains from the early stages (1964–65) of import substituting industrialization (ISI) driven by the international sanctions. The second (1970–76) reflected a static situation. The third period (1976–90) shows a noticeable decline in exogenous growth. The causes include the cumulative negative effect of sanctions, skilled labor out-migration due to the political turmoil and the restrictive regulatory and legislative environment already alluded to. The political environment after 1980 further eroded productivity through labor laws that restricted dismissals and imposed minimum wages. These changes can be considered more a nuance than significant because of the statistical nature of the shift factor. However, we can explain the apparent changes.

For most of the time covered by our analysis (1964–89) foreign exchange for investment to supply the domestic market was rationed in favor of existing firms. This created virtual monopolies as well as rent-seeking behavior in import-dependent industries. About 69 per cent of the industrial sectors had concentration ratios for the top four firms of over 80 per cent. The Herfindal index of concentration for 86 per cent of the industrial sector was over 1800, largely the result of government ownership and other policies.[6] After 1989 trade liberalization and price deregulation did not provide an impetus for organizational changes that would be significant enough to generate productivity changes. Probably more important, public enterprises which controlled power and telecommunications incurred huge losses and could not invest in modernizing the infrastructure.[7] The excess demand for telephone lines, poor service and uncertainties generated by bureaucratic procedures now generated cumulative negative externalities. Foreign investment remained sluggish, partly because of a political environment that was still considered inimical to private capital, and also because of the lack of a privatization strategy. The combination of constant returns to scale and lack of significant changes in total factor productivity up to 1990 meant growth (if it occurred) would be driven by higher factor usage.

4 Concluding remarks

We first modeled the dynamic behavior of those variables most affected by economic reform for the period up to the removal of sanctions in 1980. Then we included the impact of the two policy-determined interventions, namely independence and the implementation of reform measures. Our results show that the impact of both interventions on imports of intermediate inputs far exceeded that on exports, at least up to 1996. The production function parameter estimates show the imports should have had a positive impact on GDP of around 3.7 per cent, assuming fiscal reform had dampened somewhat the balance of payments effect. Public sector reform did not occur as had been envisioned and our model showed an acceleration of government recurrent expenditures after 1980, but a constant trend after 1990. They should have declined, with a larger share being spent on economic infrastructure. The latter actually declined in the face of budget deficit pressures. Furthermore, the reforms also failed to have a positive effect on private investment. We then incorporated these trends into a production function and found that constant returns to scale prevailed. There was no exogenous growth. These results would suggest gradual implementation of reforms should not imply a sequencing of measures if growth is not to decline in the short run. All aspects of the program should be implemented at the same time, albeit gradually. If they are not, growth may decline. But it is not necessarily correct to attribute this decline to those aspects of the program which are implemented.

Notes

1. For a detailed history of the Federation, see Hazelwood (1967), among other sources.
2. For the complete program of economic reforms, see Government of Zimbabwe (1991) *A Framework for Economic Reform*. Harare: Government Printers.
3. The FCAs for corporations were eliminated toward the end of 1997 because of a balance of payments crisis and the owners were obliged to convert them at the going exchange rate to the central bank. They were, however, reintroduced in August 1999.
4. The failure to meet budget deficit targets led to the suspension of IMF balance of payments support in the period 1995–97.
5. For a discussion of the sources of TFP, see Oulton (1997).
6. Implementing Policy Change Consortium Report (1992).
7. Confederation of Zimbabwe Industries (1991).

References

Alesina, A. and Rodrik, D. (1994) 'Distributive politics and economic growth,' *Quarterly Journal of Economics*, vol. 59, no. 2, pp. 465–90.

Barro, R.J. (1990) 'Government spending in a simple model of endogenous growth,' *Journal of Political Economy*, vol. 98, no. 5, Part 2, pp. 103–25.

Bouton, Lawrence, Jones, Christine, and Kiguel, Miguel (1994) 'Macroeconomic Reform and Growth in Africa.' World Bank Policy Research, Working Paper, No. 1394.

Box, George, E.P., and Jenkins, Gwilym, M. (1970) *Time Series Analysis, Forecasting and Control*. San Francisco: Holden-Day.

Box, George E.P., and Tiao, G.C. (1975) 'Intervention analysis with applications to economic and environmental problems,' *Journal of the American Statistical Association*, vol. 70, pp. 70–9.

Confederation of Zimbabwe Industries (1991) 'ESAP and public sector reform', *Industrial Review*, August, pp. 43–7.

Davies, R. and Rattsø, J. (1998) 'Short-run consequences of trade, liberalisation: Computable General Equilibrium model of Zimbabwe', *Journal of Policy Modelling*, vol. 20, no. 3, pp. 305–33.

Dickey, David A., and Fuller, Wayne A. (1979) 'Distribution of the estimators for autoregressive time series with a unit root', *Journal of the American Statistical Association*, vol. 74, pp. 427–31.

Dollar, David (1992) 'Outward-oriented developing economies really do grow more rapidly: evidence from 95 LDCs, 1976–85', *Economic Development and Cultural Change*, vol. 40, April, pp. 523–44.

Doroodian, K. (1993) 'Macroeconomic performance and adjustment under policies commonly supported by the International Monetary Fund', *Economic Development and Cultural Change*, vol. 41, July, pp. 849–64.

Enders, Walter (1995) *Applied Econometric Time Series*. New York: John Wiley & Sons.

Fernandez, R. and Rodrik, D. (1991). 'Resistance to reform: status quo bias in the presence of individual specific uncertainty', *American Economic Review*, vol. 81, no. 5, pp. 1146–55.

Hazelwood, A. (1967) *African Integration and Disintegration*. London: Oxford University Press.

Krueger, Anne O. (1993) *Political Economy of Policy Reform in Developing Countries*. Cambridge, Mass.: Oxford University Press.

Oulton, Nicholas (1997) 'Total Factor Productivity Growth and the Role of Externalities,' *National Institute Economic Review*, no. 162, October, pp. 99–111.

Perkins, Dwight (1994) 'Completing China's move to the Market', *Journal of Economic Literature*, vol. 8, no. 2, pp. 23–46.

Phillips, Peter (1995) 'Fully Modified Least Squares and Vector Autoregression', *Econometrica*, vol. 63, no. 5, September, pp. 1023–78.

Study of Monopolies and Competition Policy in Zimbabwe. Implementing Policy Change Consortium Report, March 1992.

Taylor, Lance (ed.) (1993) *The Rocky Road to Reform*. Cambridge, MA: MIT Press.

World Bank (1989) *Zimbabwe: Private Investment and Government Policy*. Washington D.C., May.

Government of Zimbabwe (1991) *Zimbabwe: a Framework For Economic Reform 1991–95*. Harare: Government Printers.

Government of Zimbabwe (1997) *Zimbabwe Programme for Economic and Social Transformation 1996–2000* (ZIMPREST). Draft.

4
Inflation During Structural Adjustment

Dick Durevall and Phineas Kadenge

1 Introduction

High inflation has been closely linked to the implementation of the economic structural adjustment program in Zimbabwe (ESAP) in the period 1991–95. In the 1980s, inflation was generally less than 15 per cent but by the end of 1995 it stood at around 25 per cent, having peaked at close to 50 per cent in the interim. This increase in inflation is likely to have led to a number of problems. There was, for instance, a sharp fall in real earnings per worker as nominal wages failed to keep pace with prices. Moreover, monetary policy was tightened in a bid to reduce inflation, and real interest rates rose significantly. The latter increased the cost of borrowing for industry at the precise time it needed to update its capital stock because of exposure to foreign competition, and this probably slowed down the adjustment process. The high inflation rate might also have impeded structural adjustment directly by obscuring relative price changes. After all, one of the main purposes of ESAP was to encourage a shift of production from nontradables to tradables, and this was to be generated through a change in the relative price in the two sectors.

According to the economic reform program, inflation was expected to rise to 16 per cent during the first two years, and to drop gradually thereafter. It was also pointed out that inflation would not be the result of structural adjustment but a problem the program was designed to address (GoZ, Annex III, p. 11, 1991). Given the outcome, it is not surprising that several attempts have been made to explain the incidence of high inflation during the period of ESAP. There seems to be general agreement that high budget deficits played a fundamental role in influencing the determinants of inflation, but there are many different views about what actually determined inflation itself. One explanation is that excessive money supply, in combination with gradual removal of price controls and drought-induced price increases, generated the spurt in inflation (IMF, 1993; Morande and Schmidt-Hebbel, 1994; Reserve Bank of Zimbabwe, 1996). Another explanation is that (too large) devaluations, particularly during the third quarter of 1991, increased import costs, and thereby consumer prices over an extended period of time (Bloch, 1993; Bonyongwe, 1992; Cleary, 1992; Mugova, 1992; Robertson, 1993; Dzvanga, 1995). Another analysis suggests that increases in interest rates, caused by the deregulation of the financial markets, could have caused cost-push inflation through their impact on the cost of borrowing by firms (Ncube, 1992). This argument is supported by Bloch (1992a, 1992b) who argues that high real interest rates fuel inflation because the shortage of goods make it possible for firms to raise prices in order to cover the increased cost of finance.

This chapter examines how the structural adjustment program in Zimbabwe (1991–95) affected the inflationary process. Such a study is needed since most of the above authors have based their conclusions either on anecdotal evidence or on empirical analyses not covering the period of ESAP. The models developed are to a large extent databased, and should be viewed as a first step in understanding the dynamics of inflation. Nonetheless, they do convey some interesting information. In this chapter, we analyze the dynamics of inflation by developing two single-equation error correction models (ECMs) using monthly data. The first model is estimated for the period before Zimbabwe embarked on its structural adjustment program, and is used to analyze how the estimated parameters changed during the program with recursive methods. The second ECM is estimated over the period of ESAP. We acknowledge that it would have been preferable to develop one model for both periods, but the large structural changes brought about by ESAP prevented us from doing this.

In the analysis, we allow the data to play an important role when developing the empirical models. The use of theory is limited to assuming that price formation in an open economy operates through purchasing power parity (PPP) and/or money demand, and these are used in modeling the long-run part in the ECMs. This is in line with several other studies on inflation in Sub-Saharan countries, which have been based on similar theories (see, for example, Ndung'u, 1994; Moser, 1995; Atta et al., 1996; Durevall and Ndung'u, 1999).

The chapter is organized as follows: Section 2 presents the data and discusses the postulated causes of inflation. Section 3 describes our modeling strategy. Section 4 develops the empirical models and reports the results. Lastly, conclusions are given in Section 5.

2 A look at the data

In this section we examine the behavior of inflation for the period 1985:1 to 1995:12, and present the principal variables used in the study. Since our purpose was to find an empirical model with stable parameters for the period before ESAP, we chose 1985 as the starting year for the analysis. In this way we avoid the period following independence in 1980, which began with GDP growth rates in the two-digit range and ended with a sharp contraction in the real money supply. Extending the sample further backwards would have required including the tumultuous period of civil war (1975–79).

Figure 4.1 plots the yearly rate of change of the consumer price index over 1985:1–1995:12.[1] As the figure shows, inflation fluctuated around 10 per cent from 1985 to 1990, and was never above 20 per cent. Following the launch of ESAP in 1991, it rose rapidly and peaked at almost 50 per cent in August 1992. It was during this period that most of the price controls were lifted; the share of domestic products subject to direct price controls declined from 60 per cent in late 1990 to about 10 per cent at the beginning of 1993 (IMF 1993).[2] In 1993 inflation came down, and settled at around 20 per cent until the end of ESAP.

Figure 4.2 plots the log of real money stock defined as M1 divided by the CPI, and the log of manufacturing output index, serving as a proxy for GDP, which is only available on a yearly basis. A close relationship between these variables is necessary for the monetarist model of price determination to be valid. As can be seen, the series have the same trend up until 1993, when real money starts growing much faster than output. In the short run, there are strong seasonal swings which are mainly due to the coincidence of summer vacations and Christmas celebrations in Zimbabwe. The log of manufacturing production and the log of GDP, interpolated from yearly data, were

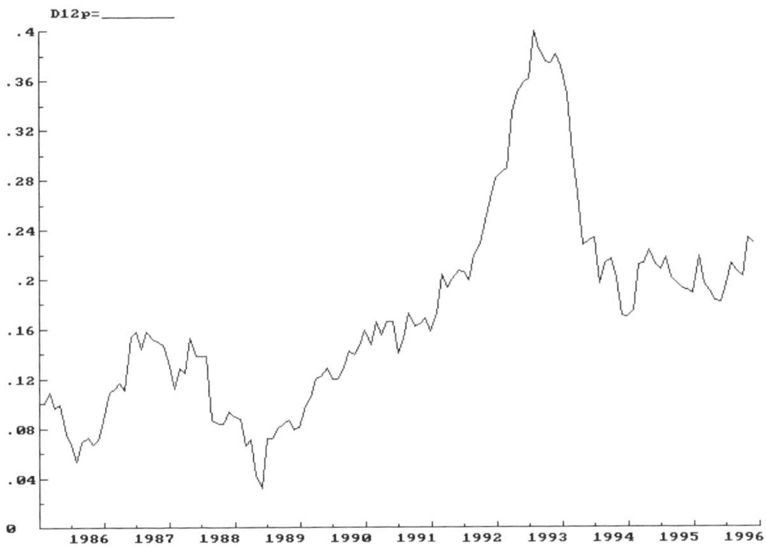

Figure 4.1 Yearly rate of change of the consumer price index (1985:1–1995:12)

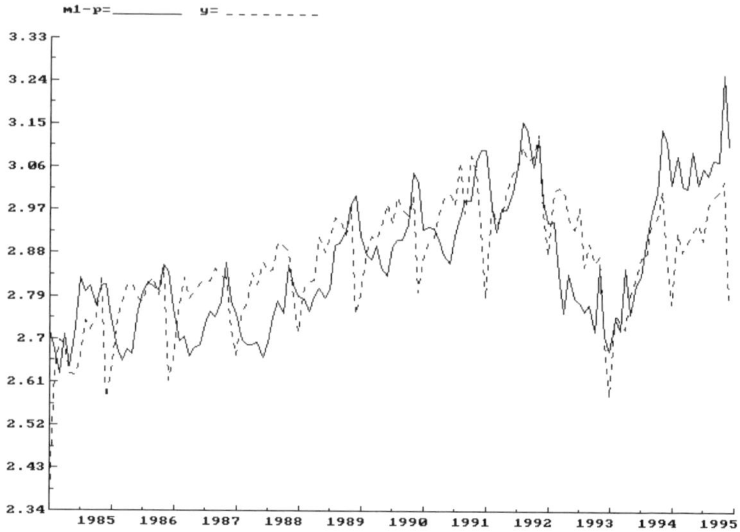

Figure 4.2 Mean adjusted log of real money stock and log of manufacturing output index

plotted and the former appeared to be a reasonable proxy for GDP, though there is a somewhat larger decline in the former in the beginning of the 1990s.

Figure 4.3 plots the log of the trade-weighted real exchange rate – that is, the log of the deviations from PPP. Before mid-1990 it followed a positive trend, implying that the Zimbabwe dollar was depreciating in real terms. The depreciation was caused by a policy of devaluing the currency, at short

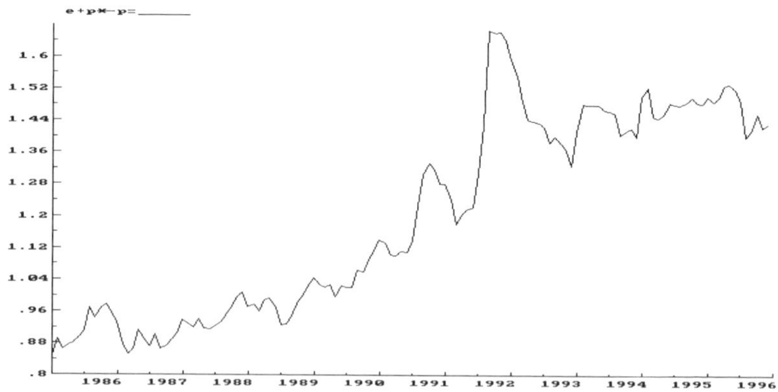

Figure 4.3 Log of the trade-weighted real exchange rate

intervals, at a faster speed than the change in the difference between domestic and foreign prices. During ESAP exchange rate policy changed; initially, the Zimbabwe dollar was allowed to appreciate in real terms, then, in the third quarter of 1991, there were several large devaluations, and these were followed by periods of stable nominal exchange rates, interrupted by major devaluations in January 1993 and 1994. At the end of ESAP the real exchange rate was relatively low, indicating that a large part of the effects of the devaluations had been annulled by domestic price increases.

Figure 4.4 plots the yearly rate of change in the price level, the exchange rate and the money stock. As argued by, for example, Morande and Schmidt-Hebbel (1994), there was rapid growth in money supply at the end of the 1980s. However, there was also an increase in the rate of devaluation of the exchange rate at the start of the 1990s, and in 1991 there were several major devaluations, making it difficult to judge the relative contribution of the two variables to the rise in inflation. At the end of 1991 monetary policy was tightened, and about eight months later inflation started to decline. However, during 1993 growth in money went up again, reaching about 50 per cent, while inflation and the rate of depreciation of the Zimbabwe dollar continued to decline, and throughout the following two years money growth exceeded inflation by a wide margin. Thus, from 1993 onwards, inflation seems to be more closely related to the development of the exchange rate than to the money supply. This change might be due to the

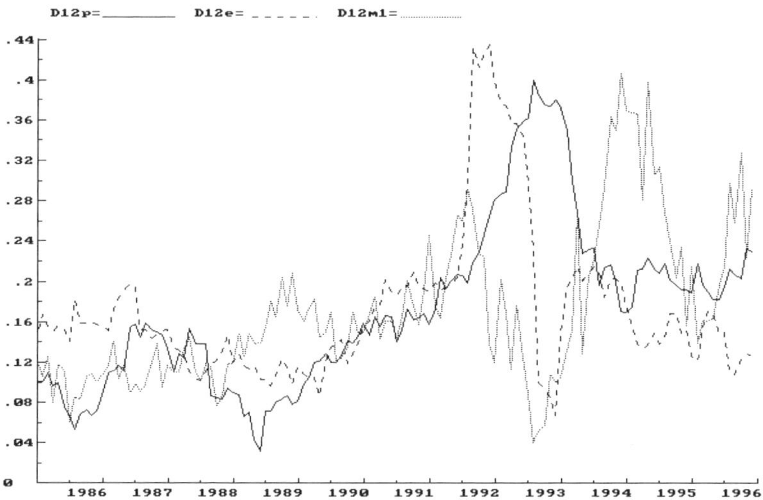

Figure 4.4 Yearly rate of change in the price level, real exchange rate and money stock

Figure 4.5 Lending rate and yearly rate of inflation

extensive measures taken in liberalizing the external sector during 1993 and the beginning of 1994.

Figure 4.5 plots the lending rate, defined as ln[1 + (percentage interest rate/100)], and yearly inflation over 1985:1–1995:12. Before ESAP the lending rate was fixed most of the time and the real interest rate, defined as the nominal interest rate minus inflation, was negative for long periods. During ESAP the lending rate was first increased in small steps. However, when the monetary policy stance was tightened in August 1992 the nominal rate was raised sharply, and after that the real lending rate remained positive. Changes in policy and financial deregulation during ESAP thus shifted the average real lending rate from being negative to positive.

Figure 4.6 plots the yearly rate of inflation and the change in the log of the index of manufacturing output measured as the three-month moving average over 1985:1–1995:12. There is a clear counter-cyclical relationship between the variables in the 1980s and the beginning of the ESAP period. This is usually attributed to two interrelated factors. First, shortages in the goods market and the system of cost-based price controls made it possible for firms to raise prices when production costs per unit increased. Second, variations in the supply of final goods were mainly due to the availability of inputs, which varied with the amount of rainfall and the degree of rationing of imports, and a decline in production reflected excess demand for inputs which raised their prices, and thus costs. However, the

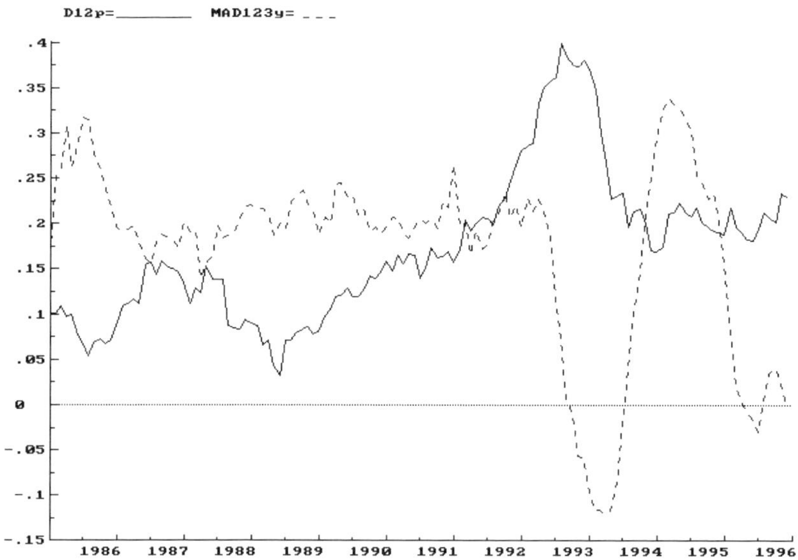

Figure 4.6 Inflation and mean adjusted three-month moving average of the rate of change of manufacturing output (1985:1–1995:12)

counter-cyclical relationship is also consistent with the view that supply-side shocks generated excess supply or demand for money, and therefore led to price changes. The disappearance of the counter-cyclical pattern during the period of ESAP is probably due to a decrease in the importance of supply shocks following the opening up of the trade account.

3 Empirical modeling strategy

In this section we describe the approach that we use to study inflation during the period of ESAP. First we briefly introduce the econometric model, and then we explain how we handled two important issues: (i) studying alterations in the process of inflation entailed by ESAP; and (ii) dealing with the problem of having many explanatory variables of interest in relation to the number of observations.

To study the dynamics of inflation we used single-equation ECMs. An unrestricted version of the model for monthly data with one explanatory variable can be written as,

$$\Delta p_t = a + \sum_{i=1}^{n} b_{1i}\Delta\, p_{t-i} + \sum_{i=0}^{n} b_{2i}\Delta\, x_{t-i} + \sum_{i=1}^{11} b_{3i}S_{it} - c_1 p_{t-1} + c_2 x_{t-1} + v_t \tag{4.1}$$

where p is the log of the price level, x the log of an explanatory variable, a a constant, S_{it} the seasonal dummy for the ith month, v_t the error term, and Δ the first difference operator, i.e., $\Delta p_t = p_t - p_{t-1}$ In this model the variables in first differences are assumed to be stationary, while those in log-levels may be nonstationary. When p and x are nonstationary they must be cointegrated, that is, they have a common stochastic trend, in order to have significant parameters and form an error-correction term. In this case, inflation, according to Equation (4.1), is determined by the rate of change of x, lagged inflation, the deterministic variables, and deviations from the average value of the linear combination of p_{t-1} and x_{t-1}, i.e., the cointegrating relation, $(p - c_2/c_1 x)$. Note that equation (4.1) is also a price equation, since in the long run p is determined by x.

In the empirical analysis the specification of the error-correction term, that is, the long-run part of the ECMs, was based on the assumption that the price level is determined in the money demand relation, i.e., the Harberger (1963) model, and/or by the exchange rate and foreign prices in the PPP relation.

The two long-run relations are defined as

$$m - p = b_1 y - b_2 R - b_3 \Delta p + b_4 OR, \tag{4.2}$$

$$p = e + p^* \tag{4.3}$$

where m is the log of the money stock, y the log of real output, R the alternative and OR the own interest rate, both defined as ln[1 + (percentage interest rate/100)], e the log of the exchange rate, and p^* is the log of the foreign price level.[3] To capture short-run effects in the ECMs we included the rate of change of the variables in the money demand relation and the PPP relation. Apart from these, we added two variables often mentioned in the debate about the causes of inflation in Zimbabwe – the lending rate and the rate of change in agricultural production. The former is assumed to act through the costs of financing working capital, and the latter through its effect on supply of inputs and consumer goods (see Reserve Bank of Zimbabwe 1996 on agricultural production).

A difficulty with estimating an ECM over a period when a structural adjustment program is being implemented is that the economic structure is, by definition, changing. This means that it is likely that the process of inflation is altered. The approach we have used is to first estimate a model for the period before ESAP with the objective of obtaining a model with stable parameters that describes the inflation process well. Then, variables believed to be important for inflation during ESAP were added, and the model was re-estimated over the whole sample. Using recursive methods, the changes taking place in the parameter estimates during the structural adjustment were then analyzed.

A weakness with this approach is that recursive estimation, although informative, was really designed to demonstrate constancy in conditional models, rather than structural change in parameter values. For example, it is possible that the lag structure changed during ESAP, and that including other lags of some variable changes the results. Hence, we also developed a model for the ESAP period only. This was achieved by using the information provided by the previous model, and then testing whether other variables and lags entered significantly. Finally, the estimated parameters of the ESAP model were compared with those of the recursive estimation of the pre-ESAP model.

Since there were several variables of interest, given our sample size, it was not possible to follow a general-to-specific methodology in a consistent way. Thus, we started with small base-line models, and then tested the significance of other variables by adding one, or more, in steps. To reduce the risk of missing variables that are only significant jointly, the variables were entered in many different combinations. As a final check we tested whether variables, and lags of variables, not included in the preferred model, were significant.

4 Results

In this section we begin by developing an empirical model of inflation for the period 1985:1–1991:1. A version of the monetarist model of Harberger (1963) is first estimated with the purpose of obtaining a base-line model. The reasons for starting with this model are that it has been used with some success in a number of studies on inflation in Africa (see, for example, Tegene, 1989; London, 1989; Ndung'u, 1994), and formed the core of the model used by Chhibber et al. (1989) in their analysis of Zimbabwean inflation. Moreover, it worked better empirically than alternative models which we examined. Then, after going through the general-to-specific procedure with the Harberger model, new variables are added and tested for their significance. The preferred model is then used to analyze how the process of inflation changed during the structural adjustment period 1991:2–1995.12. Finally, an ECM for 1991:2–1995:12 is developed and compared with previous models.

4.1 Estimation of the pre-ESAP model

The estimation results of the general Harberger model are reported in Table 5.1. It contains the first lag of the log-level of the real money stock, $(m-p)_{t-1}$, and output, y_{t-1}, and the level of the alternative, R_{t-1}, and deposit interest rates, OR_{t-1}, six lags of the first differences of each variable, seasonal dummies (not reported), and a constant. Moreover, we added the yearly rate of change of agricultural sales through the marketing boards, $\Delta^{12}ap$ to capture the effects of variations in harvests on inflation.[4] Previous runs with different models had shown that it only enters significantly at the 13th lag. Before estimation, tests for non-stationarity of the variables entering the model were carried out using Dickey–Fuller and augmented Dickey–Fuller unit root tests. The test statistics indicated that all the variables in first differences, real money stock minus output, $m - p - y$, and the spread between the alternative and the deposit rate, are stationary.[5] (See Durevall and Kadenge, 1998.)

Several diagnostic tests were done and, as shown in Table 4.1, they were all insignificant.[6] The model is over-parameterized and most parameter estimates are insignificant; the exceptions are the last three lags of output and agricultural sales. To obtain a parsimonious model, we followed the general-to-specific methodology and removed variables and lags progressively if their t-values were substantially below 2. Moreover, we imposed the restrictions that the coefficients for $m{-}p_{t-1}$ and y_{t-1} are equal but of opposite signs,

Table 4.1 General monetarist model 1985:1–1991:1

	Lag							
Variable	*0*	*1*	*2*	*3*	*4*	*5*	*6*	*13*
Δp_{t-l}	−1	−0.025	−0.109	−0.073	−0.072	0.279	−0.100	
	(—)	(0.179)	(0.196)	(0.196)	(0.175)	(0.171)	(0.177)	
Δm_{t-l}	−0.049	−0.104	−0.046	0.039	−0.105	−0.168	−0.060	
	(0.084)	(0.099)	(0.104)	(0.107)	(0.119)	(0.108)	(0.075)	
Δy_{t-l}	0.063	−0.090	−0.118	−0.149	−0.236	−0.283	−0.192	
	(0.070)	(0.108)	(0.098)	(0.101)	(0.109)	(0.102)	(0.068)	
ΔR_{t-l}	−0.365	−0.017	0.432	0.952	0.040	−0.187	−0.022	
	(0.349)	(0.557)	(0.583)	(0.580)	(0.620)	(0.581)	(0.446)	
ΔOR_{t-l}	0.489	−1.206	−1.231	−1.126	0.222	−0.615	−0.199	
	(0.629)	(0.712)	(0.705)	(0.747)	(0.801)	(0.737)	(0.547)	
$\Delta^{12} ap_{t-l}$								−0.005
						0		(0.002)
m_{t-i}		0.040						
		(0.061)						
y_{t-i}		0.027						
		(0.083)						
R_{t-l}		−0.377						
		(0.590)						
OR_{t-l}		0.745						
		(0.801)						
Constant	−0.238							
	(0.308)							

Method OLS, T = 73 [1985: 1−1991: 1] RSS = 0.0018 $R^2 = 0.8085$ F(50, 22) = 1.8578 [0.057]
$\Delta = 0.0091$ *DW* = 1.95 *AR* 1−5*F*(5, 17) = 0.5121 [0.763] *ARCH* 5 *F*(5, 12) = 0.1842 [0.963]
Normality Chi^2(2) = 3.2097 [0.201] *RESET F*(1, 21) = 0.0544 [0.819]
Note:
1. Standard errors are in parentheses. Seasonals are not reported.

and that the $\Delta^2 m_{t-i}$ enter instead of Δm_{t-i}. Table 4.2 reports the parsimonious model, diagnostic tests, and the F-test statistic for reducing the general model by 28 parameters. The model has 11 parameters apart from the constant and seasonal dummies, and there is no evidence of mis-specification. The next step was to test whether other variables enter the model significantly. This was done in steps since lack of observations made it impossible to test all the variables at once. Details about this procedure and test statistics can also be found in Durevall and Kadenge (1998).

Table 4.2 Preferred parsimonious pre-ESAP Model 1985:1–1991:1

Variable	*Parameter estimate*	*t-value*	*Instability test*
$\Delta^2 m_t$	0.062 (0.029)	2.108	0.05
$\Delta^2 m_{t-3}$	0.084 (0.031)	2.673	0.10
$\Delta^2 m_{t-4}$	0.065 (0.032)	2.003	0.07
Δy_{t-4}	−0.062 (0.036)	−1.716	0.32
Δ_{t-5}	−0.147 (0.043)	−3.384	0.11
Δy_{t-6}	−0.137 (0.038)	−3.547	0.06
ΔR_{t-3}	0.280 (0.114)	2.438	0.2
ΔOR_{t-5}	−0.707 (0.206)	−3.422	0.31
$(m-p-y)_{t-1}$	0.073 (0.024)	3.049	0.12
Δe_{t-1}	0.178 (0.070)	2.524	0.16
Δp^*_{t-3}	0.164 (0.065)	2.500	0.11
$\Delta^{12} ap_{t-13}$	−0.005 (0.001)	−3.129	0.25
Constant	0.158 (0.048)	3.286	0.13

Method OLS T = 73 [1985: 1–1991: 1] RSS = 0.0033 R^2 = 0.6492 F(23, 49) = 3.9424 [0.000]Δ = 0.0083
DW = 1.65 AR 1–5F(5, 44) = 1.7614 [0.140] ARCH 5 F(5, 39) = 0.5715 [0.721], Normality $Chi^2(2)$ = 0.8053 [0.668] *RESET F*(1,48) = 5.1521 [0.027], Variance instability test: 0.116348; Joint instability test: 3.5829 Tests of parameter constancy over: 1990 (2) to 1991 (1); Chow F (12, 37) = 1.1323 (0.36521) t(11) for a zero Forecast innovation mean = −0.414.
Notes:
1. Standard errors in parentheses. Seasonals are not reported.
2. The instability tests, variance instability test and the joint instability test are from Hansen (1992). No test is significant at the 95 per cent level.

In Table 4.2, the chosen equation for 1985:1–1991:1 is presented together with diagnostic test statistics against various forms of mis-specification. The model can be interpreted as a monetarist model, since in the long run inflation is associated with excess money supply; the error-correction term $(m - p - y)_{t-1}$ is significant and has a coefficient of 0.07. However, equation (2) does not hold exactly since the levels of the interest rates do not enter significantly. The money demand variables are also important for the determination of inflation in the short run; the sum of the coefficients of the lags of the growth rate of the money supply, $\Delta^2 m_{t-i}$, and output, Δy_{t-i}, are 0.21 and −0.35 respectively, and the first difference of the alternative and the own interest rates enter significantly with expected signs.

There are also other factors explaining inflation in the short run; devaluations and foreign inflation raise inflation within a couple of months. The value of the estimated coefficients for these variables is rather small, approximately 0.17, reflecting the extensive use of trade and exchange restrictions. Similar results were obtained by Younger (1992) in a study on devaluations in Ghana during a period of widespread controls on the external sector. The rate of growth in agricultural output enters lagged 13 months. Its coefficient is only −0.005, but that is probably due to the large variance of the variable we use; agricultural sales through the marketing boards vary much more than actual agricultural output.

The diagnostic test statistics for the model are all insignificant at the 5 per cent level, except the one for the RESET test, which has a probability value of 0.028. The other test statistics reported in Table 4.2 are instability tests of Hansen (1992), a Chow test of parameter constancy over 1990:2–1991:1, and a t-test for zero forecast innovation mean. They are all insignificant, and the model thus appears to be fairly well specified.

To further investigate the stability of the parameters we used recursive estimation over 1987:6–1991:1. Since the volume of output from this exercise is large, it is not presented here due to space constraints. It was summarized in graphs and can be found in Durevall and Kadenge (1998). First, the estimated parameter values are shown together with their sequentially estimated standard errors times plus or minus two. This output shows that they are all reasonably stable. The one-step residuals and the corresponding standard errors are depicted. Since all estimates are within the confidence intervals there is no evidence of outliers. Finally, one-step and break-point scaled Chow test statistics are presented, with the straight line through unity indicating a critical value of 5 per cent. In no case are the tests significant. Thus we conclude that the stability of the model is satisfactory.

4.2 The pre-ESAP model and structural adjustment

In this section we estimate the model recursively over the ESAP period. However, first we added three variables of interest – the real lending rate, the change in the lending rate, and the real exchange rate. Stationarity tests performed showed that they are all stationary during the 1990s (see Durevall and Kadenge, 1998). The estimation results are reported in Table 4.3. A selection of the recursive estimates of the parameters over the period 1991:2–1995:12 is plotted in Durevall and Kadenge. All the graphs indicate that large changes occurred in the inflationary process during the structural adjustment program. In particular it is interesting to note that money supply became much less important as a direct cause of inflation; the estimate of the

Table 4.3 Pre-ESAP model estimated over 1985:1–1995:12 with lending rate and real exchange rate added

Variable	*Parameter estimate*	*t-value*
$\Delta^2 m_t$	0.016 (0.015)	1.010
$\Delta^2 m_{t-3}$	0.048 (0.021)	2.299
$\Delta^2 m_{t-4}$	0.031 (0.021)	1.430
Δy_{t-4}	0.026 (0.027)	0.971
Δy_{t-5}	0.021 (0.029)	0.721
Δy_{t-6}	−0.007 (0.026)	−0.295
ΔR_{t-3}	0.078 (0.061)	1.276
ΔOR_{t-5}	0.015 (0.087)	0.087
$(m-p-y)_{t-l}$	0.016 (0.013)	1.253
Δe_{t-l}	−0.052 (0.034)	−1.517
ΔP^*_{t-3}	−0.078 (0.070)	−1.114
$\Delta^{12} ap_{t-13}$	−0.002 (0.001)	−2.234
$(e-p+p^*)_{t-1}$	0.023 (0.005)	4.396
ΔLR_{t-4}	0.130 (0.062)	2.100
$(LR-\Delta^{12}p)_{t-4}$	−0.0523 (0.019)	−2.686
Constant	0.022 (0.030)	0.738

Method OLS, T = 132 [1985: 1−1995: 12] RSS = 0.0141 $R^2 = 0.534$ F(26, 105) = 4.629 [0.000] $\Delta = 0.0116$.

Note: Standard errors are in parentheses. Seasonals are not reported.

parameter for $m - p - y_{t-1}$ drops and becomes insignificant in the middle of 1992, and the value of the parameters of $\Delta^2 m_{t-i}$ declines during 1993 to 0.05. On the other hand, the real exchange rate turns significant at the end of 1991, indicating that domestic and foreign prices, and the nominal exchange rates move together. The adjustment of prices to changes in the real exchange rate is, however, slow – that is, the parameter estimate is only 0.024. Nevertheless, the results show that ESAP has shifted the economy from being closed, in the sense that controls on the current and capital account isolated the price level from changes in the exchange rate and foreign prices in the long run, to an open economy where the PPP relation becomes central for the determination of prices.

Further, evidence of a change of economic structure is given by the shifts in the estimates of the parameters of the other variables in the money demand relation; the log-level of output does not enter the long-run relation, none of the estimates of the rate of change of output are significant, and the coefficients of the alternative and the own interest rates are both insignificant. These shifts are clearly visible in the recursive estimates.

The estimate of the coefficient of ΔLR_{t-4} is significant and positive, which indicates that increases in the cost of capital transmit into higher prices. However, the real lending rate is also significant but has a negative coefficient. Thus, the lending rate appears to influence prices via its impact on demand as well. It becomes important for the determination of inflation as from the beginning of 1993. Thus, the effect of an increase in the interest rate is a reduction of inflation, although it raises inflation in the short run.

4.3 The ESAP model

To obtain a model for the ESAP period we re-estimated our model over 1991:2–1995:12, removed the variables with very low t-values, and then repeated the procedure of adding lags of sets of variables in turn. The resulting model is presented in Table 4.4. The model has seven variables, apart from the constant and seasonal dummies, and they are all lagged. None of the diagnostic tests, the Chow tests for stability, the Chow test of forecast parameter stability, the t-test for zero forecast innovation mean, or Hansen's (1992) instability tests were significant. The recursive estimates of most of the coefficients are reasonably stable; the exceptions are the ones for agricultural production and the lending rates which become significant as from the beginning of 1993. Actual and fitted values of inflation are shown in Figure 4.7. The model tracks inflation closely during the sharp rise in 1991 and 1992, but narrowly misses the decline at the beginning of 1993. However, overall, considering the large structural changes that took place, the model explains inflation well.

Comparing the latter model with the pre-ESAP model in Tables 4.2 and 4.3, we note that the results from the previous analysis are confirmed. Money only affects inflation directly in the short run; output growth has

Table 4.4 ESAP model 1991:2–1995:12

Variable	*Parameter estimate*	*t-value*	*Instability test*
Δm_{t-3}	0.090 (0.021)	4.283	0.46
Δy_{t-8}	−0.102 (0.026)	−3.913	0.09
$\Delta(e+p^*)_{t-8}$	0.108 (0.025)	4.208	0.02
ΔLR_{t-4}	0.124 (0.042)	2.922	0.10
$(LR-\Delta^{12}p)_{t-4}$	−0.060 (0.010)	−5.513	0.17
$(e-p+p^*)_{t-1}$	0.037 (0.010)	3.555	0.09
$\Delta^{12}ap_{t-2}$	0.003 (0.001)	4.575	0.10
Constant	−0.040 (0.016)	−2.432	0.09

Method OLS, T = 59 [1991: 2–1995: 12] RSS = 0.0025 R^2 = 0.8458 F(18, 40) = 12.188 [0.000] Δ = 0.0079 DW = 2.24 AR 1 – 7 F(4, 36) = 0.8423 [0.508] ARCH 4 F(4, 32) = 0.6798 [0.611] Normality $Chi^2(2)$ = 0.7332 [0.693] Heteroscedastisity F(25, 14) = 0.6002 [0.871] *RESET F*(1, 39) = 2.6758 [0.110] Variance instability test: 0.215; Joint instability test = 3.899; Tests of parameter constancy over: 1995 (1) to 1995 (12); Chow F(12, 28) = (1.679) [0.126] t(11) for a zero Forecast innovation mean = 1.3.

Notes:
1. Standard errors in parentheses. Seasonal dummies are not reported.
2. The instability tests, variance instability test and the joint instability test are from Hansen (1992). No test is significant at the 95 per cent level.

a much smaller impact; the exchange rate and foreign prices affect inflation through the error-correction term, the change in the lending rate has a positive effect on inflation, and the real lending rate has a negative coefficient. Nevertheless, there are some differences between the two: the rate of change of output, the exchange rate, and foreign inflation enter lagged eight months in the ESAP model, indicating a change in the lag structure. Moreover, the rate of change of agricultural production enters lagged two months, and has a positive sign. This is an indication that changes in agricultural production now mainly influence aggregate demand, because of its impact on income, and that opening up the economy has alleviated supply constraints that characterized the pre-ESAP economy.

5 Summary and conclusions

This chapter has examined how the structural adjustment program in Zimbabwe, 1991–95, affected the inflationary process. One finding is that

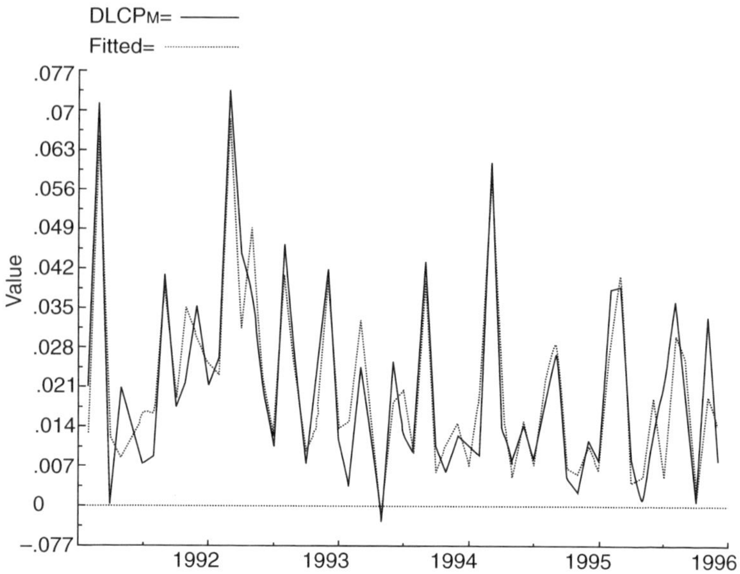

Figure 4.7 Actual and fitted values of inflation

before 1991 prices were determined by excess money supply in the long run, and that during ESAP money supply was replaced as the determinant of the domestic price level by the exchange rate and foreign prices. This change was probably due to the dismantling of the systems of import quotas and allocation of foreign exchange, and relaxation of controls on capital flows. Signs of the growth in importance of the PPP relationship are also visible in the development of the real exchange rate. During a large part of the 1980s devaluations led to an almost continuous depreciation of the real exchange rate, even though fiscal and monetary policies were quite lax. After the launch of ESAP, it depreciated only a little in spite of several large devaluations, which is a strong indication that the link between the exchange rate and prices has become much stronger as a result of liberalization.

The central role of the money demand relation during the 1980s did not preclude supply shocks from being an important determinant of inflation. The counter-cyclical behavior of inflation in relation to output is probably explained by changes in the availability of inputs, due to variations in the harvests and import rationing. There are at least two channels through which an exogenous supply shock might have affected inflation: (i) it led to a change in output which created excess demand or supply of money; and (ii) it altered the costs of production through changes in availability and prices of inputs. During ESAP the importance of output for inflation declined sharply according to our estimations. Moreover, the coefficient for agricultural production changed sign and became positive. The change in the role of output and agricultural production is likely to be a consequence of the opening up of the economy, making supply respond much quicker to changes in demand through imports.

During the latter part of ESAP, monetary policy aimed to keep real interest rates positive and fairly high in order to reduce inflation. Critics of this policy claim that increasing interest rates lead to a higher cost of financing working capital, and thus cause cost-push inflation; a mechanism emphasized in the new structuralist approach to macroeconomics (see Taylor 1991). We find support for this view in the form of a fairly large and positive coefficient for the rate of change of the lending rate. However, we also find that increases in the level of the lending rate reduce inflation as predicted by standard theory – that is, it affects aggregate demand. Over time, demand effects dominate the cost-push effects and tight monetary policy, which generate increases in interest rates and leads to lower inflation.

Our models thus highlight the difficulties in stabilizing prices during structural adjustment. A slower rate of devaluation of the exchange rate reduces inflation, but it also appreciates the real exchange rate in the short run, which is counter to the objective of the policy reforms. Raising the interest rates, on the other hand, has a weak effect on inflation, while it reduces investment and thus slows down the movement of resources from the nontradable to the tradable sector. Nevertheless, the results also indicate that inflation is mainly a domestic phenomenon and that it can be controlled with proper policies, albeit with some short- to medium-run costs. The role of the budget deficit has not been analyzed explicitly in this chapter, but, according to the experience of stabilization programs in many other countries, it is an important determinant of the proximate causes of inflation (see Bruno et al. 1991). A reduction of the budget deficit would thus be a given component of a stabilization program, though the exact links between deficits and inflation remain to be explored in Zimbabwe. The other part of the program would consist of exchange rate policies, aiming at keeping the rate of devaluation in line with targeted inflation. This is because there is some support in the literature (see, for example, Bruno et al. 1991) for the use of the exchange rate as a nominal anchor for inflation in the long run.

Notes

1. Details about data and sources are given in Appendix I.
2. We were not able to obtain enough details about the decontrol of prices to construct a variable that captures its effect on inflation.
3. Our formulation of the Harberger model differs from that given in Harberger (1963) in that we, in addition to the rate of inflation, allow the alternative and own interest rates to affect the cost of holding money.

4. The use of the yearly rate of change in agricultural production is motivated by the fact that harvests are concentrated into a few months of each year.
5. The unit-root tests, and the implications of these for cointegration between the variables, were confirmed by tests carried out with the Johansen (1988) approach. We have not reported these results because our sample is small and only covers a short time period. Moreover, the results of the Dickey–Fuller tests were consistent with both visual inspection of the series in Section 2 and the regression analysis in Section 4.
6. The diagnostic test statistics reported in Table 4.1 are for testing against the alternative hypotheses of residual autocorrelation (*AR* and *DW*), autoregressive conditional heteroscedasticity (*ARCH*), skewness and kurtosis (*Normality*), and non-linearity (*RESET*). See Hendry (1995) for details and references.

References

Atta, J.K., K.R. Jefferis and I. Mannathoko (1996) 'Small country experiences with exchange rates and inflation: the case of Botswana', *Journal of African Economies*, vol. 5, no. 2, pp. 293–326.

Bloch, E. (1992a) 'High interest rates discourage investment', *The Financial Gazette*, 30 January, p. 6.

Bloch, E. (1992b) 'Monetary policies are fueling inflation', *The Financial Gazette*, 11 June, p. 6.

Bloch, E. (1993) 'Price controls must not be restored', *The Financial Gazette*, 17 June, p. 6.

Bonyongwe, W. (1992) 'Proposals to ease the current liquidity crisis confronting the manufacturing sector', memo, Confederation of Zimbabwe Industries.

Bruno, M., S. Fisher, E. Helpman and N. Liviatan with L. Meridor (eds) (1991) *Lessons of Economic Stabilization and Its Aftermath*. Cambridge, MA: MIT Press.

Central Statistical Office (CSO) *Quarterly Digest of Statistics*, various issues.

Chhibber, A., J. Cottani, R. Firuzabadi and M. Walton (1989) 'Inflation, price controls, and fiscal adjustment in Zimbabwe', The World Bank Working Paper Series, Number 192, April.

Cleary, A. (1992) 'Fine-tuning tactics compound economic problems', *The Financial Gazette*, 27 August, p. 4.

Doornik, J.A. and Hendry D.F. (1994) *PcGive 8.0: 'An Interactive Econometric Modelling System'*, Institute of Economics and Statistics, University of Oxford, International Thomson Publishing.

Durevall, D. and P. Kadenge (1998) 'Inflation during structural adjustment: the case of Zimbabwe', paper presented at a conference on Zimbabwe: Macroeconomic Policy, Management and Performance since Independence, Harare, 18–21 August.

Durevall, D. and N.S. Ndung'u (1999) 'A dynamic model of inflation for Kenya, 1974–1996', IMF Working Paper, March.

Dzvanga, M. (1995) 'The inflation phenomenon under a changing economic environment: the case of Zimbabwe 1983–1994', an unpublished MSc in Economics Dissertation, University of Zimbabwe, 1995.

Government of Zimbabwe (1991) *A Framework For Economic Reform (1991–1995)*. Harare: Government Printers.

Hansen, B. (1992) 'Testing for parameter instability in linear models', *Journal of Policy Modelling*, vol. 14, pp. 517–33.

Harberger, A. (1963) 'The dynamics of inflation in Chile', in C. Christ (ed.), *Measurement in Economics: Studies in Mathematical Economics and Econometrics in Memory of Yehuda Grunfeld*. Stanford: Stanford University Press.

Hendry, D.F. (1995) *Dynamic Econometrics*. Oxford: Oxford University Press.
IMF (1993) 'Background paper on Zimbabwe', 6 May.
Johansen, S. (1988) 'Statistical analysis of cointegration vectors,' *Journal of Economic Dynamics and Control*, vol. 12, nos 2/3, pp. 231–54.
London, A. (1989) 'Money, inflation and adjustment policy in Africa: some further evidence', *African Development Review*, vol. 1, no. 1, pp. 87–111.
Morande, F. and K. Schmidt-Hebbel (1994) 'Zimbabwe: fiscal disequilibria and low growth,' in William Easterly, Carlos Alfredo Rodriguez and Klaus Schmidt-Hebbel (eds), *Public Sector Deficits and Macroeconomic Performance*. New York: Oxford University Press for the World Bank.
Moser, G.G. (1995) 'The main determinants of inflation in Nigeria,' *IMF Staff Papers*, vol. 42, no. 2, pp. 270–89.
Mugova, A. (1992) 'Is currency devaluation a prudent policy instrument', *The Financial Gazette*, 18 June, p. 4.
Ncube, M. (1992) 'What is the economic theory behind ESAP?', *The Financial Gazette*, 7 May, p. 4.
Ndung'u, N.S. (1994) 'A monetary model of inflation: Kenyan case', *African Development Review*, vol. 6, no. 2, pp. 109–36.
Reserve Bank of Zimbabwe (1996) 'Sources and consequences of inflation in Zimbabwe', *Quarterly Economic and Statistical Review*, vol. 17, no. 1, pp. 21–6.
Robertson, J. (1993) 'Economic structural adjustment programme and its impact on financial stability and the balance of payments,' paper presented at the conference 'On the Road Towards a Market-Based Economy', Harare.
Taylor, L. (1991) *Income Distribution, Inflation and Growth*. Cambridge, MA: MIT Press.
Tegene, A. (1989) 'The monetarist explanation of inflation: the experience of six African countries', *Journal of Economic Studies*, vol. 16, pp. 5–18.
Younger, S.D. (1992) 'Testing the link between devaluation and inflation', *Journal of African Economics*, vol. 1, no. 3, pp. 369–94.

Appendix I

The data

All data are monthly, and the sample period is 1984:1–1995:12. The data sources are the Zimbabwe Central Statistical Office *Quarterly Digest of Statistics* (*QDS*), the Reserve Bank of Zimbabwe *Quarterly Economic and Statistical Review* (*QESR*), and *International Financial Statistics (IFS)* data base from the IMF.

— Domestic price level, *P*, the unweighted average consumer price index (CPI) for the higher- and lower-income urban families for the period 1984 to 1989 and the unified CPI for the period 1990–95. (*QDS*)

— Money stock, *M*, comprises notes and coin in circulation and demand deposits with the monetary banking sector, i.e. M1. (*QESR*)

— Deposit interest rate, *OR*, the maximum interest rate paid on three-month deposits with commercial banks. (*QESR*)

— Negotiable certificates of deposit (NCD) rate, *R*, the maximum three-month NCD rate. (*QESR*)

— Lending Rate, *LR*, the maximum of the commercial banks' lending rate. (*QESR*)

— Output, *Y*, manufacturing production index. (*QDS*)

— Agricultural output, *AP*, the value of sales of principal crops and livestock to/through Marketing Authorities. (*QDS*)

— Real imports, *IMP*. (*QDS*)

— Multilateral nominal exchange rate index, *E*. The weights are import shares of the six major trading partners (Botswana, Germany, Japan, South Africa, the UK and the USA) and oil imports at the following years, 1986, 1988, 1990, 1992, and 1994. Oil imports are valued in US dollars. (*IFS*, line ae, and *QDS*)
— The foreign price, P^*, the wholesale price index of Zimbabwe's six main trading partners' imports plus spot market oil price, using the same weights as for the multilateral exchange rate (*IFS*). For Botswana the consumer price index was used.

5

Labor Market Policies and Outcomes

John Knight

1 Introduction

In 1980, the incoming Zimbabwe government adopted an interventionist approach to the labor market. Its main interventions took the form of wage policies (intended to raise the incomes of poor workers and to reduce income inequality), employment policies (intended to protect and expand employment, particularly the employment of relatively unskilled workers), and educational policies (which, in the long term, would promote the same objectives). In 1990, as part of its economic reforms program (ESAP), the government began to deregulate the labor market. There was to be less government intervention in labor relations, in wages and in employment, and the public sector was to be reduced in size. How successful were government policies in pursuing these objectives of inter-personal and inter-temporal income redistribution – of redistributing income to the African majority while encouraging rapid growth of the economy? That is our central question. Thus, this chapter analyzes labor market policies and outcomes in Zimbabwe since independence with two distinct purposes. The first is to understand the labor market in order to inform policy making and the second is to consider whether lessons from this experience can be drawn for the new millennium. However, this chapter concentrates on the first of these two objectives.

2 The political economy of labor relations

The new government had to cope with the extremely high expectations of rapid improvement in the lives of black people that had been aroused by liberation, but it also had to take a long-term view. The leadership, which had been radicalized in the liberation struggle, envisaged a gradual transition towards socialism. It decided to maintain the interventionist economic policies of the previous government, reorienting them towards socialist transformation, and to extend government intervention to the labor market. It was concerned to end racial disczimination in the labor market, to raise the lowest incomes and to reduce income differentials. Although the liberation struggle had been peasant-based, the new government expressed a commitment to workers and sought their support.

Its handling of the widespread strikes in the period 1980–82 was symptomatic of the competing pressures on government. The strikes occurred in response to a 'crisis of expectations': workers felt that improvements were now possible. At first, the government sympathized with workers' demands. It called for the establishment of workers' committees in enterprises, pledged to examine the wage structure, and set up a commission of inquiry into wages.[1] The government introduced extensive statutory minimum wages in 1980, in recognition of workers' needs and demands. When the strikes continued, however, the strikers were ordered to desist. Eventually, strikes were broken by police using force to make arrests. The government justified these measures in terms of the harm that strikes could do to economic development and political stability.

In many less developed countries not long after the attainment of political independence, government took steps to control trade unions. A common method was to confer monopoly representation on a single trade union organization and to 'incorporate' this body so that it would accept and implement government labor market policies. This strategy has both economic and political explanations – pursuit of the broader national economic interest and stifling of potential political opposition. The path taken by the Zimbabwe government had therefore been trodden before.

The government adopted a corporatist labor policy. It sought to monopolize political representation especially for black people, not only among political parties but also among trade unions. The government played a positive role in the creation of the Zimbabwe Congress of Trade Unions (ZCTU) in 1981. Trade unions aligned with the ruling party (ZANU, PF) won the ZCTU elections, and their leaders took command. The ZCTU was granted a monopoly of workers' representation in its dealings with government. With strikes effectively prevented and the government in control of the ZCTU, the trade union movement was now subordinate to government. The trade union movement was further undermined by the government's assumption of trade union functions. Its use of tripartite organizations (involving representatives of ZCTU, the Employers' Confederation of Zimbabwe (EMCOZ) and government) to discuss minimum wages and its legislation against the retrenchment of workers diminished the unions' bargaining functions. Government also attempted to compress the inegalitarian wage structure by specifying maximum percentage wage increases which tapered as the wage level rose. Thus the interventionist wage policies reduced the scope for bargaining over both unskilled and skilled wages.

The great powers over the labor market acquired by the state in the first five years of independence waned slightly over the next five years. The clique ruling the ZCTU came into disrepute owing to corruption and was ousted in elections in 1985. Thereafter the leadership showed greater, albeit muted assertiveness of its members' interests: the relationship with government evolved from subservience to conflict.

In the late 1980s the Zimbabwe government increasingly recognized the deficiencies of its interventionist development strategy, and in 1989 began to introduce less interventionist and more market-orientated policies, formalized in 1991 as the economic structural adjustment program (ESAP).

Although the government claimed 'ownership' of the new strategy, the policy reversal reflected the lobbying of local interest groups and the influence of the International Monetary Fund and the World Bank (Skalnes, 1995, ch. 7). As part of the policy reversal, government decided on some liberalization of the labor market. Zimbabwe was shifting from 'state corporatism' in labor matters, if not to free market solutions, then to 'bargained corporatism' (Shadur, 1994, p. 113).

Although the government's reversal on labor relations was part of the broader change in policy, it had some specific causes. First, there was pressure both from inside (ZCTU and EMCOZ) and outside (the ILO and the World Bank) Zimbabwe to restore collective bargaining. Second, the private interests of the leadership – becoming more involved in business – were changing. Third, the state increasingly recognized that it could not deliver rising living standards nor protect jobs. It saw an advantage in withdrawing and leaving the responsibility, and the blame, to others. Fourth, government became concerned about the slow growth of employment in relation to the rapid growth in the labor force, and the consequent rise in unemployment: a new labor market strategy was required.

In the late 1980s the government allowed the employment councils to play a larger role in setting wages and conditions. In 1990 statutory minimum and maximum wages were abolished, except for agricultural and domestic workers. The labor laws were softened by a series of statutory instruments and acts of parliament. One eased the rules on retrenchment of workers. Another established regulations for 'codes of conduct', whereby labor relations were decentralized. Codes could now be drawn up either at the industry or at the firm level. Once registered, they are binding for the settlement of disputes. Particularly as some codes of conduct are not negotiated but are imposed on employees, the codes permit employers greater flexibility with regard to wages, retrenchment, dismissal and (relatively unprotected) contract employment. The Ministry of Labor is now involved only as a last resort.

The withdrawal of government labor regulations did not strengthen the bargaining power of the unions. On the contrary, the balance of power swung considerably from employees to employers (Sachikonye, 1995, p. 64). First, the prohibition on strikes remained. Second, the threat of redundancy made workers insecure and afraid to voice discontent. Third, perhaps two-thirds of urban employees have ties with rural relations and access to land in the rural areas. The cushion that this provides reduces the capacity of unions to mobilize and negotiate on their behalf.

3 Human capital formation

The Zimbabwe government inherited a human capital stock ill equipped to cope with renewed economic growth and expanded social services. The skills shortage was exacerbated by the emigration of whites, and the exodus affected the quality of the labor force. In the 1980s a remarkable expansion occurred in primary, secondary and tertiary enrolments. Primary enrolment was doubled in 1980 and soon became universal. Secondary enrolment grew even more rapidly, the enrolment rate rising from 8 per cent before independence to 50 per cent a decade later – it was distinctly higher for the four years of junior secondary education (72 per cent in 1989).

The rapid expansion of primary and secondary education had serious implications for the labor market. While the scarcity of highly qualified labor continued, the market for primary and secondary school-leavers changed abruptly. The number of form four-leavers was under 10 000 in 1980 but exceeded 100 000 by 1987, when they represented half the 17-year-olds. These young people expected to obtain formal sector non-agricultural jobs in the way that their predecessors had done. Yet the increase in non-agricultural wage employment over the period averaged less than 20 000 per annum.

We can examine how well or badly the economy absorbs school-leavers by tracing their subsequent experience in the labor market. In 1991 a tracer survey of secondary school-leavers – those who had completed form four in 1985 and in 1988 – was conducted (Bennell and Ncube, 1992). Unemployment was extremely high among the cohort who in 1991 had been three years in the labor market – accounting for well over one-third of respondents. The proportion of those entering skilled occupations declined over time, suggesting that a process of 'filtering down' into lesser occupations was occurring among labor market entrants. The proportion entering the public sector dropped sharply, reflecting the deceleration in its growth. The public sector accounted for only one-quarter of the employment of the 1988 cohort. In the new, even harsher circumstances of the 1990s the potential of the informal sector to absorb educated young people productively has become a question much in need of an answer.

In the short term, at least, the educational policies presented a problem of educated unemployment and of potential social discontent. In the long term, however, it could be expected that the labor market would adjust as employers raised their recruitment criteria and entrants lowered their expectations. There is good evidence that educational expansion can increase human capital and thus the productivity of labor, and that, operating through the forces of supply and demand, it can erode the scarcity rents accruing to the educated (for example, Knight and Sabot, 1990, chs 3, 5, 7–9, with regard to Kenya and Tanzania). Although the evidence for Zimbabwe is incomplete, the educational expansion that has taken place since 1980 may, after adjustment lags, have raised output in the economy and the incomes of those who received the education. It may also have reduced the extreme inequality of wages that characterized Zimbabwe at the time of independence.

Whereas the expansion of education was extremely rapid after independence, the same cannot be said for formal training. Nevertheless, the case for more training was strong. Before 1980 the apprenticeship system was racially biased and produced few skilled manual workers. The number of apprentices was controlled by the white trade unions, which wished to maintain scarcity rents on skills. In order to correct the inherited distortions, the government centralized the recruitment of apprentices: prospective apprentices had to apply to the Ministry of Labor, and those selected were offered to employers, whose choices were limited. The number of indentured apprentices has fallen over time, not because of the lack of demand for places but because of the lack of supply. The explanation lay partly in an internationally observed decline in the need for apprenticeship training and partly in the hostility of employers towards the role played by the Ministry of Labor.

In 1984 the Zimbabwe Manpower Development Fund was created by means of a 1 per cent levy on the payroll of formal sector employees. It was to compensate employers for the costs of training. For instance, rebates from the levy fund are automatically available to cover the first two years of the four-year apprenticeship (King, 1990, p. 22). However, employers complained of excessive bureaucracy giving rise to reimbursement difficulties, and of the narrow range of eligible training. Moreover, a large proportion of the fund was used to finance government training institutions (Kanyenze, 1995, p. 8).

With the payroll levy, the formal apprenticeship scheme and the technical schools and colleges, the array of training institutions in Zimbabwe is impressive. Nevertheless, it appears that neither market forces nor government interventions have provided an adequate quantity and quality of training in Zimbabwe. These deficiencies are not unique to Zimbabwe: training is a perennial problem everywhere. Market solutions tend to fail because firms are reluctant to invest in workers who might leave, and because workers cannot afford to pay for their own training. Government interventions are often bureaucratic and uninformed and underfunded in relation to their objectives. The government technical schools and colleges in Zimbabwe suffer from all these problems. There is probably a case to be made for increasing government resources for training, even if they come from general education. However, there is also a case for improving the use of those training resources which are already in existence.

At the time of independence political power was transferred to Africans but economic power remained largely in the hands of non-Africans. The expansion of education and training after independence would permit the indigenization of the economy but the new government was determined to hasten the process through a policy of affirmative action. To this end, the Constitution of Zimbabwe empowered the President to direct the Public Service Commission to aim for a representative public service, and a directive to this effect was issued in 1980. The policy was vigorously implemented.

It has been suggested by some analysts that the efficiency of the public service fell over the 1980s on account of the affirmative action policy (see, for example, Strachan, 1993, p. 145). However, public service efficiency is not amenable to measurement, and anyway, the contribution made by affirmative action is difficult to isolate. It was, after all, replacing a system of negative discrimination which restricted the pool of talent, public service numbers were expanding rapidly, and there was ad hoc political interference in appointments. Moreover, with 5000 experienced white officials leaving under an incentive scheme shortly after independence, it was inevitable that normal procedures for recruitment and promotion would need to be lifted.

The same process of indigenization occurred in the parastatals and the private sector. However, employers in these sectors were not bound by the presidential directive, and the pace of black advancement here was slower. The politics of reconciliation and the potential harm to a fragile economy limited affirmative action in the private sector. The Zimbabwe government attempted to redress the racial imbalance in the private sector through exhortation and non-preferential legislation. The Labor Relations Act of 1985 made labor market discrimination unlawful. The Ministry of Labor had investigative powers but was insufficiently resourced to monitor firms effectively (Bennell and Strachan, 1992, p. 30).

The policy of affirmative action was understandable and predictable in the circumstances of Zimbabwe's independence. Nevertheless, the lesson to be drawn is that the policy can be pushed too hard and that it may have done harm as well as good to society. This experience highlights the need for education and training to level the playing field and, after the initial inevitable replacement of resigning staff, for normal adherence to the principle of promotion on the basis of merit (Strachan, 1993, p. 149; Gatherer and Erickson, 1993, p. 152). There is a need not only for legislation against labor market discrimination but also for a well-resourced enforcement body.

4 Wages and their determinants

As one of its first decisions, the newly elected government introduced a comprehensive national minimum wage in July 1980, at a time when many unorganized and spontaneous strikes and expressions of worker discontent were taking place. This minimum wage legislation was a potentially powerful policy tool because no fewer than 1 010 000 workers were then in wage employment, representing some 36 per cent of the labor force. The greatest impact occurred in 1980, when the minimum wage was initiated, and in 1982, when it reached its peak in real terms.

The period of rapid increase in the real minimum wage, 1980–82, was one of post-independence economic boom. This was followed by a period of drought and economic contraction, 1982–84. The real minimum wage was permitted to fall below its initial 1980 level in 1984. In 1986, the establishment of the tripartite Wages and Salaries Advisory Board provided a formal consultative machinery on minimum wage policy. This institutional development had the effect of strengthening the hands of technocrats relative to politicians, and it gave the employers greater influence over wage policy (Herbst, 1990, pp. 218–20). This helps to explain why real minimum wages fell again after 1985. General statutory minimum wage-setting effectively ended after 1988, and this was replaced by a policy of encouraging collective bargaining through industrial councils in all sectors. Basically the stagnation of real earnings for most of the 1980s reflects two things: the slackness of the labor market, and rising unemployment; and restraint in minimum wage-setting, as the technocrats in government gained influence. Bursts of inflation had a short-term depressing effect on the real wage but we cannot be sure, from the econometric evidence, that inflation had any long-term effect on real earnings.

For much of the 1980s, Zimbabwe had been 'living beyond its means' – the current account deficit (including factor payments) averaged 3.7 per cent of GNP between 1980 and 1989, and the budget deficit (net of grants) 8 per cent of GNP. With public debt increasing, neither was sustainable in the 1990s. The introduction of the ESAP in 1990 was intended to correct the imbalance. Part of the adjustment was directed at the labor market. It took the form of a real wage reduction in the public sector, government withdrawal from direct wage-setting in the private sector, a cut in the budget deficit and a fall in the exchange rate: all four mechanisms would tend to squeeze real incomes. Kanyenze (1995, p. 21) cites a World Bank document, which stated that a fall in real wages is 'a brutal but necessary adjustment to reflect labor unemployment caused by a growing labor force that has outstripped job creation and the need to become internationally competitive'. The real depreciation of the Zimbabwe dollar after 1990 required that real wages be flexible downwards in order to secure and maintain a competitive advantage.

The benefits of this strategy were expected to accrue over time, in the form of increased employment in the tradable sector – an issue addressed below. The costs – in the form of reduced economic welfare – were immediate and severe. Between 1990 and 1993 average real earnings in the formal economy as a whole fell by 36 per cent. This collapse occurred in all sectors – both private and public – although the tradable sector of mining was the least affected (with a decline of 'only' 24 per cent). There was only a slight reversal of real earnings in 1994 (a 2 per cent recovery overall). Although the drought in 1992 and consequent inflation were contributory, their effects were not noticeably reversed.

The majority rule government wished to reduce the extreme disparities in wages that it inherited. Therefore, the government adopted not only a minimum wage policy but also a maximum wage policy. Increases in the statutory minimum wage were usually accompanied by regulations setting out the maximum increases in rates of pay. These were tapered according to the wage level. The policy succeeded in compressing the wage structure but not to the extent implied by the regulations. Owing to skill shortages and the high labor turnover among skilled workers, employers had incentives to circumvent the controls. They did so by means of promotions, allowances and maintaining secrecy over the levels of remuneration (Shadur, 1994, p. 125).

The Zimbabwean government pursued an egalitarian incomes policy throughout this period. This was successful in compressing the wage structure in the public sector; however, it achieved limited success in the private sector. The fall in real earnings in the lowly non-manual occupations (such as clerk or typist), both absolutely and relative to the unskilled wage, may well have reflected the labor market response to the increased supply of secondary-educated labor. By contrast, the occupations requiring higher education or professional training (such as engineer and company secretary) continued to be in short supply. Employers responded to the increased scarcity by raising pay in relative as well as absolute terms.

The policy of compressing the wage structure, so widening the ratio between private and public sector pay, created severe difficulties for the public services, especially at the technical, professional and managerial levels. The policy generated a 'brain drain' from the public to the private sector: staff shortages and turnover became acute in such areas as accounting, programming, engineering and architecture (Kanyenze, 1993, pp. 165–70). Falling morale and effort and rising absenteeism and moonlighting were other predictable consequences for the public sector.

The threat of a 'brain drain' to other countries of the region emerged following the fall in the real incomes of professional staff in the public sector. In particular, the large occupational income differences between South Africa and Zimbabwe became more compelling as South Africa moved towards majority rule. The prospect of renewed economic growth and expanded social services in South Africa produced a need for more professionals – including doctors, nurses and teachers at all levels. It was reported in 1992 that some 200 Zimbabwe doctors had moved to South Africa over the previous 18 months, a very large figure given that the Zimbabwe government employed only 567 doctors in 1989/90. The median salaries of chartered accountants, programmers, employed medical doctors, engineers and university lecturers in Zimbabwe were about half of South African median salaries (Knight, 1993, pp. 290–1, tables 9.14, 9.15).

This is another example of a problem that often faces interventionist governments. The urge to intervene with some desirable objective in mind can backfire because the government does not adequately foresee the indirect effects of the intervention. One alternative was to harness market forces and to allow educational and training policies to increase the supply of skills sufficiently to compress the wage structure. This policy might nevertheless fail in the presence of a regional market for highly qualified personnel.

The liberalization of the labor market in the 1990s could be expected to widen the wage structure. In the private sector, pay in skilled jobs, both manual and non-manual, did indeed rise sharply in relation to pay in unskilled and lower clerical jobs. Although generally subject to collective bargaining in employment councils, the private sector responded to market forces. There was also some widening of pay differentials, in the public sector, with technical jobs gaining in relation to unskilled and administrative jobs. This was the result of a policy decision. In the 1990s the Public Service Commission – recognizing that valuable staff had to be attracted, retained and motivated – decompressed the civil service pay distribution. In 1995 civil service grades were restructured to allow for greater pay flexibility according to skill scarcity and individual performance. The reform was hampered, however, by political resistance to increased pay for top civil servants.

A survey of 200 industrial enterprises was conducted in Zimbabwe in mid-1993 (reported in Gunning, 1994). An earnings function analysis of the sampled employees yielded a number of interesting findings (Valenchik, 1994). First, by international standards, wages in Zimbabwe remain very unequally distributed. The coefficient of variation of hourly earnings is no less than 1.40. A major reason for this great dispersion is the remarkably high returns to human capital, a reflection of scarcity. In a human capital earnings function with the logarithm of hourly earnings as the dependent variable, earnings are found to rise with employment experience to a peak after 38 years, when the premium on experience is 400 per cent. The return to a year of education is no less than 16 per cent. Another important result of the survey is the powerful effect of firm size on earnings. Distinguishing four size groups (small: 1–10 employees; medium: 11–100 employees; large 101–250 employees; and very large: 250+ employees), the mean earnings are $2.38, $5.35, $7.15 and $10.72 respectively. It seems likely that some small firms ignore the legally binding minimum wage laid down in the relevant employment council agreement and that some large firms pay well above it. There is considerable evidence from the survey that the larger firms pay efficiency wages. The firm size effect was weaker for less skilled workers and also when controls for labor quality were introduced, and large firms had lower labor turnover. Large industrial firms in Zimbabwe are characterized by internal labor markets. The small firm sector, by contrast, not only paid lower wages but also employed less human capital and rewarded it less well.

Because some firms in manufacturing (and no doubt some other sectors) choose to pay efficiency wages that are above the market-determined level, we might expect real wages to be maintained in the face of economic recession and inflation. However, the evidence indicates that private sector real wages generally fell during the period 1990–95. One explanation is that efficiency wages may be set relative to market-determined wages – that is, the benefits to employers derive from the differential in wages and not from their level. These considerations are important to the issue of whether real wages will recover from their collapse since 1990.

5 Employment

In the period under discussion, the Zimbabwe government was concerned not only to increase output but also to increase employment. Formal sector wage employment, especially outside the sectors of agriculture and domestic service, generally offered higher wages than other economic activities, especially household farming. This generated political pressures to create more employment, particularly as the numbers of school-leavers burgeoned and urban unemployment rose. Through the 1980s formal sector employment increased by 180 000, or 18 per cent. Slightly more than half of this (100 000) was in the public sector, mainly in education and administration. To some extent, as in many other developing countries, the public sector was serving as a provider of employment and as a means of advancement for indigenous people. By comparison, the private sector was largely left alone in the politics of reconciliation.

One of the objects of the ESAP was to reduce the size of the public sector. In 1990 government embarked on a reform and retrenchment of the public service. The number of civil servants (excluding health and education) was to be reduced by 22 000 posts – that is, by 25 per cent (including vacancies). By February 1995, 18 000 public service posts had gone, including 7000 actual retrenchments (World Bank, 1995b, p. 20). Public sector employment overall declined slightly (by one per cent) over the five years, although a somewhat variable picture emerges according to the precise definition being used. However, real earnings fell dramatically in the public sector (by 39 per cent, compared with 25 per cent in the private sector), and this was the primary factor in the reduction of the public sector wage bill.

The events and policies of the 1990s had various effects on employment, making it difficult to isolate any particular contribution. In the short run, at least, the effect of the ESAP was to harm private sector output, which fell in 1992 and 1993. Similarly, the drought of 1992 contributed to economic recession. The change in relative prices associated with trade liberalization and exchange rate depreciation caused redundancies in some sectors, with the prospect of employment creation in those sectors which became more profitable. The budgetary component of ESAP caused some retrenchments in the public sector, although the net effect on public sector employment was tiny. According to our elasticity estimates, the substantial fall in real wages should have increased employment by almost 5 per cent in the formal sector as a whole. Total formal sector employment rose by 8 per cent between the second quarters of 1990 and of 1994, there being a rise of 14 per cent in the private sector. This growth is roughly half of what the authors of the ESAP had anticipated (Zimbabwe, 1991, p. 18). Prior to majority rule the policy of the state on matters of worker dismissal and retrenchment was one of non-intervention. By contrast, the new government was predisposed to intervene. Between 1980 and 1982 the government acquired considerable powers over the retrenchment and dismissal of workers. These job security regulations were, according to one view, 'among the most onerous prescribed anywhere' (Fallon and Lucas, 1993, p. 242). The government intervention on retrenchment could be expected to make employers reluctant to dismiss workers but also reluctant to recruit workers who might need to be dismissed in the future. Fallon and Lucas (1993) argued that job security regulations reduce employment, partly because they increase adjustment costs and partly because they reduce efficiency. Greater job security reduces employees' incentives to be productive and employers' ability to choose and keep productive workers.

Fallon and Lucas (1993) used econometric methods to estimate the employment effects of the employment protection legislation. It is possible to quibble with their estimates and interpretation, but they found a powerful long-run effect: on average, the legislation had reduced employment by 25 per cent in the industrial sector. Moreover, there was attitudinal evidence, based on a survey of employers, that the regulations served as a deterrent to employment (Hawkins et al., 1988, table 3.17). This appears to be another example of well-meaning government intervention having a harmful rather than a beneficial impact because of unforeseen general equilibrium effects. The employment regulations were effectively withdrawn in 1990. The immediate effect of this was to permit retrenchments associated with ESAP, but the evidence suggests that in the long run their withdrawal will be a spur to employment.

6 The labor force and its absorption

The labor force in Zimbabwe grew from 2.59 million in 1980 to 3.80 million in 1990 (Zimbabwe, CSO, 1989b, Appendix A, table A; Zimbabwe, CSO, 1989a, table 2.16). By contrast, formal sector employment grew from 1.01 million to 1.19 million. The annual percentage growth rates were 3.9 and 1.7 per cent respectively. The labor force grew on average by 122 000 per annum, whereas formal sector employment grew by 18 000. How were the additional 104 000 additional workers absorbed into the economy each year? In the 1990s the equation has become worse. How can productive employment be found for the labor market entrants?

The national household surveys of 1984/85 and 1990/91 show a very considerable difference in average household per capita income between urban and rural areas. The income per capita of urban households was 3.5 times that of households in the rural areas (mainly the communal lands) in 1984/85, and 3.6 times in 1990/91 (Zimbabwe, CSO, 1988; 1994b). The Zimbabwe labor market is best seen as one in which the preferred non-agricultural formal sector jobs are rationed by employers and the residual labor force is absorbed into open unemployment or the free-entry informal sector. The glittering urban prizes can be expected to attract migrants from the rural areas and so generate unemployment and an urban informal sector.

Unemployment is largely an urban phenomenon. According to the 1986 labor force survey, it was 18 per cent of the labor force in urban areas. Urban unemployment (on similar definitions) rose from 18 per cent to 26 per cent between 1986 and 1990/91, and from 7 to 11 per cent for the country as a whole (Zimbabwe, CSO, 1989b, Appendix A, tables A,D,E; 1994b, table 2.8). The unemployment rate was extremely high for those aged under 25 and for secondary-school-leavers. If the data were available, they would probably show unemployment to be well over 50 per cent for educated young people in the urban areas. Even if this unemployment is transitory, one cohort of school-leavers is replaced by another, larger cohort. It is always difficult to measure unemployment, partly because there are many dimensions which a single statistic cannot capture. However, the evidence is consistent with the claim that there is a trend rise in unemployment in Zimbabwe.

The introduction of ESAP in 1991 meant that the formal sector, and in particular the public sector, was unlikely to provide enough jobs and opportunities to cope with the demand. There were also demands from the group of existing and incipient black entrepreneurs for government encouragement and support of black enterprise. Middle-class frustration was perceived to be a danger to the state. The government responded to these pressures by formulating a policy of indigenization (Raftopoulos and Moyo, 1995). The Indigenous Business Development Centre (IBDC) was launched in 1990, to press for more black participation and control. It has a membership of 4000 enterprises. In 1992 the government set aside Z$150 million for black business people (Raftopoulos and Moyo, 1995, p. 28). The government report on indigenization proposed measures to assist informal sector business – such as the subcontracting of 30 per cent of government tender work to small firms and an increase in the subsidized credit provided by the Small Enterprise Development Corporation (SEDCO) – as well as measures to advance indigenous management in the formal sector (Zimbabwe, 1994a). Other things being equal, we would therefore expect informal sector growth to have been more rapid after 1990 than before.

Two nationally representative surveys of small enterprises were carried out in 1991 and 1993 covering unregistered (that is, informal sector) micro and small non-agricultural enterprises (MSEs). It was estimated that there were 868 000 MSEs employing 1 351 000 workers (McPherson, 1991, revised by Daniels, 1994, p.10). Thus employment in the non-agricultural informal sector exceeded that in the formal sector (which accounted for 1 244 000 workers). Further, the number of MSEs grew by 9 per cent and their employment by 14 per cent between 1991 and 1993 (Daniels, 1994, p.10). Thus, the informal sector provided more opportunities for the absorption of labor market entrants than did the formal sector. Is this expansion a sign of success or failure? Distinctions can be drawn between demand-pull and supply-push factors, and between high-income dynamic activities and low-income free-entry activities. The evidence from the surveys suggests that on the whole the expansion is a sign of failure: most of it occurred in free-entry activities offering relatively low incomes, such as trade in farm products, crocheting and knitting.

If the population of the communal lands grew at the national rate (3.14 per cent per annum) between the census years 1982 and 1992, then population density in the communal lands increased by 36 per cent over the decade as their population grew by 1.4 million (Zimbabwe, CSO, 1994a, table 2.2). According to the Rukuni Commission on land tenure, as the population of the communal areas had grown, so people had resorted to farming less fertile and more fragile areas. It found that 'there are over three times as many people now living in the communal areas as their environment can sustain' and that 'land resources are overutilized and their condition is deteriorating at a high rate' (Zimbabwe, 1994b, vol. 1, pp. 27, 28, 36).

As in many developing countries, rural households in Zimbabwe would be able to raise their incomes and spread their risks by diversifying into other activities. There are two main possibilities: non-farm self-employment and migration. The number of rural MSEs implies that 45 per cent of rural households ran an informal non-farm business in 1991 (Daniels, 1994, p. 10; Zimbabwe, CSO, 1994, p. 80). However, this may be misleading because the extremely low contribution of income from household enterprises (other than agriculture) to household cash income (3.2 per cent) and total income (1.5. per cent) in the communal lands in 1990/91 suggests that most rural households' non-farm activities were pitifully small (Zimbabwe, CSO, 1994b, table 3.1(a)).

The urban informal sector in Zimbabwe is small in relation to that found in comparable African economies. To a large extent this reflects the repressed state of the informal sector prior to 1980. It is also due to the relatively advanced formal sector, associated with non-African entrepreneurship and the westernization of tastes, and the remaining obstacles to urbanization and to entry to informal sector activities. Nevertheless, the 1980s saw two important urban informal sector developments. One was the growth of informal manufacturing, for instance furniture-making, repair services and tailoring, assisted by the relaxation of rules concerning the establishment of small enterprises and the weakness of formal sector competition. Secondly, rural–urban migration and the growth of urban unemployment pushed more people into free-entry informal sector activities. The informal sector is therefore heterogeneous, ranging from profitable small businesses protected by various entry barriers to low-income activities characterized by underemployment. The small businesses also generated wage employment, often paying wages below the statutory minima. The free-entry self-employed and these wage-employed workers – predominately women and youth – constituted the urban poor.

According to the 1992 census, the urban population grew by 5.2 per cent per annum over the inter-censal decade 1982–92 – from 26 to 31 per cent of the total population (Zimbabwe, CSO, 1994a, table 2.3 and p. 24). Thus the pace of urbanization remains constrained: government has blocked the establishment of shanty towns near urban areas and continues to enforce the vagrancy laws. This has put a brake on the development of an urban free-entry informal sector.

Contrary to the predictions of probabilistic migration models, the informal sector in Zimbabwe does not appear to be a stepping stone to the formal sector. No less than 80 per cent of reporting respondents from a 1984 survey of non-free entry small enterprises (Moyo et al., 1984, reported in Zimbabwe, Ministry of Labor, 1989) entered it from the formal sector, and only 20 per cent came from unemployment or rural work. Thus the formal sector is generally the stepping stone to the informal sector, possibly because it provides experience and capital. These results suggest that this productive part of the informal sector may not be easily entered by the educated unemployed youth. According to the McPherson (1991)–Daniels (1994, p. 10) surveys, in 1993, the majority of MSEs (88 per cent) made profits below the average non-agricultural earnings in the formal sector, and 67 per cent were below even the minimum wage for domestic servants (Daniels, 1994, pp. 24–5). To a considerable extent the urban informal sector serves as a residual sponge to absorb surplus labor: only a part of it can be regarded as productive. The appropriate training of would-be entrepreneurs stands out as a serious but unresolved problem. It appears that much training cannot be left to the market because of capital market imperfections, informational imperfections, the 'free-rider' problems facing existing firms, and the high risks involved. With little government intervention, little has happened. In an ILO survey of the training needs of entrepreneurs, only 6 per cent of the entrepreneurs interviewed had received training related to their business. The authors concluded that 'there appears to be a lack of interest and commitment by government to provide technical and vocational training opportunities to informal sector entrepreneurs' (Siddiqui and Nyagura, 1993, pp. 26, 34). Another ILO report (Siddiqui and Matare, 1993) concluded that current training efforts in Zimbabwe were reaching only an insignificant proportion of school-leavers. Although the system of youth training centers (YTCs) had been set up in 1981 in order to help rural school-leavers to gain artisan skills for self-employment, this was a drop in the ocean.

7 Lessons for the future

The interventionist labor market policies pursued by the Zimbabwean government soon after independence had only limited or mixed success. Many of the interventions, although well intentioned, were either ineffective or had unforeseen consequences. Interventions which harnessed market forces might well have been more successful. We consider each in turn.

Education

The remarkable expansion of education from the extremely low levels prevalent at the start of the period was perhaps the most successful intervention. However, it had two associated dangers. One concerned the quality–quantity trade-off. The faster the education system expanded, the greater the threat to standards imposed by financial and staffing constraints. The other was the economic loss and the threat to social stability associated with high and rising levels of unemployment among post-primary graduates. The expansion of the supply of educated labor relative to the demand was a powerful means of compressing the earnings structure, and one which could rely on market forces.

Wage determination

Government intervened in formal sector wage-setting. It raised the minimum wage and laid down maximum wage increases, tapering as the wage level rose, thus compressing the wage structure. However, this had little effect in high-wage sectors such as industry and commerce, where wages are generally above the minimum. These regulations were more effective in the public than in the private sector and had serious drawbacks, creating allocative inefficiency and disincentive effects that affected the quality of public services. For the future, it would be better to rely on the policy of expanding education and training and then allow market forces to narrow the dispersion of wages. The possibility of a 'brain drain' would, however, limit the reduction in professional and managerial pay.

Employment

Although the state's dismissal regulations were a well-intentioned attempt to defend jobs against employers' response to the introduction of the minimum wage, evidence suggests that they had the opposite effect. Employers were reluctant to hire if they could not fire. The net result was that the regulations both weakened workers' incentives for effort and reduced employment. There are good economic reasons why, in many circumstances, it is in the interests of both the employer and the employee to form a long-term relationship, thereby helping to build and retain firm-specific skills. However, this process does not require state intervention. Job protection appears to have been excessive in Zimbabwe. Two other policy variables governing employment are: (i) the relative protection or taxation of the labor-intensive primary sectors such as agriculture and mining vis-à-vis such capital-intensive sectors as manufacturing and services; and (ii) government interventions in the pricing of capital and labor. Evidence exists that wage increases would reduce employment considerably in agriculture but little in industry.

The fostering of a productive urban informal sector is a potentially important development strategy. With independence came some relaxation of restrictions and assistance to would-be small entrepreneurs. Nevertheless, a web of laws and regulations remained for most of the post-independence decade, which obstructed the establishment of and operation of small businesses. Thus a less regulatory and more promotional framework is required. In particular, government intervention is needed in order to help overcome the informational, credit and training constraints which hinder the educated unemployed from opting for entrepreneurial careers. It is arguable, therefore, that the most fruitful government interventions in the labor market are the result of failures in the capital market, viz. the promotion of human capital accumulation. Human capital takes various forms – education, training, and learning by doing. Whether through direct action, subsidization or loans, there is a case for government to concentrate on helping people to accumulate human capital in all its forms. It seems that the market in training for the informal sector has failed. There is a great need for government to consider the ways and means of a more active policy on training, particularly in relation to young educated workers.

Rural–urban income differentials

The substantial income gap, even for unskilled workers, between households in urban and rural areas cannot be explained simply in terms of government intervention. Efficiency wage considerations and rent-sharing by employers engaged in collective bargaining help to explain why urban formal sector wages have generally exceeded the rural supply price and, indeed, the statutory minimum wage. However, government wage interventions have at times assisted some urban workers. Moreover, 'urban bias' in government policies towards areas such as education, health sanitation and housing also contribute to the urban–rural income gap. We would expect the higher urban incomes to act as a powerful magnet to rural people. The evidence suggests that rural–urban migration has occurred but not on the expected scale. There is a good case for government intervention to control the pace of urbanization. The object is to avoid the burgeoning of a free-entry urban informal sector and the growth of urban unemployment and poverty, and their attendant problems.

Direct government interventions on wages and on employment have not been beneficial, mainly because they have had unanticipated general equilibrium effects. The labor market reforms of the 1990s reduced the extent of government intervention on wages and employment. However, it cannot be concluded that they were beneficial overall. This required an assessment of the labor market effects of the ESAP strategy. The effects on the welfare of wage earners was clearly adverse: a sharp fall in real wages and reduced security of employment. To some extent this was an inevitable correction of the unsustainable economic policies of the 1980s – that is, the 'no-change' counterfactual may with time have been even worse. On the benefit side, the employment growth that was anticipated to flow from the ESAP by government and the World Bank has not materialized. The prognosis for the future is unpromising.

Note

1. Roger Riddell (1981) *Report of the Commission of Inquiry into Incomes, Prices and Conditions of Service*. Harare: Government Printer.

References

Bennell, Paul and Mkhululi Ncube (1992) 'Assessing educational outcomes: key findings from a chronological tracer survey of secondary school-leavers in Zimbabwe', Institute of Development Studies, Sussex, UK, processed, pp. 1–33.

Bennell, Paul and Brigid Strachan (1992) 'The Zimbabwean experience: black occupational advancement', in Pierre Hugo (ed.), *Redistribution and Affirmative Action: Working on South Africa's Political Economy*. Halfway House: Southern Book Publishers.

Daniels, Lisa (1994) 'Changes in the small-scale enterprise sector from 1991 to 1993: results of a second nation-wide survey in Zimbabwe', Gemini Technical Report No. 71, March.

Fallon, Peter R. and Robert E.B. Lucas (1993) 'Job security regulations and the dynamic demand for industrial labor in India and Zimbabwe', *Journal of Development Economics*, vol. 40, pp. 241–75.

Gatherer, John and Jonathan Erickson (1993) 'Affirmative action in Zimbabwe: a private sector case study', in Duncan Innes, Matthew Kentridge and Helene Perold (eds), *Reversing Discrimination: Affirmative Action in the Workplace*. Cape Town: Oxford University Press.

Gelb, A., J.B. Knight and R.H. Sabot (1991) 'Public sector employment, rent seeking and economic growth', *Economic Journal*, vol. 101, no. 408, September, pp. 1186–99.

Gunning, Jan W. (ed.) (1994) *The Manufacturing Sector in Zimbabwe: Dynamics and Constraints*. Amsterdam: Free University Press.

Hawkins, A.M., P.J. McBurney, M.A. Shadur and W. Clatanoff (1988) *Formal Sector Employment Demand in Zimbabwe*. Harare: University of Zimbabwe Publications.

Herbst, Jeffery J. (1990) *State Politics in Zimbabwe*. Berkeley: University of California Press.

Kanyenze, Godfrey (1993) 'The Impact of Economic Stabilisation on the Wage Structure of Zimbabwe', PhD thesis, University of Sussex.

Kanyenze, Godfrey (1995). 'Human resource development in Zimbabwe: beyond the economic structural adjustment programme', Zimbabwe Congress of Trade Unions, Harare, processed.

King, Kenneth (1990) 'Inservice training in Zimbabwe: an analysis of relationships among education, training, industry and the state', World Bank, Population and Human Resources Department, Education and Employment Division, Background Paper No 90/27, Washington DC: World Bank, processed.

Knight, John (1988) 'A comparative analysis of South Africa as a semi-industrialised developing country', *Journal of Modern African Studies*, vol. 26, no. 3, September, pp. 473–94.

Knight, John (1993) 'Labor markets', in African Development Bank, *Economic Integration in South Africa*, volume 3. Abidjan: African Development Bank, chapter 9.

Knight, John (1996) 'Labor market policies and outcomes in Zimbabwe', Centre for the Study of African Economies, University of Oxford, August, processed.

Knight, John. B. and Richard. H. Sabot (1990) *Education, Productivity and Inequality: The East African Natural Experiment*. Oxford: Oxford University Press/World Bank.

McPherson, Michael A. (1991) 'Micro and small-scale enterprises in Zimbabwe: results of a country-wide survey', Gemini Technical Report No. 25, December, processed.

Moyo, N.P., R.J. Davis, G.C.Z. Mhone and L. Pakkiri (1984) *The Informal Sector in Zimbabwe – its Potential for Employment Creation*. Lusaka: South African Team for Employment Promotion (ILO/SATEP).

Raftopoulos, Brian and Sam Moyo (1995) 'The politics of indigenization in Zimbabwe', *East African Social Science Review*, vol. 11, no. 2, June, pp. 17–33.

Sachikonye, Lloyd M. (1995) 'Industrial relations and labor relations under ESAP in Zimbabwe', in Peter Gibbon (ed.), *Structural Adjustment and the Working Poor in Zimbabwe*. Uppsala, Sweden: Nordiska Afrikainstituten, pp. 38–131.

Shadur, Mark A. (1994) *Labor Relations in a Developing Country: a Case Study on Zimbabwe*. Aldershot: Avebury.

Siddiqui, Farid and Silas Matare (1993) 'Training school-leavers for self-employment', ILO/Ministry of Labor, Manpower Planning and Social Welfare, August.

Siddiqui, Farid and Levi Nyagura (1993) 'Training needs of entrepreneurs in the informal sector in Zimbabwe', ILO/Ministry of Labor, Manpower Planning and Social Welfare, June.

Skalnes, Tor (1995). *The Politics of Economic Reform in Zimbabwe*. London: Macmillan – now Palgrave.

South Africa, Central Statistical Services (CSS) (1990) *South African Statistics 1990*. Pretoria: Government Printer.

Strachan, Brigid (1993) 'Africanisation in the Zimbabwe public service', in Duncan Innes, Matthew Kentridge and Helene Perold (eds), *Reversing Discrimination: Affirmative Action in the Workplace*. Cape Town: Oxford University Press.

Valenchik, Ann (1994) 'The labor market: wages and earnings', in Jan W. Gunning (ed.) (1994) *The Manufacturing Sector in Zimbabwe*, pp. 97–145.

World Bank (1990) *World Development Report 1990*. Washington DC: World Bank.

World Bank (1995a) *World Development Report 1995*. Washington DC: World Bank.

World Bank (1995b) 'Performance Audit Report. Zimbabwe', Washington DC: World Bank, processed.

World Bank (1995c) 'Zimbabwe. Achieving Shared Growth. Country Economic Memorandum', volume 1, Washington DC: World Bank, processed.

Zimbabwe, CSO (1988) *The Economy of Households in Zimbabwe 1985: Main Preliminary Results from the Income, Consumption and Expenditure Survey 1984/85*. Harare: CSO.

Zimbabwe, CSO (1989a) *Statistical Yearbook 1989*. Harare: CSO.

Zimbabwe, CSO (1989b) *Main Results of the Labor Force Survey 1986–1987*. Harare: CSO.
Zimbabwe, CSO (1994a) *Census 1992. Zimbabwe National Report*. Harare: CSO.
Zimbabwe, CSO (1994b) *Income, Consumption and Expenditure Survey Report 1990/91*. Harare: CSO.
Zimbabwe (1991) *Second Five-year National Development Plan 1991–1995*. Harare: CSO.
Zimbabwe (1994) *The Way Forward to the 21st Century: Draft Policy on the Indigenization of the Economy*. Harare: CSO.
Zimbabwe, Ministry of Labor, and others (1989) 'The promotion of economic development, employment and equity in Zimbabwe', Harare, mimeo.
Zimbabwe (1994). *Report of the Commission of Inquiry into Appropriate Agricultural Land Tenure Systems*, 3 volumes (the Rukuni Report). Harare: Government Printer.

Part III

Financial Liberalization, Monetary Policy and Currency Crisis

6

Financial Liberalization and the Adoption of Indirect Instruments of Monetary Policy

Obert Nyawata and Clever Mumbengegwi

Introduction

At the time of its independence in 1980, Zimbabwe inherited a diversified and well-developed financial sector relative to the size of its economy: there were five commercial banks, two discount houses, four merchant banks, three building societies, six finance houses and a Post Office Savings Bank (POSB). Several insurance companies, pension funds, specialist credit and development finance institutions also existed for the purpose of directing funds to preferred sectors such as agriculture and industry. The Reserve Bank of Zimbabwe (RBZ) sat (and still sits) at the apex of the financial system and was (still is) bestowed with the full responsibilities of a central bank. However, the financial sector was subject to various controls and government-induced distortions such that the financial sector exhibited many of the characteristics of financially repressed economies. This highly regulated system remained virtually unchanged until the economic reforms adopted in 1991 under the economic structural adjustment program (ESAP). Thus, financial liberalization was an important component of the economic reform measures implemented during the 1990s.

This chapter examines Zimbabwe's experience of financial liberalization. It provides an account of the main facts and major episodes of the monetary and financial sector reforms. Preliminary assessments of the impacts of these reforms on financial intermediation are given and the implications for the conduct of monetary policy are also addressed. The rest of the chapter is organized as follows: Section 1 gives an overview of the pre-liberalization monetary policy framework in Zimbabwe and the incidence of financial sector repression. Section 2 discusses the theoretical basis for financial liberalization and provides an account of the major financial sector reforms that have been implemented. Section 3 gives a preliminary assessment of the impact of financial liberalization measures using simple criteria to assess performance. Section 4 discusses the implications of the financial sector reforms on the conduct of monetary policy, especially the move towards indirect instruments of monetary policy and the implications of financial liberalization on the stability of the long-run money demand function. Section 5 concludes.

1 The pre-liberalization financial sector and monetary policy framework (1980–1990)

Prior to financial liberalization, Zimbabwe's monetary and financial sector was highly regulated and subject to various types of controls which induced financial market distortions such as negative real interest rates, credit rationing, excessive taxation of the financial sector and capital-intensive industries. The controls included macroeconomic, allocative, structural, prudential, organizational and protective measures[1] leading to government-induced distortions and financial repression. The distortions originating from macroeconomic controls were associated with the following:

Interest rate ceilings

Interest rates were administratively fixed and subject to ceilings. The RBZ prescribed deposit and lending rates for commercial banks, building societies and finance houses. However, rates on commercial bank fixed deposits, negotiable certificates of deposit, Treasury Bills, call deposits and inter-bank loans were not directly controlled; they were allowed to be determined in the market within a narrow range. Other interest rates were also set in line with various sectoral objectives. Thus, interest rates remained more or less fixed, with marginal changes occurring only when the authorities sought a more active role for monetary policy.

Theories often cited as providing some of the economic rationale for imposing interest ceilings include Keynes' liquidity trap, Tobin's monetary growth model, Seignorage, deficit financing and planning models based on fixed input–output coefficients. Keynes' liquidity trap implies that excessive liquidity preference destroys the incentive to save and thus impedes growth.[2] Under these circumstances, economic agents find the holding of money as an asset more attractive than holding capital and, as a result, the level of investment falls. In Tobin's model of money and growth, households allocate their wealth between money and productive capital assets. A higher return on capital relative to the return on money results in a larger proportion of capital relative to money in the portfolios of households and this produces higher capital/labor ratios, higher labor productivity and higher income. From this, it is concluded that a reduction in the return on money increases welfare. Such a reduction can be achieved by reducing deposit rates, by taxing money or by increasing the growth in the stock of money.

Directed lending

The Reserve Bank (RBZ) played a key role in facilitating the allocation of financial resources to preferred projects and sectors though directed lending. Special financial institutions were created, such as the Zimbabwe Development Bank, the Small Enterprise Development Corporation (SEDCO) and the precursor to the Credit Guarantee Company and the RBZ used to issue certificates of deposit (CDs) in order to mobilize funds for on-lending to these development finance institutions. These would, in turn, channel credit to selected programmes – in some cases, this may have simply been a disguised means of catering for special interest groups.[3] Sectoral credit allocations were used, with targets being set for bank lending to particular activities and sectors. Those institutions which complied with these targets were given greater access to special funds while non-compliance could result in the denial of access. Non-price rationing and selective credit techniques were also used as a means of providing subsidized credit, especially to parastatal bodies. Preferential lending rates were set for what were considered productive activities, while unproductive activities attracted penal interest rates. The RBZ also used moral suasion to cajole commercial banks into increasing lending to mostly black-owned enterprises and newly established small to medium-sized exporters. The rationale of this measure was that large and established exporters were assured of pre- and post-shipment credit from these same banks, usually at much lower interest rates.

Statutory regulations

Legislation and statutory regulations were introduced by the Zimbabwean financial authorities to prescribe specific roles, functions, and interest rate ceilings, taxation and reserve requirements for different types of financial institutions. This hampered competition and resulted in a repressed and highly segmented financial market. For example, the RBZ provided its 'lender of last resort' function through discount houses. These institutions acted as intermediaries between the RBZ and other financial institutions. They have traditionally had exclusive access to the RBZ's facility for discountable paper. The rate at which discount houses are accommodated by the Reserve Bank determines the rate at which they, in turn, accept the call deposits of the banks. They have not been subject to reserve requirements. Similarly, building societies are also exempt from legal reserve requirements and enjoy special tax exemptions on their shares. However, they are required by law to keep 10 per cent of their assets in short-term instruments and are subject to interest rate controls on mortgages to various categories of consumers.[4] The POSB mobilizes savings and fixed deposits from small savers throughout the country and can only invest them in central government bonds or in other stock issued by public bodies. This institution has a competitive advantage in attracting deposits due to the tax-exempt status of the interest earnings on deposits held with it. Insurance companies, pension funds and other non-bank financial institutions are required to invest pre-specified proportions of their assets in government securities – a portfolio requirement that was often over-fulfilled due to a combination of weak credit demand and the lack of alternative investment opportunities. This was designed to ensure that government has ready access to non-bank financing of its budget deficits.[5] The statutory asset prescription, differential taxation of financial assets and unequal reserve and liquidity ratios on deposits from different types of financial institutions were used to achieve the same objective of directing financial resources to preferred sectors.

Seignorage[6]

The need to collect seignorage could well have been one of the principal reasons for the Zimbabwe government to repress its financial system. Blanchard and Fischer (1989) observe that seignorage accounts for as much as one-half of 1 per cent of GNP in low-inflation industrial countries and much more in high-inflation and cash-strapped developing countries. Cukierman (1992) shows, inter alia, the relative importance of seignorage and inflation as a source of revenue for both developed and developing countries. For Zimbabwe, seignorage revenue amounted to an annual average of 4 per cent for the period 1971–82 compared with an annual average of about 2 per cent for the period 1990–96. Seignorage as a proportion of GDP may be depicted as:

$$S_t = (M_t - M_{t-1})/Y_t \qquad (6.1)$$

where M_t is nominal base money at the end of period t, and Y_t is nominal GDP in period t. Seignorage revenue comprises two parts – namely, the real balance effect and the inflation tax effect. The former derives from the public's willingness to hold the government's financial liabilities while the latter derives from taxation of the outstanding stock of real balances through inflation. The exchange control regime that existed facilitated the collection of seignorage revenue. It is worth noting that financial sector and exchange regime liberalization reduces the scope for generating seignorage. The emergence of other financial assets renders the demand for money more elastic to returns on these other financial assets. The liberalization of the trade and exchange regimes eliminates rationing and thus the need for economic agents to hold speculative balances. Additionally, the removal of exchange controls eliminates the implicit tax on exports and also offers scope for currency substitution; the effect of which would have been to reduce the seignorage tax base.

The monetary policy framework prior to financial liberalization

The major objectives of Zimbabwe's monetary policy during the early 1980s were to achieve price and exchange rate stability. These were later broadened, towards the end of the decade, to include promoting economic growth and balance of payments stability.

Instruments of monetary policy

The RBZ had a wide range of instruments at its disposal through which it sought to keep money supply growth in check in order to attain the above policy objectives. In practice, the RBZ relied on direct mechanisms to implement its monetary policy, despite their well-known distortionary effects. Policy makers preferred direct instruments because of their one-to-one correspondence with the intended policy targets. This is in contrast to indirect instruments, which impact upon the underlying supply and demand conditions in the money market. The instruments included liquidity requirements, interest rate controls, direct credit controls, hire purchase arrangements, import deposits, non-negotiable RBZ Bills, the discount rate, overnight advances to commercial banks and changes in the yields on Treasury Bills and government stock, and, finally, moral suasion. The discount window and RBZ bills were elements of indirect instruments of monetary control. Treasury Bill auctions were exclusively for financing budget deficits until early 1994, when special Treasury Bill open market operations were introduced for liquidity management.

The objectives of price and exchange rate stability were directly addressed through tight exchange and price controls, which were applicable to a wide range of items. These were instrumental in keeping inflation low during the 1980s. Monetary policy was, for the most part, passive and accommodated developments on the real side of the economy. At any rate, the scope for an independent monetary policy was limited given the fixed exchange rate arrangement that prevailed. However, as monetary policy became more active, it sought to contain inflation through the proximate target of aligning monetary growth with growth in nominal GDP.

In its attempt to keep the factors affecting money supply in check, the RBZ focused directly on the demand for credit from the various sectors. This was approached from both the domestic and the foreign side. External sources of monetary expansion were easily handled through variations in the foreign exchange allocations for imports. However, with the subsequent liberalization of the trade and exchange regime, it became difficult to sterilize external sources of monetary expansion. Domestic credit objectives were achieved through direct contacts with financial institutions to ensure that credit was allocated to productive uses. Quantitative targets were set for each institution's lending to small enterprises and other purposes. Banks were generally conservative in their lending operations. This could be attributed to foreign exchange constraints as well as a tight regulatory framework. It is therefore hardly surprising that there were no reports of banks being saddled with serious problems of bad loans. However, it is equally probable that the lack of on-site inspection of banks may have facilitated the disguising of some bad loans. Conjectural and anecdotal evidence seems to suggest that the incidence of bad loans has increased over the years as some banks have aggressively extended loans to emerging businesses which previously had no access to bank credit – a legacy of the country's political history. Portfolio restrictions effectively rendered the non-bank sector a captive market for government paper, thus restricting the volume of credit to the private sector. The financing needs of the budget would be determined once amounts available from the POSB and the rest of the non-bank financial institutions were established. The financing needs of the Agricultural Marketing Authority (AMA) and other public enterprises were also established and credit to the private sector was determined as the residual.

Interest rates were more or less fixed throughout the 1980s. In 1989, the RBZ replaced the minimum lending rates (MLR) for commercial banks and finance houses with the base-lending rate (BLR). The BLR became a kind of reference rate which the lending rates for preferred activities were not allowed to exceed by more than a specified percentage.[7] At the same time, minimum lending rates were set for what were considered to be less desirable activities, including speculation. The interest rates paid on deposits in commercial banks, building societies and finance houses were set or stipulated by the RBZ. However, interest rates on commercial bank fixed deposits, negotiable certificates of deposit, Treasury Bills, call deposits and inter-bank loans were not directly controlled and thus could be determined freely in the market, albeit within a narrow range. Other interest rates were set in line with various sectoral objectives.

Liquidity ratios were the main instrument used to influence liquidity in financial markets while reserve requirements (usually kept below 10 per cent) were used mainly for prudential purposes. Prior to liberalization, these were rarely changed. Treasury, Agricultural Marketing Authority (AMA) and trade bills, government stocks with less than six years to maturity and Banker's Acceptances counted towards the liquidity requirements of banks. The RBZ used to discount all of these financial instruments. Furthermore, it would instruct each institution to take up a specified amount of RBZ bills, which were non-transferable and non-discountable.[8] In essence, these bills became the main instruments through which the RBZ could influence liquidity in the financial system in the short term.

Thus the use of direct instruments generated the tendency for monetary authorities to micro manage the banking system and in the process generate further distortions in financial markets through ad hoc controls imposed in order to enforce policy. However, these measures failed to control monetary expansion and the liquidity overhang that existed in the banking system in the latter half of the 1980s. The liquidity overhang was exacerbated by the tight exchange controls such that, by the end of the decade, it was evident that reform of the financial sector was needed for monetary policy effectiveness and the efficient functioning of the financial system. Hence financial

Table 6.1 Zimbabwe: early monetary policy reform measures

Interest rate policy	*Early 1991*	*Late 1991*	*1992*
Deposit rates			
	Increased with a view to mobilize domestic resources for investment in productive sectors	Minimum savings rate for all institutions increased to 14%. Rate on demand deposits remained at 7%	
Commercial Banks	Minimum deposit rate increased to 7% (2/91)		
Building Societies	Minimum rate increased from 9.25% to 12% (2/91) Rate on tax free PUPs increased from 9% to 11% (2/91)	Rate on tax-free PUPs inreased to 12.65%	
POSB (tax-free interest)	Rate on savings deposits increased from 9.25% to 12% (2/91) Rate on fixed deposits increased from 11% to 12.5% (2/91)	Rate on savings deposits increased to 14.25% Rate on fixed deposits increased to 14.25%	
Finance Houses (fixed deposits)	3 months increased to 11% (2/91) 6 months increased to 11.5% (2/91) 12 months increased to 12.5% (2/91)		
Deposits > 12 months and NCDs	Continued to be market-determined. Maxima on placements with POSB and Building Societies retained	Limits on holdings increased by 100% in anticipation of increased deposits	
Lending Rates			
Commercial and Merchant Banks	Increased from 12% to 15% (BSL)	Base lending rate increased from 15 to 17.25%	
Finance Houses	Increased from 14.5% to 18% (BSL)	Base lending rate increased from 18% to 21% Base lending rate ceased to be statutory and became indicative.	

Table 6.1 (continued)

Interest rate policy	*Early 1991*	*Late 1991*	*1992*
Preferential Rates			
	Continued for productive and export sectors		Government provided $400 million to Commercial banks and the AFC for the rescheduling of farmers' debts and drought relief. Z$100 million was provided to assist the start of small to medium scale enterprises at a low interest rate. Government facilitated offshore borrowing of US$ 1 million by merchant banks to finance merchant banks, tobacco purchases on the auction floors as well as pre-shipment finance for tobacco exports. Z$ 110 million was provided to building societies to finance mortgages. Building societies were allowed to issue NCDs as a means to generating funds. Government negotiated a low-income housing facility (US$50 million with USAID to assist building societies. Local commercial banks and the merchant banks granted permission to negotiate external lines of credit provide cheap foreign financing for exporters working capital needs. RBZ catered for small to medium scale exports by providing pre- and post-export finance at rates

Minimum Lending Rate (MLR)		
(Consumption – covering goods and services)	Increased from 17% to 25%	Increased from 25 to 30%
Mortgage rates		
New non-owner-occupied housing and commercial property in municipal areas including holiday resorts	From 18% to 30%	Increased to 32%
Located in any other area	Pegged at 20%	
Tourist development	Pegged at 20%	
Existing non-owner-occupied housing and commercial property in all areas	From 18% to 20%	Increased to 23%
Owner-occupied houses	From 13.75% to 14.5%	Increased to 17% for those > Z$35 000
Mortgage rate for low-cost housing or loans below Z$12 000	From 12.5% to 13%	Threshold increased to Z$35 000 and rate to 15%
Mortgage rate for industrial property	From 14.75% to 16%	Increased to 18.25%
Liquidity ratios		
(Prescribed liquid asset ratio)	Previously used as monetary policy tool – to switch to prudential purposes	For commercial banks from 40% to 25%
	Narrower definition of liquid assets with a view to reducing the ratio	For merchant banks from 40% to 20%
	Reserve assets excluded from definition 11/91	Unchanged for building societies and finance houses at 15% (10/91)

Table 6.1 (continued)

Interest rate policy	*Early 1991*	*Late 1991*	*1992*
Direct controls			
Import deposits		OGIL imports in excess of Z$15 000 to require an advance deposit to Customs. Deposit to be held in a special non-interest-earning account at RBZ. Additional funds not to be obtained from Banker's Acceptances. Aim to minimize speculative import purchasing and siphon liquidity from the banking system.	
Reserve Requirements '(RR)'			
Reserve requirements for finance houses	Unification of reserve requirements at 10% across deposit types (2/91) RR increased to 12.5% (11/91). Shift in focus towards monetary control – no longer treated as non-liquid assets Remained at 4%		RR reduced to 6.25% (3/92) RR increased again to 12.5% (6/92)
Non-negotiable Reserve Bank Bills			
	Used as a short-term fine-tuning instrument Low interest rate 5%, non-liquid and non-transferable		
Changes in the yields on Treasury Bills and govt stock			
	To ensure competitiveness with alternative investment in the market Govt. stock yields were adjusted upwards especially at the short end of the market as follows: 1–10 years – an average of about 350 basis points	Government stock issues to be by tender and all secondary trading of such stock to be done through the Stock Exchange or through other private placements. Objective to correct distortions brought about by aligning yields on Govt stock with	

		other market-determined rates and administratively linking the determination of stock prices on the secondary market to the ruling yield curve. RBZ to act as broker for stock issues and to buy and sell Govt stock at its discretion. Termination of the preannouncement of stock Issue programme: Objective to accord RBZ greater flexibility in ensuring appropriate combinations of instruments of Govt paper, maturities and amounts.	
	11–17 years an average of about 240 basis points 17–30 years an average of 130 basis points		
Indirect methods of monetary control			
Open market operations	At ruling rediscount rate 13% (2/91) and	To lend to Government at 15.75% (ruling DR)	
RBZ lending to Government to parastatals	At base lending rate for commercials and, merchant banks 15% (2/91)	To lend to parastatals at 17.25% (ruling BSL) for commercial and merchant banks	
Rediscount rate (bank rate)	Increased from 10.25% to 13% (2/91)	Rate increased from 13.65% to 15.75% Increased to 18% (10/91), 20% (12/91	Increased to 21% 1/92) and 22% (3/92) and to 25% (5/92) And
No longer referred to as the bank rate			Reduced to 22% (6/92) increased to 30% (7/92) and 29% (12/92)
Rediscount policy	Tightened the eligibility criteria for private	REPO whereby the RBZ only resold BAas to the originating house at predetermined prices was discontinued	

Table 6.1 (Continued)

Interest rate policy	*Early 1991*	*Late 1991*	*1992*
Bankers' acceptances (to reduce the number of eligible Bankers Acceptances that could be discounted by the Reserve Bank and that way restrict monetary expansion)	For rediscounting in line with change in liquidity as follows: (a) Limited eligible paper to only that relating directly to specific merchandise transactions involving exports of such goods (b) With respect to imports -only by allowing those imports backed by a firm export order or where there was evidence of continuity of exports to be eligible for rediscounting	Henceforth the RBZ could hold bills to maturity or sell them to whoever it chose Retained the policy of rediscounting TBs with some modifications on the issue: a) tender multiples reduced from Z$10,000 to Z$5,000 b) RBZ became the sole underwriter of TBs c) TBs ternder opened up to include individuals, insurance companies, pension funds, the POSB, banks, companies d) Variations in maturity and amounts of bills to be adopted	

Source: Quarterly economic and statistical reviews, policy statements.

liberalization was introduced as an integral component of the economic structural adjustment program (ESAP).

2 Financial liberalization in Zimbabwe

This section provides the theoretical basis for, and some basic facts about, the financial liberalization measures implemented in Zimbabwe during the period of ESAP. The measures that were implemented fall into two broad categories: (i) pure financial sector reforms and (ii) monetary policy reforms. However, the specific measures in these categories are not mutually exclusive; rather, they tend to act in a mutually reinforcing manner. The former aimed to increase the sector's competitiveness and market orientation to broaden and deepen financial intermediation while the latter sought to achieve macroeconomic stability.[9]

The theoretical basis for financial liberalization

The theoretical basis for financial liberalization date back to the work on financial intermediation by Gurley and Shaw (1960). Until the 1970s, this work was not widely discussed because of the assumed efficiency of financial markets.[10] Gurley and Shaw noted that commercial banking is the main form of intermediation in the early stages of financial development and that in this environment, the stock of money may be a useful proxy for financial activity since the supply of inside money is closely related to the overall level of financial intermediation. However, this is not true in the advanced stages of financial development where other institutions have emerged and provide credit as well as alternative means to hold liquidity.

The financial repression paradigm

The theoretical foundations for financial liberalization as a way to address the problems of financial repression were further laid in the work of McKinnon (1973) and Shaw (1973). Their approach is rooted in the classical view of savings as determining the level of investment and they challenged the predominant tendency of macroeconomic models to focus on the stock of money as the most relevant aggregate in the relationship between real output and the financial sector. McKinnon and Shaw (M–S) argue that financial repression in the form of indiscriminate distortions of financial prices, ceilings on interest rates and foreign exchange impedes efficient financial intermediation and economic growth.[11] In such situations, interest rates are kept low and are usually negative in real terms. The removal of interest rate ceilings and other restrictions is expected to facilitate economic development and growth by ensuring greater efficiency in the allocation of capital.[12]

The main elements of the M–S approach are:

- a saving function that is a positive function of both the real rate of interest on deposits and the real rate of growth in output;

- a negative relationship between the effective real loan rate of interest and investment and a positive relationship between economic growth and investment;
- a real interest rate that is below its equilibrium because of the nominal rate being administratively fixed by the government and;
- non-price rationing of loanable funds.

The major conclusion from their analysis is that financial intermediation can be improved by making real interest rates positive and removing other forms of distortions in financial markets. While arriving at similar conclusions, Mckinnon and Shaw differ over the transmission mechanisms of the real interest–savings–investment and economic growth nexus. McKinnon analyzes the impact of real deposit interest rate on savings, investment and growth through the complementarity hypothesis which views money and physical capital as complements. The analysis is premised on two assumptions: (i) that all economic units are confined to self-financing; and (ii) that investment expenditures are lumpy and do require prior accumulation of money balances. Thus deposits are crucial in encouraging self-financed investment. A raising of the opportunity cost of holding money by increasing real deposit rates increases the savings needed for self-financed investment.

By contrast, Shaw adopts the debt intermediation view of financial intermediaries and their ability to offer better interest rates because of the ability to reduce costs through economies of scale and risk diversification. According to this view, higher deposit rates are expected to increase deposit mobilization by banks and this in turn increases loanable funds.

Further theoretical advances which incorporate both endogenous growth and endogenous financial institutions have emerged from the renewed interest in growth theory and financial growth models. Financial intermediation is now explicitly modeled as opposed to being taken for granted or treated in simple deterministic terms as was the case with the first-generation financial repression models (Fry 1988). For example, researchers have added financial variables to the list of variables used by Barro (1991) in his endogenous growth approach to examine the determinants of growth in a cross-section study.[13] These studies also find that financial repression, in the form of discriminatory taxes on financial intermediation, reduces the growth rate.[14]

Pure financial sector reforms

Financial sector reforms were concentrated in the early stages of the reform process, between 1991 and 1992. This was even before the strengthening of the prudential and regulatory framework. The reforms adopted involved the liberalization of interest rates and the gradual lowering of barriers to entry in order to foster competition and reduce financial market segmentation. New legislation was tabled to guide the emergence of new money market instruments and financial services. Wider branch networks were encouraged in order to deepen financial intermediation. The competitiveness of capital markets was enhanced by the opening up of the Zimbabwe Stock Exchange to foreign capital so that it could become a vibrant source of equity finance. With the liberalization of the exchange and trade regime in 1993, foreigners were allowed to acquire and trade shares on the stock exchange. As a result, there were large capital inflows onto the stock exchange with the result that it became one of the best performers among emerging markets. However, some of the liberalization measures that were envisaged at the beginning of the program have yet to be implemented. For example, the Securities Exchange Commission is yet to be established. Similarly, the reform of the regulatory and supervisory framework was slow. The Reserve Bank Act and the new Banking Act only achieved parliamentary approval in 1999 and became law in 2000. The former was meant to strengthen the supervisory powers of the central bank and the latter to reduce financial market segmentation. However, by the time these changes were introduced, the financial sector had been shaken by problems, with some institutions having accumulated high levels of bad and non-performing loans in their portfolios. One bank was forced to close and another was only saved by the intervention of the Reserve Bank.

3 The impacts of financial liberalization

The theoretical expectation from the McKinnon–Shaw hypothesis is that financial liberalization improves financial intermediation, which, in turn, increases savings, investment and economic growth.[15] Thus, in implementing the financial sector reforms, the Zimbabwean government had a reasonable expectation that they would generate some real benefits to the economy; some specific to the financial sector (microeconomic) and others economy-wide (macroeconomic) in nature. Interest rates were expected to become positive in real terms as a result of the removal of ceilings on them and the adoption of prudent monetary and fiscal policies. Competition among financial institutions was expected to increase while spreads between lending and saving rates were also expected to narrow. Monetary aggregates relative to GDP were expected to increase, reflecting improvements in financial intermediation. Credit to the private sector was also expected to increase and the crowding-out that is often associated with financial repression to be reversed. Macroeconomic aggregates such as savings, investment, external capital movements and economic growth were also expected to benefit from the reforms. Financial liberalization would also engender financial innovation resulting in the use of a wider range of financial instruments which had hitherto been considered unattractive or just unavailable.

However, these expectations were not fulfilled because some key ingredients were missing during Zimbabwe's financial sector reforms. Macroeconomic instability, the partial implementation and the poor sequencing of economic and financial sector reforms, especially the slow pace of fiscal reform, have severely undermined the intended impacts of the reforms. Experiences from other countries indicate that macroeconomic stability, removal of controls on interest rates, appropriate sequencing of reforms and a strong regulatory and supervisory framework are key ingredients in any successful process of financial liberalization.

To assess the more direct effects of financial liberalization we use simple criteria and indicators, as suggested in Galbis (1995). Inflation and the budget balance are used as indicators of macroeconomic stability. The levels and trends in real interest rates, especially the maintenance of positive real interest rates and narrowing of interest rate spreads, are used as reasonably good indicators of the efficiency of financial intermediation. They also provide information about the extent of financial repression. Differentials between local and international interest rates are indicators of the extent of pressures for capital mobility (inflows or capital flight). The extent of financial deepening and broadening is indicated by the behavior of monetary aggregates. Whereas growth in monetary aggregates gives some clues about the stance of monetary policy, the ratio of broad money to GDP indicates the level of financial deepening. The levels and growth in credit to the private sector are used as indicators of financial broadening and the reversal of financial repression and the crowding-out of private investment that is often associated with it.

Financial sector reforms are further assessed on the basis of their influence on broad macroeconomic aggregates such as savings, investment volume, capital movements and economic growth. Savings and investment ratios to GDP are used as indicators of the general effects of financial liberalization on the volume of savings and investment, which are known to have implications for the rate of economic growth.

Efficiency of intermediation

Indicators of the efficiency of intermediation suggest that the efficiency of the Zimbabwean financial sector did not improve substantially, perhaps as a result of the continued oligopolistic structure of the financial sector and high unremunerated reserve requirements.

Competition and the removal of barriers to entry

The removal of barriers to entry was meant to enhance competition among financial institutions and thus reduce spreads between lending and deposit rates. As a result of the regulatory reforms that were implemented by the Zimbabwean government, some of the delineation between financial institutions has become blurred. While significant progress has been made, market segmentation and some distortions still exist due to incomplete liberalization. To date, financial institutions engaged in similar activities were still subject to differential treatment with respect to reserve requirements and taxation. For example, discount houses and building societies which have always been deposit taking but were not subject to reserve requirements. This not only undermined the use of changes in reserve requirements as a monetary policy instrument, but also accorded unfair advantages to these financial institutions.

The removal of barriers to entry also resulted in the emergence of new and indigenously owned financial institutions[16] which has led to increased competition to the extent that established financial institutions have often raised concerns that the country had become over-banked and fraught with the potential for a banking crisis. Despite this, the Zimbabwean financial sector remains highly oligopolistic in structure. At the time of writing, the number of commercial banks had only increased from five to seven, merchant banks from four to seven and discount houses from two to six. Finance houses increased by one to six and building societies increased from three to five. Thus established banks have urged the financial authorities to restrict further entry in order to avoid some of the new banks going bust. While these concerns might reflect sectarian interests by established financial institutions to protect their profits and market shares, the proliferation of new financial institutions in the absence of a strong regulatory and supervisory framework has its own pitfalls. The subsequent withdrawal of a bank licence and the temporary waiver of legal reserve requirements for some troubled institutions are cases in point which point to the dangers of liberalization in advance of a suitable regulatory and supervisory framework.

Interest rate trends

Positive real interest rates were expected to result from the removal of interest rate ceilings. Nominal rates skyrocketed in the first two years of reform, but so did inflation, with the result that most real interest rates remained negative. They only became positive after 1992 and remained so till 1998. Excessively high levels of inflation rendered them negative again thereafter. Thus liberalization and the removal of interest rate ceilings in the absence of prudent fiscal and monetary policies was no guarantee for improved efficiency in financial intermediation.

Interest rate spreads

Despite the increased competition, interest rate spreads actually widened. The spread between domestic deposit and lending rates declined marginally in 1990 but widened sharply thereafter until 1993, when they started narrowing once again. The spread between domestic commercial bank lending and international rates (LIBOR) also followed a similar pattern – widening considerably, but narrowing marginally in 1993. This, however, encouraged significant capital inflows. Indeed, some of the increase in the size of spreads could be associated with the higher loan rates needed to offset the costs of bad loans and higher unremunerated reserve requirements.

Other indicators of efficiency

Other indicators of efficiency – the ratio of reserve money to quasi money and broad money (M2) – showed a similar pattern.

Financial deepening

One of the immediate symptoms of financial repression is the extent of financial disintermediation or demonetization. Table 6.2 shows the developments in the various monetary aggregates that could be used as indicators of financial deepening. Ratios of the various concepts of money, ranging from the narrowest to the broadest (M1, M2 and M3) relative to GDP fluctuated. The trends in these variables suggest some financial disintermediation during the first two years of the liberalization program. This trend is most observable in the ratio of M2 to GDP. Table 6.2 also shows that, on average, the velocity of circulation was generally higher during the period associated with financial disintermediation but declined and stabilized thereafter. From 1993, the ratios for these monetary aggregates showed signs of recovery, reflecting, in part, the positive impact of liberalization measures.

Financial broadening

Data on the quality of bank loan portfolios and the corporate sector's financial structure would have been useful but are difficult to obtain. However, the increase in real credit to the private sector is often used as an indicator of financial broadening and a sign of reversal of the crowding-out of private investment that often occurs under conditions of financial repression. In the case of Zimbabwe, the share of real credit to the private sector marginally increased relative to that to the public sector, indicating some evidence of financial broadening. However, some of this increase might simply reflect the effects of distress borrowing as firms struggled to stay afloat in the face of high interest costs.

Savings, investment and economic growth

The negative real interest rates that prevail under conditions of financial repression impact negatively upon the rate of economic growth through their effects on savings and investment. Where ceilings exist on both deposit and loan interest rates, some form of credit rationing may arise, in which some projects with high rates of return are not undertaken because of the lack of funds while those that are undertaken may be just marginally above the interest rate ceiling. Furthermore, such ceilings may result in financial disintermediation and the emergence of informal financial markets. The liberalization of interest rates enhanced the development of financial markets and improved the allocative efficiency of investment decisions. Savings and investment ratios are used as indicators of the general effects of financial liberalization on overall development and economic growth. However, data on these variables do not readily lend themselves to an unambiguous interpretation and identification of the effects of financial liberalization. Empirical results from elsewhere have shown the interest elasticity of savings to be ambiguous. The short duration of the reforms and the limited number of observations constrain similar empirical analysis of the interest rate elasticity of savings and investment in Zimbabwe. With regard to investment, it is worth noting that the problem prior to liberalization was one of foreign exchange constraints, while after liberalization, it seems to have been credit constraints and political factors dampening investment.

Macroeconomic stability

Macroeconomic stability, as indicated by a low and stable inflation rate and the budget balance, is important for various macroeconomic aggregates such as savings, investment and economic growth. Reforms in the financial sector have economy-wide effects through their impacts on these aggregates. During the period of reforms, monetary policy experienced difficulties in obtaining its intermediate objective of maintaining a stable and low level of inflation. Inflation rose to an unprecedented 42 per cent in 1992 before declining to an average of 25 per cent and then rising again to an all-time high of 70 per cent in the last quarter of 1999. Although the monetary policy stance was tight, it had little support from the fiscal side. This fiscal inertia meant that monetary policy became overburdened with the responsibility of restoring macroeconomic stability. A weak fiscal policy stance has been the Achilles, heel of Zimbabwe's macroeconomic management, which gave rise to monetary control problems. It is this combination of a tight monetary policy and a lax fiscal policy that has undermined macroeconomic stability, the investment climate and overall economic growth. As indicated above, many real interest rates remained negative despite high nominal rates during the early part of financial liberalization. This outcome was primarily due to the high levels of inflation.

Monetary management

The adoption of indirect instruments of monetary control reinforced the development of money markets through an efficient emission of signals and offered scope for the effective conduct of monetary policy. Monetary management through indirect instruments helped promote the efficiency of financial markets and, as such, was one of the benefits of financial liberalization.[17] A distinguishing feature is that these instruments targeted the balance sheet of the central bank while direct instruments mainly target the balance sheets of commercial banks. Direct controls tended to be blunt and contributed to an inefficient allocation of financial resources.[18] This

Table 6.2 Zimbabwe: financial indicators

	1990	*1991*	*1992*	*1993*	*1994*	*1995*	*1996*
GDP growth (percentage change)	7.0	5.5	−9.0	1.3	6.8	0.1	7.3
Inflation (percentage change)	17.4	23.3	42.1	27.6	22.2	22.6	21.4
Budget deficit (% of GDP)	−5.3	−5.4	−5.0	−6.3	−3.8	−8.8	−7.6
Domestic Debt/GDP (per cent)	31.3	26.5	23.3	21.4	23.0	37.3	
Inflation tax rate (per cent)	14.8	18.9	29.6	21.6	18.2	18.4	17.6
Seignorage	1.9	1.8	0.6	3.1	1.7	0.7	3.6
M2/GDP (per cent)	23.3	17.1	16.6	23.0	23.5	25.0	25.7
Velocity of M2	4.3	5.8	6.0	4.4	4.3	4.0	3.9
Growth in money supply (%)	27.6	23.0	5.8	94.9	18.2	52.4	23.1
Domestic credit/GDP (%)	22.7	21.2	26.3	33.8	30.8	31.0	30.4
Credit to private sector/M2 (%)	99.2	153	173.6	130.0	121.1	126.2	121.3
Reserve money/quasi money	0.51	0.85	0.78	0.85	0.63	0.71	0.76
Reserve money/M2	0.26	0.34	0.34	0.30	0.28	0.23	0.28
Interest rate differential (domestic) (%)	0.5	3.0	5.0	4.5	8.5	8.5	17.8
Interest rate differential (foreign) (%)	3.7	11.3	43.6	44.2	35.3	32.5	31.6
Real bank discount rate (%)	−7.1	−3.3	−12.1	0.9	7.3	6.9	5.57
Exchange rate depreciation (− = appreciation) percentage change	15.6	47.8	40.9	27.1	25.8	6.4	15.3
Real effective exchange rate (− = depreciation) percentage change	−11.0	−15.9	−9.2	4.1	−6.9	5.5	7.9

Sources: Calculations from IFS, RBZ and CSO publications.

explains the successful adoption of indirect instruments of monetary control which could have given scope for the reduction of unremunerated reserve requirements[19] closer to the levels necessary for prudential considerations only. However, in practice they were raised periodically in an effort to deal with the problem of excessive monetary growth[20] and hence increasing the level of implicit taxation of financial institutions.

4 Post-liberalization monetary policy reforms

The liberalization of the financial sector and the trade regime posed challenges for Zimbabwean policy makers. As they grappled with the problems of high fiscal deficits, high levels of inflation, high real lending rates, large capital inflows and the associated appreciation of the exchange rate, the challenges were in terms of the sequencing and choice of monetary policy variables and the ineffectiveness of the chosen monetary policy instruments to reduce and stabilize inflation.

Monetary policy framework and financial liberalization measures

Early in the liberalization program, the Reserve Bank put in place a restrictive monetary policy to address the rapid growth in the money supply that resulted from the above problems. There was a definitive shift from an accommodating monetary policy stance to an active one, geared to contain inflation and ensure the stability of the exchange rate. The main objective of monetary policy was to reduce the rate of inflation to less than 10 per cent by 1995. Within this framework, various instruments of monetary policy were used and fine-tuned in line with other liberalization measures taking place within the financial sector.

However, these short-term instruments proved ineffective in controlling the growth in money supply. Between 1993 and 1997, broad money, M3, grew at an average rate in excess of 30 per cent per annum, reaching a peak at 58.6 per cent in August 1994. Increased recourse by government to the domestic banking sector to finance its budget deficits, increased private sector borrowing, a rise in demand deposits of both commercial banks and discount houses and the liberalization of the trade and exchange regimes were among the major factors behind this trend.

Instruments of monetary policy

Monetary policy was conducted through a gradual transition from direct to indirect instruments of monetary control designed to influence various monetary aggregates and interest rates. The operating targets were reserve money and short-term interest rates while the intermediate targets included credit aggregates, broad money and interest rates. The main instruments of policy were:

Open market operations

Open market operations were widely used to inject or absorb liquidity through the buying and selling of securities in the open market. The Reserve

Bank used government securities, special Treasury Bills as well as its own securities to curb monetary expansion.

Interest rate policy

The timing and changes in magnitudes of various interest rates are summarized in Table 6.1 above and the various nominal and real interest rates, which reflect changes in interest rate policy are given in Table 6.3. Interest rates on government stock became more market-determined rather than being set by the government. Trading in government and other commercial paper was opened up to wider participation and secondary markets for government securities were also strengthened. Deposit rates were generally increased across institutions and deposit types to attract higher savings for investment. The minimum lending rate (MLR) was increased from 17 per cent to 25 per cent, in the first instance, and further increased to 30 per cent for non-productive lending. Non-essential consumption, speculative and non-productive lending was discouraged through the imposition of high lending rates. The hike in interest rates also led to a widening of the spread between domestic rates and international rates.

Reserve requirements and liquidity ratios

Short-term, indirect money market instruments failed to contain the growth in money supply due to the fact that money growth was driven by long-standing structural imbalances in the economy. As a result, the RBZ actively used variations in statutory reserve requirements and liquidity ratios, which are the traditional long-term instruments of monetary control.[21] Prior to liberalization, reserve requirements were used mainly for prudential reasons, while liquidity ratios were a statutory instrument with which to manage liquidity in the banking system and channel financial resources to the government. With the advent of liberalization, the RBZ switched the respective roles of reserve requirements and liquid asset ratios. In addition to it being an implicit tax on the financial sector, especially where they are not remunerated, reserve requirements were now used for monetary control purposes and were adjusted in accordance with monetary policy objectives. Initially, they were unified at 10 per cent across deposit types for commercial banks and merchant banks and were no longer treated as a part of liquid assets. On the other hand, the definition of liquid assets was narrowed and the liquidity ratios substantially reduced. In an effort to curtail commercial banks' capacity to lend, and hence reduce money supply growth, the statutory reserve ratio was periodically adjusted upwards (see note 20). These high levels of reserve requirements are a tax on financial intermediation and contributed to widening interest rate spreads.

The authorities also used trade policy instruments with monetary implications. For example, in response to the strong demand for imports due to the liberalized trade regime, import deposits were required on all Open General

Import Licence (OGIL) imports in excess of Z$15 000. These deposits were held in a special non-interest-earning account at the central bank. They were not to be financed through Bankers' Acceptances (BAs). These measures constituted a double-pronged strategy to minimize speculative import purchasing and at the same time soak up some of the liquidity in the banking system.

However, there was a temporary monetary policy reversal following the supply shocks caused by the effects of the 1992 drought. The RBZ reacted to the drought by relaxing its monetary policy stance. It reduced the legal reserve requirements and relaxed its rediscounting policies. Furthermore, drought-related fiscal expenditures fueled growth in money supply, adding to inflationary pressures. At the end of 1992 inflation rose to 42 per cent and, as a result, most real interest rates became negative. However, by the end of 1992, monetary policy had turned full circle again.

Non-negotiable reserve bank bills were used as a short-term instrument for managing liquidity. They were issued at a low interest rate of 5 per cent, were non-liquid and non-transferable and, hence, were unattractive to the market. In early 1991, the yields on government stock were adjusted upwards by up to 350 basis points at the short end of the market. The objective in adjusting the yield structure was to align the yields with other market-determined rates. The RBZ also took some measures to give itself greater flexibility in ensuring an appropriate mix of paper, maturities and quantities. Reserve Bank lending to government was to be at the prevailing discount rate while that for its lending to parastatals was to be at the current base-lending rate for commercial banks and merchant banks. There has been an increase in the stock of RBZ bills and lending to the government by the RBZ.

Rediscount and overnight accommodation rates

Under the reforms, the rediscount (previously known as the bank rate) and overnight accommodation rates became active instruments of monetary policy. As indicated earlier, the discount rate applies to discount houses which are the only financial institutions with direct access to the RBZ discount window. The rediscount rate is adjusted on a day-to-day basis and it reflects the RBZ's medium-term view on the inflation level. As the rediscount rate is the benchmark for other rates in the money market, each time the Reserve Bank raised the rediscount rate, virtually all lending institutions would also raise their rates by comparable margins. Thus, all other rates have also been on an upward trend.

The RBZ sought to restrict monetary expansion by reducing the quantities of Bankers' Acceptances that it discounted. It also made its accommodation policy (RBZ provision of liquidity to banks through discount houses) more restrictive by raising the rate in order to discourage commercial banks from borrowing money from the Reserve Bank. The discount rate currently reflects the RBZ's medium-term view on inflation, and acts as the benchmark

Table 6.3 Zimbabwe: selected nominal and real interest rates, 1990–1997 (end of period, per cent per annum)

	1990	*1991*	*1992*	*1993*	*1994*	*1995*	*1996*	*1997*
Nominal discount rate	10.25	20.00	30.00	28.50	29.50	29.50	27.00	25.50
Real discount rate	−7.15	−3.30	−12.10	0.90	7.30	6.90	5.60	6.50
Nominal treasury bill rate	9.85	18.50	35.50	26.96	29.91	29.83	18.90	23.90
Real treasury bill rate	−7.55	−4.80	−6.60	−0.64	7.71	7.23	−2.50	4.90
Nominal rates on 3-month bankers' acceptances	10.20	35.00	36.75	34.25	31.00	29.60	27.10	25.60
Real rates on 3-month bankers' acceptances	−7.20	11.70	−5.35	6.65	8.80	7.00	5.70	6.60
Nominal rates on 6-month NCDs	11.50	35.00	39.00	29.00	32.00	31.00	21.75	26.00
Real rates on 6-month NCDs	−5.90	11.70	−3.10	1.40	9.80	8.40	0.35	7.00
Nominal savings rates in building societies	9.25	14.00	14.00	14.00	14.00	14.00	14.00	13.00
Real savings rates in building societies	−8.15	−9.30	−28.10	−13.60	−8.20	−8.60	−7.40	−6.00
Nominal savings rates at the POSB	9.25	14.25	14.25	19.75	19.75	19.75	17.00	14.00
Real savings rates at the POSB	−8.15	−9.05	−27.85	−7.85	−2.45	−2.85	−4.40	−5.00
Commercial banks								
Nominal rates on 3-month fixed deposits	11.50	24.00	42.50	43.00	31.50	30.00	19.25	25.35
Real rates on 3-month fixed deposits	−5.90	0.70	0.40	15.40	9.30	7.40	−2.15	6.35
Nominal rates on 12-month fixed deposits	11.00	20.00	37.00	37.00	29.00	28.00	19.00	25.50
Real rates on 12-month fixed deposits	−6.40	−3.30	−5.10	9.40	6.80	5.40	−2.40	6.50
Accepting Houses								
Nominal rates on 3-month fixed deposits	11.50	25.00	41.00	43.00	30.00	30.00	19.50	25.50
Real rates on 3-month fixed deposits	−5.90	1.70	−1.10	15.40	7.80	7.40	−1.90	6.50
Finance houses								
Nominal rates on 12-month fixed deposits	11.50	28.00	42.00	42.00	30.00	29.00	20.50	26.00
Real rates on 12-month fixed deposits	−5.90	4.70	−0.10	14.40	7.80	6.40	−0.90	7.00

Table 6.3 (Continued)

	1990	*1991*	*1992*	*1993*	*1994*	*1995*	*1996*	*1997*
Building societies								
Nominal rates on 12-month fixed deposits	10.50	14.85	14.85	15.85	15.85	15.85	15.85	13.75
Real rates on 12-month fixed deposits	−6.90	−8.45	−27.25	−11.75	−6.35	−6.75	−5.55	−5.25
Post Office Savings Bank								
Nominal rates on 12-month fixed deposits	10.25	14.50	14.50	21.75	21.75	21.75	20.00	17.00
Real rates on 12-month fixed deposits	−7.15	−8.80	−27.60	−5.85	−0.45	−0.85	−1.40	−2.00
Lending Rates								
Nominal commercial banks rate (maximum)	12.00	17.25	47.50	47.50	40.00	38.49	37.07	35.75
Real commercial banks lending rate	−5.40	−6.05	5.40	19.90	17.80	15.89	15.67	16.75
Nominal accepting houses lending rate	12.00	17.25	38.66	42.12	40.50	42.00	40.00	35.00
Real accepting houses lending rate	−5.40	−6.05	−3.44	14.52	18.30	19.40	18.60	16.00
Nominal finance houses lending rate	25.00	36.00	50.00	50.00	40.00	42.00	40.00	38.00
Real finance houses lending rate	7.60	12.70	7.90	22.40	17.80	19.40	18.60	19.00
Building societies (Mortgages)								
Nominal residential property rates	13.75	17.00	17.75	19.00	22.25	22.25	18.50	15.75
Real residential property rates	−3.65	−6.30	−24.35	−8.60	0.05	−0.35	−2.90	−3.25
Nominal commercial property rates	14.75	18.25	20.25	27.00	32.00	32.00	32.00	24.00
Real commercial property rates	−2.65	−5.05	−21.85	−0.60	9.80	9.40	10.60	5.00

Source: Central Statistical Office, and RBZ QESR.

for other interest rates while the accommodation rate is a direct indicator of prevailing liquidity conditions in the money market.

The rediscounting of Treasury Bills was modified by reducing the size of tender denominations from Z$10 000 to Z$5000, and opening up participation to individuals, companies, pension funds, insurance firms and the

POSB. The central bank became the sole underwriter of Treasury Bills. In early 1994, the RBZ was authorized to issue special 91-day Treasury Bills in order to assist RBZ bills in short-term liquidity management. The plan to review the discount rate policy and replace it with Repurchase arrangements (Repo rate) which has a more direct impact on short-term interest rates has been implemented.[22]

Special or compulsory Reserve Bank bills.

These bills were tradable only between discount houses and commercial banks. The RBZ introduced new bills which took effect on 1 September 1997. It introduced a new 30-day deposit instrument to be used if the money market surplus is below Z$50 million and the RBZ bills to be used if the surplus is above that limit. Unlike Treasury Bills, these bills are not rediscountable at the RBZ, although they are tradable elsewhere in the money market. The rate on them is not attractive and this reduces their liquidity status.

Exchange rate policy

In an effort to stabilize the Zimbabwe dollar, the Reserve Bank has sold foreign exchange in the domestic inter-bank foreign exchange market from time to time and, in the process, succeeded in withdrawing cash from the market to support efforts to curb monetary growth. For some time, the exchange rate was market-determined. However, following the crises of November 1997, when a series of economic and political events culminated in massive attack on the currency, there has been some behind-the-scenes fixing of the rate by the financial institutions, with the agreement of the authorities. The massive depreciation of the Zimbabwe dollar that followed the crisis worsened the balance of payments and fueled inflation.

Monetary policy effectiveness

Monetary policy clearly failed to achieve its primary objective of reducing money supply growth and inflation during the liberalization process. Fiscal pressures aside, the changes that took place in Zimbabwe's financial sector may have been a factor in this failure. Financial liberalization has been known to lead to changes not only in the behavior but distinctions among various monetary aggregates. This may have reduced the effectiveness of monetary policy instruments given that the use of monetary policy instruments for macroeconomic stabilization is premised on the stability of the money demand function, the controllability of the money supply and the reliability of the relationship between money supply and the ultimate policy targets. The possibility of an unstable money demand function raises interesting questions as to the efficacy and effectiveness of monetary policy. Thus, a useful exercise would be to empirically investigate whether the demand for money function has remained stable in the wake of financial sector reforms and financial innovation. The changes that have taken place could have led to a shift in the demand for money. For example, the adoption of indirect instruments of monetary policy reduces the authorities' degree of control over monetary variables. Deregulation of interest rates may generate significant portfolio shifts and change the sensitivity of money demand to incomes and interest rate changes. Elimination of credit ceilings may result not only in increased borrowing but also in increased uncertainty about the volume of credit in the economy. Regulatory reforms often induce both discrete portfolio adjustments and changes in the interest elasticity of money demand as agents reassess the relative risks of different financial assets. Financial liberalization, in general, creates a more competitive environment by reducing barriers to entry and financial market segmentation. Financial innovations may also lead to portfolio shifts away from monetary assets. Thus, empirical validation of some of these propositions through econometric estimation and statistical testing of the stability of the money demand function would help establish whether there is still scope for targeting monetary aggregates in conducting of monetary policy. A structural break or instability in the money demand function between the pre- (1980–90) and post-reform (1991–98) periods in Zimbabwe may have affected the effectiveness of monetary policy instruments during and after financial liberalization.

5 Summary and conclusions

This chapter has discussed financial liberalization and the transition to indirect instruments of monetary policy in Zimbabwe. Its major findings and conclusions are that considerable progress has been made towards liberalizing the financial sector. Market segmentation and the oligopolistic structure of the banking system have been reduced through the entry of new financial institutions. Interest rates have been allowed to adjust to market conditions and most interest rate ceilings have been removed. However, some controls, asset prescription and distortionary taxes on some financial assets still remain, thus impeding progress towards complete financial market liberalization. Overall, financial intermediation has been marginally improved, as indicated by trends in interest rates and other indicators of financial deepening. Domestic and international interest rate spreads initially increased sharply before narrowing marginally. A combination of a restrictive monetary policy stance and the oligopolistic structure of the banking system largely accounts for the wide spreads in domestic interest rates and also between domestic and international rates. Reforms also influenced such broad macroeconomic aggregates as savings, investment volume and efficiency, capital movements and economic growth. However, whereas effects on real interest rates occur with almost immediate effect, effects on these macroeconomic variables and financial deepening take longer to manifest themselves.

Despite some policy reversals, monetary control, for the most part, was on track, with the exception of some experimentation with targeting various operational instruments, such as net domestic assets of the central bank, real interest rates and reserve money. Whilst there has been a genuine transition to the use of indirect instruments of monetary policy, macroeconomic stability was not achieved because of the authorities' fiscal indiscipline. The full transition to indirect instruments of monetary policy had been premised on a successful reduction of fiscal deficits by the end of 1995. This was not fulfilled – the budget deficit remained at more than 8 per cent of GDP throughout the period. This lax fiscal policy rendered monetary policy ineffective in curbing money supply growth and inflation. The high inflation rates that prevailed affected the pace and nature of financial sector reforms.

The issue of prudential regulation and bank supervision is vitally important, especially during the implementation of financial reforms. Progress has been very slow in implementing supervisory and regulatory reforms. Delays in amending the Banking Act and the Reserve Bank Act created problems for the financial sector. The collapse of the United Merchant Bank (UMB) in 1998, which precipitated a banking crisis the exact extent of which is yet to be established, has been largely attributed to the absence of an effective regulatory and supervisory framework. It is still too early to determine whether the passage of the Banking Act and the Reserve Bank Act in March 1999 will address these outstanding issues.

Notes

1. The types of controls are not mutually exclusive since the actual measures deployed may service more than one type of control.
2. '. . . the doctrine that the rate of interest is not self-adjusting at a level best suited to the social advantage but constantly tends to be too high, so that a wise government is concerned to curb it by statute and custom and even by invoking the sanctions of moral law'. See Keynes (1936, p. 351).
3. The success of such selective credit policies turns on the ability of the authorities to segment and restrict financial markets effectively. Failure to effectively segment and restrict the financial markets negates the objectives of the policy since ample opportunities for arbitrage would be created, resulting in the rerouting of subsidized credit to uses with the highest private returns.
4. Despite financial liberalization, and the freeing-up of other interest rates, rates on commercial and residential mortgage advances have still not been deregulated.
5. For example, the Pension and Provident Fund Act stipulates that a registered fund shall at all times hold its assets in Zimbabwe and in a form that is realizable in Zimbabwe; and that it shall at all times hold not less than 35 per cent of the value of its assets in local registered securities which are issued or guaranteed by the State or issued by a local authority or statutory body or in loans approved by the registrar to a local authority or statutory body. The Insurance Act states that

insurance funds shall be held in prescribed securities as specified by the Minister of Finance who shall from time to time specify the proportions. According discretionary powers to the minister was convenient for the purposes of tightening or loosening the requirement as needed for policy purposes.

6. Seignorage refers to the amount of resources that the government obtains through the issuance of fiat money.
7. Initially the BLR was set at 13 per cent, the same level as the MLR that it replaced. Banks were allowed to charge a maximum of $2\frac{1}{2}$ percentage points above the BLR for productive lending and 3 percentage points for non-productive lending. The RBZ took into account the level of excess liquidity and inflation in setting the BLR.
8. The amount of RBZ bills issued was arrived at on the basis of assessments of the general economic conditions, money market conditions and the excess liquidity holdings of each institution. These bills more or less operated like a different reserve requirements on different institutions.
9. For a good exposition of financial sector reforms in general, see Galbis (1995).
10. Efficiency can have different meanings. Tobin (1984) defines at least three: namely, information arbitrage efficiency, fundamental valuation efficiency – referring to the idea that the current valuation of a financial asset accurately reflects future payments to which the asset gives title to – rational expectations, the Arrow–Debreu sense full-insurance efficiency and functional efficiency which, in the case of the financial system, refers to the mobilization of saving and allocation to more socially productive uses.
11. For details and a graphic exposition, see Fry (1988) and Gibson et al. (1994) among others.
12. Some critics of the liberalization school have faulted this argument as being incomplete and oblivious to the possibility that endogenous constraints in the credit market such as imperfect information could constitute significant barriers to efficient credit allocation even when banks are freed from interest rate ceilings. They also point out that financial liberalization literature has not addressed the market structure of banking systems in developing countries which tend to be oligopolistic or operate like cartels. See Cho (1986) and Stiglitz and Weiss (1981) for details. The work of Stiglitz and Weiss (1981) on credit rationing and adverse selection has shown how asymmetric information between lenders and borrowers may lead to credit rationing and optimal interest rates that are below market-clearing levels even in competitive banking systems and in environments where there are no interest rate ceilings. This challenges the view which attributes low interest rates and credit rationing solely to government intervention. Therefore, it is not obvious that the removal of government controls on interest rates leads to a dynamic and efficient financial system.
13. In Barro's approach, average growth per capita is regressed on the initial value of GDP, initial value of some measure of human capital, rate of physical capital accumulation, the ratio of government expenditure to GDP, openness, inflation, the rate of foreign direct investment and an index of political tensions. In endogenous growth models, a broadly defined concept of capital stock experiences increasing returns to scale and thus growth is a positive function of the investment ratio.
14. For examples of studies that have added financial sector variables to the endogenous growth framework, see De Gregorio and Guidotti (1992), Roubini and Sala-I-Martin (1992), King and Levine (1993).

15. Extensive work has been done to extend this basic framework in the context of macroeconomic stabilization programs with both open and closed economy models: Kapur (1976); Mathieson (1980); Galbis (1977). See Fry (1988) for an extensive discourse on these models.
16. Including many unregulated and unauthorized financial institutions such that in April 1995, the Ministry of Finance found it necessary to publish a list of authorized financial institutions and warned the public about a range of bogus institutions that had emerged.
17. Direct instruments include interest rate controls, credit ceilings, liquidity ratios, directed credits and bank-by-bank discount quotas. Indirect instruments comprise reserve requirements, rediscount window, Lombard or overdraft window, public sector deposits, credit auctions, open market operations and secondary market operations involving outright purchases and sales or repo operations.
18. See Alexander et al. (1995) for a detailed description of direct and indirect instruments and their advantages and disadvantages.
19. Reserve requirements are classified as an indirect instrument of monetary control because their monetary impact is realized through effects on the demand for reserve money. Changes in reserve requirements are effective in sterilizing excess liquidity and in enhancing the predictability of reserve money demand. However, they are not an ideal instrument for short-term liquidity management given the disruptive effects of frequent changes in reserve requirements on bank portfolio management.
20. They were raised in February 1994 from 12.5 to 13.5 per cent of banks' liabilities to the public. It was raised again in mid-June the same year to 17.5 per cent and to 20 per cent in November 1996 while those on foreign currency deposits were raised to 17.5 per cent.
21. Reserve Bank of Zimbabwe, 'Zimbabwe's Financial System and the role of the Reserve Bank of Zimbabwe', 1996, p. 16.
22. A repo is an instrument through which the RBZ accommodates the market during shortages and constitutes an advance to clearing banks for a maximum period of seven days, against security.

References

Adam, C.S. and M. Ncube (1994) 'Financial liberalization and trade expansion in Zimbabwe' unpublished mimeo.

Aghevli, B.B., M.S. Khan, P.R. Narvekar and B.K. Short (1979) 'Monetary policy in selected Asian countries', Staff Papers, International Monetary Fund, December.

Alexander, William, T. Balino and C. Enoch (1995) 'The adoption of indirect instruments of monetary policy', Occasional Paper 126, International Monetary Fund, Washington DC. June.

Barro, R. (1991) 'Economic growth in a cross section of countries', *Quarterly Journal of Economics*, vol. 104, pp. 407–433.

Bisat, Amer, B. Johnston and V. Sundararajan (1992) 'Issues in managing and sequencing financial sector reforms, lessons from experiences in five developing countries', IMF Working Paper WP/92/82.

Blanchard, O. and Fischer, S. (1989) *Lectures on Macroeconomics*. Cambridge, MA: MIT Press.

Cho Yoon-Je and D. Khatkhate (1989) 'Lessons of financial liberalization in Asia: a comparative study', World Bank Discussion Papers, no. 50, April.

Cukierman, Alex (1992) *Central Bank Strategy, Credibility and Independence: Theory and Evidence*. Cambridge, MA: MIT Press.
De Gregorio J. and P. Guidotti (1992) 'Financial Development and Economic Growth', IMF Working Paper, WP/92/101. Washington: International Monetary Fund, December.
Fry, Maxwell J. (1988) *Money, Interest and Banking in Economic Development*. Baltimore, MD: Johns Hopkins University Press.
Galbis, V. (1977) 'Financial intermediation and economic growth in less developed countries', *Journal of Development Studies*, vol. 13, no. 2, pp. 58–72.
Galbis, V. (1994) 'Sequencing of financial sector reforms: a review', IMF Working Paper, WP/94/101, September.
Galbis, V. 'Financial sector reforms in eight countries: issues and results', IMF Working Paper, WP/95/141.
Gertler, Mark (1988) 'Financial structure and aggregate economic activity: an overview', *Journal Of Money, Credit and Banking*, vol. 20, issue 3, part 2: Recent Developments in Macroeconomics.
Gibson, H. and E. Tsakalatos (1994) 'The scope and limits of financial liberalisation in developing countries: a critical survey', *Journal of Development Studies*, vol. 30, no. 3, pp. 578–628.
Government of Zimbabwe, *Digest of Statistics*, CSO (various issues).
Government of Zimbabwe (1996a) *Insurance Act, Chapter 24:07*, revised edition.
Government of Zimbabwe (1996b) *Pension and Provident Fund Act, Chapter 24:09*, revised edition.
Government of Zimbabwe (1998) *Zimbabwe Programme for Economic and Social Transformation 1996–2000*. Harare: Government Printer.
Government of Zimbabwe (1991) *Zimbabwe: a Framework for Economic Reform (1991–95)*. Harare: Government Printers, January.
Gurley, J.G. and E.S. Shaw (1967) 'Financial structure and economic development', *Economic Development and Cultural Change*, vol. 15, April, pp. 257–68.
Gurley J.G. and E.S. Shaw (1960) *Money in a Theory of Finance*. Washington, DC: Brookings Institution.
IMF, *International Financial Statistics*, various issues.
Johnston, B. and C. Pazarbasioglu (1995) 'Linkage between financial variables, financial, sector reform and economic growth and efficiency', IMF Working Paper, WP/95/103.
Kapur, B.K. (1976) 'Alternative stabilisation policies for less developed economies', *Journal of Political Economy*, vol. 84, no. 41, pp. 777–95.
King, R. and R. Levine (1993) 'Finance and growth: Schumpeter might be right', *Quarterly Journal of Economics*, vol. 108, pp. 17–37.
McKinnon, Ronald (1973) *Money and Capital in Economic Development*. Washington, DC: Brookings Institution.
Rather, P. (1998) 'Money demand and regional monetary policy in the West African Economic and Monetary Union', IMF Working Paper, WP/98/57.
Reserve Bank of Zimbabwe *Quarterly Economic and Statistical Review*, various issues.
Roubini, N. and X. Sala-I-Martin (1992) 'Financial repression and economic growth', *Journal of Development Economics*, vol. 39, pp. 5–30.
Shaw, Edward. (1973) *Financial Deepening in Economic Development*. New York: Oxford University Press.
Tobin, James (1984) 'On the efficiency of the financial system', *Lloyds Bank Review*, July, no. 153, pp. 1–15.
Tseng, W. and R. Corker (1991) 'Financial liberalization, money demand, and monetary policy in Asian countries', Occasional Paper no. 84, International Monetary Fund.

Vittas, D. (ed.) (1992) 'The impact of regulation on financial intermediation' in Economic Development Institute, *Financial Regulation, Changing the Rules of the Game*. Economic Development Institute World Bank.

Wong Chorng-Huey (1991) 'Market based systems of monetary control in developing countries: operating procedures and related issues', IMF Working Paper, WP/91/40.

7
From Liberalization to Financial Crisis

Chandima Mendis

Introduction

On 14 November 1997, the Zimbabwe dollar crashed against most major currencies, sparking a major currency crisis, followed by financial market instability. One merchant bank collapsed, and a building society was rescued amid major problems in the banking sector. The 'November' crash occurred against the backdrop of severe balance of payments pressure dating back several months, and market uncertainty regarding a potential devaluation. The local unit crashed again in July and October 1998. Selling rates of the Zimbabwe dollar against the US dollar plunged from about Z$20 to over Z$32 during August/September 1998 to peak at Z$44/US$ in October 1998. For most of 1999, it traded within a narrow band of between Z$38 and Z$39/US$, mainly due to a voluntary, informal agreement between the Reserve Bank and foreign currency dealers (mainly commercial banks) to achieve artificial stability at these levels. This is by far the biggest and most prolonged period of currency volatility in recent years.

In this chapter, we seek to examine the determinants of the recent financial crisis experienced in Zimbabwe. The emphasis will be on the causes of the financial turmoil that occurred in the latter half of the 1990s. The econometric work applies a logit model on Zimbabwean time series data to disentangle external causes from internally propagated factors.

The chapter is organized as follows: the next section briefly discusses Zimbabwe's financial sector and then reviews the theoretical literature on currency and financial crises. Some stylized features that may be of particular relevance to understanding the causes of the crash and subsequent financial crises are presented. This is followed by a discussion of the Zimbabwean financial sector crisis and the role played by external shocks. The theoretical literature is then applied to Zimbabwean data using an econometric logit model analysis. The objective is to determine what caused the crisis and to predict or point to any likelihood of future occurrence. The summary and conclusions complete the chapter.

The nature of Zimbabwe's financial sector

At independence in 1980, Zimbabwe inherited one of the most sophisticated and diversified economies in Africa. Its financial sector was fairly developed, offering a wide range of instruments and financial services. There is a primary bond market, although an active secondary and derivatives market is lacking. The Zimbabwean financial sector comprises commercial banks, merchant banks, discount houses, building societies, development finance institutions, insurance corporations and a stock exchange. The Reserve Bank sits at the apex of the financial system.

Figures 7.1 and 7.2 show aggregate measures of financial development in Zimbabwe. The ratio of narrow money (M1) to GDP increased quite significantly during the 1980s and into the 1990s, while that of the broader measure, M2 to GDP, fell during the 1990s. This aggregate view is further supported by the ratios of demand deposits to GDP and longer-term deposits to GDP.

The general trend in the 1990s was one of movement out of longer-term deposits and into shorter-term ones. This may be due to several reasons; one of which is likely to be the high levels of inflation experienced after adjustment, as well as the higher returns offered by Treasury Bills in a post-liberalization interest rate environment. This is shown in Figure 7.3 below which shows that the Treasury Bill rate rose to over 30 per cent in the early 1990s before declining.

As was the case for the economy as a whole, the financial sector was highly controlled, with most trade, foreign exchange, interest rate and price

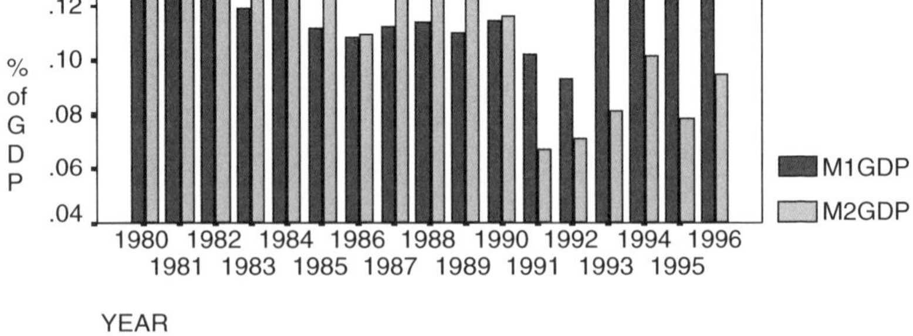

Figure 7.1 Monetary aggregates as a percentage of GDP

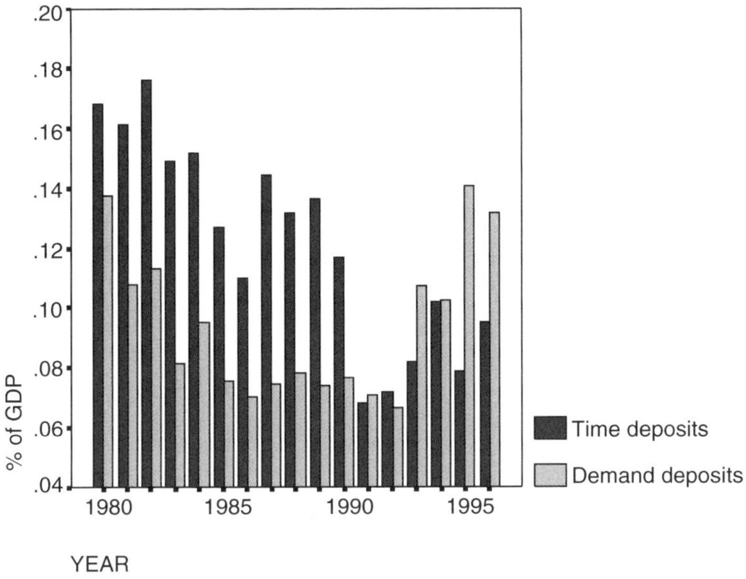

Figure 7.2 Deposits as a percentage of GDP

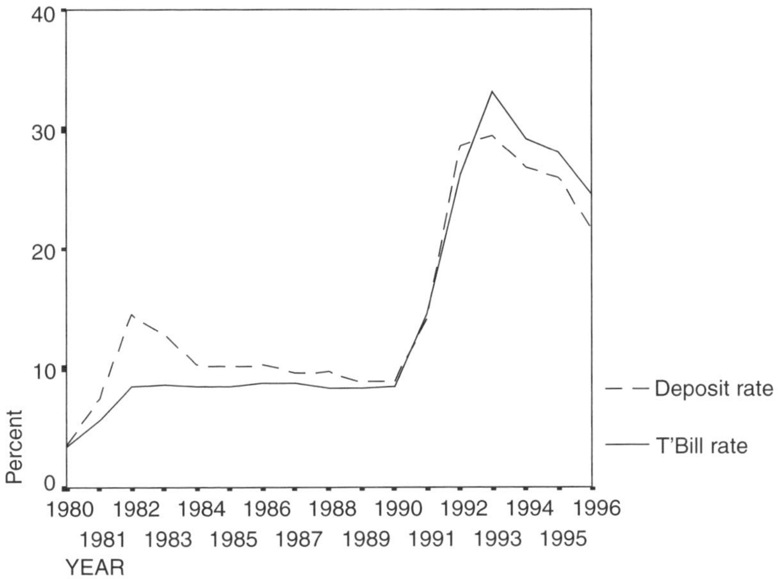

Figure 7.3 Deposit and Treasury Bill rates

controls remaining in place throughout the 1980s. Inflation remained low only because of the extensive nature of price, interest rate and exchange controls. Despite this, the financial sector is quite well developed, by regional comparison, and has continued to grow considerably since independence. The controlled economic environment discouraged investment such that gross domestic investment fell appreciably during the 1980s. As a result, the traditionally high private sector savings were channeled, through the money market, into financing the fiscal deficit. The public sector deficit ballooned as the new government sought to redress past colonial imbalances by expanding expenditure on social capital. Thus, apart from periodic droughts, the policy environment – and efforts made to change it – has played a big role in determining overall economic growth and financial sector performance. It was against the background of poor economic performance, falling foreign exchange revenues and rising unemployment, that the economic structural adjustment program (ESAP) was adopted.

Effects of liberalization on the financial sector

Liberalization of the financial sector was one of the key elements in the economic reform programme initiated by the Zimbabwean government in 1991. The main elements included liberalizing interest rates and moving towards open market operations. Monetary policy has increasingly moved from direct controls to open market operations, mainly in the form of Repurchase agreements (Repos). While the benefits of financial liberalization have been well documented on both the theoretical and the empirical fronts, the hasty liberalization of often weak financial sectors has been known to create financial crises in subsequent years. As highly regulated financial sectors are opened up, financial intermediation increases due to the entry of new intermediaries, better and more competitive rates of returns, introduction of new instruments, and other measures. While this may be beneficial, in countries with initially weak institutional structures and prudential regulations, the entry of new banks may sometimes lead to risky lending. If this happens throughout the financial system, then the banking sector may build up a large proportion of risky assets exceeding prescribed capital adequacy requirements. These loans may eventually end up as non-performing assets. This leads to risky lending and deterioration in the balance sheet of the banking sector. The inability by smaller banks to recover their loans may result in a liquidity crisis and subsequent deposit run. This may well have been the cause behind the collapse of the United Merchant Bank and the financial turmoil experienced in Zimbabwe since 1997. Before going on to analyze the effects of liberalization and causes of the financial crises, a brief review of the theoretical literature is carried out in the following section.

Theory of financial crises

There are both micro and macroeconomic theories explaining financial crises. We begin with a brief look at the micro theoretic causes of financial crises.

Micro theoretic explanations

The microeconomic theoretical framework for studying financial and banking crises comes from asymmetric information and credit market analysis. The most commonly discussed approach has been the credit rationing situation resulting from various market failures. Although this theory was initially used to explain financial and banking crises in developed countries, particularly the United States, it was later extended to examine developing country crises. In developing country studies, this micro theoretic analysis used in the asymmetric information literature has been linked with the macroeconomics of small open economies. In particular, the effects of various external shocks on monetary and banking sectors have been analyzed, as documented by numerous studies of Latin American[1] countries such as Chile and Venezuela. Besides being a small open economy with a heavy dependence on volatile primary product exports, Zimbabwe has also witnessed a steady inflow of foreign capital after the economic reforms initiated in the 1990s. The interaction of external factors with several domestic factors could be the cause of the currency crises that occurred in 1997 and 1998. There are three main channels through which market failure may affect or worsen financial fragility:

Increases in interest rates

According to Stiglitz and Weiss (1981), asymmetric information and the resulting adverse selection problem can lead to credit rationing in which some borrowers are denied loans even when they are willing to pay a higher interest rate. Since borrowers have more information about investment projects than lenders, a moral hazard problem is created because those agents with the riskiest projects are exactly those who are willing to take the highest interest rate. If these high-risk investment projects succeed, they have more to gain. Thus, at a higher interest rate, the probability of lending to riskier projects increases. If the lender cannot distinguish between high-risk and low-risk projects, then the supply of loans declines with higher interest rates. This leads to credit rationing and even if the availability of loanable funds in the banking sector increases, banks will be unable to distinguish between good and risky borrowers because any increase in lending only increases the probability of making risky investments, thereby worsening financial fragility. According to this view, credit rationing could 'trigger' the collapse of non-financial firms.

Increases in uncertainty

According to Mishkin (1996), an increase in uncertainty in financial markets – as the result, for example, of a recession, political instability, a stock market crash or the failure of prominent financial or non-financial institutions – makes it even harder for lenders to screen out good credit risks from bad ones. This worsens the adverse selection and moral hazard problems.

Asset market effects on balance sheets

Deterioration of balance sheets worsens both adverse selection and moral hazard problems in financial institutions. Factors that may reduce the value of a firm's balance sheet, both external and internal, may severely undermine its viability. Studies carried out by Calomiris and Gorton (1991), Greenwald and Stiglitz (1988) and Bernanke and Gertler (1989) show that unanticipated shocks such as stock market crashes could lead to financial crises through the impact on the balance sheets of financial institutions. According to Mishkin (1996), the problem of moral hazard and adverse selection rises under such conditions. This comes about because banks normally require collateral before issuing loans. Collateral takes the form of assets or even the net worth of a firm. The higher the net worth, the lower the moral hazard and adverse selection problem as the lender has more to lose by defaulting on the loan. However, when the value of net worth declines – for example, following a stock market crash – the moral hazard problem increases as lenders have less to lose by making a more risky investment.

These problems of moral hazard and adverse selection depend on the extent and nature of an economy's financial infrastructure. In most developing countries, supervisory institutions and regulations are often inadequate. Lack of a proper legal framework, personnel and institutions could lead to risky and connected lending exacerbating the problems of moral hazard. Political interests in banks, and connected lending, could encourage public bail-outs. Deposit insurance schemes could also lead to reckless lending due to the implicit assurance of a bail-out (Diamond and Dybvig, 1984).

Demirguc-Kunt and Detragiache (1997) have argued that these problems of moral hazard and adverse selection are attenuated after financial liberalization in developing countries.

Business cycle explanations of banking crises

The business cycle approach examines the vulnerability of a financial sector over the business cycle expansion. Since an economy's fragility depends on indicators such as liquidity, debt ratios and share of rollover debt, this might change in response to variability in interest rates and expectations about the future. The financial sector responds endogenously to movements in the business cycle (Minsky, 1977; Taylor and O'Connell, 1985). A crisis develops because of systematic forces near the peak of the cycle. In particular, interest rates rise, which in turn reduces lending. Banks also reduce their non-loan investments in relation to loans, as well as reserves. These events make a financial sector more vulnerable to a shock, such as surprise news relating to a bankruptcy.

The monetary approach to banking crises

The other approach is the monetary approach, which emphasizes the role of money growth and its variability as the principal determinant of a crisis (Friedman and Schwartz, 1963). According to this view, a financial crisis need not occur at any particular stage of the cycle, but could result from a change in the monetary base, such as a sudden and erratic tightening of reserve money which may force financial enterprises to sell assets in order to meet reserve obligations. This may reduce asset prices, raise interest rates and threaten solvency. The key feature of the monetary approach is that the determinants of financial crises are analyzed as endogenous events caused by economic policy at the time of the crises, such as the choice of the exchange rate regime (fixed and flexible) and the structure of the financial system. Although the effects of exogenous shocks, such as declines in asset prices, crises and stock market crashes, are known to 'trigger' financial crises, under this monetary approach analysis these events are not assumed to influence financial crises independently from the effects of policies already in place.

Any increase in liquidity, such as from capital inflows or trade shocks, may increase lending, but banks are still unable to differentiate between risky and good projects. Consequently, banks may end up with a large proportion of non-performing loans on their balance sheets. If liquidity dries up in subsequent years, then a large proportion of these loans would have to be written-off. Connected lending, both individual and institutional (for example, *chaebols* in Korea), have furthermore exacerbated the problem.

Balance of payments crises

According to the 'first-generation' theoretical models, balance of payments crises occurred when fixed exchange rate regimes became inconsistent with economic policies. For example, Krugman (1979) and Flood and Garber (1984) developed models in which excessive domestic credit creation led to a gradual loss of international reserves and ultimately a speculative attack on the domestic currency. This excessive domestic credit creation could, for example, arise from the need to finance a government budget deficit or even to finance off-balance-sheet events such as a rescue package to bail out failing banks. A second generation of crises models have subsequently been developed, in which macroeconomic policies are not predetermined but instead respond to agents' expectations (see, for example, Obstfeld 1994). An exchange rate regime can only be maintained as long as it is compatible with other policies, not only with economic fundamentals.

This broader set of policies includes variables such as the ability of a government to roll over debt, the access to international liquidity, government stability, and so on.

Evidence from a number of case studies seem to confirm some of these priors. Using an international panel data set, Frankel and Rose (1996) found that monetary and fiscal shocks, the size of current account imbalances, foreign indebtedness, maturity and composition of foreign debt and world interest rates to be major determinants of balance of payments crises. In another study, Sachs et al. (1996) identified low levels of international reserves relative to broad money, a large appreciation of the real exchange rate and a weak banking system as major determinants of currency crises. Table 7.1 summarizes the main groups of variables considered and their effectiveness in explaining and predicting a crisis.

Kaminsky et al. (1997) use a signals approach to construct an early warning system. Using 76 currency crashes, they construct an index of exchange market pressure indicating the probability of a crisis occurring. It allows the authors to ascertain how good an indicator is at predicting a crisis. Major factors cited by this study are real exchange rate appreciations, a fall in exports, a fall in stock market prices and an increase in the ratio of M2 to international reserves.

Most studies examine two ways in which banking and balance of payments crises are related. First a heavy loss of international reserves might lead to a

Table 7.1 Variables used in currency crises literature

Category	*Variable used*
Capital account	International reserves, capital flows, interest rate differential, FDI
Debt profile	Total debt, public foreign debt, short-term debt, share of debt, debt service
Current account	Real exchange rate, current account balance, trade balance, terms of trade, export prices
International variables	Foreign growth, interest rates, prices
Financial liberalization	Credit growth, change in money multiplier, real interest rates, bank lending spread
Other financial variables	Central bank credit, gap between money demand and supply, bond yields, inflation, shadow exchange rate, M2/reserves
Real sector	Real GDP growth, output gap, unemployment, changes in stocks
Fiscal side	Deficit, government consumption, credit to public sector
Institution	Openness, trade concentration, exchange controls, financial liberalization
Political	Elections, incumbent loss/victory, transfer of power, political instability, new finance minister

sharp devaluation. If this is not sterilized, private sector credit falls, leading to increased bankruptcies among both financial and non-financial firms. If this happens to a large proportion of firms, such a scenario may propagate a banking crisis. Furthermore, if a large number of banks have a high level of foreign exchange exposure, a devaluation may severely increase their debt in domestic currency terms. On the other hand, a banking crisis could also lead to a balance of payments crisis if authorities use domestic credit to bail out banks and depositors. The final permutation is that a balance of payments crisis and a banking crisis may occur simultaneously as a result of large swings in world interest rates, which may affect the levels of capital flows to emerging economies (Calvo et al., 1992). Mendis (1999) has also shown that terms of trade shocks, which are prevalent in developing countries, have the ability to create large fluctuations in money supply and, domestic credit which may, subsequently, lead to banking crises. During periods of positive external shocks, there may be simultaneous increases in money supply, deposits in the banking system and domestic credit, leading to an asset bubble. In the event of an outflow or negative shock, banks might be left with a maturity mismatch and a large proportion of non-performing loans.

Since Zimbabwe experienced a currency crisis followed by problems in the banking sector, it is interesting to investigate the applicability of the above-mentioned theories in the empirical analysis that follows.

Financial crisis in Zimbabwe

The above-mentioned stylized features may be of particular importance to Zimbabwe. Besides being a small open economy with a heavy dependence on volatile primary product exports, the country has also witnessed a steady inflow of foreign capital after the economic reforms initiated in the 1990s. The interaction of these external factors with several domestic factors could be the causes of the currency crises over the last few years. In fact, these factors might be useful in predicting the probability of any future crises. Thus the aim of the following sections is to use the theoretical priors from the financial crises literature in order to conduct empirical work to look at what caused the crisis as well as to try and point to any likelihood of future crises.

Taxonomy of events leading to the crisis

Financial liberalization not only deregulated interest rates, but also facilitated the entry of new financial intermediaries and banks. Although this has had the positive effect of increasing competition for financial services, prudential regulation aspects have not been reviewed. As noted earlier, this has the tendency to encourage risky lending and a potentially high level of non-performing loans. A number of banks and finance houses entered the market in the 1990s. Most of them initially specialized in some form of market activity, such as financing export credit, issuing of bills on behalf of non-financial institutions and parastatals, as did the United Merchant Bank before it was put under administration and subsequently liquidated. However, most of these new banks also engaged in deposit taking, although the scale of these operations was limited in comparison to total financial holding of the sector. Without mixing up these problems in the banking sector with the exchange rate crisis, the primary focus of this section will be on the currency crisis.

Nature of the currency crash

The nominal exchange rate regime used in Zimbabwe during the 1980s was a trade-weighted adjustable peg. The Reserve Bank periodically adjusted the rate in order to maintain export competitiveness. Average inflation rates of about 12 per cent throughout the 1980s meant the nominal rate was adjusted downwards by similar amounts. The exchange rate, in terms of Zimbabwe dollars per US dollar, is shown in Figure 7.4.

A look at changes in the nominal exchange rate reveals some interesting features. While there were frequent and minor changes during the 1980s, the major spike during the start of the 1990s reflects the onset of the economic reform program and movement towards a flexible exchange rate system. Between 1990 and 1994, a dual system, consisting of a freely

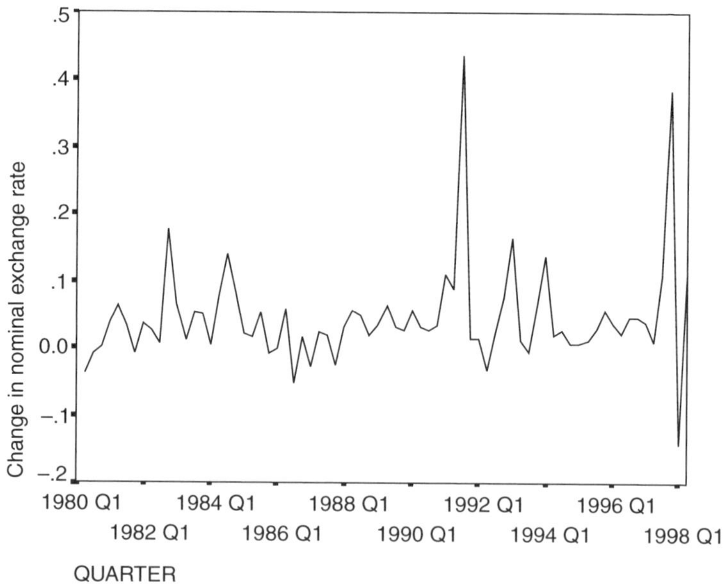

Figure 7.4 Nominal exchange rate (Z$/US$)

determined market rate and an official rate, existed. The rates basically converged to yield a market-determined rate by 1995. However, the system is not entirely based around the free market, since considerable capital controls remain in place and the amount of foreign exchange available in the market depends on the amounts of export proceeds exchanged into local currency through foreign currency accounts (FCAs) held by local exporters and by periodic central bank intervention. While authorities devalued the exchange rate periodically throughout the 1980s, major devaluations were undertaken in 1991. The upward spike in 1997 represents the crash of the local currency after market fears about dwindling reserves. This also coincided with the Asian crisis, suggesting some sort of contagion. A third crash occurred in July 1998 and the market has remained volatile ever since. Again, the general consensus was market fears pertaining to lack of adequate import cover by the Reserve Bank. According to the Reserve Bank's 1997 Annual Report, average import cover stood at around 3 months. However, market speculation mounted on rumors that the import cover had fallen to about one month, and continued silence by the Bank fueled these fears.[2] There was also considerable political uncertainty emanating from mixed signals given by the government over the fiscal implications of the war veterans, compensation,[3] lack of transparency in the implementation of the land reform program and the financial repercussions of the involvement in the Democratic Republic of the Congo conflict.

External shocks and contagion

The terms of trade

One of the most important external factors which might affect or even propagate financial crises are changes in the terms of trade. This is of particular concern to Zimbabwe. Tobacco prices have exhibited a downward trend over the past few years. Earnings from other primary commodities have also declined. Nickel prices have fallen due to dumping by Russia while the price of gold has also declined. This negative trend has put severe pressure on the balance of payments situation and on the exchange rate, which had become market-based by the mid-1990s. Figures 7.5 and 7.6 show a downward trend for Zimbabwe's terms of trade and the current account respectively.

Capital flows

Foreign capital flows increased after liberalization of the capital and current accounts. This positive trend initially cushioned the effect of lower export earnings from the main export commodities. However, most of these capital flows consisted of portfolio equity flows in the stock market by international investors. The danger of these kinds of foreign capital flows is that they can be quickly reversed during a panic or contagion (see Figure 7.7).

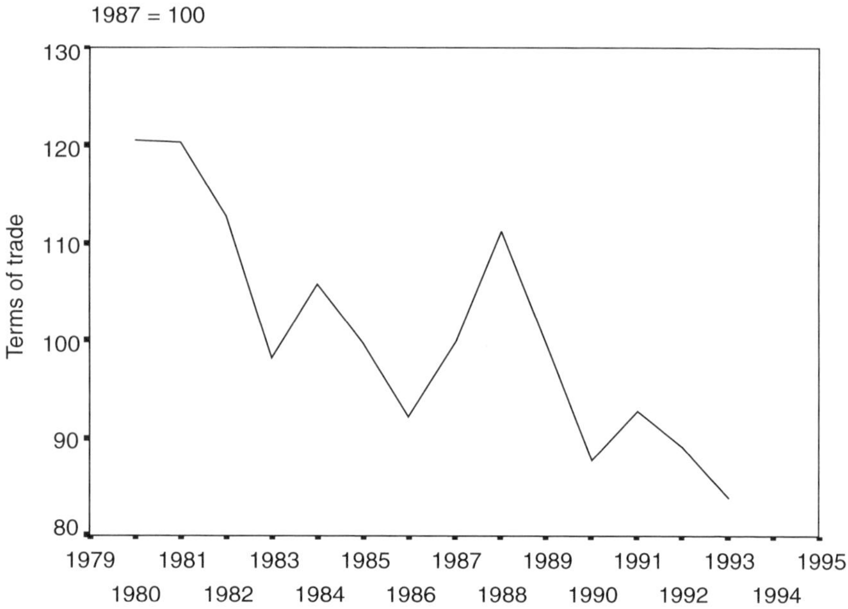

Figure 7.5 Zimbabwe's terms of trade (1987 = 100)

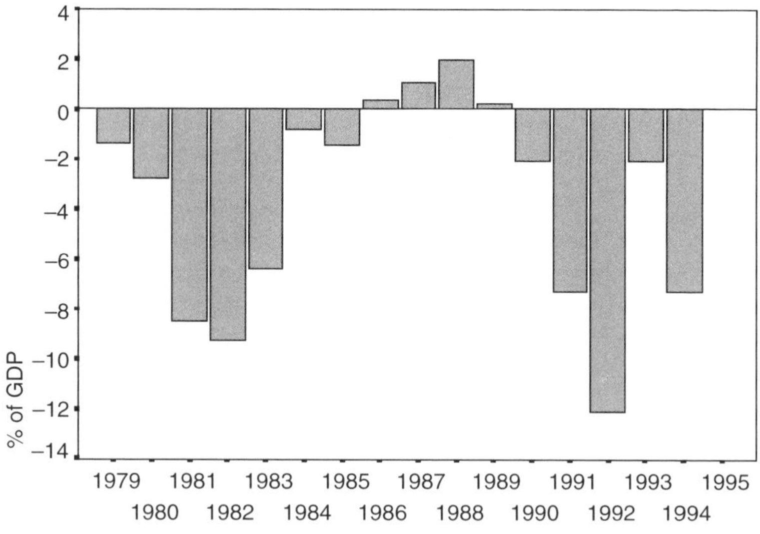

Figure 7.6 Zimbabwe's current account as a percentage of GDP

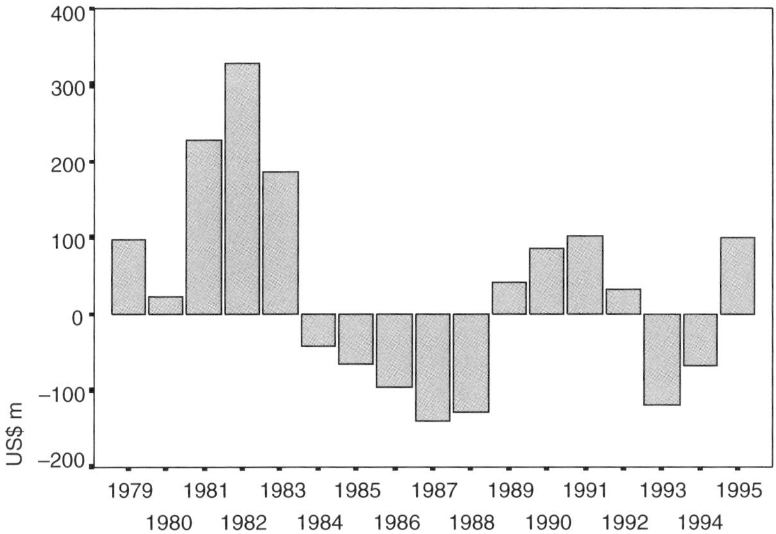

Figure 7.7 Foreign capital inflows

Contagion and the Asian Crisis

The prevalence of contagion has been studied on both the theoretical and the empirical fronts.[4] Contagious currency and financial crises are common features in the global financial system, with the crisis in Asia being the most recent case. Contagion spreads through two main routes. The first is through macroeconomic links. If agents are skeptical about the stability of one currency, then other agents may also become skeptical about the prospects of the currencies of other countries showing similar macroeconomic fundamentals. The second transmission channel is through trade linkages. In this case, attacks will spread contagiously to the other countries with which that country trades. Using an international panel, Eichengreen et al. (1996) find strong evidence for contagion to occur via the trade route channel.

The timing of the Zimbabwean currency crash – in 1997, immediately after the Asian currency crises – might suggest evidence to support the macro link channel. Increasing capital flows into East Asia during the previous decade dramatically increased the money supply and liquidity in the financial systems of these countries. Cheap credit, although mainly short term in nature, was channeled through various banking systems. The lack of well-developed financial markets meant that a large proportion of these inflows were used to finance long-term projects, such as investment in infrastructure. In some countries, this was buttressed by connected lending. Banks subsequently built up a large proportion of potentially non-performing loans in their balance sheets without regard for capital adequacy requirements. This led to system-wide maturity mismatches. The problem was further exacerbated by the fact that the fixed exchange rate regimes pursued in some of these countries eliminated exchange rate risk and encouraged both the private and public sectors to borrow from abroad. A number of countries accumulated large foreign debts – this was especially true in the case of Korea. This combination of risky (and connected) lending and foreign borrowing became incompatible with the fixed exchange rate regime and increasing current account deficits in the long run. The perceived inability of some governments to maintain the commitment to a fixed exchange rate along with the magnitude of non-performing loans in domestic banking sectors led to a string of speculative attacks, starting with one on the Thai baht in July 1997. The 'contagion' spread to other countries with similar macroeconomic fundamentals and bank liabilities.

Authorities initially tried to defend their pegs, but their efforts were ultimately unsuccessful. Since a key element of a defense strategy against a currency attack is to raise interest rates, this further adversely affected the solvency of indebted firms because they had to make higher interest repayments. Malaysia, Indonesia and Korea were forced to adopt more flexible exchange rate regimes and to agree to economy-wide reforms, including reforming their banking systems. Furthermore, subsequent devaluations increased the domestic currency debt servicing requirements of firms and governments with high levels of foreign debt.

The effects of the Asian crisis had global ramifications. The Zimbabwe dollar crashed on 14 November 1997. The timing of the crash suggests some form of contagion effect. As pointed out earlier, the crash occurred under the backdrop of severe balance of payments pressure and market uncertainty regarding a potential devaluation. It may well be possible that the contagion effect from Asia may have helped 'trigger' the crash in November. Conclusive evidence can only be obtained from empirical investigation. The next section tests this contagion hypothesis and uses the international crises in Table 7.2 for the econometric analysis to investigate if they had any effect(s) on the Zimbabwean financial system.

Table 7.2 Sources of international contagion

Crisis	*Year*
Latin America	1982
ERM	1992
Mexico	1994
East Asia	1997
South Africa	1997

Econometric analysis

The econometric model estimates the probability of a country experiencing a banking crisis using a logit model. The logit estimates whether or not a country experienced a crisis, using a dummy variable as the dependent variable. This variable takes a value of one if the country concerned experienced a crisis at a particular time and zero otherwise. The probability of a crisis (y) occurring for any period is defined as a linear function of y^*, an observed continuous random variable.
Let

$$y_i = 1, \text{ if } y^* = \text{crisis}$$

and

$$y_i = 0 \quad \text{otherwise}$$

The reduced form model becomes

$$y^* = \beta' x + u$$

Assuming errors are distributed in a logistic cumulative distribution, the model then becomes

$$\mathrm{P}(y = 1) = e^{\beta' x}/(1 + e^{\beta' x})$$

The probability of a crisis becomes the probability of the error term exceeding the vector of explanatory variables x and the vector of unknown parameters β. To find β, the following function is maximized to obtain the maximum likelihood estimator of the unknown β.

$$\mathrm{L} = \Pi \mathrm{F}[\beta'^{x}][1 - \mathrm{F}(\beta'^{x})]^{1-y}$$

where F is the cumulative distribution function linking probability that an event y occurs or not in relation to a vector of explanatory variable x.

While the signs on the coefficients in the logistic function shows the direction of change, the magnitude depends on the slope of the cumulative distribution function. This means that the probability of a crisis occurring depends on the initial probability of a crisis occurring. In other words, a change in the explanatory variable depends on the initial value of the explanatory variable.

The data and variables

The model was tested using macroeconomic quarterly data from 1980 to 1997. Since quarterly data for series such as GDP and the budget deficit are not published for Zimbabwe, the relevant series were interpolated using a quadratic method.[5] The dependent variable is the financial crisis variable, which is a dummy variable with a value of one during a period when the country experienced a 'financial or currency crisis' and zero otherwise. The choice of the explanatory variable depended on both theoretical assertions and data availability. The periods of crisis were chosen from a qualitative basis and for periods where the nominal exchange rate deviated by more than two standard deviations from the mean in a given quarter. Major changes in the exchange rate and 'crises' according to this criteria occurred during 1991 and 1997.

To test whether sudden capital outflows led to a liquidity crisis, the ratio of M2 money to foreign reserves is introduced (M2RESRVES). This is supposed to be a good measure of a country's vulnerability to a balance of payments crisis. The level of aggregate foreign reserves (RESERVES) was also tested. In order to test the contagion hypothesis, a contagion dummy variable (CONTAGION) was constructed using the years, as mentioned in Table 7.2. Finally in order to test the first-generation model priors that excessive government spending and budget deficits could become inconsistent with exchange rate polices, the ratio of the fiscal deficit to GDP (BUDGETGDP) was included.

Results

The results from the logit regressions are presented in Table 7.3. The availability of the latest data for 1998 would greatly improve the predictive

Table 7.3 Logit regression results

	1	*2*
Dependent variable Financial crisis		
Constant	−8.14	−8.1
	[2.32]	[2.30]
Reserves	—	—
	0.00019	0.00022
	[2.19]	[1.80]
Budget GDP	0.54	0.53
	[1.56]	[1.54]
CAAGDP	0.0001	0.0004
	[0.487]	[0.359]
M2Reserves	0.0004	0.0001
	[0.003]	[0.008]
Contagion		−0.817
		[0.386]
Obs	61	61
Chi squared	7.97	8.11
Prob. > chi squared	0.093	0.151
Pseudo R squared	0.333	0.339

Note: t-statistics are shown in brackets.

powers of the model as the currency and banking problems are still ongoing.

Although the results are only preliminary, they are suggestive in that they confirm some of the theoretical assertions. The level of reserves is found to be a statistically significant crucial determinant of financial sector problems in Zimbabwe. A low level of reserves increases the probability of a crisis. Although the level of fiscal deficit has the expected sign – that is, higher fiscal deficits increase the probability of a crisis – this is not significant at the 5 per cent level. The same applies for the level of current account balance which proxies the effects of exports on the dependent variable. The contagion variable did not have any effect, and reduced the explanatory power of the other variables. The M2 to reserves variables, though again of the correct sign, was not significant.

Conclusion

The main conclusions from this preliminary analysis support the view that the level of foreign currency reserves and fiscal deficit could explain some of the causes of financial crises in Zimbabwe. The level of reserves could be particularly affected by short-term capital flows and sudden movements. While the reduction of government expenditure is crucial for macroeconomic stability, it may also reduce the likelihood of future balance of payments problems. Since the evidence from the above analysis points to low net foreign assets as a contributory factor, efforts must be made to increase future foreign exchange and capital flows. These efforts will obviously depend on a variety of other political and social indicators which may affect Zimbabwe's risk rating as a destination for investment.

Although the fiscal deficit term had the correct sign, it was not significant at the 5 per cent level. This may be due to the fact that the variable could be acting as a poor proxy for fiscal mismanagement. In fact, as events unfolded, the fiscal implications of the war veterans' compensation and the involvement in the war in Congo were significant factors which undermined confidence in both the economy and the currency. These results imply that weak fundamentals were more to blame for the recent crisis as postulated by the first-generation models. While the present crisis may still not be over, there is the possibility for this to affect the viability of the entire financial sector. The proliferation of new intermediaries in the context of inadequate prudential regulation and bank supervisions laws, as well as the growing proportion of risky and non-performing loans owed by agricultural and manufacturing enterprises, is evidence that this may continue in the future.

Notes

1. See, for example, Diaz-Alexandro (1985) on the pitfalls of the period of rapid financial liberalization in Latin America. Demirguc-Kunt and Detragiache (1997) address this issue using cross-country data and show that countries that liberalized with weak institutional and regulation frameworks were more susceptible to financial crises in subsequent years.
2. Between 1990 and 1995, a dual exchange rate existed. The market and official rates eventually converged in 1996. Immediately after liberalization, importers and non-residents were allowed to hold foreign currency accounts (FCAs). However, during 1997, speculative pressure and fears pertaining to inadequate import cover, exporters delayed converting foreign currency receipts in the hope of hedging against a potential devaluation of the currency. This build-up in FCA holding was primarily responsible for the crash during 1997 according the financial media (*Financial Gazette*). The authorities, response was to abolish the FCA accounts and force their holders to sell the accumulated reserves in the open market with the hope of increasing the supply of foreign exchange. This policy was partially successful in the very short run, as market rates fell back to pre-crash levels. However, in the ensuing months, market pressure worked through the forward market, which was established in 1993. Speculation by importers continued through the issuance of Forward Contracts instead. This build-up could have been responsible for the crash in 1998. The authorities responded this time by first shortening the maximum length of a forward contract from 90 to 30 days in August 1998; and then, following continued pressure on the exchange rate, the authorities banned all forward contracts in late September 1998.
3. In August 1997, the government granted an unbudgeted Z$3 billion to ex-freedom fighters as gratuities and pensions for having fought in the liberation war against the UDI regime of Ian Smith.
4. See, for example, Eichengreen et al. (1996).
5. See Khan and Goldstein (1985).

References

Bernanke, B. (1983) 'Nonmonetary effects of the financial crisis in the propagation of the Banking Crisis', *American Economic Review*, vol. 73, pp. 257–76.

Bernanke, B. and M. Getler (1989) 'Financial fragility and economic performance', *Quarterly Journal of Economics*, vol. 105, pp. 87–114.

Calomiris, C. and G. Gorton (1991) 'The origins of bank panics: models, facts and bank regulation,' in R. Hubbard (ed.), *Financial Market and Financial Crises*. Chicago: University of Chicago Press.

Calvo, G., L. Leiderman and C. Reinhart (1992) 'Capital inflows and real exchange rate appreciation in Latin America,' IMF Staff Papers, vol. 40, pp. 108–51.

Calvo, G. and L. Leiderman (1993) 'The capital inflows problem: concepts and issues' IMF Policy Analysis and Assessment Paper, no. PPAA 93/10, Washington DC.

Caprio, G. and D. Klingebiel (1996) 'Bank insolvencies: cross-country experience,' Policy Research Working Paper 1620. Washington DC: World Bank.

Choudhri, E. and L. Kochin (1980) 'The exchange rate and the international transmission of the business cycle disturbances', *Journal of Money, Credit and Banking*, vol. 12, pp. 565–74.

Demirguc-Kunt, A. and E. Detragiache (1997) 'The determinants of banking crises: evidence from developing and developed countries,' IMF Working Paper, WP/97/106, Washington DC.
Diamond, D. and P. Dybvig (1984) 'Bank runs, deposit insurance and liquidity', *Journal of Political Economy*, vol. 91, no. 3, pp. 401–19.
Diaz-Alejandro, C. (1985) '"Good-bye financial repression, hello financial crash,"' *Journal of Development Economics*, vol. 19, pp. 1–24.
Eichengreen, B., A. Rose and C. Wyplosz (1996) 'Contagious Currency Crises', NBER Working Paper, no. 5681.
Flood, Robert P. and Peter M. Garber (1984) 'Collapsing exchange rate regimes; some linear examples', *Journal of International Economics*, vol. 17, nos 1–2, pp. 1–13.
Frankel, J. and A. Rose (1996) 'Currency Crashes in Emerging Markets; Empirical Indicators', NBER Working Paper, no. 543.
Friedman, M, and A. Schwartz, (1963) *A Monetary History of the United States, 1867–1960*. Princeton, NJ: Princeton University Press.
Ghosh Atish (1995) 'Does the Nominal Exchange Rate Matter', CSAE, IMF Working Paper 95/121, November.
Government of Zimbabwe (1998) *ZIMPREST Document*. Harare: Government Printer.
Greenwald, B. and J. Stiglitz (1988) 'Information, financial constraints and business fluctuations', in M. Khan and S. Tsiang (eds), *Expectations and Macroeconomics*. Oxford: Oxford University Press.
International Monetary Fund (various years) *International Financial Statistics*. CD-ROM.
Kaminsky, G., S. Lizondo and C. Reinhart, (1997) 'Leading Indicators of Currency Crises,' IMF Working Paper, WP/97/9.
Khan, M. and C. Reinhart, (1996) 'Capital Flows in the APEC Region', IMF Occasional Paper.
Krugman, P. (1979) 'A model of balance of payment crisis', *Journal of Money, Credit and Banking*, vol. II, no. 3, pp. 311–25.
Mendis, C. (1999) 'Monetary effects of terms of trade shocks and capital flows in small open economies', DPhil thesis, University of Oxford.
Minsky, P. (1977) *John Maynard Keynes*. New York: Columbia University Press.
Mishkin, F. (1996) 'Understanding Financial Crises', NBER Working Paper, no. 5600.
Obstfeld, Maurice (1994) 'The logic of currency arises', National Bureau of Economic Research, Working Paper, no. 4640.
Reserve Bank of Zimbabwe, *Quarterly Statistical Review*. Harare.
Stiglitz, J. and A. Weiss (1981) 'Credit rationing in markets with imperfect information,' *American Economic Review*, vol. 72, pp. 393–410.
Taylor, L. and S. O'Connell (1985) ' A Minsky crisis,' *Quarterly Journal of Economics*, vol. 10, pp. 871–85.
Sachs, J., A. Tornell and A. Velasco (1996) 'Financial crises in emerging markets', Brookings Papers on Economic Activity. Washington DC: Brookings Institution.
Veblen, T. (1904) *The Theory of Business Enterprise*. New York: Charles Scribner.
World Bank (1998) *World Development Indicators*. CD-ROM.

8
The Crisis in Asia: Are There Lessons for Zimbabwe?

James Gordon

1 Introduction

The period 1997–98 was an exceptionally turbulent period for emerging markets, with financial market instability sweeping from Thailand across Asia, and, later, affecting Russia and South Africa. Zimbabwean financial markets have not been immune from this turbulence and the question of whether there is anything for Zimbabwe to learn from the Asian crisis is the subject of this chapter. Before addressing this question, it is worth considering the likelihood of uncovering general lessons for Zimbabwe from the Asian crisis.

First, it is important not to lose sight of the obvious point that *the Zimbabwean economy is very different from the Asian crisis economies*. To begin with, the economic structures are fundamentally dissimilar, with the agricultural and mining sectors far more important in Zimbabwe than they are in the Asian crisis economies (for example, these two sectors generate over half of Zimbabwe's exports, but less than 5 per cent of exports from Korea). Moreover, in contrast to Zimbabwe, the Asian economies have grown rapidly over the past three decades, with high levels of savings and investment. The conduct of macroeconomic policies has also been dissimilar. Unlike Zimbabwe, the Asian crisis economies have a history of low inflation and generally balanced fiscal positions. These fundamental differences should serve to limit the applicability of the recent Asian experience to Zimbabwe. If, as it seems from the Asian case, financial crisis strikes fast-growing, rapidly industrializing economies, care has to be taken in drawing lessons for an economy such as Zimbabwe that does not display similar characteristics. Second, it would be ironic to be advising a country like Zimbabwe to be 'less like Asia', when until recently non-Asian developing countries were being encouraged to be 'more like Asia' (so as to emulate the 'Asian miracle'). This shift in views argues for some humility in attempting to draw lessons for Zimbabwe from the Asian crisis.

These caveats aside, Zimbabwean financial markets have encountered turbulence since 1997. Moreover, financial markets often tend to take a 'broad brush' approach to judging emerging markets. Analysts typically focus on a limited number of variables in assessing an economy's fundamentals, and in some of these areas, Zimbabwe undoubtedly exhibits weaknesses. The central question posed in this chapter is therefore worth exploring. The chapter attempts to separate the part of the recent turbulence in Zimbabwean financial markets that has been due to Asian contagion from that which can be attributed to Zimbabwe-specific factors. In addition, how a country extricates itself from financial distress is at least as interesting as how it got into that situation in the first place. The search for lessons from Asia is therefore couched not only in terms of identifying the factors that might reduce the likelihood of future crisis in Zimbabwe, but also those that seem to assist in restoring confidence after financial markets have become turbulent. The chapter comes with the consumer warning that the author has only followed the Zimbabwean economy from a distance over the past few years and will likely make errors in assessment that come from not being a close observer. For any such errors, the reader's understanding is requested. The author has, however, been involved in the IMF's recent activities in Korea, an endeavor which has been much criticized. A secondary aim of this chapter is therefore to explain the purposes of the IMF program in that Asian economy, while, all the time, searching for commonalities with Zimbabwe. Nonetheless, the views expressed in the chapter should not be taken as an official position of the International Monetary Fund.

Section 2 of the chapter explores the question of whether there were contagion effects from Asia on Zimbabwe, while Section 3 discusses the role of fundamentals in causing the Asian crisis. Section 4 describes the evolution of the IMF programs in Asia, with particular reference to Korea. Section 5 offers some conclusions.

2 Contagion effects of the Asian crisis on Zimbabwe

During 1997, financial crisis struck Thailand and then spread to other ASEAN countries (particularly Indonesia, but also Malaysia and the Philippines), and, finally, to Korea. In the second half of 1997, the currencies of these Asian Tigers lost as much as half of their value, while their stock markets dropped by similar orders of magnitude. Southern African currencies were not immune to the turbulence that swept across emerging markets in 1997 – in the second half of the year, the South African rand depreciated by 7 per cent against the US dollar. Despite heavy intervention, the Zimbabwe dollar fell by 40 per cent in US dollar terms, most spectacularly on 14 November 1997 when it dropped by 100 per cent during trading, before recovering somewhat by the end of the day (Figure 8.1). The two largest stock exchanges in Africa also recorded declines in the latter part of 1997:[1] the Johannesburg Stock Exchange (JSE) lost 16 per cent of its value, while the Zimbabwe Stock Exchange (ZSE) fell by 30 per cent (Figure 8.2),

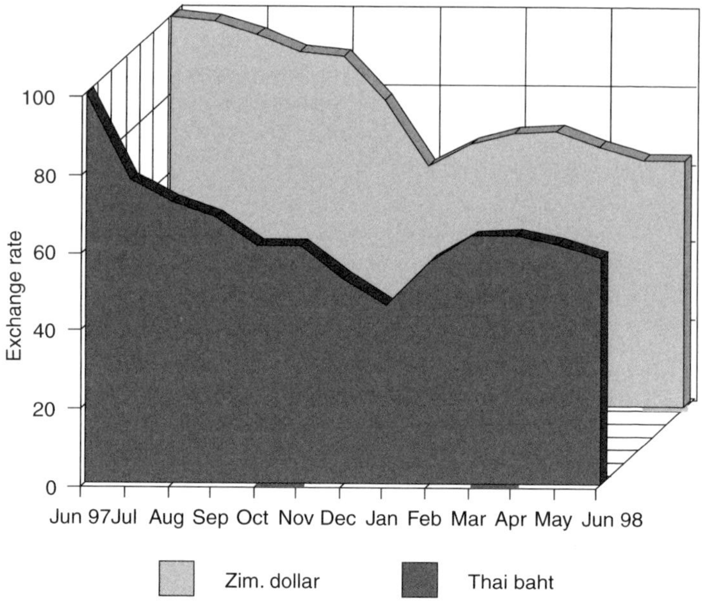

Figure 8.1 Exchange rate developments, 1997–98 (June 1997 = 100)

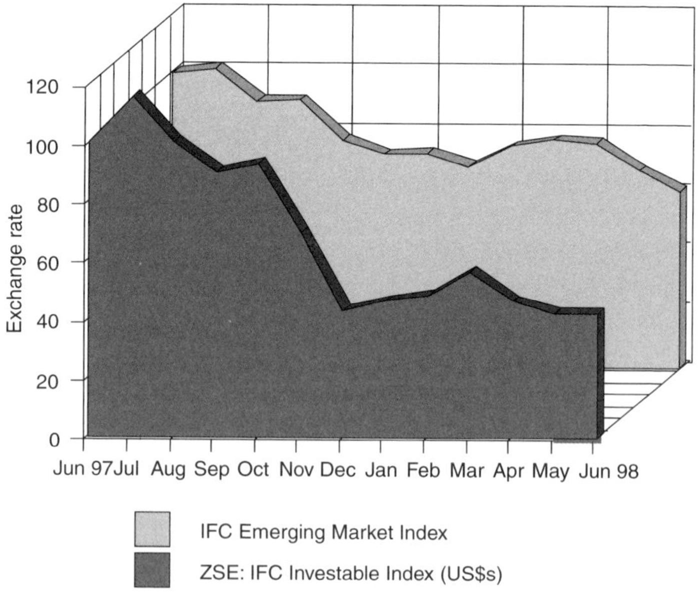

Figure 8.2 ZSE vs combined emerging markets, 1997–98 (June 1997 = 100)

Table 8.1 Changes in the exchange rate and the stock market index up to August 1998

	Thailand	*Indonesia*	*Korea*	*Zimbabwe*	*South Africa*
% change in:					
Exchange rate[1]					
Since June 30, 1997	−39	−84	−36	−41	−27
Since Dec. 31, 1997	13	−68	23	−2	−18
Stock market index					
Since June 30, 1997	−49	−40	−60	−33	−9
Since Dec. 31, 1997	−27	7	−21	−5	9

Note: 1. Local currency per US dollar.

partly reflecting foreign investors liquidating their positions.[2] In US dollar terms, foreign investors in Zimbabwean equities could have lost as much of two-thirds of the value of their investments in the second half of 1997.

Between 1998 and the time of writing, there was considerable differentiation in the performance of the Asian crisis countries. Korea and Thailand have seen their currencies strengthen, but their stock markets weaken as a result of concerns about the impact of financial sector and corporate restructuring and the weak regional outlook due to the continuing recession in Japan. Indonesia, by contrast, descended into a maelstrom of civil disorder, causing the rupiah to lose a further two-thirds of its value. In South Africa, the rand, having sustained only moderate depreciation in 1997, has, to the time of writing, been marked down severely in foreign exchange markets. By contrast, the Zimbabwean dollar initially regained some stability in 1998, before coming under renewed downward pressure in August which eventually led to an informal control of the currency from early 1999. The two regional stock markets changed little during the first half of the year (1998). Initially, the JSE benefited from some flight by emerging market investors away from Asia, but by the end of June it had given up most of these gains. Up until 1997, the ZSE had been one of the star performers among emerging markets. Foreign investment in local stocks was first permitted in December 1993 up to a 25 per cent limit, and the limit was progressively raised, reaching 40 per cent by December 1996. Liberalization of portfolio inflows, combined with a succession of good agricultural seasons, fueled a bull market from 1995, with the ZSE rising by 70 per cent in US dollar terms in 1996 alone. Capital inflows into the ZSE in 1994–96 are estimated at US$270 million. This contributed to a strengthening of the Zimbabwe dollar, which appreciated by 12 per cent in real effective (trade-weighted) terms during 1994–96, even after allowing for a build-up in official foreign reserves of US$250 million over this period.

The ZSE continued to rise steeply in 1997, seemingly unaffected by some signs of growing macroeconomic imbalance, as evidenced by the continued high fiscal deficit, and the threat of a wider trade deficit due to lower tobacco and gold exports (see EIU, 1997). By July 1997, the ZSE had reached a peak 300 per cent higher than mid-1995, implying a two-year US dollar value increase of 120 per cent. However, domestic events now began to exert a negative impact on sentiment. In August, the government promised pensions to war veterans, an unanticipated and unfunded expenditure (of more than 2 per cent of GDP) that threatened a much larger fiscal deficit, and a possible surge in inflation should it be monetized. Signs of growing labor discontent and a reopening of the land question were further eroding market sentiment, as were concerns about a possible EI Nino drought in the 1997/98 season. Monetary policy also appears to have been eased from October (EIU, 1998).

The stock market had already begun to weaken in the third quarter of 1997, as had the Zimbabwe dollar, although heavy intervention by the Reserve Bank was serving to check its depreciation. By November 1997, the realization that official reserves were almost depleted, combined with uncertainty about the future conduct of domestic economic policy, caused a sharp drop in the value of the Zimbabwe dollar and further falls in equity prices. On the other hand, by mid-November, Asian markets had already collapsed; the Hong Kong stock market (the Hang Seng Index) crashed on 24 October, and Korea was facing an increasingly grave external financing situation. No attempt is made here to attempt to separate empirically the part of the turmoil that swept Zimbabwean financial markets in late 1997 that was due to domestic factors from the part that represented Asian contagion. However, the data are consistent with the story that the stock market and real exchange rate had been run up to a level judged to be unsustainable both domestically and abroad, particularly as foreign investors were now reassessing all countries in their emerging market portfolios. In a sense there was an element of contagion from Asia, but uncertainty about the future direction of economic policies appears to have been the primary factor explaining the severity with which financial market instability struck Zimbabwe in 1997.

In early 1998, the IFC Emerging Market Index staged a recovery, with the JSE in particular benefiting from a flight to quality, but by that time a pall hung over the Zimbabwean economy as a result of labor unrest,[3] as well as the fear that the policy of forced land appropriation would diminish agricultural production and sour relations with donors. Similarly, the Zimbabwe dollar remained weak in 1998, even though most Asian currencies – the notable exception being Indonesia – have regained some value against the US dollar. Sentiment improved considerably in mid-1998 as a result of reduced uncertainty about land redistribution and improved relations with donors. It is also worth noting that an indirect effect of the Asian crisis on

Zimbabwe may have operated through the effect of weak Asian demand on the world prices of minerals that Zimbabwe exports. On the other hand, oil prices have also fallen in the wake of the crisis, and this has been to Zimbabwe's benefit. These latter types of links between Asia and Zimbabwe are not explored in this chapter. They do not represent contagion in the conventional sense, because they affect the current and not the capital account of the balance of payments, but may nevertheless have played a limited role in Zimbabwe's current difficulties.

3 The role of fundamentals in the Asian crisis

3.1 Macroeconomic fundamentals

In general, macroeconomic indicators in Asia did not provide advance warning of the impending crisis. Asian economies had long histories of sound macroeconomic management – as evidenced by low inflation, budget surpluses, and moderate levels of external indebtedness. Indeed, the strength of these countries' macroeconomic fundamentals was judged to have been a central determinant of the 'Asian miracle' (World Bank, 1993). There were also few signs of a weakening of these fundamentals in the period preceding the crisis.

In terms of the standard indicators – reserve cover, external debt ratios, and macroeconomic balance – the Asian crisis countries were judged to have had low vulnerability. Subsequent events, of course, have shown this confidence to have been entirely misplaced, and most observers seem to have been caught unaware by the virulence with which the crisis struck (see IBCA, 1998). Even Paul Krugman, who had famously questioned the sustainability of high Asian growth rates in the early 1990s (Krugman, 1994), has admitted to not having foreseen a crisis anything like as severe as that which happened (Krugman, 1998).

That most observers were surprised by the events of 1997 can be illustrated by observing the recent progression of the consensus forecast for 1998 GDP growth in Korea (Figure 8.3). Even as late as November 1997, the same month that Korea approached the IMF for a stand-by loan, the consensus was that growth in Korea in 1998 would be 5.4 per cent, only a little below that expected at that time for 1997 (5.8 per cent). The 1998 growth forecast was dramatically marked down in December. The figure also shows that the consensus forecast has tended to be lower each month in 1998, indicating that most analysts continue to underestimate the severity of the downturn and to overestimate Korea's ability to recover in the short term. As noted, macroeconomic fundamentals showed few signs of weakening in the period immediately preceding the crisis. Growth in Thailand, Indonesia and Korea continued to be robust (6 to 9 per cent in 1995–96), with Korea's per capita GDP rising above US$10 000 in 1996, the same year it became an OECD

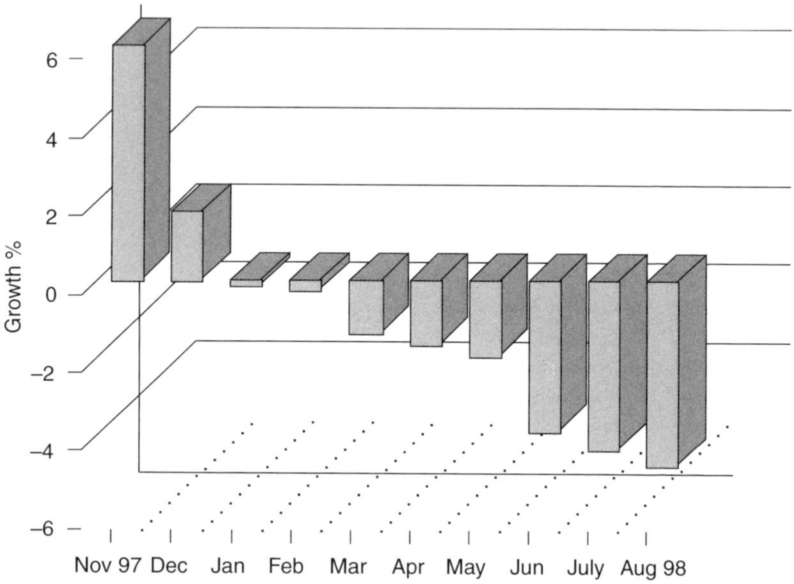

Figure 8.3 Evolution of consensus forecast of Korean GDP growth for 1998

member. Inflation remained at moderate levels (in the range of 5 to 9 per cent). Investment typically amounted to 30–35 per cent of GDP, or ten percentage points higher than in Zimbabwe, and savings were close to 30 per cent of GDP.

In 1996, there was concern about an export slowdown in Asia and current account deficits began to widen, reaching 5 per cent of GDP in Korea and 8 per cent of GDP in Thailand. Nevertheless, external positions were judged to be sustainable, either because deficits were being financed by foreign direct investment, and hence were non-debt-creating (Indonesia), or because low external debt levels were thought to allow some latitude to borrow over a short period (Korea). Investment in Asian countries was seen as highly productive, so current account deficits represented foreign savings flowing toward economies where they would be productively used. Current account deficits in Asia were less of a cause for concern than they would have been elsewhere in the world, particularly because analysts, still mindful of the causes of the Mexican crisis in 1994, were confident that they did not reflect unsustainably high levels of consumption.

There was, however, one macroeconomic indicator, the exchange rate, that was sounding a warning, although the signal is considerably clearer with the benefit of hindsight. ASEAN countries pegged their currencies to the US dollar, so the sharp appreciation of the dollar during 1995–97 (from ¥80 to ¥130 per dollar) substantially harmed their competitiveness.[4] The appreciation of ASEAN exchange rates (and, to a lesser extent, the Korean won) seemed justified at the time by the capital flowing into the region, although the negative effects on export growth and profitability were not being fully recognized. Here there is a similarity with Zimbabwe's experience, where the real effective exchange rate was allowed to appreciate during 1995–96, a strengthening which also proved unsustainable in 1997.

3.2 Microeconomic fundamentals

Two types of explanation have emerged in response to the observed phenomenon of countries with strong macro fundamentals experiencing crisis. One school of thought argues that the fundamentals of the economies were intrinsically sound and markets simply overreacted (Sachs and Radelet, 1998). Feldstein (1998) takes this position when he maintains that Korea's crisis was one of liquidity and not solvency. The other school of thought, which underlies the IMF programs in Asia, is that the economic fundamentals were not as strong as had appeared to be the case. In part, the impressive macroeconomic performance had served to mask fundamental structural problems, notably weak financial sectors and overleveraged corporate sectors. But there has also been a realization that high investment was in many cases unproductive. Overinvestment had led to excess capacity in export industries (Korea) and in the property sector (Thailand), thereby depressing the profitability of companies and the financial institutions from which they had borrowed. Financial institutions have traditionally lacked independence in Asia. Even though typically not state-owned, they were used by governments to channel credit to preferred sectors and projects, often with little regard for whether these loans made commercial sense or not. State allocation of credit was facilitated by a weak system of prudential controls and forbearance by the supervisory authorities. The result was a banking system with little commercial orientation, limited ability to price risk, and excessive exposure to key sectors and large corporations. Bank financing for large and ambitious investment projects was made available, even when such investment simply added to overcapacity. Korea made large investments in semiconductors in the mid-1990s, thereby adding to global excess supply. Chip prices fell sharply from 1996 (Figure 8.4).

As a consequence, when investment booms ended and corporate profitability came under downward pressure, either because property prices fell (in the case of Thailand) or export prices weakened (in the case of Korea), the asset quality of financial institutions deteriorated commensurately. Indeed, from 1996, the international credit ratings agencies had become increasingly concerned about the poor health of Asian financial sectors, but, on balance, most analysts judged these problems to be manageable. Directed lending had served Asian economies well in the past and few were able to foresee that the system had outlived its useful life – even though, in retrospect, this now appears very clear.

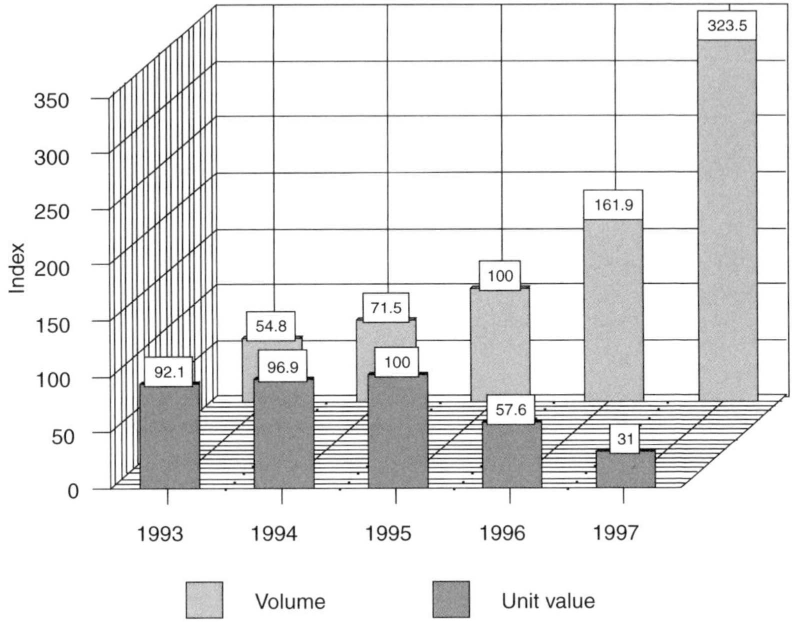

Figure 8.4 Korea: exports of electronic products, 1993–97 (Indices, 1995 = 100)

What was different in 1997 was that Asian financial institutions had become substantial short-term borrowers on the international capital markets, thus increasing their vulnerability to any financial crisis. As concerns increased about the health of Asian banks, and falling reserve levels made the tacit willingness of Asian governments to bail out banks less and less reassuring, international credit lines began to dry up, thus precipitating a foreign exchange crisis. All the facts are not yet known, but there may also have been an element of 'gambling for resurrection' in the behavior of Asian borrowers. For example, faced with increasing non-performing domestic loans, Korean financial institutions appear to have been purchasing high-yield (junk) foreign bonds with funds borrowed cheaply using Korea's high sovereign credit rating. When foreign lenders started to recall loans to Korea in late 1997, these assets proved to be illiquid, thereby aggravating the foreign currency crisis. International markets began to closely scrutinize Asian economies once confidence began to sour and the severity of the crisis was compounded by the lack of transparency that was discovered. In the corporate sector, close alliances between government and bank managers had led to non-transparent decision making and, if not 'crony capitalism', at least poor corporate governance. In Korea, a clear assessment of corporate health was precluded by complex systems of cross-corporate guarantee (used to ensure that weak subsidiaries received credit) and incomplete financial reporting (unlike conglomerates in Zimbabwe, the Korean *chaebols* were not required to publish consolidated financial statements).

With regard to official data, there was little or incomplete disclosure of key variables such as foreign reserves, external debt, forward exposure, and non-performing loans. The Bank of Thailand committed a substantial portion of its reserves in forward market intervention, but, in common with many central banks, did not publish details, resulting in a shock to the market when the data was finally released. Korea included illiquid deposits at offshore Korean banks in its foreign reserves, so that the official reserve data tended to understate the true extent of reserve loss. Official debt data was also inadequate, omitting, in the case of Korea, external debt contracted by offshore entities, a practice that appears to have understated true external indebtedness by about a half. In the financial sector, reporting practices by supervisory authorities were similarly opaque – markets placed little credibility in official estimates of non-performing loans, which were widely regarded as considerable underestimates.[5]

Once the Thai crisis had caused overseas lenders to scrutinize all Asian exposures – what Goldstein (1998) termed the Asian 'wake-up call' – the lack of transparency undoubtedly harmed Asian borrowers. Opaque and incomplete data tended to inflate fears, and although the lack of transparency was not a new development, Asian economies ceased to receive the benefit of the doubt. There may have been some overreaction on the part of the markets, but in view of the structural weaknesses outlined above, it is difficult to subscribe to the Sachs–Feldstein belief that there was nothing fundamentally wrong with Asian economies. Indeed, the list of weaknesses provided in this section broadly corresponds to the agenda for reform under the IMF-supported programs.

4 IMF-supported programs in Asia

There is no evidence that Asian governments fundamentally altered the stance of fiscal or monetary policy in the run up to the 1997 crisis. The monetary policy stance was not visibly eased in Asian countries; in Korea, for example, growth of broad money aggregates continued on a downward trend, even in 1997. With regard to fiscal policy, budget positions broadly similar to previous years were recorded in 1996 in Korea (balance) and Thailand (surplus). The Indonesian budget was in surplus by about one per cent of GDP in 1996, which was better than the average (balance) recorded during the period 1990–95.[6]

With the commencement of the IMF-supported programs, monetary conditions were tightened sharply to support the exchange rate. This is an aspect of the Asian programs that has attracted considerable criticism, even though it is common practice for countries to increase interest rates in order to defend their currencies (a recent example being Russia). Indeed, the Reserve Bank of Zimbabwe raised its rediscount rate in November 1997 after the dollar had fallen. What was different about the Asian situation is that debt was so high; debt–equity ratios in Korea and Thailand before the crisis were 200–300 per cent; and critics have accused the IMF's high-interest rate policy of having exacerbated the downturns in these economies. The rationale behind IMF advice to Asian economies regarding interest rates is clearly explained in Fischer (1998). Here it is sufficient to note that the intention was to keep interest rates high only as long as it took for exchange rates to stabilize. The strategy has had success in Thailand and Korea, where interest rates are now lower than before the crisis. The answer to the question of whether the strategy of high interest rates had negative effects on these economies that could have been avoided is unknowable; however, it is worth noting that Malaysia, without an IMF-supported program, and with interest rates raised relatively little, was facing a downturn in 1998 almost as severe as Korea's.

Since the crisis, budget positions have deteriorated substantially. In Korea, the IMF-supported program at first required that fiscal measures be taken to offset the cost of financial sector restructuring and thereby to restore budget balance. This should have allayed market concerns that public support to the financial sector would require significantly (and perhaps unsustainably) larger budget deficits. Since that time, economic activity and tax collections have contracted sharply, implying increasingly large budget deficits in the absence of further offsetting measures. However, balancing the budget is a questionable strategy when economies are undergoing severe cyclical contraction and unemployment is doubling or tripling. Under what circumstances can a relaxation of fiscal policy be justified? Two important conditions would be low initial levels of public debt, and the country having a strong fiscal track record – so that the promise to balance the budget again post-crisis is credible. In Asia, the IMF therefore supported the authorities in targeting larger deficits – estimated at 4 per cent of GDP in Korea in 1998 – so as to avoid withdrawing stimulus from the economy and to provide for the higher number of unemployed. Current fiscal policy advice in Asia provides an example of a case where IMF-supported programs have differentiated themselves according to individual country circumstances – often held not to be the case. Macroeconomic policies, of course, were not the primary cause of the Asian crisis, and the most important changes being made under the IMF-supported programs concern structural reforms.

In Korea, the primary components of the structural reform agenda are sweeping reforms of the financial sector and measures to facilitate corporate restructuring and de-leveraging. At the time of writing, considerable progress has already been made, particularly with regard to financial sector reform; in particular, a number of insolvent banks and merchant banks have been closed; other banks have devised recapitalization plans; and a resolution-trust-type institution has started to buy up bad loans.

Korea has also accelerated its program of capital account liberalization. Inward foreign direct investment in Korea, which had traditionally been discouraged, has been liberalized. Such investment promises benefits in terms of technology transfer and efficiency gains from increased competition. Capital inflows may also serve to lower Korean interest rates. But, as evidenced by the indiscriminate foreign borrowing by Korean banks in the run up to the crisis, there are also risks associated with opening the capital account. These add urgency to the task of strengthening prudential supervision. The transparency of official data has improved considerably in 1998. Key data on reserves, forward exposure, external debt and non-performing loans are now provided on a regular and timely basis. Changes planned for accounting and reporting practices should also improve the transparency of corporate affairs, leading to better informed investors and sounder financing decisions.

Finally, while political factors are largely exogenous, they have obviously given Korea and Thailand an advantage in their reform efforts. Initially, political developments aggravated the Korean situation, since the crisis occurred immediately before a presidential election. But social consensus for reform was quickly forged under the new President, including through an impressive tripartite accord between labor, business and government. Political unity and a sense of national solidarity, as evidenced by the campaign for private citizens to sell their gold, which generated export receipts of US$2 billion in the first quarter of 1998, have clearly aided Korea in recovering from the crisis.

5 Conclusion and possible lessons for Zimbabwe

Although Zimbabwe has an economy fundamentally dissimilar to the Asian crisis economies, all emerging market economies had similar experiences in the period 1997–98, and there appear to be some lessons for Zimbabwe to learn from the Asian crisis. The discussion in the chapter suggests the following:

1. *Over-appreciation of the exchange rate should be avoided*: in retrospect, smaller countries (such as Zimbabwe) should have responded to substantial swings in the yen/dollar rate by attempting to maintain stability in the effective (trade-weighted) exchange rate. To some extent this was tried by Korea from mid-1996, but its efforts were not sufficient to stave off the crisis; in any case, exchange rate policy on its own will not provide adequate protection if an economy has other problems. In view of the yen/dollar movements, and their contribution to the Asian crisis, Fischer (1998) observes that the issue of how better to promote global exchange rate stability will return to the agenda.

2. *International reserves should be sufficient to cover short-term debt*: the events of 1997 reinforce how important it is for a country that is borrowing in international markets to maintain adequate levels of official reserves, where adequacy of cover is measured with regard to expected amortization (that is, the size of the short-term debt stock), rather than to imports. With so much of its foreign borrowing from official sources, this lesson seems less important to Zimbabwe. However, if declining aid flows to Zimbabwe in the future will imply increased borrowing from international capital markets, it may become more relevant over time.

3. *Government-directed bank lending and the weak enforcement of prudential regulations can ultimately prove extremely costly*: the current distressed state of Asian financial sectors illustrates the costs of excessive government intervention in credit allocation. It also demonstrates the importance of a sound prudential supervision; of full disclosure of data on non-performing loans; and of taking visible steps to prevent a bad loan problem from recurring. While Zimbabwe moved quickly to close down a troubled financial institution, directed lending appears to persist. There may be important political and redistributive reasons for directed lending in Zimbabwe, but the Asian crisis has shown how quickly loans that are not commercially driven can sour, thereby eroding the profitability of banks, putting pressure on bank supervisors to exercise forbearance, and ultimately leading to a claim on the government budget.

4. *A lack of transparency in official data can also be costly*: faced with opaque and incomplete Asian data, markets made the judgment that 'no news was bad news'. Foreign market analysts focus on key variables such as official reserves, forward exposure, short-term external debt and increasingly on forward and derivatives exposure. Zimbabwe might well benefit from improved disclosure in these areas.

5. *Government commitment makes reforms more likely to succeed*: the Asian experience would tend to suggest that reform efforts are most credible when they come from within the country, rather than appearing to be imposed on the country by outsiders. This question of the 'ownership' of a program is a familiar one in Zimbabwe.

6. *Looser fiscal policy is not an option open to every government*: expansionary fiscal policy is currently being recommended in Asia because the countries concerned have low initial public debt levels and can credibly commit to restoring budget balance after the crisis has passed. These conditions are not typical of Zimbabwe, where budget deficits have

historically been high, public debt has increased to 80 per cent of GDP, and the government lacks credibility as a deficit cutter. The task of containing the deficit in Zimbabwe should therefore continue to be a priority.

Notes

1. The capitalization of the ZSE at the end of 1996 was slightly higher than that of the Nigerian Stock Market, and it rose 20 per cent with the Ashanti listing in early 1997 (see Oyama, 1997).
2. Changes in Zimbabwean stock prices are measured using the IFC Investable Index for Zimbabwe.
3. A fiscal package that included substantial increases in indirect taxes was announced in late 1997 as a means of financing the pension liability, but this met strong opposition from labor unions, including industrial action.
4. Exchange rate pegs also contributed to the build-up in external debt, since confidence that the pegs would be maintained increased the attractiveness of borrowing abroad at low international interest rates.
5. Nyawata (1998) notes that non-performing loan data are not readily available in Zimbabwe.
6. The policy record in Zimbabwe in 1997 is somewhat different, with evidence of an easing of monetary policy, as well as the threat of a much larger fiscal deficit.

References

Feldstein, Martin (1998) 'The IMF's Errors', *Foreign Affairs*, March/April.

Fischer, Stanley (1998) 'The IMF and the Asian Crisis'. Unpublished internet manuscript (www.imf.org), March.

Goldstein, Morris (1998) 'The Asian Financial Crisis', International Economics Policy Brief, Institute for International Economics, Washington, March.

IBCA (1998) 'After Asia: "Some lessons of the Crisis"', Fitch IBCA Sovereign, Comment, January.

IEU (1997) *Zimbabwe Country Report*. London: Economist Intelligence Unit.

IEU (1998) *Zimbabwe Country Report*. London: Economist Intelligence Unit.

Krugman, Paul (1994) 'The Myth of Asia's Miracle', Foreign Affairs, vol. 73, no. 6, December.

Krugman, Paul (1998) What Happened to Asia?, unpublished internet manuscript (www.web.mit.edu/krugman), January.

Nyawata, O. (1998) 'Financial Liberalisation and the Adoption of Indirect Instruments of Monetary Policy. The Experience of Zimbabwe', mimeo, IMF, July.

Oyama, Tsuyoshi (1997) 'Determinants of stock prices: the case of Zimbabwe', IMF Working Paper WP/97/117, September.

Sachs, J. and Radelet, S. (1998) *The East Asian Financial Crisis: Diagnosis, Remedies, Prospects*, Brookings Panel, Washington DC, March.

World Bank (1993) *The East Asian Miracle*. New York: Oxford University Press.

Part IV

Trade Liberalization: CGE Analyses

9

Macroeconomic Imbalances and Adjustment Reforms: a CGE Model Simulation

Ramos E. Mabugu

Introduction

Since 1980, the government of Zimbabwe has pursued two diametrically different policy regimes – namely, the controlled and fiscally-driven redistributive, import substitution policy regime of the 1980s followed by the structural adjustment reforms which began in 1991. The macroeconomic outcomes of the 1980s policy regime were, at best, very modest while those of the 1990s reforms were very poor. This chapter attempts to answer the question of whether the modest performance outcomes realized in the 1980s would have been sustainable without reform and addresses the issue of why macroeconomic performance in the 1990s has apparently been so poor. To analyze the nexus of these issues, we develop a computable general equilibrium (CGE) model of Zimbabwe and simulate the impact of the broad macroeconomic reforms pursued by Zimbabwe since independence. The simulated results are compared and contrasted with observed performance outcomes and from this we draw inferences and policy lessons for the future of the economic reform process.

Although CGE models vary widely with regard to model specification, they all serve two main purposes: first, they allow for ex-ante policy analysis and second, theory can be fleshed out. Since theory can give directions but cannot provide quantitative measures, models are an excellent solution. As is argued below, the benefits of structural adjustment reforms, in particular, have been many. However, the combined effects of initially adverse external shocks (bad weather and sluggish world growth) and poor policy sequencing have had significant effects on output growth, poverty and income distribution, with environmental and political repercussions that are still being worked through.[1] Compared to the previous literature on Zimbabwe, this chapter has three original features:

- First, the economic feedback on households and producer behavior is explicitly modeled. Previous works (for example, Chitiga and Mabugu

(1999), Davies et al. (1994, 1998)) have made significant steps in this direction. Although available analytical tools are still limited, this development has allowed the exploration of the consequences of reform in markets similar to those found in the Zimbabwean economy.

- Second, a counterfactual free of exogenous shocks is constructed. This allows the discussion of how policies would have impacted on the economy had there been no external shocks. A related point is that policies pursued in the 1980s are expected to have delayed effects in the 1990s and this constitutes a problem. The model allows the separation of these effects.
- Third, the model can be run under different trade regimes, one with foreign exchange rationing and one with free trade, along the lines suggested by Davies et al. (1998). This allows for the analysis of issues related to trade orientation.

Calibrating the model on Zimbabwean data, it is found that the expansive policies of the 1980s yield relatively high growth. However, this strategy is unsustainable on fiscal, equity and balance of payments criteria. The lack of growth in the 1990s is traced back to four issues – namely, subdued investment, a deteriorating balance of payments position, a lack of fiscal adjustment and negative distributional shifts. The results suggest that macroeconomic imbalances (especially fiscal imbalances) cause a contraction of sectoral outputs and real GDP beyond the levels expected from economic reform. The simulation results imply that the longer the delay in making the necessary adjustments in macroeconomic variables, the larger will be the gap between gains from adjustment and the ad hoc reform attempts of the 1990s which have been accompanied by accumulation of domestic debt.

Model development

As mentioned above, this chapter uses a CGE model. This is a real side model, distinguishing between policy instruments by the government and their general equilibrium effects on production, employment, income generation, fiscal and foreign trade balances. The model further distinguishes between five production sectors (agriculture, services, construction, exportables and importables), two types of labor (skilled and unskilled), four income groups (small-scale agriculture, profit, unskilled and skilled) and the government. The social accounting matrix (SAM) for 1991 (constructed by Chitiga and Mabugu (1997)) is used to calibrate the parameters of the model.

Production

In each production sector except agriculture (*exogenous supply, endogenous imports and flex prices*) and services (*demand-determined output and cost-plus pricing*), a representative firm maximizes its profit under the hypothesis of perfect competition. The functional form of the production technology is a constant elasticity of substitution (CES). This functional form was chosen to give a particular role to the different production factors used (skilled labor, unskilled labor and capital) in nested fashion in order to produce more or less goods. So, the firm's program is written as profit maximization under the CES. The solution gives the optimal factor demand as well as the factor price frontier under the hypothesis of zero profits. At an inferior level of the production structure, intermediate input consumption is further disaggregated under the hypothesis that it is formed as a CES composite of domestic and foreign inputs, each constituent then being allocated according to the Armington (1969) specification. The intermediates aggregate is combined with value added as a Leontief function to form output.

Consumption

Consumers receive all income from the production factors – labor, capital and land. After paying income taxes, a certain share is set aside as private saving and the rest is spent on consumption. A consumer in each category is assumed to have a utility function of the Stone–Geary type, hence

$$U(C) = \sum m_i(C_i - \theta_i)$$

where m_i (marginal propensity to consume) and θ_i (floor consumption levels) are parameters and C_i is sectoral consumption. The consumer's budget constraint is written as $Y_d = \sum P_i C_i$ where Y_d is disposable income while P_i is sectoral output price. With this constraint on total consumption expenditure, standard utility optimization yields consumption values for goods of the form

$$C_i = \theta_i + m_i/P_i(Y_d - \sum P_i\theta_i)$$

where the first term on the right-hand side is the quantities of committed consumption, the term in parenthesis is the supernumerary expenditure, that is, expenditure over and above total committed expenditure. This is the well-known linear expenditure system (LES), where the consumer always consumes a minimum amount of each good independent of price changes, and the surplus money from the expenditure budget is spent with constant coefficients for each good, although different consumers have different consumption propensities.

Government

The government collects fiscal receipts (taxes, indirect taxes on intermediate inputs, on consumer expenditures, on imports, income taxes and various non-tax charges and levies), employs skilled and unskilled labor and consumes both foreign and domestic products. The receipts are written simply according to the structure of the tax system.

Investment

The modeling of investment (while there are no adjustment costs on the capital) is general in nature, typical of that used in general equilibrium sectoral models. It is supposed that total aggregate investment is a composite good produced according to a tier structure resembling the productive sector. In this model, total investment, obtained as the sum of investment in construction and importables, is a construction–importables CES composite. This specification allows the allocation of total investment in demands for construction and importables respectively, with the shares depending on relative prices. As with final consumption and intermediate consumption, investment may come from the national territory or may be imported. Once again, the allocation is done according to the Armington specification.

Foreign trade

In modeling foreign trade, distinction is made between tradables and non-tradables. In one version of the model, a foreign exchange rationing mechanism is introduced to capture the situation in the 1980s (for details, see Mabugu (1996)). In the second, the foreign exchange rationing mechanism is removed, in order to represent the more market-oriented conditions of the 1990s (for details, see Davies et al. (1998)). The current account is now endogenous, with the nominal exchange rate fixed. All foreign currency needs for inputs, food and consumer goods are satisfied by drawing on the current account balance.

The data

The database underlying the model is a social accounting matrix (SAM) for the year 1991, extracted from the Zimbabwean national accounts. Hypotheses concerning production, consumption, investment, and so on, have been introduced to complete the initial matrix. The choices of elasticities have been realized following two principles: (i) a review of the economic literature, especially on Zimbabwe, provided an 'elasticity basket' whose validity is, a priori, guaranteed; and (ii) where an exact match could not be made, guestimates based on experience and consultations with experts were used. The remaining parameters such as distribution or scale parameters were calculated so as to precisely reproduce the benchmark SAM for 1991.

Policy analysis and simulations

Given the non-linear/non-autonomous nature of the system of the equations defining the model, there is little which can be done in the form of *analytical* investigations. Therefore, in order to find the effect of various policies directed toward economic development since 1980, recourse is made to numerical simulations. Various scenarios are run and compared to the benchmark ('no-change') scenario.

Scenario A: were the policies of the 1980s sustainable?

One question that comes to mind when considering the performance of the Zimbabwean economy in the 1980s is this: despite the variability, why was growth relatively high during this period and can these reasons be expected to bring about sustained development? To study the impact of the 1980s policy regime, a policy that simultaneously raises government expenditure and minimum wages by 5 per cent in a foreign-exchange-rationed model is simulated. The results of these policy experiments on selected variables are shown in Table 9.1. The policy increases GDP by 3.2 per cent. However, although government revenue goes up, government saving falls, implying that the positive effect of the larger tax income base does not fully offset the drastic increase in government expenditure. The minimum wage policy is effective in raising the real income of unskilled workers, whose increased demand in turn benefits the domestic-oriented sectors.

However, on a wider scale, the expansive policy with foreign exchange rationing also favors a relatively small affluent class, which typically leads to a deterioration of the current account balance.[2] This is reinforced by the observation that some of the highest production growth during this period was in the area of consumer durables.

This raises interesting sustainability questions. If expansionary policy was the major factor explaining the relatively high growth, that growth is unlikely to be sustainable for at least three reasons. First, a stagnant economy in which capacities are underutilized can increase its output for a short time

Table 9.1 Effect of a 5 per cent increase in minimum wage and government, expenditures in a model with foreign exchange rationing (percent changes, from base values)

Variable	*Scenario A*
GDP	3.2
Fiscal deficit	−2.8
Current account	—
Unskilled income	3.4
Skilled income	2.5
Profit income	2.1
Sectoral Performance	
Importables	5.8
Exportables	−1.6

as demand rises even without additional investment, so long as the balance of payments position permits such an expansion of output. However, in order for growth to be sustained, the process of capital formation must be renewed. This was not the case in Zimbabwe because net capital stock had almost ceased to grow because of the rapid decline in investment.[3] Second, the rise in current government expenditure is not matched by a corresponding rise in current receipts. With the ratio of current receipts to current expenditure declining, an increasing portion of revenue expenditure had to be financed through borrowing and other means. Consequently, interest payments as a percentage of total current expenditure rose as expansionary government policies were made possible by a rapid expansion of government internal and foreign debt. Theoretically, a fast-growing country can sustain persistent fiscal deficits without increasing its external indebtedness. This was not the case for Zimbabwe. The increase in public debt was unsustainable, especially in view of the fact that the economy could not grow itself out of the problem because of foreign exchange constraints on expansion. Third, the increase in unskilled wages and the ensuing fragile growth had a 'contamination' effect on other aspects of the labor market. During this period, Zimbabwe suffered a severe lack of skilled labor and this potentially put a brake on growth. With increased growth, the market for skilled wages became increasingly tight and wages began to rise. To the extent that this process continued, a wage spiral could have been set in motion. Recession-inducing policies would have been required to obviate the explosion. In view of this, it appears that the growth of the 1980s would most likely have been unsustainable.

Scenario B: are the policies of the 1990s sustainable?

Following the lackluster performance of the 1980s, Zimbabwe made a fundamental shift in its economic strategy in 1991. Like many other countries in Sub-Saharan Africa, it embarked on a far-reaching adjustment program. The policy framework that is currently being followed is embodied in the economic structural adjustment program (ESAP) and its successor, the Zimbabwean Program for Economic and Social Transformation (ZIMPREST). Are these changes likely to result in sustainable development? To answer this question, four scenarios described below are run in a liberalized model. The results are displayed in Table 9.2.

Scenario B1: trade liberalization (removal of foreign exchange rationing and tariff cut), with no fiscal adjustment

Trade liberalization is represented as a regime shift (that is, a shift from foreign exchange rationing to market allocation) and a reduction in tariffs on imports. Although economic efficiency and capacity utilization may be enhanced by trade liberalization, this does not improve distribution in the

Table 9.2 Stepwise impact of reform policies in a liberalized regime model (percent changes from base values)

Variable	*Scenario B1*	*Scenario B2*	*Scenario B3*	*Scenario B4*
GDP	–0.2	5.0	–3.8	10.0
Fiscal deficit	–2.3	0.1	0.4	2.5
Current account	–12.1	—	4.5	–3.7
Unskilled income	–0.4	–4.2	–1.3	2.4
Skilled income	–0.0	–1.2	–0.4	3.2
Profit income	1.1	8.0	1.4	4.0
Sectoral performance				
Importables	–10.0	–1.1	–0.3	17.2
Exportables	–1.2	12.0	4.1	5.5

medium term. There is a distributional shift towards the better-off classes, and a consequent fall in private consumption. As noted above, this tends to reduce aggregate demand, causing a depressing effect on output in standard Keynesian fashion. The recession has the effect of reducing the tax income base. However, there is only a mild worsening of the fiscal deficit as tariff revenue increases from increased imports.

A distinct feature of the results is the deindustrialization that results. The importables sector drops by 10 per cent compared to the base scenario. This is mainly due to loss of market share as consumer imports pour in, with a consequent slowdown in technological change. A closer look at the recent manufacturing performance at a disaggregated level indicates that the purely manufacturing sector (excluding ferrochrome, iron and steel, cotton lint and sugar) has become the most dynamic sector (growing by about 15 per cent between 1991 and 1995). Interestingly, the activities that led growth in the past are displaced by imports and continue to struggle. These include textiles and nonferrous metals. Consistent with predictions of liberalization, there is a dismantling of the industrial structure that existed before the reform *in tandem*.

The impact on the current account is detrimental. The measures increase imports (and import demand) while exports are hurt by a relative real appreciation, so that the trade balance worsens. It deteriorates until it is almost 8 per cent of GDP, which is an unsustainable level. The lesson here is that trade liberalization on its own is not enough. The ensuing balance of payments crises, deindustrialization from reduced demand and loss of market share and stagnant investment need to be addressed.

Scenario B2: Scenario B1 plus a currency devaluation

It is common for countries liberalizing their trade policies to devalue their currency in order to compensate for the liberalization impact on the balance of payments. To investigate this phenomenon, a scenario in which there is a 25 per cent nominal devaluation[4] in addition to the policy changes carried in the preceding scenario B1 is simulated.

The GDP growth rate now reaches a respectable 5 per cent. The main partial effect is an increase in total exports due to a direct positive effect in production prices for exported goods. There is a scale effect as well as a substitution effect, since the relative prices between the export and domestic markets increases. In assessing the devaluation response to a balance of payments pressure, we should note that it leads to some deindustrialization as importables decline. But this reduction is offset by the increase in export volume and increase in domestic demand. The required economy-wide elasticity of exports for this to happen would be 0.3. Based on econometric evidence on export elasticity in Zimbabwe reported in Chhibber et al. (1989), it would appear that traditional exports would be this responsive. However, devaluation results in severe income redistributions and inflationary pressures. The share of profit in total income rises at the expense of wage workers, especially unskilled workers. The potential inflationary and negative redistribution effects of devaluation are likely to constrain the use of nominal exchange rate policy, with the result that sustained reforms are likely to involve deterioration in the external balance until there is an export response.

Under the assumptions of the model, a devaluation would have favorable effects on both the macroeconomic balance and output. It would, however, exert an inflationary impact and lead to worsening income distributional shifts. The crucial question here is what would happen to wage costs when devaluation is undertaken. This brings us to the structure of the labor market, the role of trade unions and their readiness to co-operate with policy makers in some form of social accord. Allowing wages to increase would fuel inflation and hurt growth. The benefit for the external balance would almost completely vanish. Provided an accord is reached, devaluation appears to be a good idea.

This is fine as far it goes, but Zimbabwe must also develop a comparative advantage in some manufacturing branches. This is very difficult in an economy where the price system has been badly distorted in the past. Partly because of this difficulty, more attention should be given to the extent of 'natural' as opposed to policy barriers to exports in particular. Natural barriers include higher transport costs associated with distance, or with inefficiencies associated with the proliferation of small firms and the lack of competitiveness in the transport sector. It also covers delays and costs associated with customs procedures, and the costs and procedures associated with trade financing. These supply-side measures need to be focused on a particular group of firms in order to have the maximum effect. Basically this boils down to an exercise in finding areas where Zimbabwe may have a comparative advantage. However, picking winners ex ante is very difficult, so that euphoric expectations about the effects of supply-side policies should be discouraged. The point is that the Zimbabwean reform package has not given as much attention to such infrastructural deficiencies as it has to the reform of direct policies.[5]

Scenario B3: Scenario B2 plus cut in government expenditure

In this scenario both government consumption of goods and use of labor is reduced by 5 per cent, on top of the policy changes in scenario B2. This is one aspect of the overall reform package not successfully carried out by authorities as the budget deficit is still far from being in line with that stipulated in the reform program. The first-order effect of a reduction in government employees is a reduction in GDP, which falls by almost 9 per cent. This entails a negative demand effect on the economy. The negative output effects of this demand reduction are enhanced by the multiplier mechanism. Reducing government expenditure partially increases government revenues, but other tax income sources are adversely affected by the economic contraction, so that there is an overall reduction in government revenue. However, government savings increase because of the reduction in expenditure. Imports fall in line with the decline in output, while the real exchange rate depreciates, and hence exports increase. This explains the relatively large improvement in the trade balance.

Thus, if care is not taken, government stabilization policies could easily come into conflict with the growth objective. Avoiding fiscal adjustment is not the solution either, as experience has shown. The way stabilization policy has been carried out in Zimbabwe points to a trade-off between growth and price stability. Monetary policy has been very tight during the 1990s, yet fiscal adjustment has been difficult to achieve. This has led to a situation where nominal interest rates are so high that it can be argued that they tend to choke growth.

Reducing just the *level* of expenditure has favorable effects on the macroeconomic balance but generates adverse effects on growth. This policy reform needs very careful assessment before implementation. Attention must be devoted to other types of intervention. For example, there may be a need to change the composition of the budget and realign it towards investment in order to compensate for the demand contraction from the policy. If the economic outlook is gloomy, it may be advisable to postpone to a latter period this part of the reform because it may compromise the chances of any social pact formation between government and the people, which is crucial for reform success. A number of voices have recently suggested that the success of reforms will have more to do with the willingness of government to undertake the appropriate macroeconomic policy adjustment. Similarly, economic reforms have to be matched by reforms of political institutions and social safety nets.[6]

Scenario B4: Scenario B3 plus an increase in investment

This scenario investigates the implications of increased investment by letting investment rise plus the full ESAP scenario B3. The total effect of all the economic reform policy changes in this scenario is positive compared to the benchmark. GDP is higher and its composition is turned more towards manufacturing production which is 17.2 per cent higher than in the base-line scenario. The increased growth leads to a worsening of the current account balance. When GDP grows in the Zimbabwean case, it results in increased imports. To the extent that the latter consists of producer goods used by the export industry the deficit on the current account will only be temporary. But since increased incomes tend to boost the imports of consumer goods and cause a real appreciation, this tends to blunt the domestic output response and result in pressures on the current account. Should this become serious, a further devaluation (as opposed to a tight monetary policy) may be required to avoid growth becoming stunted before it becomes sustained.

Over and above these issues there hangs a much more important question mark. The growth-generating force advocated in this scenario is investment, which, by definition, is exogenous and hence not under the direct control of the policy maker. As is well known, the determinants of investment are difficult to model. In the model, positive signals are coherent macroeconomic policy making, not least of which are those policies contained in scenario B3. On top of this, a solidly-based revival of the capital formation process depends on three principal variables that policy should further address: (i) the real return to investment for the economy as a whole and for the individual producer; (ii) the real cost of investment finance on the capital market; and (iii) relative stability (lack of uncertainty).

On a related matter, investment in the 1990s neither went into the more productive sectors nor was it driven by productivity trends, especially in the formal sector. This implies that reforms on their own may be insufficient to create signals necessary to channel investment efficiently. If most of the investment is distributed to sectors with low marginal productivity of real capital, the increase in the stock of real capital will contribute little extra production to the GDP – a chilling observation synonymous with recent experience.

Some observations about model outcomes compared with actual performance

In this section, we compare our model simulation results with actual performance and try to explain the reasons for the divergence. Table 9.3 shows that, on average, the growth and budget deficit performance during the 1990s was worse than that of the previous decade and certainly worse than that predicted by scenario B4 of our model.

A number of reasons, ranging from negative exogenous shocks to poor program design and implementation, account for this divergence. For

Table 9.3 Actual vs model predicted performance (average percentage change)

Indicator	*Actual 1980–1990*	*Actual 1991–1998*	*Model prediction*
GDP	4.0	2.0	10.0
Budget deficit/GDP	10.0	11.6	2.5

example, the country was hit by a massive drought, at the very outset of the reforms, in 1991/92 and again in 1994/95. In addition, there was a sharp worsening in terms of trade against agricultural and other primary exports by about 21 per cent. However, exogenous factors alone are insufficient to explain the poor actual performance. Although reforms were aggressively implemented in the early phases, the reform momentum could not be sustained. Zimbabwe found some reforms much easier to implement than others, leading to further difficulties in the sequencing of various stages of reform. To date, not all elements of the reform package have been implemented. In particular, the country has stalled over the issue of fiscal adjustment, resulting in persistently large fiscal deficits. The different policy scenarios investigated in this chapter suggest that implementation failure, especially in the latter half of the 1990s, accounts for the apparently poor actual performance. Zimbabwe is yet another example of the dangers of adjusting/liberalizing when macroeconomic (in particular fiscal) balances are not under control. Authorities failed to act decisively on the fundamentals: the public sector deficit remained high and this failure to reduce the deficit undermined the effort to tackle inflation such that the real exchange rate was allowed to appreciate. Further, high domestic borrowing by the public sector raised real interest rates and expanded the share of financial profits in the economy (at the expense of shares of labor and of non-financial profit).This financing of the fiscal deficits necessarily resulted in the extraction of funds from the capital markets that would otherwise have been utilized for new capital formation. The rise of the public sector borrowing requirements generated additional pressures on asset markets which resulted in higher interest rates for transactors than those prevailing in world markets. This increased uncertainty in the economy and a risk premium emerged between the domestic and international interest rate, with consequent distortions on savings and investment. Poverty increased because of falling wages and incomes in urban and rural areas; informal sector employment grew as formal employment stagnated. In general, these changes made the poor worse off.

Summary and conclusions

The modeling approach presented in this chapter provides a viable example of an integrated treatment of overall economic and fiscal reform policies. It is now a well recognized feature of modern macroeconomic thought that the incorporation of firms and household behavior and an explicit recognition of the budget constraint of the government simultaneously within an open-economy framework is crucial. We were able to address questions relating to how economic reforms affect rates of growth, income distribution and consumer welfare in a theoretically consistent manner.

This chapter developed a CGE model whose simulations helped us to understand the performance of the Zimbabwean economy since independence. In the first set of simulations, it was found that the expansive policies of the 1980s yielded relatively high rates of growth. However, this was found to be unsustainable on fiscal, equity and balance of payments criteria. Further, the country was slipping into a domestic debt trap, employment was inadequate and investment had stagnated at very low levels. It was hard to see how the economy could have continued for much longer at this rate.

The second set of simulations enabled us to identify the reasons for the observed failure of the Zimbabwean economy during the 1990s. This failure manifested itself in three main forms: contractionary output, deindustrialization and worsening poverty. The lack of growth in the 1990s can be traced back to four issues: namely, subdued investment, a deteriorating balance of payments position, a lack of fiscal adjustment and negative distributional shifts. The simulation of full implementation of the reform package results in a GDP level 10 per cent higher than that recorded in the base-line scenario. The failure to achieve the growth rate implied by the model can largely be traced back to poor co-ordination of the overall reform process, and in particular to the weak fiscal controls and the failure to radically change the whole budgeting process. This leads us to the conclusion that the poor performance realized was not the result of the reform programme, but, rather, the failure to implement it is full. However, the strategy implied by our simulations puts growth ahead of employment and redistribution, thus acknowledging that, unless the economy grows, no employment will be created and there will be nothing to redistribute to the poor. The growth-generating forces are investment and exports, both of which are outside the direct control of the government. Investment is difficult to model while export forecasts are just as problematic because of the simple reason that Zimbabwe, being a small open economy, by definition, has no control over international markets. We thus conclude that even if reforms are implemented in full, policy makers are still going to have to rely on luck, given that they lack complete control over some of the most critical growth components.

Zimbabwe is yet another example of the dangers of adjusting/liberalizing when macroeconomic (in particular fiscal) balances are not under control. This, in our opinion, should be the starting point for any consideration of how Zimbabwe should manage macroeconomic policies in the first decade of the twenty-first century. Fiscal deficits will be eliminated only when budgetary practices are improved. But budgetary practices do not just improve on their own. Fiscal authorities must play an active role in eliminating inertia and poor budgetary practices by offering incentives for developing new fiscal instruments and institutions.

To the extent that reforms aim at eliminating distortions in the economy, they should, in future, be implemented in full. Reforms that improve production efficiency can be expected to benefit the economy in that while other resources may deteriorate in quality/quantity, others would show growth and improvement. Further, the elimination of distortions would make economic analysis of poverty problems much more transparent. However, partial implementation of reforms cannot be relied upon to guarantee improvement in overall well-being. If, as the Zimbabwean experience with economic reforms shows, important distortions are allowed to persist, the elimination of a policy failure in a given sector would not necessarily lead to improvements in welfare.

Notes

1. There have been other general policy statements and plans since the reforms started, most notably *Vision 2020*. These do not seem to have had much impact beyond their high profile upon launching.
2. This does not happen here because of foreign exchange rationing.
3. To further complicate matters, foreign savings were negative while domestic savings were higher than 17 per cent of GDP.
4. This amount of devaluation constrains the current account balance to stay unchanged at the base level.
5. In a paper, Milner (1997) evaluates to what extent the effectiveness of the trade reforms have been constrained by avoidable infrastructure deficiencies or by the design of trade policy reform itself in the context of African reforms.
6. For example, Rodrik (1998) views the industrial/enterprise policies (such as lifetime employment) and provision of social services to avoid extremes of income inequality as a reason why the East Asian countries have been able to become more outward oriented despite external shocks.

References

Armington, P. (1969) 'A theory of demand for products distinguished by place of production', *IMF Staff Papers*, 16, 159–76.

Central Statistical Office (1997) *National Accounts 1985–1996*. Harare: Economic Publication Unit.

Chhibber, A.J., J. Cottani, R. Firuzabani and M. Walton (1989) 'Inflation price controls and fiscal adjustment in Zimbabwe', Working Paper 192, Country Economics Department. Washington DC: World Bank.

Chitiga, M., and R. Mabugu (1999) 'Minimum wages and trade regimes: CGE results for Zimbabwe', in S. Kayizzi-Mugerwa (ed.), *The African Economy: Policy, Institutions and the Future*. London: Routledge, Chapter 7.

Chitiga, M. and R. Mabugu (1997) 'A Social Accounting Matrix for Zimbabwe: 1991', mimeo, Department of Economics, University of Zimbabwe.

Davies, R., J. Rattsø and R. Torvik (1994) 'The macroeconomics of Zimbabwe in the 1980s: A CGE-Model Analysis', *Journal of African Economies*, vol. 3, no. 2, pp. 153–98.

Davies, R., J. Rattsø and R. Torvik (1998) 'Short run consequences of trade, liberalization in Zimbabwe: a CGE model analysis', *Journal of Policy Modelling*, vol. 20, pp. 305–33.

Krueger, A.O. (1997) 'Trade policy and economic development: how we learned', *American Economic Review*, vol. 87, pp. 1–22.

Mabugu, R.E. (1996) 'Tax policy in Zimbabwe: applying general equilibrium models', PhD thesis, Gothenburg University, Sweden.

Milner, C.R. (1997) 'On natural and policy-induced sources of trade regime bias', *Weltwirtschaftliches Archiv*, vol. 132, pp. 740–52.

Prebisch, R. (1950) 'Commercial policy in the underdeveloped countries', *American Economic Review*, vol. 49, pp. 251–73.

Rodrik, D. (1998) 'Globalisation, social conflict and economic growth', *The World Economy*, vol. 12, pp. 1–16.

Singer, H. (1950) 'The distribution of gains between investing and borrowing, countries', *American Economic Review*, vol. 40, pp. 473–85.

10

Trade Liberalization and Investment Response in Zimbabwe

Halvor Mehlum, Jørn Rattsø and Ragnar Torvik

1 Introduction

On the basis of liberalization experiences in many countries, there has been an increasing concern about the investment response to a process of liberalization, as summarized in, for example, Serven and Solimano (1993). Since the main reason governments embark on trade liberalization programs is to increase the productive capacity of the economy over time, a shortage of investment may prevent the expected favorable growth outcome.

Since establishing new industries typically takes a longer time than closing old ones, trade liberalization often leads to decreased output and employment in the short run. A strong investment response can be thought to diminish the adjustment problems, since demand is added in the transition phase. In this way, a strong investment response can counteract the contractionary aspects of liberalization packages. On the other hand, when investment is concentrated on imports, increased investments may contribute to problems with external accounts. Furthermore, through appreciating the real exchange rate, increased demand may slow structural adjustment away from previously protected sectors towards new tradables industries.

In order to investigate effects of trade liberalization and investment response, a CGE model for Zimbabwe is utilized. This allows a quantification of different effects both of liberalization and investment. Based on our perception of the stylized facts of the Zimbabwean economy, the CGE model emphasizes real side sectoral balances and macroeconomic interactions thought to be important with liberalization. The model is constructed to represent the import compression regime at work through the 1980s in Davies et al. (1994). Import rationing allocates intermediates and investment goods, and also includes importables and food, and the domestic markets for importables and food are protected from international competition. Davies et al. (1998) developed the model to study trade liberalization as a regime shift imposed on the benchmark import rationing model eliminating controls. The starting point of this chapter is the simulated effects of the liberalization of intermediates in 1991 documented in Rattsø and Torvik (1998a).

In order to study medium-run dynamics, the original model is modified by including investment functions and capital dynamics, replacing Rattsø and Torvik's simplifying assumption about fixed investment demand and fixed capital stock. The dynamics for trade reform are given as follows: trade liberalization shifts relative prices in favor of the export sector at the expense of the other sectors. Given that increased profits in the export sector induces investments, the periods following reform exhibit growth and a gradually improving current account balance. The investment response, however, is dependent on the perceived credibility of the reforms. Given that physical capital cannot be shifted between sectors without friction, the expected permanence of a new trade regime is decisive in determining the investment response. As Dixit among others has shown there will be '...a zone of inaction and caution before reorienting capital in response to relative price shifts.' (1989 p. 309). Hence, the positive long-run effects of trade reform only materialize if the reform is perceived to be credible. Without a positive investment response the economy will not recover from the contracted short-run state.

Section 2 discusses theoretical considerations on trade liberalization and investment, while section 3 discusses the background to and macroeconomic experiences of trade liberalization in Zimbabwe. The CGE model and its use are presented in section 4. The analysis follows in sections 5 and 6. Section 5 is devoted to the short-run effects of trade liberalization by simulations in a static model version. First, the effects of liberalization and the drought that coincided with it are simulated. Second, the short-run effects of investment response are investigated in a simulation where the investment level increase by 5 per cent with liberalization. Section 6 studies the medium-run dynamics, taking into account the link between investments and production capacity. The model is simulated with both a fixed and a flexible exchange rate, and issues related to expectations, credibility and the self-fulfilling failure of reform are discussed. Concluding remarks are given in section 7.

2 Trade liberalization, output and investment: some theoretical considerations with relevance for Zimbabwe

The standard welfare analysis of trade liberalization is based on a model assuming the full utilization of resources. Trade liberalization is shown to improve resource allocation, since imperfections disturbing marginal efficiency conditions are eliminated. Static misallocation costs of trade restrictions are generally shown to be small. The introduction of rent-seeking has added to the estimates of possible gains. CGE studies addressing trade liberalization include Benjamin (1992), Condon et al. (1985), and Grais et al. (1986).

The more recent literature emphasizes the macroeconomic context of the liberalization, as in Collier and Gunning (1992). Even in models of full employment, credibility problems may lead to unfavorable outcomes regarding trade balance and investment. In the case of Zimbabwe it is realistic to assume unemployment of unskilled labor, opening up for possible effect on total employment. Theoretical studies by Buffie (1984) and Ocampo (1987) have shown that trade liberalization can be contractionary in this situation – Ocampo emphasizes demand switching, while Buffie assumes higher intermediate import costs. Demand switching may reduce the output from import-competing domestic industries. This mechanism can be seen as an example of forced import substitution following from restrictions on imports. The total employment effect depends on the strength of the supply responses in other sectors, particularly exportables.

The core of the action during trade liberalization takes place in import-dependent and import-protected sectors, typically manufacturing in Sub-Saharan Africa. On the supply side, rationing of intermediates means less efficient production, since the reduced availability of imported intermediates can be compensated only imperfectly by domestic intermediates. The rationing system offers the producers commodity-specific licenses for intermediates, and they are not allowed to resell. Clearly this system motivates rent-seeking, and costs associated with rent-seeking is another possible source of less efficient production, as suggested by Grais et al. (1986). In Zimbabwe the license holders were old clients of the government, and observers agree that costs associated with rent-seeking have not been important in this instance. License holders do get an implicit rent as a result of the rationing. Rationing means a higher price of the finished good in the protected domestic market than otherwise would be the case. This leads us to the other important aspect of import rationing – effects on the demand side through protection of domestic final goods markets. The import compression had come close to eliminating both importables and non-competitive consumer goods imports. Furthermore, a domestic market for the imports allowed has been almost absent, which is surprising.

Two effects of this protection are especially important because of their impact on the demand side. First, demand switches to domestic goods when foreign goods are not available. Since consumer imports are rationed, the ratio of imported to domestically produced consumption was lower than desired at the prevailing prices. The notional price of consumer imports was higher than the actual. Second, when demand for imports is not satisfied, part of the income can be set aside as savings – in the expectation of less severe rationing in the future. A theoretical justification for this phenomenon is offered by Torvik (1997a). Empirical evidence is identified by Chhibber et al. (1989) and Morande and Schmidt-Hebbel (1991).

Trade liberalization in Zimbabwe can be understood as having eliminated the rationing in two steps. The first step, intermediates liberalization, removed with the rationing of intermediate imports. Improved access to imported intermediates is expected to be expansionary, especially in an economy with unemployment. The notional price of imported inputs falls. This is the opposite effect of the contractionary liberalization analyzed by Buffie (1984). In his model, a higher relative price of imported inputs accounts for the possible contraction in output.

The second step, full liberalization, adds free trade in importables, non-competitive consumer goods and food to intermediates liberalization. The elimination of protection mainly affects demand towards domestic producers. Two counteracting forces can be identified. On the one hand, private savings rates are reduced when foreign goods are made available, and the consumption demand goes up given the income level. Since the stock of wealth accumulated under rationing can be higher than desired under liberalization, the immediate flow-effect on consumption can be quite large. If demand expansion dominates, also the second phase of liberalization is expansionary. On the other hand, demand switches to imports since consumers have hitherto been forced to hold an inefficient mix of domestic and foreign goods before liberalization. This effect tends to shift the demand away from domestic producers, with output contraction as a result of the second step of liberalization.

Production in the exportables sector is expected to increase following the removal of rationing. When domestic producers produce more efficiently as a result of intermediates liberalization, the costs of production fall. In this way, liberalization depreciates the real exchange rate even in the absence of devaluation. Furthermore, the opening up of the domestic market for finished goods means a lower price of importables, which pulls in the same direction. If the liberalization is combined with devaluation, the output response is strengthened. A sufficiently strong exportables expansion can help counteract contractionary effects from the opening up of imports to the final goods market.

The output response, as well as the structural shift away from importables and towards exportables, can affect investment decisions. Investments in the importables sector are expected to decrease, while investments in the exportables sector may increase. With limited capital mobility between sectors, the isolated effect of the structural shift from importables to exportables on the investment level should be positive. The reason is that the exportables sector should enter a phase where the capital stock increase rapidly over time, until the new desired capital stock is reached. This catch-up requires increased investments.

The liberalization also affects the cost of investment goods. Liberalization of imported intermediates reduces the cost of production for domestic producers, implying cheaper domestically produced investment goods. On the other hand, if liberalization is accompanied with devaluation, the cost of the imported content of investments increases. The effect may be significant in countries where imported goods make up a large fraction of investments.

The dynamics following reform is determined by whether investments respond to the changing profit rates. Two investment response scenarios, linked to the credibility of reform, are analysed. The linkage between credibility and investment response builds on Dixit's (1989) argument that investment response will be weak when the credibility of reform is weak. The relevance of this argument for the case of trade reform is emphasized by Rodrik (1992, p. 90): 'Trade reform is frequently met with scepticism on the part of private sector. The Argentine reform of the late 1970s, for example, had such low credibility that it is reported many enterprise managers apparently chose not to respond.' Hence, the two investment scenarios are:

1. Reform is not credible. Investment levels and capital stocks are unaffected by reform, as it is expected that the reform will be reversed, re-establishing the historic profit rates.
2. Reform is credible. Capital accumulation is endogenous, responding to changes in profit rates.

These two investment scenarios are explored within the model of two exchange rate regimes – one where the exchange rate is fixed and one where the current account balance is fixed and the exchange rate floats. The emphasis on these four polar cases enables a clear-cut analysis clarifying the main alternatives and trade-offs.

3 Trade liberalization in Zimbabwe

Regulation of foreign trade has been a key feature of the Zimbabwean economy for three decades. During the period of Unilateral Declaration of Independence (UDI) between 1965 and 1980, international sanctions, and domestic policies to cope with them, induced a policy of import-substituting industrialization. A sophisticated import control system was built up, which the new government continued to use after independence in 1980. The post-independence boom (1980–82) was unsustainable on foreign exchange grounds, and the government resorted to administered foreign exchange allocation to control the current account deficit. This policy led to macro-economic stability, but restricted growth. Green and Kadhani (1986) wrote the authoritative account of the early independence period. Since the mid-1980s, a number of institutional responses to deal with the linkage between import capacity and economic growth have been introduced, basically aimed at export promotion. The measures were not without effect, and the relaxation in the foreign exchange constraint can be observed as rising growth rates in the last part of the decade. In view of the relative success of the modified protectionism, this looked like a long-run solution of a government with socialist inclinations and rhetoric.

To the surprise of most observers, the government then chose to go for a policy of full trade liberalization – one that was, in fact, more radical than most developing countries. It must be understood in the context of increased political pressure to join the international trend of liberal economic reform. Outside Zimbabwe, both donors and the Bretton Woods institutions argued for liberalization and could add on funding. Inside the country, the powerful Confederation of Zimbabwe Industries changed its opposition to one promoting trade liberalization around 1987–88. Skålnes (1995) reports increasing concerns within the ruling party ZANU(PF) about the growth effects of regulation.

The adopted program contains all the elements of the orthodox Washington package, and trade liberalization has been the main area of action. The seriousness of the policy intentions was shown in October 1990, when raw materials and inputs to industries were put on a list of Open General Import License (OGIL). Industries in key sectors such as cement, textiles and mining were given free access to imported inputs. As early as the fall of 1991, the liberalization had been extended to include imported final goods. At first the extension was part of the gradualist approach, and new items were put on the OGIL list. The Export Retention Scheme (ERS) introduced in the spring was broadened, and all exporters were now entitled to 15 per cent of export revenues in foreign exchange. Internal trade with ERS imports developed and an unofficial foreign exchange market was started.

Later, the trade liberalization assumed its own momentum. In the summer of 1993 the process accelerated with new extensions of the export retention and free trade with ERS entitlements. Individuals were allowed to open foreign exchange accounts, and a dual foreign exchange market developed with both an official and an ERS exchange rate. Later the corporate sector has been allowed to open foreign exchange accounts. External borrowing was allowed and exchange controls were relaxed (for example, travel). The opening up for foreign capital flows was partly motivated by the high cost of available domestic private credit. During 1994, the exchange rates were unified, one of the last moves towards the liberalized economy as we know it at the time of writing.

Although it is too early to evaluate the long-term growth effects of the new economic environment, the short- and medium-term macroeconomic responses are indicated by the most recent national accounts data. Table 10.1 shows the promising start of the program with the liberalization of intermediates in 1990 and 1991. Output growth was strong, even in per capita terms, and the manufacturing sector grew along with the rest of the economy. According to the national accounts, gross fixed capital formation (GFCF) grew by 35 per cent in 1990 and 23 per cent in 1991 in real terms. Although the increased imports worsened the trade balance, the first two years of ESAP must be characterized as successful. From 1992 onwards the economic development summarized in Table 10.1 appears to be less favorable.

Table 10.1 Economic development indicators 1990–1997

	1990	*1991*	*1992*	*1993*	*1994*	*1995*	*1996*	*1997*
GDP growth per cent	7.0	5.5	−9.0	1.3	6.8	−0.9	7.6	4.4
Per capita	3.7	2.3	−11.8	−2.2	3.2	−4.1	4.3	0.4
Percentage of manufacturing in GDP	20.5	20.0	20.1	18.3	18.8	16.8	16.3	16.0
Percentage of exports in GDP	22.9	23.9	27.2	30.7	34.6	38.1	36.6	37.3
Percentage of imports in GDP	22.8	27.2	36.5	32.4	36.5	40.8	36.4	40.1
Trade balance per cent of GDP	0.1	−3.3	−9.3	−1.7	−1.9	−2.7	0.2	−2.8
Percentage growth gross fixed capital formation	34.7	23.1	−8.5	+7.1	+2.4	+2.0	−11.1	−9.3

Four observations can be extracted from the table: contraction, deindustrialization, external imbalance and erratic investments. The move towards liberalization of finished goods went hand in hand with a serious drought, and GDP fell by 9 per cent in 1992. To date, the economy has not fully recovered from this contraction. Although growth has been mostly positive, even in per capita terms, GDP per capita in 1997 was still about 10 per cent lower than before liberalization was launched in 1990.

When imports of finished goods where liberalized, domestic producers lost their sheltered home market. As expected, many could not face the new competition, and closed down. The growth of new firms has not been sufficient to keep production up, and the structural shift observed must be characterized as deindustrialization. The share of manufacturing in GDP has dropped from above 20 per cent to 16 per cent.

In a few years the openness of the Zimbabwean economy has increased rapidly, measured by both the import and export shares of GDP. But the share of imports has increased faster and more than the share of exports. While the trade balance was positive every year from 1985 to 1990, the liberalized economy of the 1990s has produced trade deficits. The lack of devaluation and the uncertainty of the process contributed to the hoarding of imported goods, and combined with the drought in 1992, the deficit grew rapidly. Since then, the trade deficit has fluctuated at around 2 per cent of GDP. The foreign debt has accumulated in a country that developed a tradition of prudent control and independence of international financial markets in the first decade after independence.

Investment response has been erratic from 1992 onwards. Part of the reason for this is probably the uncertain political and economic conditions, such as whether the program is on track, the exchange rate development, and land reform. The latest numbers on GFCF show that investments are lower in real terms now than at the beginning of the 1990s. GFCF in the first half of the 1990s made up about 22 per cent of GDP, compared to about 15 per cent in the years before liberalization took place. By 1997 the latest numbers suggest that gross capital formation make up 16 per cent of GDP. The behavior of investments are crucial for the long-term growth prospects of the economy, as well as the more short- and medium-run responses analyzed in this chapter.

On the monetary side, which is outside the scope of this study, inflation early in the program reached a peak close to an annual rate of 50 per cent. The drought must take some of the blame for this development, together with deregulation of domestic markets. The inflation has led to dramatic cuts in real wages and thereby a shift in the income distribution away from urban unskilled labor. The interest rate level drifted up with inflation and reached a peak with an extreme real loan rate of about 20 per cent, related to the continued public deficit of about 10 per cent of GDP.

The trade liberalization has substantially changed the conditions for production and distribution. The first step of liberalization gave easier access to imported intermediates and raw materials, and an overall expansion of import-dependent activities was expected. The delayed devaluation kept imported inputs cheap, although some tariffs and charges were imposed. Opening up for free imports of inputs basically allowed the protected domestically oriented industries to expand and involved little structural change. Firms with the most restricted access to imports before the liberalization of course benefited most. Only a small shift from domestically oriented to export activities was observed, with a marginal increase in exports as a share of GDP in 1991.

The liberalization in 1992 dramatically changed the conditions for import-competing industries. They had previously been protected from competition. The inflow of imported final goods made many domestically oriented manufacturing firms unprofitable. Imports have crowded-out domestic production. The negative effect on industrial production was influenced by the 1992 drought which reduced agricultural income and demand, and reduced the access of inputs from agriculture to industrial processing. Other aspects of the adjustment process were also important. The interest rate shock associated with financial liberalization raised the costs of working capital, and real wages dropped substantially with the overall rise in inflation. Our analysis can throw some light on the economic responses to the trade reform. By integrating import rationing policies in an economy-wide model, the effects of liberalization can be traced out, while at the same time a counterfactual analysis of investment response can be undertaken.

4 Modeling trade liberalization

The full economy-wide interactions are captured in a computable general equilibrium model emphasizing the real side. The benchmark model with import regulation is constructed and documented by Davies et al. (1994), and 1985 is used as the base year. The model brings together two types of dual models familiar from development economics. The dependent economy model, distinguishing between traded and nontraded goods, can be seen as a starting point. With a view to including terms of trade effects and differences in import rationing, traded goods production is disaggregated into importables, exportables and food agriculture. De Melo and Robinson (1989), Bevan et al. (1990) and Devarajan et al. (1991) argue for a disaggregation of the traded sector in developing countries. The exportables are often raw materials, agricultural crops and so on, while the importables have the characteristics of manufacturing goods and, in Sub-Saharan Africa, foodstuffs. Since production structure and demand linkages differ, nontraded production is disaggregated to services and construction. The dual flexprice–fixprice approach of Taylor (1983), distinguishing between agriculture and the rest of the economy, is taken into account with a specific food agriculture sector. Our formulation is different from Taylor since both food agriculture and most nonagricultural outputs are supply-driven in the Zimbabwean context.

The sectors are disaggregated into the following categories: food agriculture, nontraded consumer goods ('services'), nontradable capital goods ('construction'), exportables, and importables. The supply side of the import-dependent sectors construction, importables, and exportables, captures the role of import regulation. The formulation allows for substitution possibilities in a hierarchical system including imported and domestic intermediates, skilled and unskilled labor and real capital. The exportables sector is a price taker in the world markets, and output and exports adjust to clear the market. In the construction sector, a falling demand curve combined with the rising supply curve equilibrate supply and demand. The same is the case for the importables sector because of imperfect substitution between domestic and imported importables goods. A combination of imports and domestic production equilibrate supply and demand for the composite good. With imperfect substitution there is room for endogenous determination of the domestic price. The importables sector has some of the characteristics of a nontraded sector. Output of food agriculture is exogenous in the short run. Foreign trade in food is regulated and the domestic price clears the market. The service sector is characterized by mark-up pricing and demand determined output.

A separation is made between skilled and unskilled labor in formulating both production and distribution technologies. In the labor market, skilled labor is in short supply, and the wage rate adjusts to clear the market. Unskilled labor is in permanent excess supply, and the use of unskilled labor is demand-determined given an institutionally determined nominal wage rate. In addition to skilled and unskilled labor, income is distributed to profit earners and small-scale agriculturalists. The income groups have different savings rates, implying that income distribution affects aggregate demand in a standard structuralist fashion.

The foreign exchange available, export revenues and an exogenous trade deficit, is allocated to satisfy priority needs (investment goods, intermediates for the exportables sector and food). The importables sector is protected, and only a limited volume of importables is allowed to be imported. Any remaining foreign exchange is allocated as policy-determined shares, to meet requirements for imported intermediates by construction and importables, and to noncompetitive consumer imports. When imported intermediates are rationed in the construction and importables sectors, these sectors are forced to substitute towards domestic goods, resulting in an inefficient mix of inputs. The availability of imported intermediates, dependent on the existing capacity to import, influences the supply curves. The description is consistent with Davies (1991) and Pakkiri and Moyo (1986). A theoretical framework for analyzing import compression is suggested by Rattsø (1994a), with additional aspects developed by Rattsø (1994b) and Torvik (1994, 1997b). Gibson (1985) was the first to link up export performance and import-dependent industries in his model of Nicaragua.

The imports of food are part of government policy to regulate domestic food markets, in particular in response to drought. We have made food imports endogenously dependent on food shortages, the gap between a target for food consumption and the actual.

Investment imports are assumed to have priority. In the static model the investment level is exogenous, and the import share responds to relative prices. In order to clarify the short-run effects of increased investments, an exogenous shift in investment demand are shown in a counterfactual experiment below. Thereafter, in the dynamic model, we endogenize the investment response and study the capacity-increasing effects and the medium-run dynamics.

Based on this model of import regulation, trade liberalization can be analyzed as a regime shift. Davies et al. (1998) documents the alternative model regimes and offers ex-ante liberalization experiments using the model. Rattsø and Torvik (1998a) offer an ex-post evaluation of the trade liberalization. The present chapter utilizes the revised data now available, which shows that the contraction in 1992 was considerably stronger than the earlier data indicated. The static model is simulated to investigate the effects of trade liberalization and drought, and a counterfactual experiment is undertaken to trace out how investment response influences the short-run effects of liberalization.

Liberalization is basically modeled as a change in model closure from a situation of rationing to a situation where demand functions are allowed to operate. Unfortunately, the degree of rationing before the regime shift cannot be observed, and assumptions must be made. A detailed documentation of the regime shifts and assumptions made, as well as sensitivity analysis, is available in Davies et al. (1998) and Rattsø and Torvik (1998a).

In the dynamic model capital stocks are calibrated and investment demand functions are included in order to analyze the medium-run effects of trade liberalization. The dynamic model introduces additional linkages through effects from profitability on investment demand.

The investment demand functions are conventional, containing positive dependence on the profit rate (see, for example, Rosensweig and Taylor 1990). The profit rate is significant as a proxy for expected future returns. This assumption is standard in much of the neo-Keynesian growth literature (for example, Robinson 1962). The extrapolation of the present in forming long-term expectations was also emphasised by Keynes: '[...] our usual practice being to take the existing situation and to project it into the future, modified only to the extent that we have more or less definite reasons for expecting a change' (1936, p. 148). In a developing country like Zimbabwe, an additional mechanism may add to the significance of the profit rate. As pointed out by Taylor (1991), developing countries often have highly controlled and/or poorly developed financial sectors. Current profits may therefore be the prime source of financing and the main determinant of the investment level. Since the present version of the CGE model only covers the real side, effects on investments from financial markets and the interest rate are not included. Hence, portfolio considerations and monetary effects cannot be accounted for. As will be discussed in more detail below, however, the investment behavior is assumed to be affected by the credibility of reform.

Investment goods are supplied by the construction sector, by domestically produced importables, and by imports. Collier and Gunning's (1996) study of African trade liberalization shows that the investment composition is responsive to shifting relative prices, hence the composition of investment is assumed to show some scope for substitution. The exact specification of investment demand and composition is presented in Mehlum (1999).

The analysis focuses on production capacity and the capital stock dynamics, and leaves out other, possibly important, dynamic effects. The consequences of accumulation of debt and financial wealth on the hands of government, private sector, and the foreign sector are not accounted for. Over time these asset changes will change the flow of interest payments and hence affect income levels and the current account. Moreover, changing wealth will possibly affect the savings/consumption decision directly. In the labor market the unskilled wage is likely to be changed over time depending on how the rate of unemployment develops. In addition, given substantial export growth, the export sector will probably experience price drops and bump into capacity constraints (for example, arable land, exploitable mines). Inclusion of these and other dynamic effects could to some extent modify the present medium-run results and improve on the realism. They are left out, however, in order to focus on the important linkage between investment, capacity, production and growth.

5 Trade liberalization, output and investment: static CGE model, simulations for Zimbabwe

The starting point for the empirical analysis is the imported intermediates liberalization of 1991. As shown in Table 10.1 and in Rattsø and Torvik (1998a), the economy responded favorably to the opening up of intermediate imports. In the annual data recorded in the official statistics, 1992 represents the first year of major liberalization of final goods. We assume that 'full' liberalization starts in 1992. The model is calibrated to reproduce the intermediates liberalization of 1991 as in Rattsø and Torvik (1998a), and this represents our base run.

The first model experiment undertaken is to investigate the effect of the opening up of final goods markets in 1992. At the time of writing, the most recent national accounts indicate that the drop in GDP was 9.0 per cent in that year. However, much of this contraction must be attributed to the serious drought in 1992. The effect of the drought is accounted for by the simulation by including the actual drop of 23.2 per cent in agricultural output. The results are shown in Table 10.2, as deviations from the model simulations for 1991.

When finished goods are added to the trade liberalization, four implications of previous rationing are modified. First, the protected importables sector faces competition from abroad. In the benchmark rationed situation, the sector is treated as non traded with exogenous imports and domestically determined prices. Now, imperfect substitution is assumed between domestically produced and imported importables, and the composite is a CES aggregate. It follows that output supply can respond to cost and price conditions with a combination of domestic production and imports. Second, non competitive consumer imports come in. The demand function

Table 10.2 Model simulation results

	Liberalization and drought	*5 per cent increased investments*
Growth in total GDP	−9.3	0.2
Growth in GDP services	−7.2	0.2
Growth in GDP construction	−3.0	3.1
Growth in GDP exportables	2.1	−0.1
Growth in GDP importables	−14.7	0.5
Growth in private consumption	0	0.2
Change in trade surplus as percentage of GDP	− 6.2	−0.6

for non competitive consumption goods allocates consumer spending between domestic and foreign goods, and liberalization allows more of a given demand to be directed towards imported goods. Third, the new access to imported goods is assumed to reduce private savings rates, inducing higher consumer demand given the income level. Fourth, trade in food is assumed to be determined by market forces. The flexible food price implied by import controls is replaced by one fixed by the world market. Imports and exports of food vary to clear the domestic market, rather than its price.

The model predicts that the combined liberalization and drought would reduce total GDP by 9.3 per cent, about the same contraction that was observed in 1992. Rerunning the model without the drought, but with the same liberalization, gives a fall in GDP of 4 per cent. According to the model, 57 per cent of the contraction was due to drought, while 43 per cent of the contraction was due to the liberalization. The trade liberalization implies expenditure switching from domestic to foreign goods that adds contraction to the drought. The short-run effect of liberalization of finished goods is output contraction.

The contraction can be traced back to the importables sector, with a decrease in value added of 14.7 per cent. The previously protected importables sector is a key player in the liberalization process. In the old regime, both intermediate inputs and finished importable goods were rationed. The sector expanded when it got free access to intermediates. When the final goods protection is removed, a serious contraction follows. Although the effect of the liberalization of intermediates in 1991 is expansionary according to Rattsø and Torvik (1998a), the contraction that follows with the extended liberalization and the drought is of a larger magnitude. Deindustrialization is the net result.

Output in the service sector is mainly driven by domestic demand. Both the drought and the deindustrialization push income down. When output and income decrease in the rest of the economy, the sector follows along. In addition, the new access to consumer imports mean demand switching away from the sector. The total effect is a decrease in output of 7.2 per cent.

Of the contracting sectors, construction is the sector that is least affected, with decreased output of only 3 per cent. The opening up of the importables market mean some switching toward importables goods in investment. Demand effects because of reduced income in the rest of the economy is limited when total investments are held constant. The simulated contraction in the construction sector with the liberalization of finished goods is less than the simulated expansion in the construction sector for 1991 in Rattsø and Torvik (1998a). Consequently, the net effect of liberalization is higher output in the construction sector. The reason for this is that liberalization brings with it a higher content of domestic goods in investment. The result is the same as in Collier (1992), but the reason is different. In Collier (1992), the higher domestic content of investment is due to devaluation that lowers the relative price of domestic to foreign investment goods. Here we get the same result without devaluation. Two counteracting forces are operating. Intermediates liberalization means a more efficient production in the construction sector, and a lower price. This pulls in the direction of higher domestic content in investment. Liberalization of finished goods means that imports replace some of the construction goods in investment, and pulls in the other direction. The effect of intermediates liberalization dominates the effect of liberalization of finished goods shown in Table 10.2, and the net effect of liberalization is a higher domestic content in investment, and therefore increased output in the construction sector. When liberalization in addition affects the level of the investment aggregate, additional forces operate, as discussed below.

In the model simulation, private consumption is unchanged, even with a drop in total output of 9.3 per cent. The reason for this is that when previously rationed consumer imports are made available, a higher proportion of a given income is consumed. This effect explains why decreased income does not push consumption down. According to the official national accounts data, however, consumption did fall. This is in contrast to what many feel is going on, because there seems to be a widespread belief that liberalization started a consumption boom. It is a puzzle that data show that the opposite where happening. Part of the explanation may be that private consumption is calculated residually in the national accounts, and therefore is subject to much uncertainty.

Not surprisingly, the combination of drought, domestic contraction and import liberalization has a major impact on the trade balance. The model predicts a rise in the deficit of 6.2 per cent of GDP, the combined result of agricultural market balancing and increased imports. The trade reform generated structural adjustment away from nontradable and importable goods towards exportables. In the model, the fall in domestic demand depreciates the real exchange rate and stimulates exportable supply. But the expansion of 2.1 per cent in exportables production is too little to compensate for the loss of domestic market shares in the short run. The current account deficit is comparable to the first years of independence, when it went up to about 10 per cent of GDP (Davies et al., 1994, table 2). A deficit of this magnitude is hardly sustainable. Although the deficit is brought down after 1992, Zimbabwe is still in a position where foreign debt is accumulated. The deficit and the deindustrialization associated with it are a high short-run price of liberalization, even if the long-run effects may be favorable. Furthermore, the short-run deindustrialization may induce unfavorable long-run effects. For example, if there are external economies of scale in the manufacturing sector, the short-run deindustrialization moves the economy to a development path with lower growth of potential output. Rattsø and Torvik (1998b) investigate external economies of scale in manufacturing in a model designed to reproduce the structural characteristics of the typical Sub-Saharan African economy.

As pointed out by Collier and Gunning (1992), trade liberalization may be incompatible. When private agents observe the large effect on the trade balance, they will expect future devaluations. Hence, imports are temporarily cheap, even worsening the trade balance more, and making the liberalization even less sustainable. On this background, it is not hard to understand the hoarding of imports that took place during 1992.

As seen in Table 10.1, the investment response has been erratic after the opening up of final goods markets, and it is hard to identify what the effect of liberalization on the investment level has been. The latest available numbers for 1997 indicate that the investment share of GDP is back to pre-liberalization levels.

When investment responds to trade liberalization, additional channels to those above are in operation. Table 10.2 shows the effects of liberalization with investment response, presented as deviations from the results shown in liberalization without investment response. As expected, increased investments push total production up. However, as seen from Table 10.2, the effect is moderate, with GDP increased by 0.2 per cent compared to the liberalization without investment response. On the other hand, it is seen that the effect on the trade balance is fairly strong, with a worsening of 0.6 per cent of GDP. Two implications follow. First, if increased investments response should help avoid the contraction, there would have to be a massive increase in the investment level. Second, if there was a massive increase in the investment level, the trade balance would have worsened much more than it actually did with liberalization. Consequently, a strong investment response would probably have made stabilization even more difficult after liberalization. The short-run effect of increased investments is mainly a worsening of the trade balance. To a large degree, the small output response and the large trade balance response from increased investments are two sides of the same coin. The import share in investment is high, so the first-round effects of increased investments are relatively little output growth and a relatively large weakening of the trade balance.

Furthermore, an increased investment level raises the import content in investment even more. Increased demand pushes the price of domestically produced investment goods up, and investors substitute toward imported investment goods. This substitution effect weakens the output response and strengthens the trade balance response.

In addition, the increased domestic demand appreciates the real exchange rate, making the export sector less competitive. The decreased production of exportables adds to the other forces that weaken the trade balance. When investments increase with liberalization, the structural adjustment away from nontradable and importables goods towards exportables is weakened. Also in this sense, a strong investment response may complicate the adjustment of the economy.

6 Dynamic CGE model simulations

6.1 Trade liberalization with fixed exchange rate

As a result of the demand shifts following trade reform, the profit rates also change. The expansion in the export sector gives higher profits. In the importable sector, which is the one most adversely affected by the removal of trade barriers, the profit rate decreases. Given that reform is credible, investments in each sector are increasing functions of the profit rates. Capital accumulation will increase in the export sector and decrease in the importable sector. Given an elasticity of unity, investments in exportables almost doubles following the increased profit rate. (An investment–profit elasticity of one is in range both with the assumption in Rosensweig and Taylor (1990) and the estimates in Jenkins (1998).) The reduced profitability in importables reduces their investments by about 13 per cent.

The short-run effect depends on the total investment demand. The net effect is not a priori clear because investments go up in some sectors and decline in others. Given the present calibration, however, there is an overall increase in the level of investments. As about half the investment goods are imported, increased investments inevitably worsen the current account balance. This effect is discussed above, and clearly illustrated in Figure 10.1. (The dashed curve labelled DEF/EXP captures the dynamics of the ratio of current account to exports. Compared to the case without investment response (the dashed horizontal line), the increased imports of investment goods adds four percentage points to the worsening of the deficit ratio. The increased investment demand is also partially directed towards the domestic suppliers. This has a significant effect on the construction sector that increases production by 5 per cent. This expansionary effect also shows up in the GDP figures and the recession is moderated by 0.4 percentage points compared to the case with fixed investments. This slight expansion reduces

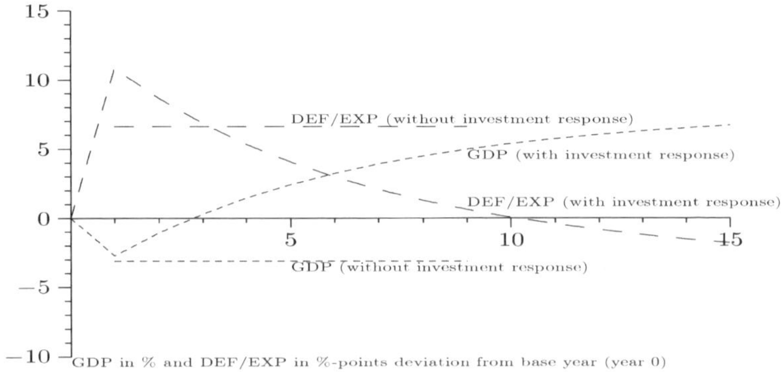

Figure 10.1 Short-run effects of trade liberalization

exports, as domestic expansion both results in a real appreciation and increased domestic use of exportables. In addition to these short-run demand effects, the investment response also affects the dynamics of the economy following reform. The investment response in the export sector is critical for the medium-run dynamics. The export sector, facing infinitely elastic demand in the world market, increases its output year by year as capital builds up. This growth stimulates the other sectors as both consumption and the supply of intermediate goods increases. Hence, overall GDP grows steadily after the first setback. From year three and onward there is an improvement compared to the starting point.

These medium-run movements are the main subject for the present analysis. For completeness (acknowledging that important factors are left out) we will briefly discuss the model's long-run properties: GDP shows stabilization at around 8 per cent above the benchmark. The expansion of GDP stops when the competition for resources has reduced profit rates to their steady state levels. With exports being the driving sector in GDP growth, the DEF/EXP ratio declines steadily and after ten years it shows an improvement.

The medium-run (and possibly long-run) result of trade reform when capital accumulation responds is increased production and an improved current account balance. As the liberalization implies an instant import boom, the short-run effects are recession and worsening of the current account balance. The strength of the investment response is critical in determining how fast the positive effects of liberalization materialize. If the investment is not responsive, the economy will remain in the state with depressed production and worsened current account balance.

Short-run compatibility issues

Irrespective of the investment response, the short-run consequence of trade liberalization, with a fixed exchange rate, is a worsening of the current account. If the funds are not available for the financing of the deficit, the country must cut into its reserves. This is a limited source and if the deficit gets sufficiently large the trade liberalization is not sustainable. Following Rodrik (1991, p. 238), countries may then have no choice but to abort the reform when the reserves fall below a certain threshold. This illustrates one important compatibility problem of trade reform. Without the access to sufficient financing, a trade liberalization giving a substantial worsening of the current account balance will not be feasible. Agents that take this into account will not consider the reform to be credible. They will therefore fail to respond to the new incentives by not investing and trade liberalization will by default not be credible.

The chance of running into a short-run compatibility problem is higher the stronger the overall investment response. A trade reform that stimulates total investments requires substantial imports of investment goods on top of the imports directly following from reform. Hence, depending on the foreign exchange constraint, it may be the case that only trade reforms that fail to stimulate investments are compatible with the short-run foreign exchange constraint. In that case reform can only be sustained if it is perceived as not credible. Hence, the following paradoxical situation can arise: reform will be sustainable, given the financing constraint, only if it is regarded as not credible. This paradoxical situation can be solved by introducing (as in Rodrik, 1991) a subjective probability of cancellation that is an increasing function of the trade deficit. Assuming further that the investment response is a decreasing function of the probability of cancellation makes interior solutions possible.

The external financing problem generating these incompatibilities can, at least to some extent, be counteracted by combining the trade liberalization with a depreciation of the currency. This is the option explored in the next section.

6.2 Trade liberalization with a flexible exchange rate

The worsening of the current account is a result of the shift in demand away from domestically produced goods as imports become relatively cheaper. This worsening of the current account balance is only possible if the foreign sector is willing to fill in the needed finances at acceptable terms. Assuming that these finances are not available, the closure of the model is changed. In this second regime the current account balance is exogenously fixed at its pre-reform level and the currency floats in order to bring exports and imports in accordance with the foreign exchange constraint. A real depreciation of the currency increases the competitiveness by reducing domestic costs relative to the world market price level. A depreciation is in effect tantamount to a reduction in the real wage of unskilled workers. In this regime a nominal wage inflation will have no real effect, as it will be exactly offset by a nominal depreciation. Hence, the unskilled workers will eventually carry the burden of remaining the current account at the status quo level. The dynamic pattern following trade liberalization when the exchange rate is flexible is illustrated in Figure 10.2.

Fixed investments

Again the horizontal lines capture the case without investment response. As long as investments are fixed, the trade liberalization requires a real depreciation of 26 per cent if the current account balance is to remain unchanged. This partly stimulates exports and partly moderates the increase in import demand. Exportables production increases by 12 per cent. The other sectors are also helped by the depreciation as their competitiveness in the domestic market improves. The output response following the depreciation more than offsets the recession analyzed above and GDP grows by 0.25 per cent. The increased exports also show up in the DEF/EXP ratio, which improves by 2.4 percentage points. The devaluation changes the income distribution effects

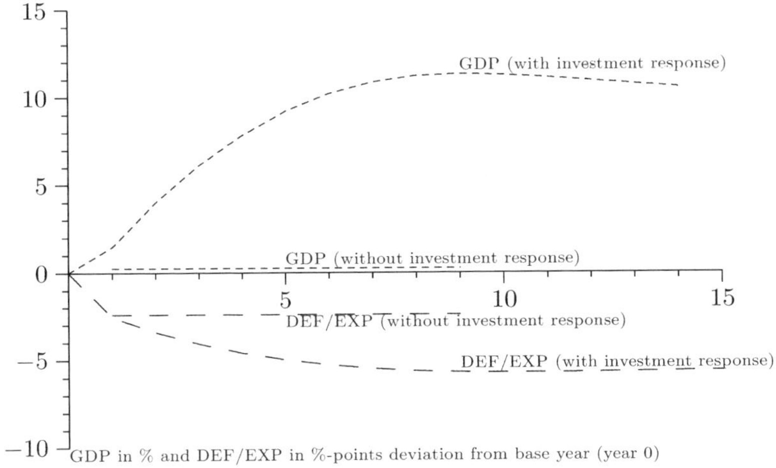

Figure 10.2 Dynamic pattern: trade liberalization with flexible exchange rate

of trade liberalization. The slight output expansion increases the demand for skilled labor increasing their wage while the depreciation directly reduces the real wage of unskilled workers. The profit income increases helped by increased profits in the export sector, and as profits rise tax revenues also rise. As the depreciation increases the price of agricultural goods, the income of small-scale agricultural firms increases. Hence, the prime loser is the unskilled labor. As the price of food is given by the world market, the purchasing power for the unskilled workers in terms of food will decline in the same magnitude as the depreciation – that is, by 26 per cent.

Endogenous investments

When trade liberalization is combined with depreciation, the positive effect on the profit rate in the export sector is strengthened. As a result of the substantial increase in the price of imported capital goods, profit rates in the rest of the economy decline. (The profit rate is defined as current profits relative to the replacement value of the capital stock.) The increased investments in exportables dominates and overall investments increase. In the case of fixed exchange rate the short-run effect of increased investments is a worsening of the current account balance. In the present regime an increase in investment works differently. Given a fixed current account balance, increasing import demand must be met by depreciation. Hence, the leakage represented by the import is neutralized and all demand expansions are channeled directly or indirectly to the domestic market. As approximately half the investment goods are imported, a substantial depreciation is required when investment increases. A total depreciation of 36 per cent is needed to offset both the effects of trade liberalization and the increased import demand generated by the increased investment. This strong devaluation gives a GDP growth of 1.5 per cent as exportables production increases further and as the other sectors experience modest demand increases due to substitution effects. The construction sector, being the main domestic supplier of investment goods, increases production by 6.4 per cent.

Over time exports grow as the capital stock in the exportable sector grows. As discussed above, this has positive repercussions on the rest of the economy. Hence, GDP grows steadily over time, and as the volume of exports steadily grows the exchange rate rule allows a gradual appreciation. The appreciation, combined with the increased competition for labor, reduces the margins in the export sector. Investments gradually fall and the economy reaches a new steady state where gross investments exactly offset the capital depreciation.

Short-run compatibility issues

The flexible exchange rate regime solved the financing problem of the fixed exchange rate regime. A depreciation in the range 25–36 per cent, however, cuts drastically into unskilled workers' real wages. Hence, by a depreciation the short-run financing problem is transformed into a possibly destabilizing deprivation of a large section of the population. The short-run compatibility problems of the fixed exchange rate regime can resurface in the form of social unrest and strikes if the real wage drop becomes too large. These mechanisms may in part explain the 1998 food riots in Zimbabwe following the November 1997 depreciation. Such unrest may force the government to reverse the trade liberalization. In that case, reform can only be made credible if the government is known to be firmly committed to liberalization. The cost of a firm government, however, can be continued strikes and unrest that may seriously depress investments as it generates contraction and cuts into profits. Thus, short-run compatibility problems can take many forms and reforms can bump into many constraints. If these constraints cannot be relaxed, the difficult (and sometimes impossible) policy challenge is to create a reform design that steers clear of all of them.

6.3 Expectations, investment response, and self-fulfilling failure

The analysis above illustrates how the investment response is critical for the effects of trade liberalization both in the short term and the medium term: (i) In the short term a positive investment response generates increased demand for imports. Given that the exchange rate is fixed, this substantially worsens the current account balance. If the current account balance is to be held constant, a substantial devaluation is required, depressing unskilled wages. (ii) In the medium run a positive investment response generates growth.

It has already been shown that the short-term consequences of trade liberalization can generate compatibility problems that may undermine reform. Thus, it may be the case that the trade reform is not internally consistent and therefore, quite inevitably, is perceived as not credible. However, the distinction between consistent and inconsistent reforms is not necessarily as clear-cut as in these examples. The abortion of reform may also be the result of self-fulfilling expectations. That is, trade reform succeeds if it is expected to succeed while it fails if it is expected to fail. The reason can, for example, be the so-called 'honeymoon' hypothesis (Williamson, 1994). According to this hypothesis, the voters' patience is limited and the reform government has to generate positive results within a certain time span, otherwise they are replaced by conservatives who restore the old trade regime. In a one-party state like Zimbabwe, the reversal may come about as the reformist wing of the ruling party loses power and the conservatives regain their influence, when reform not delivered as announced (for a discussion of these mechanisms in the case of Zambia, see Bates and Collier, 1995).

In the present context the argument can work as follows: Consider the case where trade liberalization is reversed if the GDP figures, after a 'honeymoon' period of three years, show no growth. If the economy is on a growth path, however, reform is continued. As seen earlier in Figures 10.1 and 10.2, in either regime the condition for continuation will only be met if investments have responded positively to the trade liberalization. Now, if the investment response is positive only if reform continuation is expected the mechanism for self-fulfilling expectations is established.

- *Self-fulfilling success:* Reform continuation is expected. The investment response is therefore positive and so is growth. As a result the reform is continued. Hence, the expectations about continuation are fulfilled.
- *Self-fulfilling failure:* Reform reversal is expected. There is no investment response and therefore no growth. As a result reform is cancelled and the trade controls are reintroduced. Hence, the expectations about reform reversal are fulfilled. The same mechanism is formulated in the following way by Rodrik '. . . trade reforms that lack credibility may prove difficult to sustain. First of all, macroeconomic balances will come under further stress, forcing some of the best intentioned governments to abort the reform process' (1992, p. 93).

In game theoretic terms the possibility of a self-fulfilling failure is a result of a co-ordination problem. Sen (1967) has labeled this kind of co-ordination problem in many person games 'the assurance problem': 'To get out of the problem all that is necessary is that each individual is assured that the others are doing the "right"' thing, and then it is in one's own interest also to do the "right" thing' (p. 122). Faced with a potential assurance problem the challenge for the policy makers is to induce the private agents to co-ordinate around the optimistic equilibrium. The problem can alternatively be solved by convincing the investors that the reform will be continued irrespective of the investment response. This will brake the possibly self-fulfilling vicious circle. One way of achieving this is for the government to act tough and convincingly fight back any opposition. Another possibility is to design a reform that generates an outcome that can be sustained even when reform has low credibility. As discussed in detail in Mehlum (1999), a gradual program is one way of achieving such a robust reform. In a stylized model it is shown that if reform implementation is sufficiently gradual, the sustainability of the program is not dependent on an immediate investment response. Hence, a gradual reform may be sustainable even if it is perceived as not credible and will therefore not fail as a result of self-fulfilling expectations. The self-fulfilling mechanism above relied on whether reform-generated GDP growth or not. This story is relevant in both the flexible and the fixed exchange rate regimes. Depending on the exchange rate regime also other mechanisms are possible. We will sketch two: (i) In the fixed exchange rate regime a positive investment response is required for the current account balance to improve over time. As already discussed, if the current account balance fails to improve the government may be forced to reinstate the trade controls. Hence, expectations about failure may prove self-fulfilling because the lack of investment response itself generates a prolonged trade deficit leading to the abandonment of reform. (ii) Another mechanism arises in the fixed current account regime, where a substantial depreciation was required following trade reform. Given positive investment response the exchange rate appreciates over time. Without investment response, however, the exchange rate will remain at its highly depreciated level. A depreciation is, as already pointed out, in effect a reduction of the unskilled workers' real wage. These workers' patience may be limited and given a weak investment response the real wage will remain depressed. This may eventually generate political pressure sufficient to force the government to abort the programme. Again, the lack of investment response, due to low credibility, may itself generate the cancellation of reform.

7 Concluding remarks

By 1997 GDP per capita in Zimbabwe was 10 per cent below the level before ESAP. The expected favorable effect of liberalization on living standards is yet to be seen. The short-run contractionary effects of liberalization have been larger and longer lasting than many expected. The consequences for both industrial structure and macroeconomic balance should worry observers.

Trade liberalization is meant to improve the efficiency of the economy by having imports substitute domestic import-competing industries and by stimulating exports. The reduction of import-competing activities is typically faster than the rise of new export activities, and short-run output contraction and unemployment are to be expected. In Zimbabwe this output contraction is associated with deindustrialization, which may be particularly strong because of the historical background. The international sanctions during the UDI period led to a broad manufacturing base, but also to the development of more inward-looking industries than in most countries. The import rationing of intermediates using quotas implied a static manufacturing production sector.

Increased investments with liberalization involves little output expansion, but a relatively strong weakening of the external position. The reason is high import content in investments, which would have increased further with investment expansion because of substitution towards foreign goods. A real exchange rate appreciation, reducing competitiveness, would also have contributed to a larger trade deficit. Had the liberalization succeeded in raising investments more than it actually did, the need to correct economic imbalances would have been even greater.

Trade liberalization increases the profitability of the export sector. To the extent that investments are stimulated, the result is increased exports and growth. Hence, the potential gains from trade liberalization materialize only over time, because the exploitation of the new opportunities requires capital accumulation. A positive investment response is crucial in order for this to happen. If investors have doubts about the credibility of reform, the investment response will be weak and the negative short-run effects will prevail. Therefore, trade liberalization needs to appear credible in order to be successful.

The credibility of reform can be undermined for a variety of reasons. The trade liberalization may by default be incompatible with other economic constraints (for example, foreign financing constraints). Furthermore, the low credibility of trade reform may also be a result of self-fulfilling expectations. Several possible self-fulfilling mechanisms are explored in the analysis. One example is the case where reform is abandoned if it fails over time to generate improvements in the current account balance. If reform is considered not credible, the level of investments will be low, there will be no export growth and the reform will be cancelled.

In the present analysis the self-fulfilling mechanisms resulted from the linkage between expectations, investments and export performance. However, as several authors have pointed out (for example, Collier and Gunning, 1992 and van Wijnbergen, 1992), a temporary trade liberalization generates a scope for the speculative hoarding of the temporarily cheap imports. Such hoarding worsens the current account balance and may indeed make the trade liberalization a temporary event. Import hoarding has an additional negative impact if the accumulation of import stocks crowd out fixed capital formation. These and other mechanisms, left out of the present analysis, should be considered in a more thorough description of trade reform.

References

Bates, R.H. and P. Collier (1995) 'The politics and economics of policy reform in Zambia', *Journal of African Economies*, vol. 4, no. 1, pp. 115–43.

Benjamin, N. (1992) 'What happens to investment under structural adjustment: results from a simulation model', *World Development*, vol. 20, no. 9, pp. 1335–44.

Bevan, D., P. Collier and J.W. Gunning (1990) *Controlled Open Economies: a Neoclassical Approach to Structuralism*. Oxford: Clarendon Press.

Buffie, E. (1984) 'The macroeconomics of trade liberalization', *Journal of Development Economics*, vol. 17, pp. 121–37.

Chhibber, A., J. Cottani, R. Firuzabadi and M. Walton (1989) 'Inflation, price controls, and fiscal adjustment in Zimbabwe', Working Paper 192, Country Economics Department, The World Bank.

Collier, P. (1992) 'Trade , Price and Financial Reforms in the transition from African socialism', mimeo, Oxford University.

Collier, P. and J.W. Gunning (1992) 'Aid and exchange rate adjustment in African trade liberalisations', *Economic Journal*, vol. 102, pp. 925–39.

Collier, P. and J.W. Gunning (1996) 'Trade liberalisation and the composition of investment: theory and African application', Working Paper 96:4, CSAE, Oxford University.

Condon, T., S. Robinson and S. Urata (1985) 'Coping with a foreign exchange crisis: a general equilibrium model of alternative adjustment mechanism', in A. Manne (ed.), *Economic Equilibrium: Model Formulation and Solution*. Amsterdam: North-Holland.

Cripps, F. and W. Godley (1978) 'Control of imports as a means to full employment and the expansion of world trade: the UK's case', *Cambridge Journal of Economics*, vol. 2, pp. 327–34.

Dailami, M. and M. Walton (1989) 'Private investment, government policy, and foreign capital in Zimbabwe', Working Paper 248, Country Economics Department, The World Bank.

Davies, R. (1991) 'Trade, trade management and development in Zimbabwe', in J. Frimpong-Ansah, S.M.R. Kanbur and P. Svedberg (eds), *Trade and Development in Sub-Saharan Africa*. Manchester: Manchester University Press.

Davies, R., J. Rattsø and R. Torvik (1994) 'The macroeconomics of Zimbabwe in the 1980s: a CGE-model analysis', *Journal of African Economies*, vol. 3, no. 2, pp. 1–46.

Davies, R., J. Rattsø and R. Torvik (1998) 'Short run consequences of trade liberalization: a CGE model of Zimbabwe', *Journal of Policy Modeling*, vol. 20, pp. 305–33.

de Melo, J. and S. Robinson (1989) 'Product differentiation and the treatment of foreign trade in computable general equilibrium models of small economies', *Journal of International Economics*, vol. 27, pp. 47–67.

Devarajan, S., J.D. Lewis and S. Robinson (1991) 'External shocks, purchasing power parity, and the equilibrium real exchange rate', Working Paper No. 611, Department of Agricultural and Resource Economics, University of California at Berkeley.

Dixit, A. (1989) 'Intersectoral capital reallocation under price uncertainty', *Journal of International Economics*, vol. 26, pp. 309–25.

Dornbusch, R. (1990) 'Policies to move from stabilization to growth', World Bank Conference on Development Economics, Proceedings 1990, pp. 19–48.

Gibson, B. (1985) 'A structuralist macromodel for post-revolutionary Nicaragua', *Cambridge Journal of Economics*, vol. 9, pp. 347–69.

Government of Zimbabwe (1991) *Zimbabwe: a Framework for Economic Reform 1991–95*. Harare: Government Printer.

Grais, W., J. de Melo and S. Urata (1986) 'A general equilibrium estimation of the effects of reductions in tariffs and quantitative restrictions in Turkey in 1978', in T.N. Srinivasan and J. Whalley (eds), *General Equilibrium Trade Policy Modeling*. Cambridge, MA: MIT Press.

Green, R. and X. Kadhani (1986) 'Zimbabwe: transition to economic crises 1981–1983. Retrospect and prospect', *World Development*, vol. 14, no. 8, pp. 1059–83.

Gunning, J.W. (1996) 'The trade policy review of Zimbabwe', *World Economy*, pp. 157–66.

Jenkins, C. (1998) 'Determinants of private investments in Zimbabwe', *Journal of African Economies*, vol. 7, no. 1, pp. 34–61.

Keynes, J.M. (1936) *The General Theory of Employment, Interest and Money*. London: Macmillan.

Krugman, P. and L. Taylor (1978) 'Contractionary effects of devaluation', *Journal of International Economics*, vol. 8, no. 3, August, pp. 445–56.

Mehlum, H. and J. Rattsø (1995) 'Import compression and growth constraints in Zimbabwe', mimeo, Department of Economics, University of Trondheim.

Mehlum, H. (1999) 'The political economy of failing reforms', PhD thesis, Department of Economics, University of Oslo.

Morande, F. and Schmidt-Hebbel, K. (1991) 'Macroeconomics of public sector deficits: The case of Zimbabwe', Working Paper 688, Country Economics Department, The World Bank.

Neary, J.P. and K.W.S. Roberts (1980) 'The theory of household behavior under rationing', *European Economic Review*, vol. 13, pp. 25–42.

Ocampo, J.A. (1987) 'The macroeconomic effect of import controls: a Keynesian analysis', *Journal of Development Economics*, vol. 27, pp. 285–305

Pakkiri, L. and Moyo, N.P. (1986) 'Foreign exchange policies: the case of Zimbabwe', paper presented at IDRC Workshop on Economic Structure and Macroeconomic Management, Harare.

Rattsø, J. (1994a) 'Medium run adjustment under import compression: Macroeconomic analysis relevant for Sub-Saharan Africa', *Journal of Development Economics*, vol. 45, pp. 35–54.

Rattsø, J. (1994b) 'Devaluation and monetary policy with import compression', *Open Economies Review*, vol. 5, pp. 159–75.

Rattsø, J. and R. Torvik (1998a) 'Zimbabwean trade liberalization: *ex post* evaluation', *Cambridge Journal of Economics*, vol. 22, pp. 325–46.

Rattsø, J. and R. Torvik (1998b) 'Dynamic interactions between agriculture and industry: theoretical analysis of the consequences of discriminating agriculture in sub-Saharan Africa', mimeo, Department of Economics, Norwegian University of Science and Technology.

Robinson, J.V. (1962) *Essays in the Theory of Economic Growth*. London: Macmillan.

Rodrik, D. (1991) 'Policy uncertainty and private investment in developing countries', *Journal of Development Economics*, vol. 36, pp. 229–42.

Rodrik, D. (1992) 'The limits of trade policy reform in developing countries', *Journal of Economic Perspectives*, vol. 6, no. 1, pp. 87–105.

Rosensweig, A. and L. Taylor (1990) 'Devaluation, capital flows, and crowding-out: a CGE Model with portfolio choice for Thailand', in Lance Taylor (ed.), *Socially Relevant Policy Analysis*. Boston, MA: MIT Press.

Sen, A. (1967) 'Isolation, assurance and the social rate of discount', *Quarterly Journal of Economics*, vol. 80, pp. 112–24.

Serven, L. and A. Solimano (eds) (1993) *Striving for Growth after Adjustment: the Role of Capital Formation*. Washington DC: World Bank.

Skålnes, T. (1995) *The Politics of Economic Reform in Zimbabwe*. London: Macmillan – now Palgrave.

Taylor, Lance (1991) *Income Distribution, Inflation and Growth: Lectures on Structuralist Macroeconomic Theory*. Cambridge, MA and London: MIT Press.

Taylor, Lance (1983) *Structuralist Macroeconomics*. New York: Basic Books.

Torvik, R. (1994) 'Trade policy under a binding foreign exchange constraint', *Journal of International Trade and Economic Development*, vol. 3, pp. 15–31.

Torvik, R. (1997a) 'Real exchange rate dynamics and trade liberalization: the case of multiple tariffs and unemployment', *Journal of International Trade and Economic Development*, vol. 6, pp. 329–44.

Torvik, R. (1997b) 'Agricultural supply led industrialization: a macromodel with Sub-Saharan Africa characteristics', *Structural Change and Economic Dynamics*, vol. 8, pp. 351–70.

van Wijnbergen, S. (1992) 'Intertemporal speculation, shortages and the political economy of price reform', *The Economic Journal*, vol. 102, pp. 1395–1406.

Williamson, J. (ed.) (1994) *The Political Economy of Policy Reform*. Washington DC: Institute for International Economics.

11

The Income Distribution Effects of Trade Liberalization: A Computable General Equilibrium Analysis[1]

Margaret Chitiga-Mabugu

1 Introduction

The liberalization of foreign trade, removal of import licensing, quantitative restrictions on imports, foreign exchange allocation and currency controls were major components of the economic structural adjustment programs implemented in Zimbabwe in the 1990s. An important issue for policy makers in Zimbabwe was how these adjustment reforms would affect the incomes of various economic and social groups, especially during the transition period. Indeed, the question of whether those already in poverty would be more adversely affected was, and continues to be, addressed by many. Thus, the identification of those groups most likely to be adversely affected becomes an important item on the research agenda. The design and implementation of appropriate policy interventions to protect the most vulnerable groups from any possible short-run negative effects of trade liberalization are issues relevant to policy making.

This chapter addresses these issues with the aid of a computable general equilibrium (CGE) model for Zimbabwe. The focus of this chapter is on a number of counterfactual experiments to draw out the implications of trade liberalization on aggregate output and the incomes of selected social groups. The aim of the CGE experiments is to identify those groups that would have been most adversely affected by the move from a controlled to a liberalized economy. Suitable policy interventions are suggested. The chapter is organized as follows: Section 2 outlines the structure of the CGE model used, and, in particular, the changes made to the initially controlled trade regime so as to reflect the liberalized trade environment. Section 3 reports on the simulated results of the experiments and the predictions generated by the liberalization of the foreign trade. Section 4 concludes with a summary and some policy suggestions.

2 The model

The model used is based on Chitiga (1996), which is a modified version of the Davies et al. (1994b) model. The base model captures the main features of a controlled economy, prior to reform. Trade is not yet liberalized and the economy is characterized by foreign currency shortages. Thus, foreign exchange rationing rules are explicitly modeled. Other constraints are the shortage of skilled labor and the inflexibility of unskilled wages. The base-year run is 1985, with all the controls still in place. The economy is then transformed into a liberalized one by removing the foreign currency rationing rules (Davies et al. (1994b)). The relaxation of these rationing rules produces the simulated results of liberalizing the model. Thus, the way we move from a foreign-currency-controlled economy to a liberalized one can itself be best thought of as a counterfactual experiment in this chapter. The experiments discussed below, in which the economy undergoes a full trade liberalization in non-competitive consumer goods, food and imported intermediate inputs, are compared against the base run in order to determine the impact of the reforms on output and incomes of various social groups.

The Davies et al. (1994b) model consists of five sectors – food agriculture, services, construction, importables and exportables. It has four income groups: skilled and unskilled workers, small-scale farmers and profit earners. Production in the sectors is a mixture of multilevel CES and Leontief functions. In the food agriculture sector, output is given by capacity and is produced by labor only. In the other sectors, output is produced by labor, capital and domestic and imported inputs. In the services sector a flexible price clears the market.

Several modifications to the Davies et al. model allow us to analyze the issues addressed in this chapter. In the version of the model we used, the economy is disaggregated into seven sectors and seven income groups as follows:

Sector 1: Commercial food agriculture.
Sector 2: Communal food agriculture.
Sector 3: Nontradable consumer goods (services, electricity, and transport).
Sector 4: Nontradable capital goods (construction).
Sector 5: Importables (all manufacturing not included in sector six (67.5 per cent)).
Sector 6: Exportables (mining, and parts of manufacturing (32.5 per cent)).
Sector 7: Agricultural exports (agro-exports).

Output in sectors 1 and 2 is fixed and prices are subject to government control, via the stock adjustment mechanism. Output adjustment in the services sector is demand-determined. The construction and importables sectors adjust through both demand and supply. The imported inputs for construction and importables are rationed, implying that their supply side is constrained by the amount of imports available. In the export sectors adjustment is through the export of residual output. These two export sectors are not rationed – they use whatever foreign inputs they require.

The disaggregation of income groups is carried out according to functional categories as follows:

1 Small-scale commercial farmers (SSCF).
2 Communal farmers.
3 Agricultural wage workers.
4 Unskilled wage workers in industry and mining.
5 Skilled wage workers.
6 Industrial profit earners.
7 Large-scale commercial farmers (LSCF).

These functional income groups were selected on the basis of their sources of income as well as the need to separate urban from rural incomes. Thus, groups 1, 2, 3 and 7 are rural while groups 4, 5 and 6 are urban. We further re-aggregated these functional income groups into two: low-income and high-income groups. The low-income groups are groups 1, 2, 3 and 4, while the high-income groups are 5, 6 and 7. The two groups are assumed to have different savings and consumption patterns. The low-income group saves less and spends proportionately more on food than does the high-income group. The latter in turn consume more non-competitive consumer imports than the former. Intra-group differences in incomes and performance, especially in the communal areas, are not captured because of aggregation. Lack of reliable data and the need to keep the model manageable prevented further disaggregation.

The model equations and variable definitions are presented in Appendix A at the end of this chapter. This is a short-run model of the real side of the Zimbabwean economy. Production of food is given by capacity in the short run and prices are regulated by the government. The market clears through stock adjustment and food imports as shown in equations 1 and 2. In sector 3, services are characterized by excess capacity. Both skilled and unskilled labor, capital and domestic intermediates are used for production in this sector. The price is specified as a fixed mark-up over costs, as shown in equation 3.

In the rest of the sectors, output is produced on a multilevel basis. Thus, at the first level, output is a Leontief combination of value added and intermediate inputs as in equation 4. Value added is a CES combination of labor and fixed capital (equation 4). Labor is itself combined by a CES function as skilled and unskilled labor. Intermediate inputs are a CES combination of domestic and imported inputs, as in equation 5. Exportable sectors are governed by world prices adjusted by the exchange rate (equation 6). In the remaining sectors, prices are equated to marginal costs as in equation 7.

The aggregate income groups, as described above, that is, the low- and the high-income groups, form the two consuming groups. Consumption demand for each group is modeled as a linear expenditure system (LES) with different propensities to consume for each different income distribution group, as shown in equations 8 and 9. It is assumed that the low-income group have relatively low propensities to save and high propensities to consume compared to the high-income groups.

Public sector revenue from both direct and indirect taxes is described by equation 10 while expenditure is on goods, services and wages. Investment is exogenously determined and savings adjust to meet the investment requirements. As foreign savings are assumed to be exogenous, it is domestic public and private savings that must adjust. Equation 12 is a consistency check for the full model. It equates savings to investment and it balances the whole model.

The modifications to the above model necessary to perform a counterfactual experiment on the base year are now discussed. The foreign currency rationing rules that characterize the basic model are removed. The current account is endogenized, with the nominal exchange rate remaining fixed as before. All foreign currency needs for inputs, food and consumer goods can be satisfied by an increased current account deficit. The demand for intermediate inputs for construction and importables, the previously rationed sectors, are now determined in the same way as for exportables and agro-exports. The marginal cost of the aggregate input is an aggregate of the domestic and imported inputs prices. Non-competitive consumer imports are determined by demand, unlike in the basic model, in which rationing rules determined the availability of imports.

Food imports and exports now balance the food market. The price of food is flexible and responsive to food imports. A target on food consumption is stipulated by policy in the model and is satisfied by food imports. This ensures that food prices can, to some extent, still be influenced by policy makers. In this liberalized case, food stocks are now exogenous and therefore are not controlled by the government.

Importables are formulated as a composite of domestically produced and imported goods. They imperfectly substitute each other in a CES function. Several assumptions about how much consumers shift from domestic to imported goods and how much savings fall due to a liberalization are important in determining the demand responses of the model. On the supply side, assumptions about how much the previous rationing rules affected firms, performance are also important. Thus, we end up with a model whose base run is now a counterfactual – that is, a trade liberalization implemented on the base year, 1985. We can thus compare the before (controlled) and after (liberalized) output and incomes of the various groups in order to determine the short-run effects of trade liberalization.

It is important to understand the changes that occur when the economy is liberalized. The interaction of supply and demand forces are now at work. On the supply side, there is now unlimited availability of imported inputs for the previously rationed sectors – that is, importables and construction. Instead of the previously inefficient mix of resource use in the controlled regime, costs of production decline and supply expands. Firms can now use optimal combinations of foreign and domestic inputs. Previously under-utilized capacity can also now be used. The sectors most likely to show positive response to imported input availability are those which previously experienced rationing.

Liberalization makes previously scarce non-competitive consumer goods more widely available in the economy. Before, there was forced saving due to the lack of imported consumer goods. People saved in the hope that these goods would be available in the future (Chhibber et al. (1989) and Torvik (1994a)). Thus, on the demand side, there are two opposing effects at work. First, savings fall and demand increases since people can now consume more than in the previously rationed economy. Second, demand switches from domestic goods to foreign goods, which consumers had been denied for a long time. The net demand effect of these two effects could be either an increase in demand for domestic goods (if the second effect is weak) or a fall in demand for domestic goods output (if the second effect is strong). If both supply and demand expand, then the net effect of a liberalization is an increase in output. However, if demand contraction is stronger than the supply increase, the net effect of liberalization is a fall in domestic output. These output effects, in turn, affect the distribution of income in the economy.

3 The results

3.1 Trade liberalization with no devaluation

The first set of results, reported in Table 11.1, represent a full trade liberalization with no devaluation. Full trade liberalization with no devaluation produces a recession – as aggregate output falls by 1.1 per cent.[2] Although output supply should increase as a result of increased foreign currency availability, in the short run, this is counteracted by demand-reducing factors – leading to a recession. The fact that imported intermediates are now more freely available fails to produce a supply response of sufficient magnitude partly because the previous inputs rationing was not strictly binding in the sectors concerned. On the demand side, consumption shifts towards imported goods. This shift in domestic consumption towards imported goods is sufficiently large that it cannot be met from previously 'forced' savings. Thus, consumption of domestic goods has to fall to compensate for the increase in demand for imported goods. This leads to reduced output, especially in the tradable import-competing sectors, which is exacerbated further by increases in relative prices of nontradables. Thus, the reduction in domestic demand

Table 11.1 The income distribution effects of trade liberalization with no devaluation

Variable	*% change*	
	Change	*Real*
Communal farmer income	−4.5	−2.7
SSCF income	−4.5	−2.7
Agric. workers' income	1.1	2.9
Unskilled income	−2.5	−0.7
Skilled income	−3.8	−1.6
LSCF income	1.3	3.5
Profit income	−2.7	−0.5
	Change	*Real*
Total profit income*	−2.4	−0.2
Total low income	−3.0	−1.2
Total urban income**	−2.8	−1.0
GDP	−1.1	
Budget deficit	32.1	
Low-income CPI	*−1.8*	
High-income CPI	*−2.2*	

Notes: *Total profit income consists of industrial profit income and large-scale commercial farmers' income.
**Total urban income includes skilled and unskilled incomes.

dominates and, as a result, domestic prices fall, reducing the production costs of agro-exports and other exportables. This increases export profitability, as reflected in the rise in incomes and wages in the large-scale commercial farming sector (LSCF) of 1.3 per cent and 1.1 per cent respectively. However, this is not enough to cause an overall output increase – GDP falls by 1.1 per cent. Apart from the demand-reducing substitution effects just discussed, the fall in output leads to reduced incomes and a further fall in demand. Services and construction suffer the most from this effect.

The consumer price indexes (CPIs) for both the low-income and high-income groups fall, by 1.8 per cent and 2.2 per cent respectively. This result is due to the fall in domestic demand, which partially mitigates the decline in real incomes, but not by a substantial magnitude because the change in real incomes for most groups remains negative.

The reduction in output leads to reduced demand for labor and for other production inputs. Employment and wages of both skilled and unskilled labor fall, which partly explains the reduction in services demand. Food prices fall due to reduced demand. Thus incomes of communal farmers and small-scale commercial farmers (SSCF) also fall. Profit earners' incomes also decline due largely to the fall in industrial profits. The abnormal profits that were possible in the protected regime are no longer available in the liberalized and competitive environment.

Income distribution and inequality between the two aggregate income groups has worsened. Table 11.1 shows that, on aggregate, the low-income group suffers the largest reduction in incomes, compared to the base case, while profit earners suffer the least. Further, urban incomes as a group fall, implying increased poverty in the urban areas – at least in the short run. Thus, the model predicts that all income groups suffer a decline in incomes, with the incidence being greatest among the poorer groups.[4]

The current account deficit increases in this initial step of liberalization from 2 per cent to 8.4 per cent of GDP in order to accommodate the import requirements of the economy. Such a policy is hardly sustainable in the long term. A devaluation would have to be implemented in such a case. The high current account deficit is a result of increased imports and the contraction of the domestic economy. Even though there is an increase in exports, this is not sufficient to offset the current account deficit increasing the effects of the former. One reason for these rather gloomy predictions is that there was no devaluation in this experiment to accompany trade liberalization. It is possible to check by how much the exchange rate should be devalued in order to reduce the current account deficit. Zimbabwe devalued by 67 per cent in nominal terms during the second half of 1991.

3.2 Trade liberalization with a devaluation

In the next experiment, we simulate such a devaluation to see by how much the current account deficit, output and incomes would change. The results are reported in Table 11.2. The output effects of a trade liberalization with a devaluation is expansionary – GDP increases by 5.1 per cent. The devaluation raises the relative prices of tradables and stimulates, especially, a favorable export response. Thus, most of the output growth is contributed by export sectors, with a lesser input from the importables sector. Incomes increase substantially compared to the 'No devaluation' case. The devaluation, however, is associated with inflation and higher CPIs of 26.5 per cent and 27.5 per cent for the low- and high-income groups respectively. All income groups except unskilled workers experience an increase in real incomes. The reason for this brighter picture is that a real depreciation is achieved. The exchange rate depreciates by more than the percentage increase in the consumer price index. However, the high-income group gains, on aggregate, relative to the low-income group, which suffers a real income decline of 5.6 per cent. This result is similar to what was also found in the case of trade liberalization with no devaluation.

The current account deficit is reduced by 3.6 per cent (from 8.4 to 4.8 per cent of GDP). The budget deficit also improves, falling by 40.6 per cent, due to the growth in the economy. This analysis shows that, in the short run, trade liberalization reduces incomes of most groups in the economy. The low-income groups are those worst hit by the reforms.

Table 11.2 The income distribution effects of trade liberalization: with devaluation

Variable	*% change*	
	Change	*Real*
Communal farmer income	33.1	6.6
SSCF income	33.6	6.1
Agricultural workers' income	27.4	0.9
Unskilled income	15.5	–11.0
Skilled income	35.4	7.9
LSCF income	32.6	5.1
Profit income	32.2	4.7
	Change	*Real*
Total low-income	20.9	–5.6
Total high-income	33.3	5.8
GDP	5.1	
Budget deficit	–40.6	
Current account deficit	–38.6	
Low-income CPI	*26.5*	
High-income CPI	*27.5*	

4 Summary, conclusions and policy lessons

This chapter used a liberalized CGE model in which there are no foreign currency controls. An initial experiment of liberalizing the model by removing the foreign currency constraints to the construction and importables sectors is performed. At the same time, food and non-competitive imports are liberalized by removing the foreign exchange rationing rules. The current account is endogenized and balances the import needs of the economy. The effects of the total liberalization are a fall in the output and the incomes of the non-exporting sectors and groups. This is because of a consumption shift towards the previously scarce imports, thereby reducing demand for domestic goods. This shift reduces prices and benefits the exporting sectors. The removal of protection to some sectors increases competition, which leads to efficiency. Profit earners no longer enjoy the abnormal profits afforded to them in the previous regime.

In general, the predictive powers of the model are very satisfactory. Similar results that ESAP has adverse effects on the poor were also obtained by Davies et al. (1994). The results of our CGE experiments suggest that the short-run effects of trade liberalization are negative for the poor, communal farmers and wage earners. Although an accompanying devaluation would improve incomes, the low-income groups benefit relatively less than the high income groups.

Profit earners, particularly those in exportables, make the greatest gains. This result is consistent with the realized actual outcomes since the onset of the reforms – the share of wages in total GDP has fallen while profit shares have risen since the onset of ESAP. While in the period 1980–84 wages were 56.7 per cent of GDP and gross profits were 41.6 per cent of GDP, in the period 1990–96, wages were only 45 per cent of GDP and gross profits made up 54.8 per cent of GDP. The Poverty Assessment Survey Study (1995) conducted by the Ministry of Manpower, Labour and Social Welfare (MPLSW) shows that output contraction, unemployment and low wages accounted for increases in poverty among 33 per cent of very poor households and 47 per cent of the poor households (MPSLSW, 1996; Marquette, 1997). Our model results predict a loss of jobs and a fall in wages in some sectors due to the trade liberalization. Although our results suggest that a concurrent devaluation would have cushioned the poor from some of the adverse effects, this does not seem to have been the case after the devaluations of the early 1990s. The most probable reason for this discrepancy between our results and actual outcomes is that many other factors, not explicitly modeled in our study, were at play. For example, there were massive retrenchments of labor as well as other exogenous factors like the 1992 and 1995 droughts. These may have counteracted the potentially positive effects of the devaluations making it difficult to isolate their effects.

Although at the time of writing, the ZIMPREST program had not taken root or had much effect, one is tempted to conclude that it will have the same sorts of effects, since it involves many of the policies of its predecessor, ESAP. Thus, in the short run, trade liberalization has negative effects on the poorest and most vulnerable groups. Recognition of this result is important for government initiatives to mitigate the effects of these reforms and cushion the poor and selected vulnerable groups. There is scope for government intervention to achieve this goal. Some of these have been discussed in Chitiga (1996). Among them is boosting the poor's incomes through direct budgetary transfers. Government could raise the necessary resources to do this by reducing its expenditure in other areas, by taxing the rich, by increasing the general level of taxes for everybody or by simply printing more money. However, these measures are not without their costs. Results from Chitiga (1996) show that each of these methods has high costs to the government or to society. It appears that the policy of transferring income from profit earners to the poor has the most positive gains for the poor while that of increasing the budget deficit has the second-best results. However, even these two policies are problematic. Too much taxation on profit could lead to disincentives to invest while a high budget deficit has the well-known effect of increasing inflation – which in turn impacts upon the poor. Chitiga (1996) also shows that targeted transfers are better than universal transfers in terms of cost and gains to the poor groups. These lessons may well be of cautionary value to government in the light of persistent calls from several domestic quarters for generalized subsidies on food.

Notes

1. This chapter draws on my PhD thesis submitted at Gothenburg University. I would like to thank Professor Bigsten, Professor Rattsø, Dr R. Mabugu, Dr R. Torvik, Dr H. Mehlum, Professor Davies, and colleagues at Gothenburg University for extensive and valuable comments. Any errors remain my responsibility.
2. Torvik (1994b) discusses the effects on output of changes in several parameter values and finds that results hold for a wide range of realistic parameter values.
3. Since total urban income includes one class in the low-income group and another in the high-income group, the two CPIs are averaged to calculate the real income change of the two groups taken together.
4. The low-income, or poor, group consists of communal farmers, small-scale commercial farmers, agricultural workers, and unskilled workers. The high-income, or rich, group consists of skilled workers, large-scale commercial farmers and profit earners.
5. This is a short version of the full model, which is available on request from the author. This version serves to give an idea of the type of model used and some of the driving forces behind the results.

References

Adelman, I. and S. Robinson (1978) *Income Distribution Policy in Developing Countries: a Case Study of Korea*. Stanford, CA: Stanford University Press for the World Bank.

Bourguignon, F., W.H. Branson, and de Melo (1988) *Macroeconomic Adjustment and Income Distribution: a Macro–Micro Simulation Model*. Washington: World Bank.

Brown, C., G. Gilroy and A. Kohen (1982) 'The effect of the minimum wage on employment and unemployment,' *Journal of Economic Literature*, vol. xx, no. 2, pp. 487–528.

Chhibber, A., J. Cottani, R. Firuzabani and M. Walton (1989) 'Inflation, price controls and fiscal adjustment in Zimbabwe,' Working Paper 192, Country Economics Department, World Bank.

Chitiga M. (1996) 'Distribution policy under trade liberalisation in Zimbabwe: a Computable General Equilibrium Analysis'. PhD thesis, Gothenburg University.

Collier, P. and J.W. Gunning (1992) 'Aid and exchange rate adjustment in African trade liberalizations,' *Economic Journal*, vol. 102.

Davies, R. and J. Rattsø (1993) 'Zimbabwe: from liberation to liberalisation,' in L. Taylor (ed.), *The Rocky Road to Reform: Adjustment, Income Distribution and Growth in the Developing World*. Cambridge, MA: MIT Press.

Davies, R. and J. Rattsø (1994a) 'Distribution, stabilisation and growth: some issues for Zimbabwe.' WIDER project on sustainable development.

Davies, R., J. Rattsø and R. Torvik (1994b) 'The Macroeconomics of Zimbabwe in the 1980's: a CGE-model analysis,' *Journal of African Economies*, vol. 3, no. 2, pp. 154–98.

Davies, R., J. Rattsø and R. Torvik (1994c) 'Short-run consequences of trade liberalization in Zimbabwe: a CGE-Model analysis,' mimeo, Department of Economics, University of Trondheim.

Elbadawi, I.A. and K. Schmidt-Hebbel (1991) 'Macroeconomic structure and policy in Zimbabwe.' Working Paper 771, Country Economics Department, World Bank.

Government of Zimbabwe (1981) *Growth with Equity*. Harare: Government Printers.

Government of Zimbabwe (1989) *The Promotion of Economic Development and Equity in Zimbabwe*. Harare: Government Printers.
Government of Zimbabwe (1991) *Policy Reform Document*. Harare: Government Printers.
Government of Zimbabwe (1993) *Poverty Alleviation Plan*. Harare: Government Printers.
Loo, T and E. Tower (1990) 'Agricultural liberalisation, welfare, revenue and nutrition in the developing countries,' in I. Goldin and O. Knudsen (eds), *Agricultural Trade Liberalisation: Implications for Developing Countries*. Paris: OECD.
Marquette, C.M. (1997) 'Current poverty, structural adjustment and drought in Zimbabwe,' *World Development*, vol. 25, no. 7, pp. 1141–9.
Mehlum, H. and J. Rattsø (1993) 'Import compression and growth constraints in Zimbabwe,' mimeo, Department of Economics, University of Trondheim.
MPSLSW (1996) *1995 Poverty Assessment Study Survey: Preliminary Report*. Harare: MPSLSW.
Pakkiri, L. and N.P. Moyo (1986) 'Foreign exchange policies: the case of Zimbabwe,' Paper presented at the IDRC Workshop on Economic Structure and Macroeconomic Management, Harare.
Rattsø, J. (1990) 'Conflicting claims and dynamic inflationary mechanisms in India', in L. Taylor (ed.), *Socially Relevant Policy Analysis: Structuralist Computable General Equilibrium Models for the Developing World*. Cambridge, MA: MIT Press.
Rattsø, J. and R. Torvik (1992) 'An applied General Equilibrium Model for Zimbabwe – Documentation of Model, Social Accounting Matrix 1985 and Calibration,' mimeo, Department of Economics, University of Oslo and Trondheim.
Rattsø, J. and R. Torvik (1995) 'The Zimbabwean trade liberalization: ex post evaluation,' mimeo, Department of Economics, University of Oslo and Trondheim.
Taylor, L. (1979) *Macro Models for Developing Countries*. New York: McGraw Hill.
Taylor, L. (ed.) (1990) *Socially Relevant Policy Analysis: Structuralist Computable General Equilibrium Models for the Developing World*. Cambridge, MA: MIT Press.
Thorbecke, E. and D. Berrian (1992) 'Budgetary rules to minimize societal poverty in a general equilibrium context,' *Journal of Development Economics*, vol. 39, pp. 189–205.
Torvik, R. (1994a) 'Trade policy under a binding foreign exchange, constraint,' *Journal of International Trade and Economic Development*, vol. 3, pp. 15–31.
Torvik, R. (1994b) 'The macroeconomics of foreign exchange shortages: a study with reference to Zimbabwe', PhD Thesis, Department of Economics, University of Oslo.
World Bank (1991) *World Development Report 1990: Poverty*. Washington DC: World Bank.

Appendix A: Summary of the CGE model equations and variable definitions[5]

Equations

$$X_i + XB_i \quad i = 1, 2 \tag{12.1}$$

$$DS_i = ad_i + hh_i(p_i/pG_i) \quad i = 1, 2 \tag{12.2}$$

$$P_3 = (1 + t_3)\,(1 + t_3)/\{1 - (1 + t_3)(1 + t_3)a_{33}\}[Sa_{i3}P_i + q_3b_3] \quad (i = 1, 2, 3, 4, 5, 6, 7) \tag{12.3}$$

$$X_i = 1/(1 - n_i)\,[m_{1i}L_i^{-(1-h_i)/h_i} + m_{2i}K_i^{-(1-h_i)/h_i}]^{-h_i/(1-h_i)} \quad (i = 4, 5, 6, 7) \tag{12.4}$$

$$N_i = [e_{1i}.II_i^{-(1-d_i)/d_i} + e_{2i}DI_i^{-(1-d_i)/d_i}]^{-d_i/(1-d_i)} \quad (i = 4, 5) \tag{12.5}$$

$$P_i = eP_i^* \quad (i = 6, 7) \tag{12.6}$$

$$P_i = MC_i \quad (i = 4, 5, 6, 7) \tag{12.7}$$

$$C_i^{Low} = Q_i^{\mathrm{Low}} + m_i^{\mathrm{Low}}/Pi(D_i^{\mathrm{Low}} - DB_i^{\mathrm{Low}}) \tag{12.8}$$

$$C_i^{\mathrm{High}} = Q_i^{\mathrm{High}} + m_i^{\mathrm{High}}/Pi(D_i^{\mathrm{High}} - DB_i^{\mathrm{High}} \tag{12.9}$$

$$\mathrm{GREV} = t_l Y_l + t_u Y_u + t_{\mathrm{SK}} Y_{\mathrm{SK}} + T^{\mathrm{IND}} \tag{12.10}$$

$$T^{\mathrm{ind}} = S\,(\text{from i} = 1 \text{ to } 7)\ t_i/(1 + t_i)P_i X_i \tag{12.11}$$

$$\begin{aligned} P_4 J_4 + P_5 J_5 + P_0 J_0 + S\,(\text{from } i = 1 \text{ to } 7)\ P_i DS_i \\ = s_c Y_c + s_R Y_R + s_{aw} Y_{aw} + s_u Y_u + s_a Y_a + s_{sk} Y_{sk} \\ + s_l(1 + t_1) Y_1 + \mathrm{GREV} - \mathrm{GEXP} + \mathrm{DEF} \end{aligned} \tag{12.12}$$

where the variables are as defined below

Exogenous variables

DEF	trade deficit
e	exchange rate
K_i	capital $i = 4$–6
P_i^*	foreign price of sectoral goods, $i = f, 5, 6$
XB_i	output level sector 1 and 2
P_i^G	target price of government for food (i = 1, 2)

Endogenous variables

C_i^{High}	consumption level for high-income groups i =1–7
C_i^{Low}	consumption level for low-income groups i =1–7
D_{High}	consumer spending by high-income groups
D_{Low}	consumer spending by low-income groups
DB_{High}	spending for floor consumption by high-income groups
DB_{Low}	spending for floor consumption by low-income groups
DI_{i}	domestic intermediate goods aggregate sectors i = 4–7
DS_{i}	change in stocks for sector i = 1, 2
GEXP	government expenditure
GREV	government revenue
II_i	intermediate imports sectors $i = 4$–7
MC_i	marginal cost sectors $i = 4$–6
N_i	intermediate goods aggregate to sectors i = 4–7
P_i	sectoral price levels i = 1–7
X_i	sectoral output levels i = 1–7

Y_c	communal farmers' income
Y_R	resettled farmers' income
Y_{aw}	wage income for agricultural workers
Y_u	wage income for unskilled workers
Y_a	commercial farmers' income
Y_s	wage income for skilled workers
Y_l	industrial profit income

Parameters

ad_i	constant in stock adjustment function, $i = 1, 2$
hh_i	food stock adjustment parameter sectors $i = 1, 2$
m_i^{High}	marginal propensity to consume by high-income groups sectors, $i = 1–7$
m_i^{Low}	marginal propensity to consume by low-income groups sectors, $i = 1–7$
t_i	indirect tax rates sectors, $i = 1–7$
t_l	tax rate of industrial profit income
d_i	elasticity of substitution in intermediate goods aggregate sectors, $i = 4–7$
$\hat{I}_{1i}$	distribution parameter of intermediate imports in intermediate goods aggregate sector, $i = 4–7$
$\hat{I}_{2i}$	distribution parameter of domestic intermediates in intermediate goods aggregate sectors, $i = 4–7$
h_i	elasticity of substitution in value-added aggregate sectors, $i = 4–6$
q_i^{High}	floor consumption levels for high-income groups, $i = 1–7$
q_i^{Low}	floor consumption levels for low-income groups, $i = 4–7$
m_{1i}	distribution parameter of labor in value-added aggregate sectors, $i = 4–7$
m_{2i}	distribution parameter of capital in value-added aggregate sectors, $i = 4–7$
t_3	mark-up rate sector for services sector.

Part V

Sectoral Perspectives

12
Macroeconomic Policies and Agricultural Performance

Clever Mumbengegwi

1 Introduction

This chapter examines the impact of macroeconomic policies on agricultural performance in Zimbabwe since independence, with a specific focus on the growth in aggregate output, price incentives and export performance. Agriculture is the backbone of Zimbabwe's economy – it contributes about 16 per cent to GDP. However, this grossly understates its importance because over 70 per cent of the population derive their livelihoods either directly or indirectly from agriculture and it accounts for at least one-third of formal sector employment. Not only does it provide about 60 per cent of industrial raw materials; it is also an important source of intermediate and final demand for manufacturing output. Thus, agriculture has strong forward and backward linkages with manufacturing and the rest of the economy such that policies that negatively impact on agriculture would have large economy-wide multiplier effects.

Furthermore, Zimbabwe's agriculture is highly tradable. It produces a wide variety of exportable commodities, such as tobacco, cotton, coffee, tea, horticulture and livestock products. Tradable import-competing food crops like maize and wheat are also produced, as are nontradable crops like sorghum, millet and minor grains. At least 40 per cent of the country's export earnings come from agriculture, with tobacco and cotton contributing 75 per cent of total agricultural exports and 30 per cent of total export earnings. A significant proportion of the nation's food requirements (especially wheat, rice and, occasionally, maize) are also imported. Thus, sufficient reasons exist to suspect that macroeconomic policies that affect the relative profitability of tradables vis-à-vis nontradables are likely to have significant impacts on agriculture.

The policy objectives for agriculture since independence have been consistent: to increase the rate of growth in aggregate output; to achieve diversification in output composition; to maintain food security and self-sufficiency; to raise farm incomes and employment; and to increase the sector's role as a source of raw materials and foreign exchange earner. More than two decades later, many of these objectives remain unfulfilled. Although there have been periods of spectacular growth and diversification, at the aggregate level, growth has been unimpressive and has actually declined in per capita terms. Despite being generally food self-sufficient in most years, food security remains precarious, especially during drought years. Export performance has been equally unimpressive, with the country facing chronic foreign exchange shortages. Formal agricultural employment has actually declined while the majority of the rural population has sunk deeper into poverty and deprivation. This is despite the widely acknowledged fact that Zimbabwe has pursued generally positive sectoral policies with respect to agricultural pricing, marketing, credit, input supply and infrastructural provision over the greater part of the post-independence period. Why has agriculture's performance has been so unimpressive given these favorable sector-specific policies? An attempt to provide an answer to this question is the subject matter of this chapter.

We argue that the tendency for aggregate agricultural stagnation has had more to do with the macroeconomic policy environment facing agriculture than with the effects of sector-specific policies. Although rarely targeted directly at agriculture, macroeconomic policies have been known to have a significant influence on the sector's performance through their effects on the structure of incentives facing producers (Jaeger, 1992; Valdes, 1986; Bautista and Valdes, 1993; Oyejide, 1986). Despite the shift in the macroeconomic policy framework from a controlled to a market-based economy that started in 1991, the common feature of both macroeconomic policy regimes has been their bias against agriculture. The macroeconomic policy framework of the 1980s was characterized by extensive controls on prices, exchange rates, foreign trade and administrative allocation of foreign exchange. The objective was to protect domestic industry from foreign competition. The effects of these controls would have been to turn incentives against agriculture. After the adoption of market-based reforms, the macroeconomic policy environment for agriculture was increasingly defined by expansionary fiscal and restrictive monetary policies. The incompatibility between these two approaches took on special significance in determining the levels of key macroeconomic variables of importance to agriculture such as inflation, interest rates and the overall rate of economic growth. Whereas positive sector-specific policies were continued within the new context of market reforms, the macroeconomic instability experienced during the 1990s created a highly unfavorable environment for agriculture and indeed for the economy as a whole. This would have acted to distort agricultural incentives, which exerted a significant negative impact on the sector's performance. The rest of the chapter is organized as follows: In section 2, we review agricultural sector-specific and economy-wide policies both before (1980–1990) and after the adoption of economic reforms (1991–2000). In section 3, we assess the sector's aggregate performance and, in the process, try to identify the major factors contributing to the observed outcomes. In section 4, we provide some econometric evidence on the impact of macroeconomic variables on agricultural performance. Section 5 provides the summary, conclusions and major policy lessons for the future.

2 Agricultural policy since independence: an overview

Zimbabwe's agricultural policy environment over much of the post-independence period has been characterized by positive sector-specific policies on the one hand and a generally negative macroeconomic policy framework on the other. This applies as much to the control regime of the 1980s as it does to the structural adjustment period of the 1990s. Agricultural policy has been strongly influenced by the country's inheritance from the colonial period. It inherited a highly controlled agricultural pricing and marketing policy framework that had evolved over several decades. Most agricultural commodities were designated as either 'controlled' or 'uncontrolled'. 'Controlled' products were those required by law to be marketed through statutory marketing boards such as the Grain Marketing Board (GMB), the Cotton Marketing Board (CMB), the Dairy Marketing Board (DMB) and the Cold Storage Commission (CSC) (for beef and livestock products). Producer prices of 'controlled' products were administratively fixed by government. These were announced after a lengthy process of negotiation with farmers' organizations. The desire to provide incentives for white farmers to stay on the land usually resulted in prices being fixed above world market prices or those that would have prevailed under a free market system. Consumer prices, on the other hand, were also fixed at low levels to ensure cheap food for urban consumers and low raw materials prices for domestic agro-industrial manufacturing firms. A negative outcome of this pricing policy framework was massive losses on marketing boards' trading accounts, which were met by direct subsidies from the fiscus. In later years, the unsustainable magnitudes of these 'food and parastatal subsidies' became an important factor in the adoption of agricultural policy reforms implemented in the 1990s.

Other aspects of Zimbabwe's agricultural policy inheritance were well-developed credit, input supply, research institutions and extension services unparalleled in Sub-Saharan Africa (with the exception of South Africa). Cheap credit was provided through the precursors to the Agricultural Finance Corporation (AFC), research and extension services through various predecessors to the departments of Research and Specialist Services (R&SS) and Agricultural Extension and Technical Services (AGRITEX) respectively. Zimbabwe also inherited a dualistic agricultural sector, with a predominantly white-owned large-scale commercial farming sector (LSCFS) on the one hand and an exclusively black smallholder farming sector (Communal Areas) on the other. The major weakness of these institutions was the discriminatory provision of their services in favor of the former to the neglect and detriment of the latter.

2.1 Agricultural sector-specific policies during the 1980s

The new government adopted the controlled pricing and marketing policy framework which only changed after the adoption to the economic structural adjustment in 1991. While this system was not unique, but common to most of Sub-Saharan Africa at the time, the distinguishing feature of the Zimbabwean system was the extent of farmer involvement in fixing producer prices. Whereas elsewhere in Africa, such controls were designed to extract a surplus from agriculture, in Zimbabwe they were meant to support farmers' incomes – a historical legacy from the 1930s Great Depression when they were introduced at the instigation of white farmers. Thus, the new government had a relatively easier task of reorienting existing rather than creating new agricultural policy and support institutions. The agricultural sector-specific policies pursued during the 1980s involved:

i. the extension of non-discriminatory, positive pricing policies to include the previously discriminated communal farmers;
ii. the lateral expansion of marketing depots of the Grain Marketing (GMB) and Cotton Marketing Boards (CMB) to increase their geographic coverage to remote communal areas;
iii. provision of agricultural credit to communal farmers through the Agricultural Finance Corporation;
iv. extension services to communal farmers through the department of Agricultural, Technical and Extension Services (AGRITEX); and
v. the distribution of free inputs such as seed packs and fertilizers to communal farmers.

The government's successes in widening the provision of the pricing, marketing, credit, input supply and agricultural support infrastructure to communal farmers became the key to Zimbabwe's short-lived agricultural success story during the early to mid-1980s. The tremendous communal farmer production and marketed supply response, especially for maize and cotton, made them the largest producers of these crops in the country within a relatively short time period. Thus the agricultural control regime served producer interests reasonably well such that for several years, Zimbabwe was considered one of Africa's agricultural success stories at a time Africa was facing its most serious 'food crisis' (Eicher, 1986; Mumbengegwi, 1986).

Ironically the sectoral policies and successes achieved up to the mid-1980s had in-built mechanisms which brought about their own reversal. The budgetary resources required to support an expanded positive pricing and controlled marketing policy framework originally intended to serve a tiny minority of white farmers, soon became binding constraints on the further growth of agriculture. Marketing board trading deficits, necessitating massive subsidies, contributed substantially to an unsustainable budget deficit problem. The fiscal deficit generated inflationary pressures and other macroeconomic problems, which were kept under control by virtue of the network of price controls. The resource allocation inefficiency this system generated added to pressures for economic reform. This came in the form of the economic structural adjustment program (ESAP) adopted in 1991.

2.2 Agricultural sector-specific reforms during the 1990s

ESAP was a broad package of economy-wide reforms, which had agricultural sector-specific components. These sector-specific reforms included:

Price reforms

Price reforms involved the gradual phasing-out of controls on agricultural product prices, since they had become inconsistent with the market liberalization measures taking place elsewhere in the economy. Although government continued to announce producer prices, these assumed an indicative role and, in some cases, served as the floor price, with market forces free to determine the actual levels.[1] Furthermore, these price reforms had the aim of achieving resource allocation efficiency than supporting farmer incomes, as had previously been the case.

Marketing reforms

Market reforms were introduced as a necessary complement to and in order to improve the effectiveness of price reforms. Without them, the transmission mechanisms through which price and macroeconomic reforms are translated into agricultural incentives would have been impaired. Thus, market reforms involved the liberalization of agricultural marketing channels and the phasing-out of controls on 'controlled' products. Restrictions on the movement of, especially, foodgrains between non-contiguous areas were eliminated.

Private agents were allowed to enter the market and buy produce from producers and sell directly to consumers. The single channel marketing and pan-territorial pricing system that had prevented the entry of private agents into agricultural marketing activities was abolished. The monopoly of agricultural parastatals over pricing and marketing of farm products was abandoned. The objective was to 'improve incentives for farmers ... and thus stimulate production, marketing and exports' (Government of Zimbabwe, Agricultural Policy Framework, 1995–2020).

The elimination of agricultural subsidies

Subsidies on foodgrains were gradually reduced and eventually removed as an aspect of budgetary and public enterprise reforms. Marketing boards such as the DMB and CMB were privatized, while the GMB and CSC were commercialized with the eventual goal of privatization. Thus, the deregulation of agricultural prices and markets made possible the elimination of subsidies. However, in the case of the latter two parastatals, the subsidies issue remains a problem due to the government's continued desire to use them for achieving other social policy objectives. In similar vein, agricultural input markets were liberalized.[2]

Institutional reforms

Reforms of institutions that provide services to agriculture, such as credit, research, extension and infrastructure, were incidental to measures undertaken elsewhere in the structural adjustment reform program. Severe cuts to budgetary allocations to institutions such as the AFC (credit), R&SS (research) and AGRITEX (extension services) were the most significant aspects of institutional reforms. Many of the gains realized during the 1980s as a result of funding to these institutions were eroded in a bid to reduce government expenditure. Their delivery capacity to farmers became compromised. The poor agricultural supply response, especially during the early part of structural adjustment, may be partly explained by these developments as productivity improvement and farmer response to price incentives depend to a great extent on the non-price incentives availed by these institutions. With this exception, the agricultural sector-specific reforms implemented during the 1990s constituted positive agricultural policies in the context of a liberalized market environment.

2.3 Macroeconomic policies and agriculture since independence

Economy-wide policies, though rarely targeted at agriculture, have been shown to have significant effects on performance, perhaps more than sector-and/or commodity-specific policy interventions (H. Binswanger (1989)). Macroeconomic policy is a major component of economy-wide policies. It consists of two main components: that is, (i) determining the size, composition and financing of the government budget (*fiscal policy*) and (ii) managing the nation's money supply (*monetary policy*). The interaction between the budget and monetary policy is what determines the levels of other major macroeconomic variables, such as inflation, interest rates, economic growth and the sectoral distribution of that growth (Galston, 1985). Ultimately, it creates the environment within which agriculture (*and indeed the rest of the economy*) must operate.

Zimbabwe's fiscal policy stance has been consistently expansionary both before and after the structural adjustment reforms. It has been dominated by high government expenditures not matched by fiscal revenues, resulting in unsustainable budget deficits which have averaged 8 per cent of GDP over most of the post-independence period. Its monetary policy stance has been contractionary, in a vain attempt to curtail growth in money supply and inflation. During the 1980s, an artificial semblance of macroeconomic stability was achieved through the network of price, interest rate, domestic credit and exchange controls. These latent macroeconomic imbalances became more evident after the adoption of the economic structural adjustment program. However, the adoption of ESAP did little to reverse the expansionary fiscal policy and restrictive monetary stance. The budget deficit continued to grow, inflation escalated and interest rates soared. Macroeconomic instability became an endemic feature of Zimbabwe's economy during the reform period. This negative macroeconomic environment acted to constrain agriculture's performance below its potential.

The macroeconomic environment for agriculture during the 1980s

The major elements that defined the macroeconomic policy environment for agriculture during the 1980s were:

- unsustainable budget deficits
- the administrative allocation of foreign exchange
- quantitative restrictions on foreign trade
- a controlled and overvalued nominal exchange rate
- economy-wide controls on prices, wages, interest rates and
- other macroeconomic variables known to influence the structure of, agricultural incentives.

The sector-specific controls outlined earlier were only one aspect of the controlled macroeconomic policy regime. The most significant mechanisms for resource transfers out of agriculture were the combination of foreign exchange allocation and nominal exchange rate overvaluation. These, more than anything else, were the de facto instruments for import substitution and the protection of domestic industry. Tariffs and other trade taxes were ineffectual as the foreign exchange constraint effectively rationed imports. They only served more as revenue-raising measures than protective devices. The nominal exchange rate, which is a potentially important instrument of policy, remained relatively inactive for most of the decade and as such was constrained to provide adequate signals to improve agricultural incentives. Direct taxation of agriculture has traditionally been very low with no direct export taxes levied on agricultural commodities. The only export intervention was a requirement for exporters to remit export earnings to the Reserve Bank of Zimbabwe at the official (overvalued) exchange rate. However, implicit taxation of agriculture through the protection of domestic industry as measured by nominal protection coefficients for major export crops has been estimated to have been high (Jansen and Muir 1994). This may have had a great impact on incentives facing agriculture, with negative effects on supply response, especially of exports.

As already observed, high government expenditures not matched by fiscal revenues were yet another aspect of Zimbabwe's macroeconomic environment during the 1980s. Fiscal deficits averaging 8 per cent of GDP created money supply problems, with latent inflation kept under control by virtue of the price control regime. Whereas the macroeconomic effects of price controls are usually offset by the emergence of parallel markets, this was not the case in Zimbabwe's agricultural product markets, essentially because policy makers seem to have got the controlled agricultural prices right. Parallel markets, as an indicator of negative policies, were witnessed only in foreign exchange markets, consistent with the overvalued official nominal exchange rate. Clearly, policy makers had got this price 'wrong'. These economy-wide policies of the 1980s distorted incentives to agriculture, which could have constrained the sector's performance to levels below what is consistent with its technological and natural resource potential. By the end of the decade, it had become evident that sector-specific policies alone were insufficient to sustain the initial growth spurt in agriculture.

The macroeconomic environment for agriculture during the 1990s

The economy-wide reforms implemented since 1991 were meant to eliminate the anti-agriculture bias of the controlled macroeconomic policy environment of the 1980s. The most significant of the reforms relevant to agriculture were:

Trade liberalization. Trade liberalization was meant to achieve a real devaluation to boost exports and agriculture would have been a direct beneficiary of this measure. This entailed the elimination of quantitative restrictions on foreign trade, including import-licensing regulations and the administrative allocation of foreign exchange. A tariff-based system combined with a flexible exchange rate policy were put in place instead. Since Zimbabwe had few restrictions or taxes on exports, reforms for the export sector centered on providing a set of export incentives. Key among these was the Open General Import License (OGIL) scheme that provided exporters with relatively easier access to foreign exchange.[3] The OGIL system was the first step towards eventual abolition of import controls and the administrative allocation of foreign exchange that had hampered the export sector.

Exchange rate policy. The nominal exchange rate is the intervention variable available to policy makers to effect a real devaluation. The Zimbabwe dollar has depreciated in nominal terms by almost 1000 per cent over a decade – from Z$5.00 to Z$50.00 per US$. It depreciated by 91 per cent in nominal terms and by 36.8 per cent in real terms between June and September 1991. The nominal exchange rate remained stable for most of 1992 and depreciated by a further 17 per cent during the first quarter of 1993. It continued to depreciate during 1994 and 1995 against a trade-weighted basket of 14 currencies. However, despite these nominal devaluations, the real effective exchange rate appreciated by about 33 per cent due to the high domestic inflation relative to that of trading partners. The potential for the emergence of parallel exchange rate was inhibited by the introduction of the export retention scheme (ERS), which allowed exporters to retain part of their export earnings in foreign currency to finance their imports. ERS entitlements were tradable on the market at higher rates and as they were progressively increased, the official and ERS exchange rates gradually gravitated towards convergence. By June 1994, the foreign exchange market had become unified and the exchange rate became market-determined. This remained the case until January 1999 when it became fixed through an informal arrangement between the government and foreign exchange dealers (mainly commercial banks). As the exchange rate policy was intended to support the export drive, agriculture would have also been a beneficiary.

Public enterprise reforms. Public enterprise reform was an area of adjustment meant to reduce the public sector claim on scarce resources. The commercialization and privatization of agricultural marketing boards discussed above was a step in the broad agenda for reforming the network of 51 mostly loss-making public enterprises. This, however, has fallen far short of expectations and remains unfinished business at the turn of the twenty-first century. Direct benefits to the agricultural sector aside, public enterprise reforms would assist in efforts to reduce government expenditure and the budget deficit to achieve macroeconomic stability and a favorable policy environment for agriculture.

Fiscal and monetary policy reforms. Fiscal policy reforms aimed to reduce the budget deficit to below 5 per cent of GDP. Monetary policy was used as a demand management measure to curb inflation that reduces export competitiveness. However, in the events that followed, the deficit problem has not been resolved. The government failed to seriously address its expenditure levels. To make matters worse, the financing of the deficit shifted away from borrowing from the non-bank financial sector to borrowing from the banking sector. As a result, money supply growth escalated leading to runaway inflation. This prompted the Reserve Bank to adopt a tight monetary policy stance but without the necessary support from the fiscal policy front. The failure of this aspect of macroeconomic policy reforms had detrimental effects on the structure of incentives facing agriculture, especially exports. Although these economy-wide reforms were meant to create a more favorable environment for agriculture, and, indeed, the economy as a whole, policy implementation failures have produced opposite results.

3 Macroeconomic policies and aggregate performance: theoretical and empirical evidence

3.1 Aggregate output

Although Zimbabwe's agricultural performance since 1980 has been less disastrous than elsewhere in Africa, the data suggests that it has failed to keep pace with population growth. Over the twenty-year period as a whole, aggregate growth has averaged about 3 per cent per annum. Given a population growth rate of 3.2 per cent, per capita aggregate production has remained stagnant. The most significant achievement of the period has been the integration of communal smallholder farmers into the market economy and the spectacular rise in their share of production and marketed output, especially of maize and cotton. Table 12.1 summarizes the average annual growth rates for aggregate and per capita agricultural production and for all crops, food and cereals. These figures, however, conceal the wide fluctuations that occur with overwhelming regularity due to frequent droughts, as depicted in Figure 12.1. From Table 12.1, it is possible to identify four sequential growth episodes.

The initial growth episode (1980–1985)

Aggregate agricultural production grew by an average of 8.3 per cent per annum, even after factoring in the effects of the two consecutive droughts that occurred in 1982/83 and 1983/84. Much of this growth was accounted for by smallholder communal farmers in response to both policy and exogenous non-policy factors; the details of which have been well documented in Rohrbach (1989). This period also reflects the strong sectoral incentives arising from sector-specific policy interventions. It is plausible that the incentive effects of sector-specific policies were sufficiently large as to offset the anti-agriculture bias from the controlled macroeconomic policy framework. The positive pricing and marketing policies extended to communal farmers was a decisive factor. The provision of cheap credit and free seed packs encouraged the usage of purchased inputs such as hybrid maize seeds and fertilizers, thus raising their yields. The expansion of GMB marketing depots and improvements in rural feeder roads made for easier access to markets. AGRITEX also expanded its extension and advisory services to the communal sector. As a result, communal maize area planted expanded by 85

Table 12.1 Average growth of total and (per capita) agricultural production

	Aggregate		*Food crops*		*All crops*		*Cereal crops*	
Period	*Total output*	*Per capita*	*Total output*	*Per capita*	*Total output*	*Per capita*	*Total output*	*Per capita*
1982–1985	8.3	5.1	11.4	8.1	10.9	7.6	32.2	28.2
1986–1990	0.8	−2.4	1.6	−1.6	0.2	−2.9	5.2	1.96
1991–1995	−2.2	−4.5	−3.6	−6.1	1.7	−1.2	−38.3	−41.2
1996–1999	11.3	8.9	10.1	7.8	17	14.5	23.2	20.2

Source: Calculated from the *FAO Production Yearbook*.

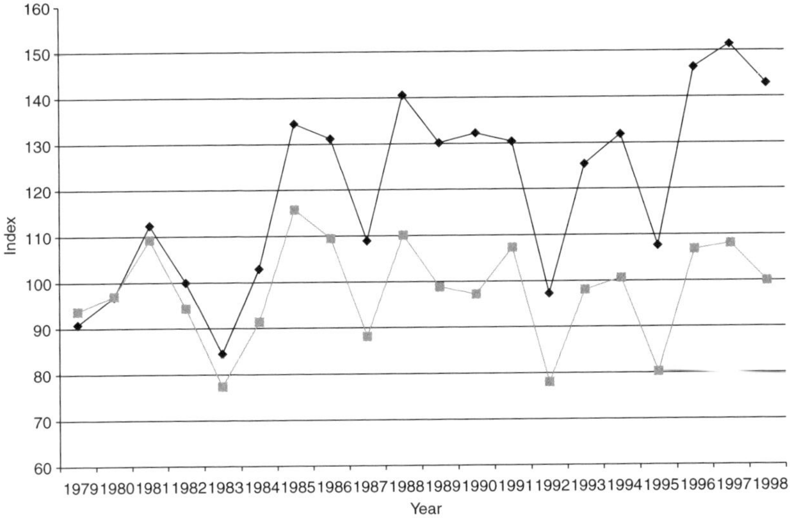

Figure 12.1 Index of aggregate agricultural and per capita output (1980 = 100)
Source: FAO Production Yearbook.

per cent, thus offsetting the decline in hectare in the large-scale commercial farming sector. These factors apply equally in the case of cotton.

The period of stagnation (1986–1990)

During the second half of the 1980s, the aggregate output index stagnated; with a mere 0.8 per cent average growth per annum. In per capita terms, it actually decreased by 2.4 per cent per annum. This period is associated with dampening sectoral incentives and an increasingly negative macroeconomic environment. The macroeconomic uncertainty reduced incentives for private investment and capital formation in agriculture, especially in the large-scale commercial farming sector.

Fiscal constraints implied shrinking budgetary allocations to agriculture in real terms. Agricultural support services could not be sustained at their previous levels. Real producer prices declined by 20 per cent. The GMB was forced to cut back on its marketing depots in communal areas. Similarly, the AFC reduced credit to communal farmers. Extension services became overstretched, while the distribution of free seed packs was abandoned. These developments reduced the use of fertilizers, hybrid seeds and other purchased inputs such that communal area yields stagnated. However, that aggregate output did not decline was due to a doubling of maize area planted such that foodgrain production registered a respectable average annual growth of 5.2 per cent and 1.6 per cent per capita, respectively.

The period of decline (1991–1995)

The third episode ironically coincides with the economic structural adjustment reforms (1991–1995). Growth in aggregate output, crop, cereal and total foodgrain production was negative, as indicated in Table 12.1. This gloomy picture is the result of two main factors. Firstly, the reform period was complicated initially by the occurrence of two consecutive droughts in 1992/93 and 1993/94 and deteriorating terms of trade for most agricultural exports. Secondly, the non-implementation and poor sequencing of key aspects of the reforms had a hand in agriculture's poor performance. The fast pace of trade liberalization with no fiscal reform, the persistently high budget deficits and tight monetary policy, cut backs in government spending on agricultural support services, high inflation and interest rates all made for an unstable macroeconomic environment. This macroeconomic uncertainty and instability turned incentives against agriculture, which adversely affected performance.

The recovery period (1996–)

This trend partly reflects recovery from drought and perhaps the delayed effects of macroeconomic reforms beginning to bear fruit. Based on data for the first two years of the programme, there are signs of agricultural growth recovery. The aggregate index of production rose by 11.3 per cent between 1996 and 1998. However, in per capita terms, agricultural production remains at the same level as in 1985.

3.2 Aggregate agricultural exports

Table 12.2 and Figure 12.2 respectively show the average growth and the time profile of the real value of agricultural exports since 1980.

Despite the initial boost to exports in the aftermath of independence, the real value of agricultural exports declined in the period 1983–85. Export growth averaged a mere 0.5 per cent per annum over the first five years of independence. Thereafter, exports failed to recover to their pre-1982 levels until after the introduction of economic reforms in the 1990s. The 6.6 per cent average growth between 1986 and 1990 merely reflects a recovery from the 26.6 per cent decline that had occurred between 1982 and 1985. Over the decade, average real growth in exports was only 3.6 per cent. In per capita terms, real agricultural exports stagnated over the 1980s. However,

Table 12.2 Average growth rates in real agricultural exports (%)

			Period			
1980–85	*1986–90*	*1991–95*	*1996–97*	*1980–90*	*1980–95*	*1980–96*
0.5	6.6	8.5	31.7	3.6	5.2	6.7

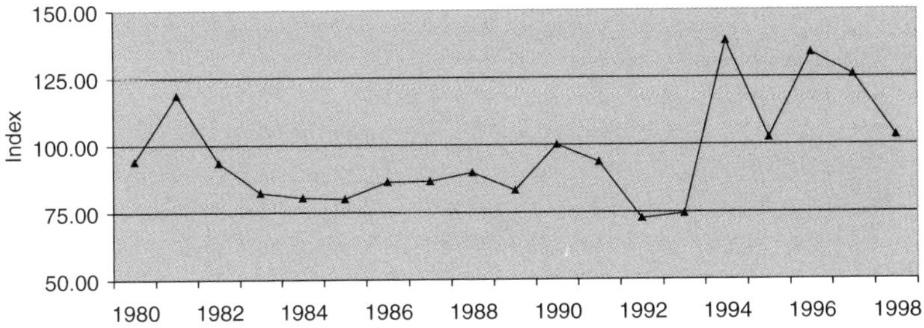

Figure 12.2 Index of real value of agricultural exports (1990 = 100)
Source: FAO.

the adoption of ESAP gave a real boost in exports, especially after the 1993/94 drought. Export growth accelerated to 8.5 per cent during ESAP and accelerated even further during the first year of ZIMPREST. Overall growth for the period 1980–96 was 7 per cent per annum.

3.3 Explaining long-term growth performance

The failure to sustain the initial growth impetus requires a more formal explanation. Our contention is that economy-wide policies played the more decisive role in determining the structure of incentives facing agriculture. A large proportion of Zimbabwe's agricultural output is highly tradable and hence sensitive to policies that impact on relative prices. The unfavorable macroeconomic policies that prevailed both before and after economic reforms negatively impacted on the structure of agricultural incentives sufficiently to counteract the positive effects of sector-specific policy interventions, thus accounting for the rather poor growth performance. The mechanism through which macroeconomic and other economy-wide policies affect agricultural performance is through the real exchange rate.

The real exchange rate is defined as the ratio of the domestic price level of tradable to the domestic price of nontradable goods (Bautista, 1985; Valdes, 1986). This ratio provides the long-term signal for the reallocation of resources across and within various sectors. An appreciation of the real exchange rate causes the relative prices of tradable agricultural output to fall, thereby discouraging production, especially of exportables and unprotected import-competing substitute crops. It depresses agriculture's price incentive structure relative to nontradables. The commonly used proxy for the price of tradables (P_T) are the wholesale prices of a country's trading partners while that of non tradables (P_{NT}) is the domestic consumer price index. The ratio (P_T/P_{NT}) is then used as a measure of the real exchange rate. Figure 12.3 depicts the ratio of weighted wholesale price indexes of Zimbabwe's five major trading partners to the domestic consumer price index.[4] Although technically, this does not measure the real exchange rate accurately (since

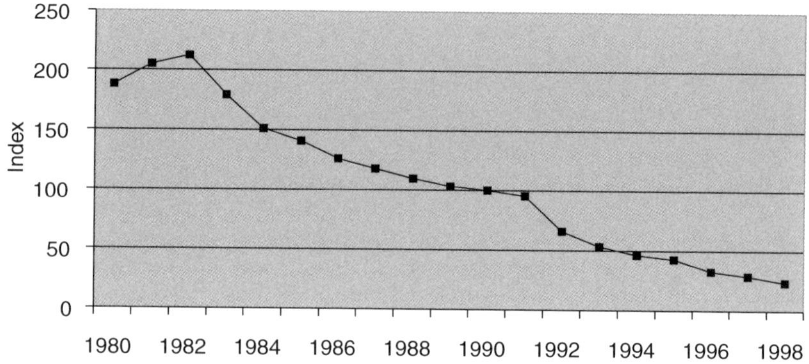

Figure 12.3 Index of the ratio of weighted wholesale prices to Zimbabwe's CPI (1990 = 100)

the former are not expressed in domestic currency), the monotonic downward trend provides a graphic picture of the effects of inflation differentials on the tendency for the real exchange rate to appreciate. This behavior of the real exchange rate had much to do with domestic macroeconomic policies, in particular the high government spending and budget deficits coupled with incompatible monetary policies.

The foreign exchange allocation and other trade restrictions during the 1980s were other factors accounting for the initial appreciation. The non-implementation of crucial aspects of reforms during structural adjustment, especially on the fiscal side, allowed the real exchange rate to continue to appreciate due to severe domestic inflation.

Government expenditure is an important component of aggregate demand. It increases domestic absorption directly. Furthermore, if revenues do not match expenditure, a budget deficit results. Depending on how it is financed, the deficit will have an added indirect effect on absorption through its impact on money supply. Financing from borrowing from commercial banks or from abroad as occurred during the 1990s, results in increased money supply, which ultimately affects domestic absorption through changes in prices and interest rates. The exact effects of increased domestic absorption on prices also depend on the composition of government expenditures and the supply responsiveness of domestic production. If the composition of government expenditures is more concentrated on nontradable (home) goods and if the latter's supply is more inelastic than that of tradables, then the rise in domestic absorption has greater incidence on home goods. This puts upward pressure on home goods prices, causing the relative price ratio between tradables and nontradables to fall, thus lowering the real exchange rate. A fall (rise) in the real exchange rate signifies an appreciation (depreciation), which causes the production of agricultural exportables to become less (more) profitable relative to non-tradable goods.

Similarly, an appreciation (depreciation) causes imports to become cheaper (more expensive) in terms of domestic currency, encouraging (discouraging) competition with domestic production, especially of unprotected import substitutes. This discourages (encourages) their domestic production. Thus, high government spending and budget deficits have negative effects on domestic production of both agricultural exportables and importables through their effects of appreciating the real exchange rate. Figure 12.4 shows the transmission mechanism from macroeconomic policies to the real exchange rate.

3.4 Real exchange rate and agricultural performance: descriptive evidence

We begin our empirical analysis of the impacts of the real exchange rate on agricultural performance, first, by examining the behavior, over time, of three important variables of interest – that is, the real exchange rate, aggregate agricultural output and aggregate agricultural exports. In Section 4, we provide some econometric evidence.

An accurate measure of the real exchange rate that fully separates tradables from nontradables is difficult to construct due to data limitations, especially for developing countries (Masters, 1994). The standard empirical methodology is typically to use international price comparisons with wholesale price indexes of a country's major trading partners used as the proxy for tradable goods prices while the domestic consumer price index is the proxy for nontraded goods (Edwards, 1989). Thus, we define the real exchange rate as the ratio of the weighted average of wholesale price indices of Zimbabwe's major trading partners to the domestic consumer price index.[5] This ratio is converted into local currency by the nominal exchange rate. This procedure essentially involves adjusting the bilateral nominal exchange rates for relative inflation differentials between Zimbabwe and each of her major trading partners and finding a weighted average.

$$\text{i.e. } RER = \sum_{i=1}^{n} wi(Pfi/Ph)t^{*} NER_{it}$$

where:

NER_{it} = bilateral nominal exchange rate (Z$ per unit of country *i*'s currency

$P_{f,i}$ = index of foreign goods prices for trading partner i

$P_{h,t}$ = index of home goods prices (CPI)

w_i = trading partner's share of trade with Zimbabwe

Figure 12.4 shows the time profiles of the three major variables of interest to our analysis.

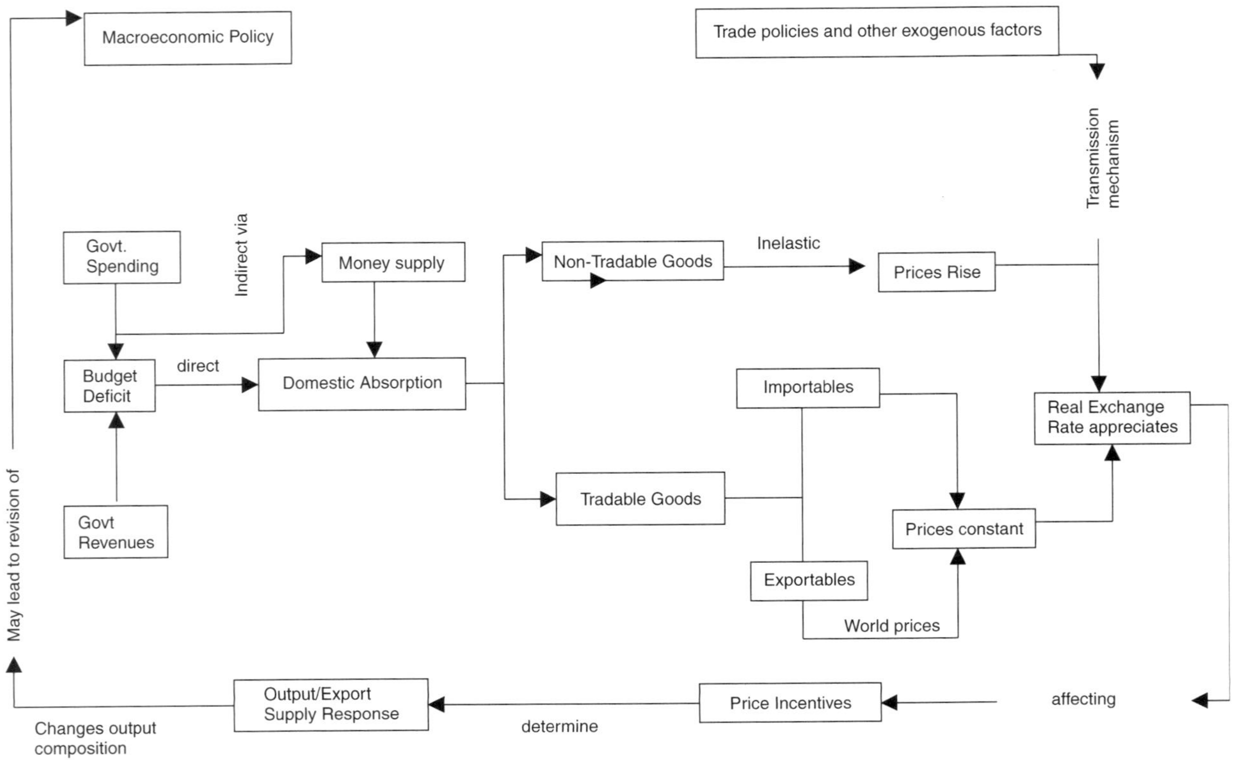

Figure 12.4 Macroeconomic policies and agriculture – transmission mechanisms

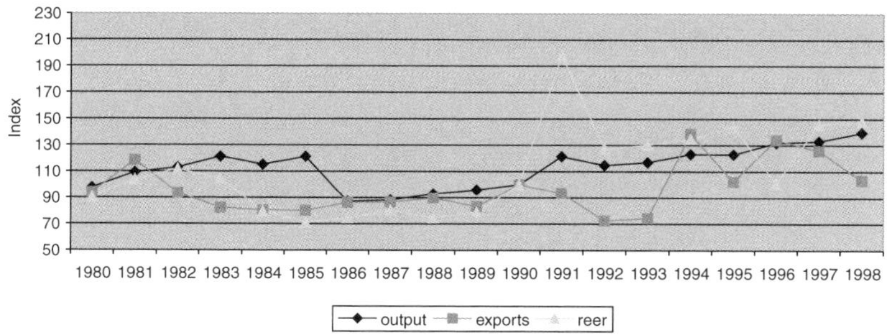

Figure 12.5 Real exchange rate, aggregate output and exports indexes (1990 = 100)

Time profile of the real exchange rate

The real exchange rate measure we use is more sensitive to changes in the trade policy intervention variable, the nominal exchange rate, than would a conceptually correct measure such as (P_T/P_{NT}). Figure 12.2 would be closer to the actual behavior of the latter. However, the real effective exchange rate tells the general thrust of the story. Soon after independence (between 1980 and 1982), the index rose (depreciated) largely due to low domestic inflation relative to Zimbabwe's major trading partners and a 20 per cent devaluation in 1982. Thereafter, the real exchange rate drops (appreciates) sharply reaching an all-time low in 1985. For the rest of the decade, the real exchange rate follows an alternating cycle of depreciation followed by appreciation in the wake of each nominal devaluation. This cycle lasts roughly two years each. There is a mild depreciation up to 1987 and a brief appreciation in 1988. The decade ends with a weak depreciation due to tentative moves towards liberalization that occurred in 1989 and 1990. Thus, despite the further nominal devaluations undertaken throughout the 1980s, the real exchange rate index remained below its 1982 level until after the adoption of structural adjustment reforms in 1991. The inflationary pressures depicted in Figure 12.2 relative to those of trading partners rendered these nominal devaluations ineffective. The index was about half its 1980 level for the rest of the decade, showing the unfavorable effects of macroeconomic policies, which caused the real exchange rate to appreciate.

After the adoption of the economic structural adjustment program (ESAP) there is a massive rise (depreciation) in the real exchange rate due to a huge (91 per cent) nominal devaluation in 1991, although this was short-lived. In 1992, it appreciated by about 23 per cent before depreciating again in 1993 and 1994, only to fall in 1995 and 1996. The effects of the collapse of the Zimbabwean currency that occurred in 1997 and 1998 were partially nullified by excessive domestic inflation. As such the real exchange rate rose (depreciated) modestly only to decline again in 1999 due to the fixed nominal exchange rate regime implemented in January 1999. However, for the decade of the 1990s, the real exchange rate index remains above the 1980s levels, showing the improved incentives from economic reforms. However, the behavior of the real exchange rate in the face of the massive nominal devaluations of the 1990s indicates a deterioration in external competitiveness as a result of domestic inflation and the unstable macroeconomic conditions prevailing during the implementation of reforms.

Time profiles of aggregate agricultural output and exports

The positive co-movement between the indexes of aggregate agricultural output and exports on one hand and the real exchange rate on the other, are quite suggestive of the impacts of economy-wide policies on agriculture. Both indexes increase in the very early 1980s with a rising (depreciating) real exchange rate. However, the index of aggregate output continues to rise despite the appreciation of the real exchange rate that occurred up to 1985. This is consistent with our earlier contention that positive sector-specific policy interventions played a more significant influence on agricultural incentives than economy-wide policies during the early to mid 1980s. These offset the negative effects of a real exchange rate appreciation. On the other hand, aggregate exports decline by 9 per cent at the same time that the real exchange rate is appreciating, indicating perhaps that they are more responsive than output to the economy-wide policies that affect international competitiveness.

The output index declines from 1985, initially sparked by the 1984/85 drought and remains below its early 1980s peak until after the introduction of economic reforms. The export index remains virtually stagnant between 1986 and 1989. It is striking that both indexes closely follow movements in the real exchange rate index, rising with a depreciation and falling with an appreciation. This suggests the increasing importance of economy-wide policies on agricultural incentives over sector-specific policy interventions during the second half of the 1980s. However, there seems to be a distinct one-period lag between the real exchange rate and export supply response.

The reforms of the 1990s gave a boost to the aggregate output index which increases steadily throughout the decade; interrupted only by the effects of frequent droughts.

However, aggregate growth was less than warranted by the massive nominal devaluations due to the tendency of the real exchange rate to appreciate and turn incentives against agriculture. The recovery in the index from the decline and stagnation of the late 1980s and early 1990s was just enough to restore it to its earlier peak. The index in 1995 was almost at its 1985 level.

In contrast, the export index declines during the ESAP period, especially between 1991 and 1993, despite the depreciation of the real exchange rate. This might be attributed to the 1992–94 drought years, the generally depressed outlook of the world economy and an increasingly negative and unstable macroeconomic environment. After 1994 and throughout the period of ZIMPREST (1996–2000), average total agricultural export grew by 2.7 per cent per annum. This low export response suggests that the real exchange rate depreciation following the introduction of reforms failed to stimulate exports. The intensifying macroeconomic instability and political uncertainty that has been experienced towards the end of the 1990s had an aggravating effect. The macroeconomic instability characterized by negative overall real growth, high budget deficit, high inflation and interest rates, and low foreign reserves leading to the massive currency crash of 1997 and 1998 acted to remove the export incentive effects of those events. However, after 1995 both the export and real exchange rate indexes follow a more erratic pattern, with the exports index moving in a fluctuating and counter-cyclical manner to the real exchange rate. The descriptive evidence seems to suggest that the real exchange rate may have been a significant negative factor in the behavior of agricultural output and exports. Below we provide supportive econometric evidence.

4 Econometric analysis

This section specifies and estimates a real exchange rate equation in which macroeconomic and other economy-wide policy indicators are the major explanatory variables. The main hypothesis is that the macroeconomic policies pursued since independence were responsible for the observed tendency for the real exchange rate to appreciate. Agriculture would have been adversely affected since farmers produce tradable crops using mostly nontradable land and labor (Masters, 1994). This reduces returns to production of tradable farm products relative to these inputs, thereby reducing and transferring incomes from farmers to producers of nontradables. Further, the real exchange rate appreciation would have negatively impacted upon the price incentive structure facing agricultural exportables and importables relative to nontradable goods. This adverse incentive structure would have discouraged production and exports.

4.1 The real exchange rate equation

The estimated reduced form equation for the real exchange rate derives its theoretical justification from the familiar three-sector general equilibrium framework developed by Edwards (1989) in which Zimbabwe's agricultural sector can be characterized as producing exportables, importables and nontradable crops. The real exchange rate is modeled as a function of the following variables.

Macroeconomic policy

Indicators of the fiscal and monetary policy stance are the variables of interest. The mechanisms through which they are transmitted to the real exchange rate have been explained above. The fiscal policy stance is proxied by total government expenditure (GEXP) or alternatively by the budget deficit (BDEF) as a percentage of GDP. The monetary policy effects are proxied by the difference between the rate of growth of money supply (M2) and the lagged real rate of growth of GDP (GM2). For reasons mentioned earlier, a negative relationship is expected.

The nominal exchange rate

As the policy intervention variable, the level and direction of change over time of the nominal exchange rate (NER) indicates policy makers' intentions. A nominal devaluation (appreciation), ceteris paribus, improves (worsens) competitiveness and stimulates (discourages) domestic production of exportables and importables. Thus, changes in the nominal exchange rate are expected to have a positive impact on the real exchange rate.

Trade policy variable

Trade policy interventions in the form of trade taxes (tariffs and export taxes), import quotas, quantitative restrictions and administrative foreign exchange allocation reduce the degree of openness of the domestic economy. This affects the real exchange rate, depending on the severity of the trade restrictions. The system of foreign exchange allocation meant that import quotas were binding, thus raising the domestic prices of importables. This induced higher demand for nontradables from the protected manufacturing sector, resulting in the rise of prices of nontradable goods relative to exportables. Thus the system had the effect of favoring importables and nontradables at the expense of exportables. This could have caused the real exchange rate to appreciate, depending on the composition of importables and exportables in the basket of tradable goods. Due to difficulties in obtaining a well-defined measure of trade restrictions, most empirical studies have used, as we do, the degree of openness as a proxy for trade policy – that is, the ratio of exports plus imports to GDP (OPEN). Alternatively we use a dummy variable which takes the value 1 for the period 1980–90 and 0 for 1991–98 to proxy the severity of trade restrictions. A negative relationship is expected.

Terms of trade

Changes in the terms of trade (TOT) can significantly affect the real exchange rate. However, due to the complexity of the relationship between the substitution and income effects of a terms of trade shock, its expected impact on the real exchange rate it is difficult to determine, a priori. If the income (substitution) effect dominates, positive shocks in the terms of trade would normally result in a negative (positive) co-movement in the real exchange rate. Negative shocks or deterioration in the terms of trade would have the opposite effect. A negative terms of trade shock reduces output and creates excess demand of nontradable goods, thus raising their prices relative to tradable goods. This leads to an appreciation of the real exchange rate. On the other hand, a positive terms of trade shock lowers the relative price of imports, which may result in a decline in the cost of imported imports used in the production of nontradable goods. This will cause the real exchange rate to depreciate.

Capital inflows

Capital inflows increase disposable income, which in turn will increase the demand for both tradable and nontradable goods. The net effect on the real exchange rate also depends on the composition of domestic absorption, as discussed earlier. If higher capital inflows result in higher demand for home goods, it pushes their relative prices up and consequently appreciates the real exchange rate and vice versa. We use the current account deficit (CAD) as a proxy for capital flows since persistent deficits have to be financed through capital inflows. Although the relationship between the real exchange rate and current account deficit is often volatile at times, a negative relationship is expected.

Real per capita income

Real per capita GDP is included as a proxy for technological progress. From a long-run perspective, real per capita GDP captures the effects of technical change on productivity growth in the production of tradables and nontradables. Thus, technological progress affects the real exchange rate through the impact of productivity growth. An increase in productivity, especially in the tradable goods sector, improves the trade balance, which then requires the real exchange rate to appreciate in order to keep the trade account at a sustainable level.

Thus the real exchange rate is modeled as a function of the size of the budget deficit (or government spending) as a percentage of GDP, money supply growth, the nominal exchange rate, a trade policy variable, foreign capital inflows, the terms of trade and per capita GDP. A log linear specification is used such that the coefficients are easily interpretable as elasticities.

$$\begin{aligned}\ln(RER) = {} & \beta_0 + \beta_1 \ln(BDEF) + \beta_2 \ln(NER) + \beta_3 \ln(TOT) \\ & + \beta_4 \ln(CAD) + \beta_5 \ln(GM2) + \beta_6\, OPEN + \beta_7 \ln(GDP) + \epsilon\end{aligned}$$

where the variable definitions should be clear from the text.

4.2 Data and estimation

The data used to estimate the above equation were obtained from various sources such as the CSO *Quarterly Digest of Statistics*, the RBZ *Economic and Statistical Review*, the IMF *International Financial Statistics*, FAO *Production Yearbook*, FAO *Trade Yearbook* and the World Bank *Book of Tables*. Due to the short span of the time series used (1980–98), more recent econometric techniques involving testing for stationarity, cointegration and error correc-

Table 12.3 Real exchange rate equation – OLS results

	Const	*ln (BDEF)*	*ln (GM2)*	*ln(NER)*	*ln(TOT)*	*ln(OPEN)*	*ln(CAD)*	*ln(GDP)*
Coeff.	3.31	−0.269	−0.09	0.405	−0.256	−0.32	−0.030	−0.41
SE	0.784	0.105	0.04	0.134	0.46	0.508	0.018	0.185
T ratio	4.22	−2.568*	−2.25*	3.025*	−0.556	−0.63	−1.697	−2.216*

$R^2 = 0.92$; Adj. $R^2 = 0.88$; DW = 1.97; F = 14.83.
* = statistically significant at that 5% level.

tion models were considered inappropriate. The equation was estimated using Ordinary Least Squares (OLS). Tests for violations of the classical assumptions underlying OLS estimation were conducted and remedied using standard techniques. The problem of multicollinearity was encountered more often in preliminary estimations and was resolved using the Hildreth–Lu procedure. The Durbin–Watson statistic showed evidence of serial correlation and was corrected for. However, the dangers associated with spurious regressions if the series are non-stationary still remain. Therefore, caution should be exercised in interpreting the results.

4.3 The results

The results are presented in Table 12.3. Alternative proxies for fiscal and monetary policies were tried and the best results are reported below. These include using total government spending/GDP in place of the budget deficit/GDP and substituting the real interest rate for the monetary policy variable. In general the results conform with a priori expectations and those from other studies. The R^2 of 0.92 shows that 92 per cent of the variations in the real exchange rate are explained by the included explanatory variables. With an F statistic of 14.8, not all parameters are equal to zero and the whole regression is statistically significant. Most of the variables had theexpected signs. The coefficient of the budget deficit (BDEF) has the expected negative sign and is significantly different from zero at the 5 per cent level.

This result was also obtained when we used total government spending. This indicates that increases in government spending leading to persistently high budget deficits had the effect of appreciating the real exchange rate. The elasticity of −0.269 is, however, small, implying that a one per cent increase in the budget deficit would lead the real exchange rate to appreciate by 0.269 per cent. The proxy for monetary policy stance (GM2), as expected, also has a small negative and significant sign. This suggests that the restrictive monetary policies that were pursued in an attempt to cure domestic inflation were perhaps unsuccessful due to excessive monetary growth arising from the method of budget deficit financing. The coefficient of NER is large, positive and highly significant at the 5 per cent level, indicating that nominal exchange rate depreciations compensated for the tendency for the real exchange rate to appreciate. The terms of trade variable (TOT) has a positive and statistically not significant coefficient, suggesting that the income and substitution effects offset each other. The ln OPEN, which proxies the restrictiveness of trade policy, has the expected negative sign but is also not statistically significant. Per capita GDP, which was used as a proxy for productivity, has a large negative and significant coefficient of −0.41, suggesting that increases in productivity cause the real exchange rate to appreciate. However, given declining per capita incomes during the 1990s, this would have acted to dampen the extent of real exchange rate overvaluation. The current account deficit (CAD) which proxies net capital inflows is negative but not significant.

Thus, the overall implications of these results are that an increase in government expenditure transmitted through increased budget deficits or total absorption levels has the effect of appreciating the real exchange rate. On the other hand, nominal devaluations tend to lead to real devaluation, but this may be offset by inflationary pressures such that in the long run there may be no clear relationship between the nominal and real exchange rates.

4.4 The real exchange rate and agricultural price incentives

To test the impact of real exchange rate appreciation on price incentives, we specify and estimate equations in which the real exchange rate is an explicit explanatory variable. Our approach to modeling agricultural price incentives has been guided by two sets of considerations. Firstly, the literature is not unanimous as to how the real exchange rate affects agricultural output and exports. Some authors have argued that the real exchange rate, per se, does not affect them directly but indirectly through its impact on producer prices relative to those of non-agricultural nontradable goods (Fosu, 1992). Others have preferred to include the real exchange rate as an explicit variable in supply response equations and proceed to draw inferences about the price incentive structure from the real exchange rate coefficient. The former may seem more plausible for Zimbabwe, given that most producer prices were not market-but policy-determined, during the greater part of the period under consideration – that is, 1980–95. Real exchange rate changes may not have been translated into changes in relative prices as a result of producer price controls. However, while policy makers may have control over producer price levels, the incentive structure (relative prices) is an endogenous variable outside their control. Therefore, our approach is to explicitly model the price incentive structure that includes the real exchange rate as an explicit explanatory variable.

The second consideration arises from the tradable nature of most agricultural commodities in Zimbabwe and the concept of a tradable good itself. It assumes that it is a composite good, or a weighted average of importables and exportables.

In Zimbabwe, where there has been a history of differential policy interventions in exportable and importable goods markets, it is reasonable to suspect that movements of the real exchange rate may affect price incentives for importables and exportables differently. Snape (1988) has argued that in such circumstances, these goods' prices can no longer be aggregated to get the appropriate tradable goods price. Collier (1992) also argues that if trade restrictions are actively used, tradables cannot be treated as a single aggregate commodity. Furthermore, in cases where import-competing goods are not good substitutes for imports (such as maize), a composite relative price will not accurately reflect changes in the price of exportables and importables. Thus, estimating a composite price incentive equation would be inappropriate, as this would be to assume that real exchange rate changes have the same effect on the price incentive structures for importables and exportables. To take this into account, we disaggregate the price incentive model into two equations – one for agricultural exportables and the other for importables. This disaggregation may enable us to more accurately capture the effects of real exchange rate changes on their respective prices relative to nontradable goods.

The exportables price incentive structure (P_X/P_{NAH}) is measured by the weighted average of the domestic price indexes of tobacco and cotton divided by the domestic non-agricultural nontradable price, proxied by the non-food component of the CPI. The weights are the share of each commodity in total exports. Similarly, the price incentive structure (P_M/P_{NAH}) for importables is measured by the ratio of the weighted domestic price indexes for maize and wheat to the domestic non-agricultural, nontradable goods price also proxied by the non-food component of the CPI. The weights are their respective shares in agricultural trade. An important point worth noting is the price incentive equations partly reflect the behavior and considerations of policy makers when fixing producer prices. Domestic producer prices were not market- but policy-determined during the price control regime that existed until the decontrol and complete liberalization of agricultural markets in 1995. Although no precise formula was used, several factors were taken into account. These include the expected size of the crop, the expected demand conditions, providing incentive prices to farmers, the expected effect of the proposed set of producer prices on agricultural marketing boards' trading accounts and on domestic wage goods, especially food prices and international price competitiveness (Mumbengegwi, 1986). Thus, the equation is specified as a function of the real exchange rate (RER), lagged output (Q_{t-1}, wage goods (W_t) proxied by food component of the consumer price index and world prices (Pw_{t-1}) constructed using the weights and logic stated above. The specifications for the two incentive equations are as follows:

$$\ln(P_X/P_{NAH})_t = f[\ln(RER_t), \ln(P_{wt-1}) \ln(Q_{t-1}), (W_t)] \quad \text{(exportables)} \qquad (12.1)$$

$$\ln(P_M/P_{NAH})_t = f[\ln(RER_t), \ln(P_{wt-1}) \ \ln(Q_{t-1}), \ (W_t)] \quad \text{(importables)} \qquad (12.2)$$

Estimation and results

The data were obtained from the same sources as previously cited. The two equations were estimated using the Seemingly Unrelated Regression (SUR) technique to take into account the possibility of contemporaneously correlated disturbances. All the explanatory variables are exogenous and assuming independence among the error terms within each equation, this gives more efficient estimates than OLS. The results are shown in Table 12.4. Figures in parenthesis are t-ratios.

Table 12.4 Price incentives equation – OLS results

	Constant	*ln* (RER_t)	*ln* $(Pw)_{t-1}$	*ln* (Q_{t-1})	*ln* (W_t)
1 Exportables price	1.23	−0.87	0.44	−0.45	−.002
incentives equation	(2.53)	(−3.21)	(4.02)	(−1.89)	(−0.031)
	$R^2 = 0.61$	Adj $R^2 = 0.48$	Dw = 2.1;	F = 12.3	Obs = 19
	Constant	ln (RER_t)	ln $(Pw)_{t-1}$	ln$(Q_{t-1}(Q_{t-1})$	ln (W_t)
2 Importables price	−2.56	−0.49	0.39	−0.42	−.007
incentives equation	(2.31)	(−2.21)	(5.2)	(1.77)	(−0.96)
	$R^2 = -0.65$	Adj $R^2 = 0.59$,	Dw = 1.89,	F = 12.7	Obs = 19

The most interesting feature of these results is that in both equations, the coefficient of the real exchange rate is negative and statistically significant at the 5 per cent level. This shows that, contrary to our hypothesis, the real exchange rate adversely affected the incentive structure for both importables and exportables. The magnitudes of elasticities of −0.87 and−0.49 are statistically different from each other, which suggests that exportables are more responsive to changes in the real exchange rate than importables. This might be due to the differential levels of government interventions in the respective markets. Tobacco, which constitutes 75 per cent of our proxy for agricultural exportables, has had minimal government controls compared to either cotton or foodgrains (maize and wheat). The coefficients on the lagged output are, as expected, negative and significant, indicating that a higher output in the previous year has the effect of depressing the price incentive price structure. The world market price has a positive and also significant coefficient but domestic wage goods are negative and statistically insignificant.

5 Summary and conclusions

This chapter has reviewed the policy environment facing agriculture in Zimbabwe since the attainment of independence in 1980. Agricultural sector-specific policies have been generally positive both before and after economic reforms. Despite this, there has been a general tendency for low growth and stagnation in aggregate output and exports. This is attributable to the negative macroeconomic environment, which exercised a significant influence on the structure of agricultural incentives. This acted to counteract the positive effects of sector-specific policies.

During the 1980s, the macroeconomic environment was defined by an elaborate system of economy-wide controls on prices, foreign exchange allocation and other trade restrictions designed to protect domestic industry. High government spending not matched by fiscal revenues, coupled with restrictive monetary policies, were other important features of the macroeconomic environment. Inflation was only kept under control by virtue of the network of price, interest rate, domestic credit and exchange controls. This combination of policies distorted the incentives facing agriculture. The economic structural adjustment reforms of the 1990s were meant to eliminate this anti-agriculture bias inherent in the controlled macroeconomic policy regime. However, policy implementation failures, particularly the non-implementation of fiscal policy reforms, resulted in macroeconomic instability characterized by high budget deficits, money supply growth, unprecedented inflation and low economy-wide growth. The reforms were implemented under the assumption that they would stimulate the production of tradables, especially exportables. Agriculture, being a highly tradable sector, was expected to benefit and to more than compensate for the anticipated contraction in the nontradable and protected import-competing sectors. That this did not occur to any significant degree was the result of the effects of the unstable macroeconomic environment, which dampened incentives of agricultural tradables relative to nontradable domestically produced goods.

The mechanism through which macroeconomic policies are transmitted to agricultural incentives is the real exchange rate. This chapter has also highlighted the sharp appreciation in the real exchange rate over this period, which accompanied the low growth and stagnation in agricultural output and real exports. This tendency for the real exchange rate to appreciate is located in the negative macroeconomic policies pursued both before and after the reforms. The descriptive evidence and econometric results presented in this chapter confirm this view. This appreciation negatively affected the price incentives structure facing producers such that the anticipated positive effects of economic reforms on agriculture could not be observed. Agriculture's performance was constrained below levels consistent with the country's resource and technological potential. Otherwise, it would have been better than that realized during the economic reform period.

The major conclusion and policy lesson Zimbabwe can learn from its experience with macroeconomic policy is that policies which cause a long-run appreciation of the real exchange rate are particularly harmful to agriculture. Thus, policy makers need to take a more serious view of the significance of macroeconomic factors in their design of policies aimed at stimulating agricultural performance. At the turn of the twenty-first century, it should be evident that the current mix of high budget deficits and tight monetary policies hold little promise for improving agricultural incentives. Favorable sector-specific policies coupled with a negative macroeconomic environment are unlikely to yield the desired results. Thus, reducing government expenditure and cutting the budget deficit seem to be the most important moves that policy makers can do for farmers and indeed the economy as a whole.

Notes

1. For details of the product-specific reform measures and their sequencing, see Takavarasha (1996).
2. For an analysis of the impact of input market liberalization, see D. Gisselquist and J. Rusike, 'Zimbabwe's agricultural inputs industries (1990–96): regulations, reforms and impacts' paper presented at the 'Zimbabwe: Macroeconomic Policy, Management and Performance' Conference held in Harare, 19–21 August 1998.
3. Under this scheme, firms could import raw materials, intermediate inputs and capital goods without recourse to a specific import license. Raw materials were placed on OGIL first, followed by intermediate inputs with capital and consumer goods following suit towards the end of the reform program.
4. The countries included are the United Kingdom, the United States, South Africa, Germany and Japan.
5. The countries included are the United Kingdom, the United States, South Africa, Germany and Japan. These account for over 50 per cent of Zimbabwe's foreign trade.

References

Balassa, Bela (1988) 'Incentive policies and agricultural performance in Sub-Saharan Africa'. PPR Working Paper, No. 77. Washington DC: World Bank.

Bautista, R.M. (1985) *Effects of Trade and Exchange Rate Policies on Export Production Incentives in Philippines Agriculture*. Washington DC: IFPRI.

Bautista, R.M. and A. Valdes (eds) (1993) *The Bias against Agriculture: Trade and Macroeconomic Policies in Developing Countries*. San Francisco: ICS Press.

Binswanger, Hans (1989) 'The policy response of agriculture', Proceedings of the World Bank Annual Conference on Development Economics 1989. Washington DC: World Bank.

Bond, Marian E. (1983) 'Agriculture responses to prices in Sub-Saharan African countries'. IMF Staff Papers, vol. 20, no. 4. Washington DC: World Bank.

Chhibber, Ajay (1988) 'The aggregate supply response in agriculture', in S. Commander (ed.), *Structural Adjustment in Agriculture: Theory and Practice*. London: James Currey Publishers.

Chibber, A. and S. Wilton (1986) 'Macroeconomic policies and agricultural performance', *Development*, vol. 23, no. 3, September.

Cleaver, Kelvin M. (1985) 'The impact of price and exchange rate policies on agriculture in Sub-Saharan Africa', World Bank Staff Working Papers, No. 728. Washington DC: World Bank.

Collier, P. (1983) 'Africa and the study of economics', in R. Bates et al. (eds), *Africa and the Disciplines*.

Edwards, Sebastian (1989) *Real Exchange Rates, Devaluation and Adjustment: Exchange Rate Policy in Developing Countries*. Cambridge, MA: MIT Press.
Galston, W.A. (1985) *A Tough Row to Hoe: the 1985 Farm Bill and Beyond*. Lanham, MD: Hamilton Press.
Jaeger, W. (1991) 'The impact of policy in African agriculture an empirical investigation', WPS 640, March, World Bank.
Jaeger, W.K. (1992) 'The effects of economic policies on African agriculture', World Bank Discussion Papers, Africa Technical Department Series, No. 147.
Jaeger, William and Charles Humphreys (1988) 'The effect of policy reforms on agricultural incentives in Sub-Saharan Africa', *American Journal of Agricultural Economics*, vol. 70, no. 5, December, pp. 1036–43.
Jansen, Doris (1988) *Trade and Exchange Rate and Agricultural Pricing Policies in Zambia*. Washington DC: World Bank.
Jansen, Doris and Kay Muir (1994) 'Trade, exchange rate policy and agriculture in the 1980s', in M. Rukuni and C. Eicher (eds), *Zimbabwe's Agricultural Revolution*. Harare: University of Zimbabwe Publications.
Lecaillon, Jacques and Christian Morrisson (1986a) *Economic Policies and Agricultural Performance: the Case of Burkina Faso*. Paris: Development Center of the Organisation for Economic Co-operation and Development.
Lecaillon, Jacques and Christian Morrisson (1986b) *Economic Policies and Agricultural Performance: the Case of Mali*. Paris: Development Center of the Organisation for Economic Co-operation and Development.
Lopez, R., R. Ali and B. Larsen (1991) 'How trade and economic policies affect agriculture: a framework for analysis applied to Tanzania and Malawi, WPS 719, July, World Bank.
Masters, W.A. (1994) *Government and Agriculture in Zimbabwe*. Westport, CT: Praeger.
Oyejide, A.T. (1986) 'The effects of trade and exchange rate policies on agriculture in Nigeria', Research Report 55. Washington DC: International Food Policy Research Institute.
Rohrbach, D. (1989) 'The economics of smallholder maize production in Zimbabwe: implications for food security', MSU International Development Paper No. 11. East Lansing, MI: Michigan State University.
Sharply, Jennifer (1986) *Economic Policies and Agricultural Performance: the Case of Kenya*. Paris: Development Center of the Organisation for Economic Co-operation and Development.
Takavarasha, T.M. (1996) 'Assessing policy effects during transition from a controlled to a market driver crop pricing and marketing system using the multiple objective policy analysis framework methodology', unpublished DPhil thesis, Department of Agricultural Economics and Extension, University of Zimbabwe.
Valdes, A. (1986) *Impact of Trade and Macroeconomic Policies on Agricultural Growth: the South American Experience*. IFPRI Reprint No. 96. Washington DC: IFPRI.
Valdes, Alberto and Ammar Siamwala (1988) 'Foreign trade regime, exchange rate policy, and structure of incentives', in Price J. Gittinger, Joan Leslie and Caroline Hoisington (eds), *Food Policy: Integrating Supply Distribution and Consumption*. Baltimore: John Hopkins University Press.
World Bank (1991) *Zimbabwe Agricultural Sector Memorandum*, Report No. 9429-Zim, May. Southern Africa Department, Agricultural Operations Division, World Bank.
Yerfi Fosu, K. (1992) 'The real exchange rate and Ghana's agricultural exports', African Economic Research Consortium Research Paper, No. 9.

13
Macroeconomic Policies and the Manufacturing Sector

Hans Bjurek, Dick Durevall and Daniel Ndlela

1 Introduction

Zimbabwe constitutes a good case for evaluating the impact on productivity of a change from import substitution to market-oriented policies. It has a very well-developed manufacturing sector, which at the end of the 1980s contributed over 25 per cent to GDP and produced about 7000 different products. Before the implementation of the structural adjustment program (ESAP) in 1991, controls were widespread. The overwhelming majority of firms produced under conditions where there was no foreign or domestic competition. Moreover, foreign exchange rationing severely constrained access to imports of machinery, spare parts and raw materials, resulting in chronic breakdowns and low capacity utilization (Riddell, 1988). Hence liberalization in general, and trade reform in particular, should have had a strong impact on productivity.

In this chapter we first examine how macroeconomic policies impacted on the manufacturing sector over two distinct periods: the inward-looking macropolicies of the 1980s and the outward-oriented policies of the 1990s. The aim is to classify and identify the set of policies that will promote growth, competitiveness and the acquisition of appropriate technologies by firms.

In the second part of this chapter we analyze if ESAP contributed to an increase in total factor productivity in the manufacturing sector. In order to do this we first estimate indexes of total factor productivity for 31 manufacturing sub-sectors for the period 1980–95. Total factor productivity is measured with Malmquist productivity indexes, obtained by a non-parametric (DEA) approach. Following this, we use panel data methods to test for the effects of trade reform and other variables related to the ESAP, such as foreign aid and imports, on total factor productivity growth, while controlling for exogenous variables. This two-step procedure is used because the sub-sectors are heterogeneous and have their own specific technology.

The following section evaluates the role of macroeconomic policies during the 1980s and 1990s. Section 3 presents the methodology used to measure productivity and reports results from our estimations of the growth rates of TFP. In Section 4 we first discuss the explanatory variables used in the panel data analysis, and then carry out the regressions. Conclusions are drawn in the final section.

2 Macroeconomic policy and the manufacturing sector

2.1 Inward-looking policies of the 1980s

The serious economic disruptions and deep social inequality that characterized the Zimbabwean economy prior to its independence in 1980 posed heavy challenges for the government with regards to the performance of the economy. The new government sought to ensure the stability necessary for economic growth, while at the same time articulating structural, economic and social changes consistent with the attainment of equity. It was in order to address these imbalances, particularly in the ownership structure of the country's wealth, that the government opted for a highly inward-looking 'socialist' strategy. The main thrust of government policy was to continue with import-substitution strategies, which in the pre-independence period had resulted in considerable diversification of economic activities and enhancement of skills. The foreign currency allocation system was embraced as a mechanism to control investment with the hope that it would orient the production structure to serve the needs of the majority of the population.

The government's objective for the manufacturing sector were set out in Volume I of the Transitional National Development Plan (TNDP) 1982/83–1984/85. These were: growth and expansion, export expansion, job creation, further import substitution, skills training, decentralization, less foreign ownership and control, and more efficient energy utilization. In the TNDP, these objectives were to be executed mainly through the instrument of a 'comprehensive industrial strategy' which was going to be further translated into short-term implementation instruments. Explicit mention was made of the need to address the question of the 'need, capacity and potential of the manufacturing sector to become more export-oriented than it is now' (TNDP, Section 13.8). However, in practice the stated plan objectives were never implemented explicitly – for example, the promised 'comprehensive industrial strategy' was only published in February 1999, eight years after the launch of ESAP.[1] To achieve the above assumptions and policy objectives the following became the mainstay of the government's policy instruments:

Foreign exchange allocation and exchange rate policy

In the 1980s the policy framework for resource allocation involved a high degree of indirect and direct controls over productive activities. Foreign exchange allocation became the most important policy instrument affecting short- and long-term decisions of enterprises in both the private and the public sectors. Through the existing system of administrative allocation of foreign exchange, government allocated all foreign exchange to firms for both working capital and investment purposes according to the assessed global foreign exchange available and the perceived priorities of the economy. Current allocations were based upon historical allocations to firms as well as specific assessments of the current needs of enterprises and foreign exchange shortages.

The system of foreign exchange rationing created distortions and, as the core of the policy environment, it had a pervasive influence on the whole structure of prices and pattern of production in the economy. In a projected period, say six months, government deducted legally committed uses (for example, external debt service, profit remittances), set aside enough to maintain international reserves at an adequate level and allocated foreign exchange to priority uses (for example, imports of medicines and fuels). The remainder was then allocated to industry, agriculture, mining and commerce on the basis of assessed need, using historical shares as a starting point for the firm-by-firm allocation, but modified for new entrants and for changes in the needs of existing firms (World Bank, 1986).

The demand for foreign exchange allocation invariably exceeded supply. Established enterprises were favored by the allocation system at the expense of new firms, a policy which led to a high degree of product concentration. Thus in the mid-1980s, half of over 6000 Zimbabwean products were manufactured under monopolies and an additional 30 per cent under oligopoly conditions (figures from UNIDO, 1986). Over half of manufactured output and employment was in the 11 per cent of firms with more than 500 workers. Established firms enjoyed protection not only from foreign competition but also from actual and potential domestic competitors. As a result both domestic and international competition was curtailed.

From 1982 onwards the Zimbabwe dollar was devalued at a faster speed than the rate of inflation, resulting in the real exchange rate steadily depreciating over the years. In the mid-1980s the real effective exchange rate reached a lower value than its 1980 level. Despite this real depreciation in the local currency there was still excess demand for foreign exchange for both current and capital account transactions at the current exchange rate, making it essential to ration foreign exchange in order to maintain external balance (World Bank, 1986).

Investment policies

Foreign exchange rationing also implied that investments were controlled. The administrative approval of all new investments or expansions was carried out by the Investments Projects Committee (IPC). The main criteria for approval were that, ex ante, the project should not be a net user of foreign exchange during any twelve month period of its expected life and that it should not compete with local production unless it also produced for export.

Projects requiring more than a certain sum – Z$2.5m or US$1.6m – and projects with more than 15 per cent foreign ownership required the approval of additional committees. Foreign investment in Zimbabwe was also administered by the Foreign Investment Committee (FIC), a body consisting of cabinet ministers assisted by a working party of senior government officials. The policy was to administratively direct foreign investment to preferred sectors, to maximize the use of local raw materials, to transfer appropriate technologies and to generate employment.

The rationing of foreign exchange was responsible for low levels of investment throughout the 1980s and became a major barrier to international trade. Investment declined from about 25 per cent of GDP in the early 1970s to less than 20 per cent of GDP in the mid-1980s, with a continuing decline in private sector investment (12 per cent of GDP in 1985, 8 per cent of GDP in 1987). In 1984 the foreign exchange component of industrial projects submitted to the Industrial Projects Committee (IPC) was some 70 per cent of total project value, and for every project approved, four were rejected. The high rejection rate was attributed largely, though not exclusively, to foreign exchange constraints.

The tax system offered some incentives for foreign investment in the form of refunds of sales tax or import tax on capital goods imported by industry for investment in priority areas. However, these incentives were more than offset by restrictions on the remittance of dividends and exchange rate controls. According to these restrictions, the local branches of companies incorporated outside Zimbabwe were permitted to remit only 25 per cent of net after-tax profits on the equity charged before 1979. This percentage was 50 per cent on the investments made after 1979. Foreign companies also had to pay a branch profit tax in addition to the income tax and an income tax surcharge. Furthermore, gross foreign dividends were subject to an income tax rate of 20 per cent. In addition, there were some restrictions on local borrowing by non-resident-owned companies.

Thus the foreign exchange allocation system acted as the most effective disincentive to foreign investment. No allocation of foreign exchange was available to foreign firms if they competed with domestic firms. Given the very low level of foreign ownership necessary for a company to be defined as foreign-controlled (25 per cent), there was no incentive for local firms to be integrated with those foreign firms which had both the skills and the technological know-how required for international competition.

Price controls

The Zimbabwean price system was characterized by extensive controls over most commodities. The government determined a maximum selling price for most basic commodities, while other commodity groups required government approval before price increases could be initiated. In order to cushion the revenue effects of these price ceilings on manufacturing firms, the government operated a system of commodity subsidies, especially on agricultural products used as direct and essential inputs in the manufacture of basic foodstuffs and items deemed necessary to be within the financial reach of the majority of the people. However this system, which was meant to facilitate the socioeconomic objectives of a command economy met with limited success in terms of overall performance of the manufacturing sector. These price controls were usually set below equilibrium levels, thereby rendering the market system ineffective in allocating resources. As a result severe artificial shortages were created because producers deliberately cut down on production and held back supplies to the market in an effort to minimize their losses. Others thrived through a fast increasing parallel market, charging highly inflated prices to desperate consumers and also capitalizing on the prevailing situation in order to make good their gains from such transmissions. The net effect of this system was a deterioration in the economic stability of the country. Investment growth took a downward trend because potential investors no longer had the confidence to invest in the economy and the incentive to expand present production capacities through the intensive use or acquisition of new technologies was hampered by the repressive price system.

The policy framework described above had a pervasive influence on the overall pattern of economic activity in Zimbabwe. The centerpiece of the policies was the administered system of foreign exchange allocation that conferred a high degree of protection on activities oriented toward the domestic market, from both imports and potential entry by domestic firms. This situation favored domestically oriented manufacturing activities (largely in the service sector), but it worked against the agriculture and mining sectors.

Labor market regulations

The main policy instrument of the Zimbabwe's government's Labour Market Regulations was the statutory minimum wage legislation of 1980. Under this, the government set up minimum wages and regulated wage and salary increments for various income brackets. The compensation structure favored those in lower-income brackets in the face of the rising inflation caused by subsidy removals and higher administered agricultural producer prices. Although the minimum wage was introduced when most firms were already paying their employees above the level of the minimum wage, the net policy effect was to increase the overall wage bill as firms sought to maintain certain differentials among different groups of their employees. Firms which experienced rising salaries and wages as a proportion of their net output – such as textiles, basic metals, non metals and certain groups of chemicals – suffered negative effects on their internal cash flow and investment. The ripple effects of such a trend are likely to have had a major contribution to the decline in investment growth that gripped the economy in the period 1982–87, during which all sectors except foodstuffs and chemicals registered negative growth rates.

In terms of employment growth, performance was poor. Barely 2 per cent employment growth was achieved over the decade, although it was fastest in the second half of the 1980s. This translated to about 4000 new jobs per year – a small figure in the context of 200 000 to 300 000 annual school-leavers. However, the fastest employment growth rates were registered in the following sectors: clothing and footwear, paper, printing and publishing, chemical and petroleum products and transport equipment.

Trade policy and export incentives

In addition to the foreign exchange controls the Zimbabwean government applied stringent import restrictions, with only a limited number of incentives aimed at boosting the country's manufactured exports. There was little change in the tariff structure inherited from the colonial government. Imports of raw materials were subject to 10 per cent or less while the average rate on capital goods was about 20 per cent. There was a wide variation in customs duties on consumer goods. Essential consumer goods were admitted either duty free or at very low rates while some prepared foodstuffs, beverages and spirits, photographic equipment, furniture, jewellery and other consumer durables were subject to high rates of duty, in order to protect existing firms. A surtax on imports was introduced to the tariff structure during the 1980s, rising from 5 per cent in August 1981 to 20 per cent in July 1983. In the case of certain commodities, the suspension of duty under certain regulations reduced the actual levied duty rates by varying percentages.

Some manufactures received considerable concessions on duties of imported inputs and raw materials through an extensive set of rebates. Customs duties were not used as an incentive to promote manufacturing industries in Zimbabwe. The effective mechanism was the foreign exchange allocation system, which involved stringent quantitative restrictions on imports. While the tariff regime was not the principal means of protecting industry from import competition, the habit of providing extensive rebates meant that tariff revenue and with that, the value of the import quotas, were often passed on to firms.

Of all the export incentives introduced in the early 1980s the most important was the Export Revolving Fund (ERF) which was introduced in July 1983. The purpose of this Fund was to promote manufactured exports by ensuring that exporters had the foreign exchange for their import requirements. Under the ERF exporters received an automatic foreign exchange allocation for such imports. The scheme was modified later to grant the same benefits to indirect exporters that had a strong link with the direct exporters. Those firms producing inputs, such as packaging for manufacturers of exports, were eligible for a guaranteed foreign exchange allocation for the importation of the required raw materials. The other export incentives of the 1980s included the Export Incentive Scheme (EIS) introduced in 1984 and the incremental bonus scheme introduced in 1988. Under the EIS an exporter received a tax-free cash payment of 9 per cent of f.o.b. price in Zimbabwean dollars; under the incremental export bonus scheme manufacturing firms could retain 5 per cent of the incremental export earnings for their imports needs.

This wide range of export incentives had a small but influential role in expanding exports, despite the foreign exchange allocation system overwhelmingly determining the pattern of resource allocation. Whereas exports declined between 1981 and 1986, they grew by 6.8 per cent between 1986 and 1990, which was quite modest given the wide range of export incentives available during the latter part of the 1980s. The slow and cumbersome bureaucratic procedures involved with these incentives to acquire import and export licences dominated the time of entrepreneurs and managers. By the end of the decade, a high budget deficit due to high recurrent expenditure – in particular, subsidies to parastatals – had become a major characteristic of the economy. These effects were behind the intense pressure for economic policy reform (see Robinson, 1993 and Ndlela, 1994).

The overall strategy to utilize the system of controls had met with only limited success. In the 1990s, this led the government to consider changing to a new socioeconomic system in which market forces played an increasingly dominant role. Thus the first phase of economic reforms, the economic structural adjustment program (ESAP), was adopted in 1991.

2.2 The outward-oriented policy framework of the 1990s

Zimbabwe emerged from the 1980s with a highly diversified manufacturing sector which, with high firm and product concentration, accounted for over 26 per cent of the country's GDP. However, the sector had limited exposure to international competition and access to 'state-of-the-art' technology. The policies discussed above, and in particular, the foreign exchange allocation system had prevented domestic industries from modernizing their plant and machinery. As such, at the beginning of the 1990s, many domestic industries were, by international standards, still utilizing traditional technologies and obsolete plant and equipment (Ratnayake, 1994).

The specific policy measures under ESAP affecting the manufacturing sector included:

- a variety of measures meant to improve the investment climate such as removal of restrictions on capital mobility especially the repatriatability of dividends and profits, the deregulation of investment controls, prices, interest rates and abolition and or modification of bye-laws and other regulations that hamper investment;
- the liberalization of trade and exchange rates;

- a market-based system of foreign exchange allocation;
- a shift from import licensing and quotas to a tariff based system of protection;
- reform of public enterprises (PEs) and elimination of subsidies to achieve greater operational efficiency through commercialization and privatization;
- achieve a stable macroeconomic environment by adopting prudent fiscal and monetary policies, reducing the budget deficit, slowing down credit creation and monetary expansion to reduce inflation;
- financial sector reforms that encourage savings and improve the efficiency of financial intermediation;
- labour market reforms that increase the flexibility and efficiency of the labour market.

While ESAP opened new growth opportunities for the manufacturing sector and created a sustainable economic policy framework, performance was influenced, to a great extent, by a combination of exogenous factors and policy implementation failures. The manufacturing sector had an initially encouraging response to the reforms, especially with respect to pure manufactured exports. While total exports grew by only 2 per cent between 1991 and 1995, due to depressed world prices for Zimbabwe's non-manufacturing exports (gold, tobacco and other primary commodities), pure manufactured exports (excluding ferrochrome) grew by an impressive 32 per cent in 1991/92, 30 per cent in 1993, 20 per cent in 1994 and 10 per cent in 1995. However, policy implementation failures and difficulties in other aspects of the reform package (especially fiscal policy and lagging public sector reforms) saw pure manufactured exports decline over the second half of the 1990s. They declined by 11 per cent in 1996, culminating in a massive collapse of –41 per cent in 1998. This decline was closely associated with decreasing export incentives because the real exchange rate was allowed to appreciate up until the currency crisis of November 1997. No significant trade-enhancing policy reforms were initiated after the initial trade liberalization measures of the early 1990s.

The introduction of ESAP was immediately followed by the region's most severe drought in 1992, which affected manufacturing output. After growing by 6.1 per cent in 1991, the volume of manufacturing production fell by 8 per cent due to the drought; and so did agricultural and mining output – by 22 per cent and 1.4 per cent respectively. Overall, GDP growth plunged by 7.7 per cent compared to 4.9 per cent in the first year of ESAP. In 1991 the fastest growing sub-sectors were: drink and tobacco, clothing and footwear, wood and furniture, printing and publishing, transport equipment, but progress in these areas was offset by declines in the large metal sub-sector and nonmetallic mineral products. Between 1992 and 1993 gross manufacturing output continued to register negative growth rates, while in 1993–94, there was a modest growth of 9.6 per cent, followed by a decline between 1994 and 1995 due to another drought year. The average fall between

February 1992 and February 1995 was 25 per cent bringing the manufacturing volume index down to a level last recorded in 1985 (Ndlela, 1994).

The government's fiscal policy stance also impacted negatively on manufacturing sector firms. The high budget deficits not only fueled inflation, but its financing also significantly reduced the availability of financial resources for both existing and emerging indigenous enterprises. Government also failed to remove the more fundamental constraints on output growth that were required in order to make a breakthrough in both the level and the composition of manufacturing production. Little effort was put into introducing changes in industrial technologies and the transformation of the whole range of characteristics often associated with increased industrial and entrepreneurial capabilities (legal systems, tax structures, financial skills, managerial skills, marketing skills, as well as technical skills.

3 Total factor productivity

Trade reform and liberalization were expected to have a positive impact on the economy and, hence, should have had a strong impact on productivity. In this section we analyze if ESAP contributed to an increase in total factor productivity in the manufacturing sector. When reviewing the effects of opening up to international trade, Harrison and Revenga (1995) concluded that economists have not reached a consensus on the relationship between liberal trade policies and productivity. They indicated that this might be due to two flaws common in many studies – lack of good data on trade policy and endogeneity problems with the measures used. For Zimbabwe, there exist data on administrative allocations of foreign exchange and these constitute a good measure of trade policy during the 1990s. Furthermore, controls on international trade were to a large extent dismantled, as planned in the original structural adjustment program, so it is unlikely that trade policy responded to total factor productivity growth.

The general understanding of total factor productivity (TFP) is that it is measured by an index of outputs divided by an index of inputs, or as the shift in the production function. These two approaches are identical when the production function is defined on continuous time and production is assumed to be efficient. Technological change is also defined and measured as the shift in the production function and is thus often used synonymously with TFP. When production is allowed to be inefficient, however, TFP change also includes technical efficiency change.

There are many possible causes for changes in productivity; in the short run, productivity can increase as a result of higher capacity utilization, which might be due to higher domestic and international demand, or access to rationed inputs. More fundamental sources of increased productivity are the use of new techniques, scale economies, investments in human capital and a more efficient allocation of resources in relation to relative factor prices.

TFP can be measured in several ways. One way is to use the so-called Malmquist index, first defined as a quantity index in a consumer context by Malmquist (1953), and then proposed as a productivity index by Caves et al. (1982). Compared to indexes like the Fisher ideal index and the Törnqvist index, the Malmquist index has several advantages. No assumptions regarding market structure or economic behavior – for example, cost minimizing or revenue maximizing – needs to be made. Moreover, the Malmquist index requires no information on prices. However, the index requires specific assumptions of the technology, which can be specified as, for instance, a translog technology (see Caves et al., 1982; Nishimizu and Page, 1982), or a non-parametric technology (see Färe et al., 1994; Bjurek, 1996).

In this chapter, we measure TFP by means of the Malmquist productivity index based on a non-parametric technology, which is well motivated since price information is weak and we know little about the economic behavior of the firms and about the market structure in the different sectors. Moreover, we measure productivity relative to a common constant returns to scale technology and do not separate technical change and technical efficiency change (see Bjurek and Durevall, 1998). Thus, for each sub-sector, productivity is measured relative to the most productive observations during the entire period. In most applications, panel data sets are used and the index is decomposed into technical change and efficiency change. Although, it is possible to decompose the index, in the case with only time series data, there are serious identification problems.

The productivity change is estimated for 31 manufacturing sub-sectors, at the 4-digit level of ISIC, for the years 1980 to 1995. For each sub-sector we have 16 observations on production, measured in 1990 manufacturing prices, capital stock, labor and materials. The capital stock is calculated using the perpetual inventory method using investment data from the Census of Industrial Production as far back as 1967. In the calculations of the capital stock, we used the value of real output in 1967 as a proxy of the initial capital stock, and a depreciation rate of 5 per cent. Since the sub-sectors are heterogeneous, each sector has its own specific technology and we cannot estimate TFP using a panel. Thus, the non-parametric technology is also justified because of the restricted number of observations, which excludes the estimation of a translog function or other flexible functions.

3.1 Total factor productivity results

Total factor productivity change for the manufacturing sub-sectors are reported in Table 13.1 for the periods 1981–85, 1986–90, 1991–95 and 1994–95. During the periods 1981–85 and 1986–90 productivity increased in most sub-sectors, while during the period 1991–95 more than half of the sub-sectors show decreasing productivity. We have also reported the yearly productivity change for 1994–95, when the trade reform was more or less completed. During this period productivity increased for approximately

Table 13.1 Total factor productivity change in the manufacturing industry 1981–95 (per cent per year).

	1981–85	*1986–90*	*1991–95*	*1994–95*
Meat	1.4	0.2	2.8	0.0
Grain mills	–0.2	–1.2	0.7	2.6
Bakery products	4.2	0.2	0.0	11.1
Confectionery	2.4	–0.5	–0.2	3.3
Miscellaneous foods	1.4	1.6	0.0	0.2
Alcoholic beverages	18.3	0.0	–7.7	–4.7
Soft drinks	3.7	4.6	–1.1	2.9
Tobacco products	5.2	–5.2	5.6	16.5
Cotton textiles	0.0	0.0	–0.4	3.6
Knitted products	0.0	1.4	–0.1	7.9
Other textile products	2.8	0.0	–4.4	–7.1
Wearing apparel	1.2	–0.1	–2.8	1.5
Footwear	4.9	–2.4	–5.8	–3.6
Wooden products	–3.3	4.9	0.0	0.0
Furniture	0.1	0.8	0.0	12.0
Paper products	0.9	0.0	–2.0	–2.2
Printing	0.0	0.0	–4.0	–9.5
Fertiliser	0.7	–3.0	0.7	–5.5
Paints	5.7	–0.1	–8.1	–5.2
Soaps-pharmaceuticals	0.1	0.2	–2.4	1.1
Miscellaneous chemicals	3.3	–1.3	–3.4	–1.9
Basic chemicals	–1.7	1.2	0.5	8.4
Rubber products	0.9	–2.2	–0.8	–3.8
Plastic products	3.0	0.9	–7.8	–4.2
Structural clay products	6.7	0.0	–5.0	1.9
Nonmetallic mineral products	–1.2	1.2	2.3	15.6
Basic metals	–1.1	0.2	1.2	9.3
Metal products-machinery	–0.7	–0.1	0.1	6.6
Electrical machinery	0.9	0.6	–0.2	0.3
Motor vehicles	1.7	–1.0	2.8	0.8
Other vehicles	0.6	0.0	–3.3	5.1

Source: *Census of Industrial Production* (various issues).

two-thirds of the sub-sectors. In general the growth rates vary greatly both over time and across sections. The overall impression is that total factor productivity growth was lower during the period of ESAP than during the period 1986–90. However, during the last two years, 1994–95, more sub-sectors experienced higher productivity growth than during 1986–90. The observed differences between the periods could be a result of liberalization, but they could also be due to changes in exogenous factors such as changes in demand, foreign aid and weather conditions. Thus, in the following section we test for the determinants of TFP.

4 Econometric analysis

To investigate if market liberalization in general, and trade reform in particular, have contributed to an increase in TFP growth, panel data methods were used to estimate fixed-effects models. The purpose was to evaluate the impact on TFP growth of variables related to ESAP, while controlling for others. Since little is known about the determinants of TFP the analysis was exploratory and several different models were estimated.

Our primary measure of trade liberalization is the share of total imports financed through the administrative allocation of foreign exchange – direct local market allocation (DLMA). It should capture the process of opening up during the 1990s well, since its evolution is quite close to the plan laid out by the Zimbabwean government (GoZ, 1992). However, during the 1980s variations in the degree of import rationing are likely to have affected the share between the government and private imports, resulting in relative decreases in allocations for reasons that are unrelated to trade liberalization. Thus, in constructing the variable we kept its values for the period 1981–89 constant, for example, the average value for the latter part of the 1980s was used. This means that we do not measure changes due to export promotion programs implemented before ESAP, such as the Export Revolving Fund and the Bonus Scheme Imports. Since these only constituted minor changes within the import-substitution policy regime they are not of central interest to our study.

As an additional measure of trade liberalization we used the premium on the parallel foreign exchange market. It is not ideal because it can also reflect factors not directly related to trade policy, such as changes in monetary policy. However, the behavior of the premium during the 1990s is closely related to that of the share of foreign exchange allocations, and thus gives support to the results obtained with the latter.

We also used two step dummies to test for the impact of trade reform. One dummy was set to zero up to 1993, and to unity in 1994–95, when the DLMA had been abolished and a unified foreign exchange market had been established. The other dummy was set to unity for the whole period of ESAP (1991–95). Both dummies are, of course, more likely than the two other measures to capture the impact of reforms in general.

One goal of trade reform is to achieve higher TFP growth through increased foreign competition. There is hardly any doubt that competition has increased in many of the sub-sectors in Zimbabwean manufacturing, as indicated both by anecdotal evidence and data on imports of manufactured goods. For instance, calculations made by Durevall et al. (1998) showed that imports of manufactured goods increased by 35 per cent in current US dollars between 1993 and 1995. This should have resulted in reduced market power for domestic firms and decreases in their mark-ups. Thus, an indirect way of testing the effects of trade reform is to include mark-ups in the empirical model.

Since independence, Zimbabwe has received a great deal of foreign aid, and during the first years of the implementation of the structural adjustment program the level of foreign aid increased considerably; in real terms foreign aid was more than 40 per cent higher during the period 1991–95 than during the previous five years. The most direct effect of foreign aid on TFP is probably through balance-of-payment support and commodity-import programs, which intend to alleviate bottlenecks due to the shortages of imported inputs and to allow the authorities to maintain a stable currency. However, foreign aid can affect TFP in many other ways, from increasing demand to having a positive impact on infrastructure. To capture these effects we added the rate of change in the real value of foreign aid in our estimation model.

Two variables were included to capture the availability of inputs: the growth in imports and the amount of rainfall. During most of the 1980s import rationing kept capacity utilization down, and thus the possibility to import inputs more freely during the 1990s should have increased productivity. However, import growth is also likely to measure increases in foreign competition, in particular for 1994 and 1995, and thereby capture two of the channels through which trade reform affects TFP. Ideally, we would have liked to disaggregate imports into goods produced by the different manufacturing sectors and their imported inputs, but this was not feasible for the whole sample period due to the paucity of data.

Rainfall is the most important determinant of yearly changes in agricultural production in Zimbabwe, and it is used instead of marketed agricultural output, of which there is a lack of information following the liberalization of the agricultural markets. Since many industries use inputs from the agricultural sector, the size of the harvests can have a direct effect on productivity through variations in both availability and price of agricultural raw materials. Moreover, changes in agricultural production also affect exports and imports. Good harvests boost exports and reduce the need to import food. During the period of import rationing, this resulted in more foreign exchange being made available to the manufacturing sector for imports of intermediate goods and capital. After liberalization, the result is probably cheaper imports through the impact on the value of the currency. Over the course of ESAP, inflation rose from about 15 per cent to close to 50 per cent and then dropped to about 25 per cent. As a result, both the variability and the dispersion of relative prices probably increased during this period. This is likely to have had a negative effect on the efficiency of price signals and could have affected decisions to invest in new technology by increasing uncertainty (Dixit and Pindyck, 1994). Thus, to control for the impact of the rapid growth in inflation during ESAP we included the rate of change in inflation as a proxy for price variability. Studies of developing countries have shown that variations in demand due to business cycles can affect total factor productivity in the short run. A sector in manufacturing is likely to experience decreases in productivity during booms and vice versa (Roberts and Tybout, 1997). The reason is that when demand is high the less efficient firms increase their market shares, and during recessions they lose shares. Moreover, more new firms enter the market when times are good and, in general, they have lower productivity than the average of old firms, though this is not likely to have been an important factor in Zimbabwe before liberalization because of the difficulties of entering the DLMA system. To capture the effect of business cycles we included two variables – the deviations from trend of the log of GDP in Zimbabwe and industrial production in the industrialized countries. The trends were obtained with the Hodrick–Prescott filter.

Output growth is usually found to have a strong effect on TFP growth (see Tybout, 1992; Weiss, 1992). This is known as Verdoorn's Law, which states that high output growth increases TFP growth through scale economies. We share Tybout's (1992) concern that the empirical results might reflect a spurious correlation since output growth also enters on the left-hand side of the equations estimated – that is, in the measures of productivity. However, as an additional check on the robustness of our results we estimated models with output growth as an explanatory variable.

4.1 Econometric results

In Table 13.2 we report a selection of the estimated models. They were estimated as 'one-way' fixed-effect models using least squares with White's robust estimation of the covariance matrix under the assumption that variances are equal within groups. We also estimated models that allowed for a more general form of heteroscedasticity and an autocorrelated error structure, but these gave results very similar to those reported. The columns numbered (1) to (4) in the table present estimates of our base-line model and the four variables measuring trade reform – that is, the share of imports financed through the DLMA, the premium, and the two step dummies. Neither of these measures is even close to being significant at the 5 per cent level, indicating that trade reform by itself has not contributed to growth in TFP. However, the results do suggest that the increase in the growth of imports and foreign aid that occurred during ESAP raised TFP. An increase by one percentage point in imports or foreign aid raises TFP growth by about 0.2 and 0.1 percentage points, respectively. The results also show that increases in the growth rate of inflation reduce TFP growth, that there is a strong and clearly significant negative effect from the foreign business cycle, and that there is a positive effect from rainfall.

In column (5), the domestic business cycle lagged one year has been added to the model, but it is not significant. This result is dependent on the inclusion of the foreign business cycle, which dominates the domestic one. We also tried adding business cycles contemporaneously but that reduces

Variable	*(1)*	*(2)*	*(3)*	*(4)*	*(5)*	*(6)*	*(7)*	*(8)*	*(9)*
Share of imports financed by DLMA	−0.011				−0.040	0.021	0.066	−0.011	0.023
	(−0.241)				(−0.764)	(0.490)	(0.835)	(−1.354)	(0.591)
Premium on parallel exchange rate market		−0.118							
		(−0.803)							
Dummy for trade liberalization			0.005						
			(0.277)						
Dummy for ESAP				−0.009					
				(−0.771)					
Growth in imports	0.191	0.186	0.185	0.199	0.211	0.257	0.232	0.255	0.166
	(2.716)	(2.644)	(2.412)	(2.842)	(2.924)	(3.831)	(2.956)	(3.814)	(2.805)
Growth in foreign aid	0.103	0.101	0.103	0.102	0.105	0.099	0.099	0.102	0.041
	(4.201)	(4.140)	(4.203)	(4.179)	(4.295)	(4.462)	(4.257)	(4.431)	(1.932)
Growth of inflation	−0.228	−0.198	−0.228	−0.250	−0.266	−0.269	−0.262	−0.284	0.047
	(−2.531)	(−2.024)	(−2.562)	(−2.778)	(−2.792)	(−3.148)	(−3.149)	(−3.341)	(0.588)
Foreign business cycle lagged one year	−1.179	−1.244	−1.143	−1.149	−1.463	−1.500	−1.345	−1.406	−0.856
	(−4.653)	(−4.668)	(−4.040)	(−4.490)	(−4.230)	(−6.126)	(−3.980)	(−5.586)	(−4.025)
Log of rainfall	0.079	0.082	0.079	0.064	0.120	0.0672	0.0667	0.055	−0.019
	(2.376)	(2.617)	(2.409)	(1.911)	(2.519)	(2.104)	(2.116)	(1.734)	(−0.663)
Domestic business cycle lagged one year					0.366				
					(1.203)				
Mark-up						0.445	0.434	0.500	
						(5.460)	(5.139)	(5.584)	
Mark-up dummy (1994–1995)							0.073		
							(0.580)		
Mark-up dummy (1991–1995)								−0.137	
								(−1.670)	
Growth in production									0.342
									(12.513)
Standard deviation	0.118	0.118	0.118	0.118	0.118	0.112	0.112	0.111	0.099
R^2	0.095	0.096	0.094	0.096	0.097	0.196	0.189	0.199	0.363

Note: The dependent variable is the growth rate of total factor productivity. The sample runs from 1981 to 1995 and there are 31 groups, giving 465 observations. All equations were estimated with Least Squares allowing for fixed effects. The standard errors are corrected for heteroscedasticity assuming variances are equal within groups. T-statistics are reported in parenthesis. All results were obtained with LIMDEP 7.1.

the t-values considerably. In any case, our measure of trade liberalization was not significant in any of the models estimated.

Column (6) reports estimation results when the mark-up is included in the model of column (1). It is clearly significant, having a t-value of 5.5. But the coefficient is positive, not negative as we predicted. Since there might have been a change in the relation between the mark-up and TFP during ESAP, we constructed two interaction dummies – one for the period of no quota restrictions (1994–95) and one for the entire period of ESAP (1991–95). As shown in columns (7) and (8), the coefficient on the mark-up does not appear to have changed during the structural adjustment program. It is interesting to note that adding the mark-up only marginally affects the estimates of the parameters of the other variables.

Finally, we included output growth to control for potential dynamic scale economies. As reported in column (9), it is highly significant and has a strong positive effect on TFP growth; its coefficient is 0.32. The inclusion of output does not change our main findings; the trade reform variable remains insignificant, and imports, foreign aid and the foreign business cycle still affect TFP. However, the coefficient on foreign aid has dropped from 0.1 to 0.04, perhaps reflecting the impact of foreign aid on the demand for manufactured goods. Moreover, inflation and rainfall are no longer significant. This casts doubts on our earlier findings about the relevance of inflation for TFP growth, because changes in inflation might result from changes in output. Rainfall, on the other hand, is not caused by output, only correlated with it. The insignificance of rainfall is probably due to output growth being sector-specific, and thus more correlated with TFP growth.

5 Conclusion

The inward-looking strategies of the 1980s were not compatible with an industrial strategy that emphasized growth, resulting in a failure to spur growth, to diversify the manufacturing base and to resolve the problem of weak competition. The most important impact of the strategies was to create disincentives to investment by manufacturing firms. They resulted in supply constraints on local and foreign demand for technological capacity, leaving firms to face fewer options and restrictive procedures for both raw material and capital expansion. This was accentuated by the restrictive labor regulations, which had a negative effect on the firm's savings flows. Nevertheless, the government's trade and investment incentives had a positive impact on manufacturing output growth during the second half of the 1980s, despite the highly repressive foreign exchange allocation system.

Following the introduction of the outward-oriented trade policies of the 1990s, the policy environment did not live up to expectations, as this was followed by a lackluster performance of the manufacturing sector. The effects of the severe drought of 1992 exposed the lack of industrial policy and the weakness of the macroeconomic policies – that is, high interest rates and rising input costs resulting from deregulation. In spite of this, there are several reasons to expect that ESAP generated substantial TFP growth in manufacturing. The disappearance of the chronic shortages of imported inputs and capital goods; the removal of the foreign exchange allocation system, price controls and several regulations in the labor market; and the increase in domestic and international competition, should all have contributed to a substantial increase in productivity.

Nonetheless, the TFP growth rates, estimated for 31 different manufacturing sectors over the period 1980 to 1995, do not show a clear tendency to increase during the implementation of ESAP – in fact, more than half of the sub-sectors experienced declines in TFP during the period 1991–95. The performance during 1994–95 was clearly better, and the average growth rate was higher than during the latter half of the 1980s.

Since the growth performance of TFP is determined by many different factors, not just market reforms, we estimated a panel data model to control for exogenous variables. We then tested formally to see if TFP growth was higher after the implementation of ESAP than before. None of our measures of trade reform turned out to be significant. However, two variables related to ESAP had an impact on TFP growth – the growth rate of imports and foreign aid.

We also tested if the mark-up influenced TFP. The hypothesis was that trade liberalization leads to increased competition, causing mark-ups to decline and TFP to grow faster – that is, they should be negatively correlated. Our finding was that the correlation is positive, not negative, and it does not appear to change during the period of ESAP. One explanation for the positive correlation is that changes in labor input and wage costs coincide, and that these have strong influences on TFP growth and the mark-up, respectively. An alternative explanation is that increasing foreign competition leads to lower sales for domestic firms. If the domestic firms are slow to adjust but stay in the market, productivity might decline. This would also imply a positive correlation between mark-up and productivity.

Another result is that both domestic and foreign business cycles, lagged a year, have a negative effect on TFP growth. This is in accordance with the findings reported by Roberts and Tybout (1997) for other developing countries. It could be due to a reallocation of market shares over the cycle as inefficient plants expand more than efficient ones when aggregate demand grows, and contract more during recessions.

We also found that rainfall increases TFP growth, and that the change in inflation decreases it. However, these results were not robust to the inclusion of the rate of change in output. In the case of rainfall, this is not surprising since it is obviously correlated with output growth. For the change in inflation, the lack of robustness implies that inflation decreases when output grows. Since causality is most likely to run mainly from output to inflation, we have no evidence that inflation growth reduces TFP growth.

The adoption of ESAP was meant to allow industrial firms to acquire their required inputs at world-market prices but in practice restrictions have persisted, and high budget deficits have resulted in crowding-out effects for many firms. However, given the still solid industrial infrastructure in Zimbabwe and the evolving policy framework, there are reasons to believe that adoption of an outward-looking industrial policy has good prospects to be successful as Zimbabwe enters the twenty-first century.

Note

1. Government of Zimbabwe (1999) *A Policy for Industrial Development, Trade and Investment in Zimbabwe*. Harare: Government Printers.

References

Bjurek, H. (1996) 'The Malmquist total factor productivity index', *Scandinavian Journal of Economics*, vol. 98, no. 2, pp. 303–13.

Bjurek, H. and D. Durevall (1998) 'Does market liberalization increase total factor productivity growth: evidence from the manufacturing sector in Zimbabwe', Working Paper, No. 10, Gothenburg University.

Caves, D.W., L.R. Christensen and W.E. Diewert (1982) 'The economic theory of index numbers and the measurement of input, output, and productivity', *Econometrica*, vol. 50, pp. 1393–1414.

Central Statistical Office (CSO) *Census of Production*, various issues.

Dixit, A.K. and R.S. Pindyck (1994) *Investment under Uncertainty*. Princeton, NJ: Princeton University Press.

Durevall, D., H. Bjurek and T. Godana (1998) 'Structural adjustment and productivity: a study of the manufacturing and agricultural sectors in Zimbabwe', *Country Economic Report 1998: 1*, Sida, Stockholm.

Färe, R., S. Grosskopf, M. Norris and Z. Zhang (1994) 'Productivity growth, technical progress, and efficiency change in industrialised countries', *American Economic Review*, vol. 84, no. 1, pp. 66–83.

Government of Zimbabwe (GoZ) (1992) *A Framework for Economic Reform, 1991–1995*. Harare: Government Printer.

Harrison A. and A. Revenga (1995) 'The effects of trade policy reform: what do we really know?', NBER Working Paper, No. 5225.

LIMDEP (1995) version 7.0, Econometric Software, Inc. Castle Hill, Australia.

Malmquist, S. (1953) 'Index numbers and indifference surfaces', *Trabajos de Estadistica*, vol. 4, pp. 209–42.

Ndlela, D.B. (1980) 'The Rhodesian economy in a historical perspective, Part 1', in *Zimbabwe Towards a New Order: an Economic and Social Survey*, Working Papers, Volume II, United Nations.

Ndlela, D.B. (1994) 'Stabilization and structural adjustment programmes in Africa: the case of Zimbabwe', paper presented to the International Centre for Economic Growth (ICEG) in Collaboration with Southern African Regional Institute for Policy

Studies (SARIPS) Conference on Economic Reform and Liberation: Perspectives from the African Experiences, Harare, 12–15 June.
Nishimizu, M. and J.M. Page Jr (1982) 'Total factor productivity growth, technological progress and technical efficiency change: dimensions of productivity change in Yugoslavia, 1965–1978', *The Economic Journal*, vol. 92, pp. 920–36.
Ratnayake, R. (1994) 'Effective protection of manufacturing industries in Zimbabwe', paper prepared for monitoring and implementation unit of the Economic Structural Adjustment Program, 1994.
Republic of Zimbabwe *A Policy Framework for Industrial Development, Trade and Investment in Zimbabwe*. Harare: Government Printer.
Republic of Zimbabwe (1982) *Transitional National Development Plan 1982/83–1984/85*, Volume 1. Harare: Amalgamated Press.
Riddell R. (1988) 'Industrialisation in Sub-Saharan Africa: country case study – Zimbabwe', ODI Working Paper, 25. London: ODI.
Roberts, M.J. and J.R. Tybout (1997) 'Producer turnover and productivity growth in developing countries', *The World Bank Research Observer*, vol. 12, no. 1, pp. 1–19, February.
Robinson P. (1993) 'Adjustment and long-term industrial development', paper prepared for International Labor Office, Geneva.
Thompson, C.H. and H.W. Woodruff (1955) *Economic Development in Rhodesia and Nyasaland*. London: Dennis Dobson Limited.
Tybout, J.R. 'Linking trade and productivity: new research directions', *The World Bank Economic Review*, vol. 6, no. 2, pp. 189–212, May.
United Nations Industrial Development Organization (UNIDO) (1986) *The Manufacturing Sector in Zimbabwe*, Document prepared by the Regional and Country Studies Branch Studies and Research Division.
Weiss, J. (1992) 'Trade policy reform and performance in manufacturing: Mexico 1975–88', *Journal of Development Studies*, vol. 29, no. 1, pp. 1–24, October.
World Bank (1986) *Zimbabwe: an Industrial Sector Memorandum*, Industrial Development and Finance Division, Eastern and Southern Africa Region.
Zimbabwe Congress of Trade Unions (1996) *Beyond ESAP: Framework for a Long-term Development Strategy in Zimbabwe Beyond Structural Adjustment Programme (ESAP)*. Harare: ZCTU.

14
Macroeconomic Policies and the Health Sector

Gladys Mutangadura

1 Introduction

The objective of this chapter is to assess the impact of macroeconomic policies on the health sector in Zimbabwe since 1980. It tries to link the changes in health sector performance to macroeconomic policies. We trace health indicators, beginning with the expansionary budgetary spending policies of the early 1980s, moving through the stagnation of the late 1980s and ending with the contractionary period associated with the structural adjustment policies of the 1990s. The chapter is organized as follows: In Section 2, we provide an overview of the health sector at independence and the changes that have taken place since. This is followed, in section 3, by a review of macroeconomic policies relevant to the health sector. The conceptual framework and empirical evidence on Zimbabwe's health performance under different sets of macroeconomic policies are presented in Section 4. Since the HIV/AIDS pandemic has been an important intervening factor, making precise causal links between macroeconomic policies and health sector performance difficult to establish, Section 5 addresses how the pandemic has placed additional pressures on the health sector and its implications for health policy. Finally, Section 6 presents the conclusions and outlines some policy lessons for the future.

2 The health sector in Zimbabwe: an overview

In Zimbabwe, health services are provided largely by the government through *rural health centers* (primary level), *district hospitals* (secondary level), *provincial hospitals* (tertiary level), and *central hospitals* (quartenary level). Municipalities, rural district councils and churches also operate primary-level clinics and maternity hospitals. There is also a vibrant private sector that provides general and specialist medical services from private clinics, hospitals and specialist medical centers. Some employers, especially in the mining industry, also provide health care facilities for their employees.

The government, through the Ministry of Health and Child Welfare, plays both a funding and a supervisory role to all health facilities operated by non-governmental institutions (see Table 14.1 for details on the number of health facilities by type of institution).

The health sector in the 1980s

At independence, in 1980, Zimbabwe inherited a two-tiered and racially structured health sector. Health services for the relatively affluent and predominantly white, urban minority were well developed. They enjoyed easy access to an efficient and a well-funded health delivery system. In contrast, the predominantly black, rural population had poor and limited access to heath care services. The policy emphasis was on the curative health needs of affluent whites with insufficient attention being given to the preventive health care needs of the poor black majority (World Bank, 1981). Thus, the provision and distribution of services was highly skewed and inequitable along racial lines. It has been estimated that in 1977/78, the Harare (Salisbury) group of hospitals, mainly for whites, served only 8.7 per cent of the population but consumed 29.7 per cent of the government's health budget. In the same year, 86.7 per cent of the Z$40.2 million government health budget was spent on curative services and only 9 per cent on preventive services (MacGarry, 1993). The rural population depended mainly on a few mission hospitals that provided two-thirds of the rural hospital beds. Mission clinics, some partially funded by government grants, were responsible for 73 per cent, or 2600 out of 3560 hospital beds in rural areas. In 1980, there were 600 persons per hospital bed in the rural areas while the comparable figure for urban areas was 300, producing a national average of 500 persons per hospital bed. Furthermore, hospitals run by the Ministry of Health cared mostly for in-patients at substantially higher unit costs than local authority health facilities which served roughly an equal number of outpatients.

In an attempt to redress these disparities in the distribution of health services, 'Equity in Health' was adopted as an integral aspect of government's overall development strategy of 'Growth with Equity'. The objective was to achieve health for all by the year 2000. Since about 90 per cent of health ailments in 1980 were from preventable diseases (World Bank, 1995), there was a deliberate policy shift from curative to preventive and primary health care. As the health delivery system was under serving the rural poor, health care services were expanded to the rural areas. Large numbers of village health workers were recruited and trained. In addition to diagnosing and treating simple common diseases, they also educated the community about nutrition, hygiene and personal health care. More local clinics and district hospitals were built. To improve access and affordability, no user fees were charged to patients from low-income households of below Z$150 per month (a little below the 1980 poverty datum line). This brought health services much closer to the people.

Table 14.1 Health facilities in Zimbabwe by type of institution

Year	*Central hospital*	*General hospital*	*Maternity hospital*	*District hospital*	*Rural hospital*	*Private mine hospital*	*Special instn*	*Mission hosp and clinics*	*Govt clinics*	*Council clinics*	*Municipal clinics*
1983	6	12	11	29	60	44	14	97	—	407	57
1985	4	12	6	28	56	173	10	46	—	424	55
1986	4	12	6	28	56	173	10	46	—	424	55
1987	4	12	6	28	56	168	9	45	—	334	55
1991	4	7	—	41	58	14	6	97	—	—	—
1992	6	7	6	37	57	175	10	120	377	452	102
1993	6	7	3	37	58	204	11	126	370	451	105
1994	6	7	3	37	58	204	11	126	370	451	105
1995	6	7	3	37	58	204	11	126	370	451	105
1996	5	7	3	34	59	209	13	128	349	497	102

Source: Central Statistical Office, Harare.

Expanded primary health care to cover rural areas, improved health education and prevention, community mobilization against disease and improved equity in health provision led to some dramatic improvements in health indicators. Infant mortality declined from more than 90 to around 53 per thousand, child malnutrition (stunting) declined from 30 per cent to less than 20 per cent and the number of fully immunized children increased from 25 per cent to 80 per cent. Thus, as the indicators in Table 14.2 show, Zimbabwe achieved very significant improvements in the health status of the nation between 1978 and 1998.

However, these achievements could only be achieved at a cost to the economy as a whole. Expansionary fiscal policies, with increased budgetary allocations to health and other social sectors, became major highlights of macroeconomic policy during the 1980s. As a result, the budget deficit, financed by borrowing, grew considerably. By the end of the 1980s, the country was beginning to experience major economic difficulties that made continued high social sector expenditures unsustainable. Stagnant

Table 14.2 Zimbabwe: key health performance indicators (main demographic and social indicators)

Indicator	*1978*	*1988*	*1994*	*1995*	*1998*
Life expectancy at birth (years)	57	61	62	57	49
Population million	7.539[3]	9.18	10.78	11.01	11.04
Population growth rate	3.4[3]			3.13	
Rates per thousand					
Crude death rate	15[3]	8		9.6	20
Adult mortality rate			9.49[1]		
Maternal mortality	130[3]	70[2]	170		
Infant mortality rate	83	52.7	49.6	85	62
Under five mortality rate	103.6	75.1	74.8	83	
Immunization rate (%)	25[4]		80		
Access to sanitation rural	100			98	
Access to sanitation urban	5			50	
Access to clean water rural (%)	14		36	65	
Access to clean water urban	100			99	
Access to health services	71	80			
Population per physician			46060		
Dependency ratio	102.9		94.4		
Human Development Indicator			47.4	53.9	57.3

Note:
[1] 1992.
[2] 1990.
[3] 1982.
[4] 1980.
Source: CSO, *Quarterly Digest of Statistics* (several issues); World Bank, *African Development Indicators* (1997); MoHCW (1995); UNDP, (1998).

investment, low GDP growth rates, weak export performance, foreign exchange shortages and rising unemployment added to the problems associated with the large budget deficits to persuade the government to adopt the economic structural adjustment program (ESAP) in 1991.

2.1 The health sector in the 1990s

The policies that were pursued under the structural adjustment program (ESAP) had serious negative implications for health sector performance. Conceptually, it is useful to distinguish between the macroeconomic reform policies affecting the supply of health services and those that affect the demand side: supply-side effects affect the environment within which health services are produced while demand-side effects operate more indirectly through changes in households' characteristics and their ability to afford these services.

In general, SAPs almost always involve elements of stabilization policies with measures designed to reduce aggregate demand. Cutbacks in overall government spending, and in particular the reduction in the health budget in particular and the introduction of cost recovery measures, were measures that affected the health sector directly. Table 14.3 summarizes some of the macroeconomic policy measures implemented under ESAP, their primary intended effects and their impacts on the public health sector.

2.2 Supply-side effects

An overall reduction in government spending may translate into reduced health services supply through a variety of channels and transmission mechanisms. Reduction in the health budget affects the quantity or supply of health services directly, while the distributional incidence of expenditure

Table 14.3 Structural adjustment policies and their impact on the public health sector

Macroeconomic policy	*Intended effect*	*Actual effect*	*Comment on impact on health sector*
Trade policy Currency devaluation	Encourage exports	High costs of imported inputs	High costs of imported medical equipment and drugs
Tight fiscal policy Cut government spending	Reduce the budget deficit	Reduced spending on health sector Cost recovery on health services Retrenchments	Cutback in the provision of essential health services Cost recovery a burden to users Drop in real incomes of average people
Deregulation of prices, goods and services Decrease in food subsidies	Improve efficiency	Increase in prices of basic consumer products	Purchasing power of low-and middle-income groups collapse

cuts between recurrent and capital expenditures and between preventative primary health care and curative services affects both the nature and quality of services delivered. Expenditure cuts that are concentrated on primary health care services would be expected to have more severe consequences for the great majority of the population and the health status of the nation.

Another avenue is through the effects on the incentive structure of the health profession. The reduction in the public sector salaries and wage bill, common to most SAPs, often has the adverse effect of reducing work incentives, leading to loss of the more talented and experienced personnel, initially from the public to the private health sector and ultimately abroad. Trade liberalization and currency devaluation inevitably increase the costs of imported medical drugs and equipment. Cost recovery measures, apart from imposing additional burdens on low-income households, only bring beneficial supply effects in the long run. Thus, the short-run effects of the policies pursued during the 1990s were to decrease both the quantity and quality of health services.

2.3 Demand-side effects

Income is perhaps the single most important factor determining the consumption of goods and services, including health services. Policies that adversely affect incomes indirectly affect the health of individuals. Macroeconomic policies that reduce real wages through inflation and unemployment (retrenchments) have an adverse effect on the demand for health services. Poverty and deprived social circumstances that lead to poor nutrition, hygiene, sanitation and housing result in higher levels of childhood deaths, maternal ill-health and inadequate health care for the family. As incomes and the consumption of basic goods (including health services) improve, so does family health status and vice versa. Devaluation, price decontrols, the elimination of subsidies, and civil service reform all have indirect impacts through their effects on the supply of and demand for health services.

Structural adjustment programs are intended to alter relative prices of goods and services in favor of tradables. These changes inevitably affect the income status of health service users in the short run. In particular, trade liberalization and devaluation improve the relative prices and profitability of tradables vis-à-vis nontradable goods. In agriculture, the largest sector of the Zimbabwean economy, this may encourage the increased production of tradable cash crops such as cotton, tobacco and horticulture. This may not be beneficial to all farmer groups. The incomes of small farmers, who primarily grow non-tradable food crops, may be adversely affected compared to the large-scale commercial farmers who produce exportables.

Domestic deregulation, which is another component of ESAP, usually leads to higher prices and costs of basic commodities. Price increases reduce individuals', purchasing power, with negative implications for their nutrition and health status. While high-income households and individuals may cope with temporary or even longer-term income reduction, low-income households lack the resources to de-link declining incomes from a deterioration in their access to basic needs (Pinstrup-Andersen, 1993). Therefore, their health status is very vulnerable to macroeconomic policies which erode incomes. The experience of the Zimbabwean health sector during the period of ESAP accords rather well with these predictions. Real allocations to the Ministry of Health and Child Welfare decreased from 6 per cent of total government expenditure in 1990 to about 4 per cent by 1995 (see Table 14.4). Health expenditures per capita and as a percentage of GDP decreased throughout the 1990s and have remained consistently below the 1990 levels. This has placed severe constraints on the ability of the health sector to offer effective health services. Whereas investment in health in the 1980s resulted in substantial gains in health indicators, the cutbacks experienced in the 1990s threaten to reverse these gains. While immediate post-independence developments increased allocations to preventive services from about 7 per cent in 1980; peaking at 12 per cent in 1994/95 this has recently decreased to about 11 per cent (see Table 14.5). The incidence of cutbacks

Table 14.4 Real recurrent health expenditure, 1980/81–1995/96, Ministry of Health and Child Welfare (1990 prices)

Financial year	*Total real health exp. (Z$million)*	*Total real health exp. per capita*	*Health exp. as percentage of GDP*	*Health exp. as percentage of total govt. exp.*
1980/81	256.24	35.62	2.0	5.3
1981/82	306.60	41.44	2.2	5.6
1982/83	300.10	39.44	2.1	4.8
1983/84	289.61	36.74	2.2	4.8
1984/85	291.97	35.92	2.3	4.9
1985/86	331.00	39.48	2.5	5.3
1986/87	355.64	41.14	2.8	5.1
1987/88	384.10	43.08	2.8	5.5
1988/89	412.18	44.82	2.6	5.4
1989/90	478.88	50.50	2.8	5.9
1990/91	564.49	57.72	3.0	6.2
1991/92	511.97	50.76	2.5	5.1
1992/93	458.18	44.00	2.4	5.3
1993/94	412.88	38.45	2.2	5.1
1994/95	424.33	38.31	2.2	4.5
1995/96	409.71	35.86	2.2	4.2
1996/97	415.0	34.7	1.7	9.9
1997/98	314.0	25.45	1.25	9.9
1998/99	299.0	23.45	1.16	11.36

Sources: S. Chandiwana, G. Woelk, P. Sikhosana et al., 1997; *Quarterly Digest of Statistics*.

Table 14.5 Ministry of Health and Child Welfare expenditure by sector (million nominal Z$)

Sector	*1979/80*	*1980/81*	*1981/82*	*1983/84*	*1986/87*	*1990/91*	*1994/95*	*1995/96*	*1997/98*[1]
Administration and general	1.71	2.53	3.89	5.19	11.72	15.13	30.80	32.09	185.90
Medical care services	45.54	74.91	95.71	114.26	195.59	382.59	1246.80	1160.79	3186.72
Preventive services	4.52	5.60	7.94	16.33	24.55	59.13	183.60	156.15	427.26
Research	0.54	0.70	0.54	0.81	1.16	2.61	6.00	5.89	18.16
Total	52.31	83.73	108.08	136.59	233.02	459.47	1467.20	1354.92	3818.05
Expenditure as percentage of total									
Sector	*1979/80*	*1980/81*	*1981/82*	*1983/84*	*1986/87*	*1990/91*	*1994/95*	*1995/96*	*1997/98*[1]
Administration and general	3.27	3.01	3.60	3.80	5.03	3.29	2.10	2.37	4.87
Medical care services	87.05	89.46	88.56	83.65	83.94	83.27	84.98	85.67	83.46
Preventive services	8.64	6.69	7.35	11.95	10.53	12.87	12.51	11.52	11.19
Research	1.02	0.84	0.50	0.59	0.50	0.57	0.41	0.43	0.48
Total	100	100	100	100	100	100	100	100	100

Note: [1]Estimates.
Source: Central Statistical Office, *Statistical Yearbook 1989*.

matters for their impacts on health. If they are in preventive and primary health care, then such cutbacks can have significant adverse effects on the poor. The government has also been reducing its grants to cities, municipalities and mission hospitals, forcing them to seriously address the issue of what services to provide and to whom.

These spending cutbacks resulted in numerous problems for the Zimbabwean health system. There is inadequate laboratory equipment at the top of the referral pyramid system and frequent breakdowns of theater equipment which take inordinately long periods to replace or repair. There has been a reduction in the numbers of appropriately trained medical personnel within the public health sector. The poorly maintained or inadequate number of ambulances lead to delays in referrals, especially from rural areas. The shortage of drugs and simple medical accessories such as gloves, needles and syringes have sapped the morale of the medical professionals within the public sector.

Rural hospitals and clinics with neither well-qualified staff nor drugs, and central hospitals with inadequate staff to manage the country's referral system,[1] have led many to observe that Zimbabwe's health system is near to collapse. Significantly, one of the major grievances in the September 1999 junior doctors' strike, which lasted for six weeks, was the increasingly deteriorating state of the health system – a situation which made it difficult for them to adequately discharge the responsibilities of their profession.

As a result, there has been an exodus of well-trained medical staff from the public health sector due to the deteriorating salaries and conditions of service. With inflation reducing the real value of their incomes, the depreciation of the domestic currency made health personnel remuneration less attractive relative to those in neighboring countries, such as South Africa. Real incomes for health personnel fell by about one-third (Government of Zimbabwe, 1998a). This disincentive induced the highly qualified and experienced doctors to migrate to neighboring countries, notably South Africa, with increasing numbers of nurses migrating to the United Kingdom. Of the doctors trained at the University of Zimbabwe Medical School, 80 per cent no longer work in the public sector. Vacancy occupancy rates for pharmacists rarely exceeded 70 per cent and the same applies for other staff such as nurses, laboratory technicians and radiographers. This has increased the number of people serviced by one of these medical personnel. As is evident from Figure 14.1, the number of people per doctor, per nurse, per laboratory staff and per X-ray staff has increased substantially since 1983, indicating that medical personnel resources are being increasingly overstretched.

User fees have increased since 1991 in line with the requirements of ESAP. The total revenue generated by fees has typically been 2 per cent of total expenditures on public health services (Normand et al., 1996). Zimbabwe's user fee structure is designed to support the referral system, by encouraging patients to seek services at the lower levels of the health system (Chisvo and

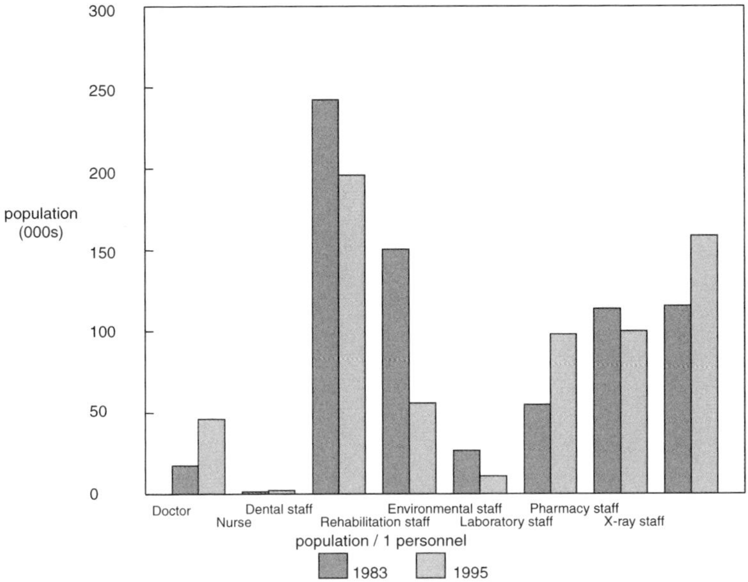

Figure 14.1 Population per health personnel (1983 and 1995)

Munro, 1994). However, Normand et al. and Chisvo et al. indicate that the user fee system fails to meet this function because many health users still consult secondary-level health care without being referred by primary health facilities. Other problems facing the user fee system include the following: (i) user fees are not based on the costs of providing the service; (ii) exemption levels are not based on any empirically objective criteria; (iii) all fees collected are not available for direct utilization by MoHCW-creating enforcement problems; and (iv) the user fees are so low that they do not even cover the costs of administering the system (Iliff, 1995). In 1994, study by the Blair Research Institute on the effects of hospital user charges on Health Care Delivery in Zimbabwe found that outpatient attendance at the eight hospitals and one clinic in their sample had dropped by 18 per cent, while antenatal attendance had dropped by almost 40 per cent. On the other hand, the in-patient numbers increased by 12 per cent. Their conclusion was that people were cutting down on what they thought were unnecessary services, only to come later with more serious conditions.

The higher fees also forced people to seek alternative sources of health service, such as traditional healers. Similar behavior has been reported in other countries. For example, in Nigeria, the introduction of SAP was followed by a decrease in antenatal clinic attendance, an increase in neonatal tetanus, an increase in the prenatal mortality rate and an increase in the number of babies delivered at home (Iliff, 1995). In Kenya, the cost recovery program resulted in decreased attendances, confusion, and even harassment of patients, to such an extent that it was discontinued after ten months. Attendance of men at sexually transmitted diseases (STD) clinics dropped to 40 per cent of previous levels and rose again after the abolition of charges (Iliff, 1995). This implies that user fees can discourage use of health service and can therefore potentially contribute to the deterioration of national health services.

The conclusion from the above is that Zimbabwe made impressive gains and consistent progress in health indicators in the 1980s. However, these have deteriorated since 1991. Whether this is largely attributable to the short-run effects of structural adjustment on health costs, incomes and standards of living of the population is an ongoing debate. While it is true that adjustment policies have had an important role to play, other intervening factors, especially the outbreak of the HIV/AIDS pandemic, have played an equally significant contribution to the deteriorating health indicators in the 1990s. It is to this issue that we now turn.

3 The HIV/AIDS pandemic and the health sector

The HIV/AIDS pandemic complicates the analysis of the impacts of macroeconomic policies on the health sector. Whereas the demand-side effects of ESAP have been to decrease demand for health care services, the HIV/AIDS pandemic has done the opposite. HIV/AIDS patients demand three major types of care.[2] These are: (1) palliative treatment and relief of symptoms like headache, pain, diarrhoea, and so on; (2) prevention and treatment of opportunistic infections associated with AIDS, such as tuberculosis and pneumonia; and (3) antiretroviral (ARV) treatment, which attempts to control HIV infection and slow down the progression to AIDS and AIDS related death. Health services for (1) are least expensive. Treatment for (2) is somewhat expensive but because some of the diseases are infectious, it is in the government's interest to treat them regardless of an individual's HIV status. Antiretroviral therapy is expensive, averaging at Z$18 000 per month (up from Z$6000 per month in 1996) on drugs alone with additional cost for viral load testing averaging Z$2000 per month.[3] These costs make the use of ARV prohibitive. In 1990, an estimated 4.3 per cent of hospital beds was occupied by AIDS patients (NACP, 1997) and the average length of stay in hospital of an AIDS patient is about 37 days. As the epidemic increases, it is estimated that the proportion of hospital beds occupied by AIDS patients will rise to two in every three hospital beds by 2005 (NACP, 1997).

Zimbabwe is rated as one of the Sub-Saharan African countries experiencing the highest HIV/AIDS rates, with an estimated 1.7 million of the 11.6 million being HIV positive (NACP, 1998). Since the outbreak of HIV/AIDS, the number of reported AIDS cases, STI episodes and new TB cases have been increasing (see Table 14.6). Many cases go unreported, however, and it is estimated that, by the end of 1998, more than 400 000 had developed AIDS (NACP, 1998). HIV has spread throughout the country, and AIDS cases have been reported from every district. The relative ease with which people travel between urban and rural areas may have contributed significantly to the rapid spread of the disease, as well as factors such as high levels of untreated STIs. In 1997, UNAIDS country data indicated that Zimbabwe's adult HIV rate to be 25 per cent, where adults aged 15–49 accounts for 48 per cent of the total population of 11.6 million. The estimated AIDS deaths in 1998 were 82 000, cumulative deaths at 400000 and AIDS orphans were 450 000.

The supply-side effects of AIDS are to reinforce the macroeconomic-induced reduction in the supply of health services. Phenomena such as staff absenteeism, mortality, training and replacement of medical staff, attrition due to stress and burnout, all increase the costs of providing health care. In some countries high levels of HIV seroprevalence have been recorded among health workers. Some countries report that health personnel leave the profession because of the high risk of exposure to HIV infection.[4] The overall effect is to increase the price of health care as demand increases and supply decreases.

Direct costs of treating palliative and inexpensive opportunistic infections for HIV positive patients were estimated to be US$300 per case per year, in Sub-Saharan Africa.[5] A 1996 study by CIMAS medical aid society on health claims submitted by 4933 positively identified AIDS cases who died during the year under review indicated an average of Z$7220 per AIDS case – an increase from Z$4928 and Z$3095 of 1995 and 1994 respectively. General

Table 14.6 Zimbabwe: reported AIDS cases, STI episodes and new TB cases

Year	*Reported AIDS cases*	*Projected new AIDS cases*	*STI episodes*	*New TB cases*
1986			559 500	
1987	119		668 422	
1988	202		971 790	6 002
1989	1 311		107 829	6 812
1990	4 362		963 436	9 132
1991	4 557		1 240 596	12 198
1992	8 180		878 366	15 237
1993	9 174		879 307	20 125
1994	10 647		813 698	23 959
1995	13 356	53 609	873 218	30 831
1996	12 029	68 021	846 166	35 829
1997	6 732	82 668	814 032	43 287
1998	7 291	94 973	828 652	47 077

Sources: NACP – Ministry of Health and Child Welfare (1998); HIV, STI, and AIDS Surveillance Zimbabwe, *Quarterly Report*, March 1996; *Quarterly Digest of Statistics*, December 1997.

practitioner and hospital costs account for the highest proportion of total costs – that is, 29 and 21 percent respectively.[6] These costs are prohibitive for average- and low-income households in Zimbabwe. Thus they have to be met by the public health sector.

Basing on the AIDS Impact model (AIM), and CIMAS 1995 health costs per AIDS patient, the NACP projected that AIDS patient care costs will be Z$841 million in the year 2000 (NACP, 1997). Using the 1994/95 MoHCW budget, the NACP calculated that by the year 2000 about 56 per cent of the entire budget will be required to meet the needs of AIDS patients. (These figures are based on private sector health costs.) This will put pressure on the budget and further macroeconomic instability.

In addition to the direct medical costs of AIDS, huge indirect costs fall on households. Death of a breadwinner might force a household into poverty, thereby making household members susceptible to disease and poor health. AIDS also affects major demographic indicators, such as mortality and life expectancy. Whereas total death rates had fallen to 9 per thousand in 1992, it rose to 12.5 in 1997 and will continue to rise in the medium term as those who are currently HIV positive develop AIDS and die. The population growth rate in 1997 was estimated at 2.2 per cent and projections based on the number of HIV cases in the country indicate that the rate will fall to about one per cent by 2000 (Jhamba, 1997). Life expectancy which had improved to 62 by 1994, has fallen to 53.4 and 44.1 in 1996 and 1997 respectively due to the HIV/AIDS epidemic (UNAIDS, 1998). This has pushed national health welfare back to levels below those prevailing at the time of independence and thus pose as a major threat to reversing all the progress which had been achieved in the health sector since independence (see Table 14.2). The government's response to HIV and AIDS in Zimbabwe has been very slow. It has generally considered HIV/AIDS to be a health problem and largely left it to the Ministry of Health and Child Welfare (Mombeshora, 1998). The creation of the NACP was the Zimbabwean government's main response to HIV/AIDS. However, resources allocated to the program have been very low; accounting for 8.4 per cent of NACP's total expenditure, with the rest coming from donors. It was not until the 2000 budget that the government announced an income tax surcharge of 3 per cent as an 'Aids Levy' to fight the disease. Thus, given the negative impacts that AIDS has on development, the national economy, sectoral and household levels, there is need to strengthen government commitment in the fight against the disease. Most important is to intensify preventive interventions since prevention is the most cost-effective response.

4 Conclusions and lessons for the future

Macroeconomic policies are a major determinant of health sector performance. Policies that were supportive of the health sector resulted in outstanding performance in the 1980s. However, while the economy made some progress in other sectors, social sectors, particularly health, have been under severe stress since the adoption of ESAP, the advent of the AIDS pandemic and the incidence of chronic droughts. Cuts in the health budget, a decline in health workers' real wages, massive retrenchments, real increases in the costs of drugs and imported equipment, inflation, health cost recovery – all of these factors seem to have worked against the health sector, resulting in its poor performance throughout the 1990s.

A number of issues that complicate government's priority setting and resource allocation need to be addressed. There are multiple national objectives which often involve trade-offs between efficiency and equity. The health sector competes with other sectors for resources. Within the health sector itself, AIDS competes with other health problems and within the AIDS budget, expensive antiretroviral treatments compete against prevention and treatment of opportunistic infections. Thus, a major challenge facing policy makers is prioritizing programs across different sectors and within the sector. This is by no means an easy task, especially during times of tightening national budgets and the AIDS epidemic. Investments in health have direct effects on productivity, and hence the whole economy. Health has an important role in meeting the equity objective. If the HIV/AIDS epidemic is not arrested, the economy can be adversely affected. Thus the Zimbabwean government's long-term strategy should be to address the underlying structural factors which fuel the spread of AIDS and exacerbate the impact of the disease on households. Unemployment, poverty, low incomes, restricted access to agricultural land, credit and markets are all linked to a macroeconomic strategy to promote growth. It will also be necessary to promote income generation and other mitigation activities which will ensure that household expenditure patterns are maintained.

Within the health sector itself, there is also a need to prioritize all health programs in order to ensure that more cost-effective and efficient programs are selected. Primary health care programs as opposed to curative care must be emphasized because they are cost-effective and offer accessibility to more people. There is also a need to improve the efficiency and effectiveness of existing health institutions through increased budgetary allocations. Health institutions should have the autonomy to utilize the funds raised from cost recovery measures rather than going into general revenue.

AIDS is much more than a health issue. Macroeconomic policies that do not take into account the fight against AIDS will prove unsustainable. The demand for welfare expenditure is likely to be increased because of the HIV/AIDS epidemic and rising levels of poverty. Thus, a high level of government commitment is required to plan and implement responses to fight the AIDS epidemic.

As government resources become scarce due to the increasing need to reduce the budget deficit, strong partnerships with the private sector will need to be developed in order to promote diversity and competition in health care delivery. The promotion of health depends fundamentally on the elimination of poverty and underdevelopment. If Zimbabwe is to improve the health status of its population, macroeconomic policies that promote growth, create employment, raise incomes and reduce poverty will be required to rescue the health sector from the downward trend that has been taking place throughout the 1990s.

Notes

1. Iliff (1995).
2. Ainsworth and Over (1997).
3. Annual costs in the USA for antiretroviral therapy were estimated to be US$19 803; Ainsworth and Over (1997).
4. Barnett et al. (1996).
5. Ainsworth and Over (1997).
6. SAfAIDS News (1997).

References

Ainsworth, M. and M. Over (1997) *Confronting AIDS: Public Priorities in a Global Epidemic*, A World Bank Policy Research Report. New York: Oxford University Press for the World Bank.

Barnett, T., E. Blas and A. Whiteside (1996) *AIDS Briefs: Integrating HIV/AIDS into Sectoral Planning*. Geneva: World Health Organization.

Behrman, J. (1993), 'Health and economic growth: theory, evidence and policy', in World Health Organization, *Macroeconomic Environment and Health*. Geneva: World Health Organization.

Campino, A.C.C. (1993) 'Social emergency and investment funds in Latin America and the Caribbean', in WHO, *Macroeconomic Environment and Health*. Geneva: World Health Organization.

Central Statistical Office (1994) *Indicator Monitoring Survey 1993*. Harare: Government of Zimbabwe.

Central Statistical Office (1995) *Inequality among Households in Zimbabwe: an Assessment using the 1990/91 Income Consumption and Expenditure Survey*. Government of Zimbabwe, Harare in collaboration with Centre for the Study of African Economies, University of Oxford.

Central Statistical Office (1989) *Zimbabwe Statistical Yearbook 1989*. Harare: Central Statistical Office.

Chandiwana, S., G. Woelk, P. Sikosana et al. (1997) *The Essential Step: an Interim Assessment of Equity in Health in Zimbabwe*. A report prepared for the workshop on a Situational and Trend Analysis of Equity in Health and Health Care in Zimbabwe. Harare: Government Printer.

Chisvo, M. and L. Munro (1994) *A Review of Social Dimensions of Adjustment in Zimbabwe 1990–1994*. Harare: UNICEF.

Consumer Council of Zimbabwe. *Low Income Urban Earner Monthly Budget for a Family of Six*, Various years.

Cornia, G.A., R. Jolly and F. Stewart (1987) *Adjustment with a Human Face: Protecting the Vulnerable and Promoting Growth*, A study by UNICEF. Oxford: Clarendon Press.

Eilerts G. and E. Vhurumuku (1997) *Zimbabwe Food Security and Vulnerability Assessment 1996/97*, USAID Famine Early Warning System (FEWS) Project.

Government of Zimbabwe (1996) *National HIV/AIDS Policy Document*. Harare: Government Printer.

Government of Zimbabwe (1981) *Growth with Equity: an Economic Policy Statement*. Harare: Government Printer.

Government of Zimbabwe (1991) *Zimbabwe: a Framework For Economic Reform (1991–1995)*. Harare: Government Printer.

Government of Zimbabwe (1998a). *Zimbabwe Budget Estimates Presented to Parliament*. Harare: Government Printer.

Government of Zimbabwe (1998b) *ZIMPREST: Zimbabwe Programme For Economic and Social Transformation 1996–2000*. Harare: Government Printer.

Gregson, S., T. Zhuwau, R.M. Anderson and S.K. Chandiwana (1996) *The Early Socio-Demographic Impact of HIV-1 Epidemic in Rural Zimbabwe*.

Hore, R. (1997) 'AIDS and private health costs in Zimbabwe', *SAfAIDS News*, vol. 5, no. 3.

Iliff, P. (1995). *Health for Whom? Mother and Child Care in Times of AIDS, Poverty, and ESAP*, Silveira House Social Series no. 11.

Jackson, J.C. and P. Collier (1988) *Incomes, Poverty, and Food Security in Communal Lands of Zimbabwe*, Department of Rural and Urban Planning. Harare: University of Zimbabwe Press.

Jhamba, T. (1997) *Mortality and Mortality Determinants in Zimbabwe: Policy Implications*, Policy Research, Department of Sociology, University of Zimbabwe, Harare.

Keogh, E. (1997) *Geographical Targeting of Districts in Zimbabwe for Community Action Project*, Prepared for The Social Dimension Fund, Ministry of Public Service, Labour and Social Welfare, Government of Zimbabwe.

Loewenson, R. and R. Kerkhoven (1996) *The Socio-Economic Impact of AIDS: Issues and Options in Zimbabwe*. Harare: SAfAIDS and TARSC.

Loewenson, R. and A. Whiteside (1997) *Social and Economic Issues of HIV/AIDS in Southern Africa: a Review of Current Research*, A consultancy report prepared for SAfAIDS.

MacGarry sj, B. (1993) *Growth Without Equity: the Zimbabwe Economy and the Economic Structural Adjustment Programme*. Gwern, Zimbabwe: Mambo Press in association with Silveira House.

Ministry of Finance (1997) *The Budget Statement Presented to the Parliament of Zimbabwe on 24 July 1997, By the Minister of Finance*. Harare: Ministry of Finance.

Ministry of Health and Child Welfare (1984a) *Evaluation of the Village Health Worker Programmes, 1983*. Harare: Government of Zimbabwe.

Ministry of Health and Child Welfare (1984b) *Planning for Equity in Health: a Sectoral Review and Policy Statement*. Harare: Government of Zimbabwe.

Ministry of Health and Child Welfare (1995a) *The Effects and Impact of Hospital User Charges on Health Care Delivery in Zimbabwe*, Report prepared for The Blair Research Institute by ARA-TECHTOP. Harare: Ministry of Health and Child Welfare.

Ministry of Health and Child Welfare (1995b) *Report of the Secretary for Health and Child Welfare for the year ended 31st December 1995*. Harare: MoHCW.

Ministry of Public Service, Labour and Social Welfare (1997) *Zimbabwe Poverty Assessment Study Survey (PASS) 1995*. Harare: MPSLSW.

Mutangadura G. (1993) 'Macro-economics and sustainable smallholder agriculture in Zimbabwe', unpublished Master of Development Economics, Williams College, USA.

National AIDS Coordination Programme (1997) *HIV/AIDS in Zimbabwe: Background, Projections, Impact and Intervention.* Harare: Ministry of Health and Child Welfare.

Normand C., G. Chapman, O. Mudyarabikwa, M. Chalwa and J. Needleman (1996) *Health Sector Resource Mobilisation Study: Zimbabwe,* Data for Decision Making Project, Harvard School of Public Health, USA.

Pinstrup-Andersen, P. (1993) 'Economic crises and policy reforms during the 1980s and their impact on the poor', in WHO, *Macroeconomic Environment and Health.* Geneva: World Health Organization.

Renfew, A. (1992) *ESAP and Health: the Effects of the Economic Structural Adjustment Programme on the Health of the People of Zimbabwe,* Silveira House Social Series No. 3. Gwern, Zimbabwe: Published by Mambo Press in association with Silveira House.

Sichone, M. (1997) *Health Reforms and HIV/AIDS in Zambia,* presentation at SAfAIDS Regional Advisory Council, October, Harare, Zimbabwe. United States Bureau of Census (1996) *HIV/AIDS Surveillance Data Base,* June.

Woelk, G.B. (1994) 'Primary health care in Zimbabwe: can it survive? An exploration of the political and historical developments affecting the implementation of PHC', *Social Science Medicine,* vol. 39, no. 8, pp. 1027–35.

World Bank (1981) *Zimbabwe Country Economic Memorandum,* World Bank Report No. 3234b-ZIM. Washington DC: World Bank.

World Bank (1985) *Zimbabwe Country Economic Memorandum, Performance, Policies and Prospects,* World Bank Report No. 5458-ZIM. Washington DC: World Bank.

World Bank (1995) *Zimbabwe Achieving Shared Growth,* Country Economic Memorandum, The World Bank, Report Number 13540-ZIM. Washington DC: World Bank.

World Health Organization (1997) *Report of The Meeting on Policy-Oriented Monitoring of Equity in Health and Care.* Geneva: WHO.

Zimbabwe Ministry of Health and Child Welfare (1996) *HIV, STD and AIDS Surveillance, Quarterly Report March 1996,* Health Information Unit and National AIDS Coordination Programme. Harare: Ministry of Health and Child Welfare.

Index